The Criminal Event

Second Edition

The Criminal Event

Second Edition

Vincent F. Sacco
Queen's University

Leslie W. Kennedy
University of Alberta

ITP Nelson

an International Thomson Publishing company

Toronto • Albany • Bonn • Boston • Cincinnati • Detroit • London • Madrid • Melbourne
Mexico City • New York • Pacific Grove • Paris • San Francisco • Singapore • Tokyo • Washington

I(T)P® **International Thomson Publishing**
The ITP logo is a trademark under licence
www.thomson.com

Published in 1998 by
I(T)P® **Nelson**

A division of Thomson Canada Limited
1120 Birchmount Road
Scarborough, Ontario M1K 5G4
www.nelson.com

Cover photo: © Jean Louis Batt / Masterfile

Canadian Cataloguing in Publication Data

Sacco, Vincent, 1948–
    The criminal event : an introduction to criminology

2nd ed.
Includes bibliographical references and index.
ISBN 0-17-607280-2

1. Criminology. 2. Crime – Canada. I. Kennedy, Leslie W., 1951– . II. Title.

HV6025.S23 1997   364   C97-932151-4

Publisher and Team Leader	Michael Young
Executive Editor	Charlotte Forbes
Senior Production Editor	Bob Kohlmeier
Project Editor	Evan Turner
Production Coordinator	Brad Horning
Art Direction	Sylvia Vander Schee
Cover Design	Steve MacEachern
Senior Composition Analyst	Alicja Jamorski

Printed and bound in Canada
  2 3 4 (WC) 01 00 99 98

To
Tiia, Daniel, Katherin, and Ema
Ilona, Alexis, Andrea, and Grandparents

CONTENTS

Preface   xiv

PART ONE   INTRODUCTION

**Chapter One   What Is Criminology? Defining and Constructing the
Problem of Crime   5**

Introduction   6
What Is Criminology?   7
Classical and Positivist Views of Offenders   8
Defining Crime   11
    Crime as Lawbreaking   11
        Crime and Law   11
        Evolving Perceptions of Crime   12
        The Focus on Offenders   12
        Context   13
        Individual Accountability   13
        Self-Defence   15
        Insanity   15
        Legal and Social Controls   15
    Crime and Morality   18
    Crime, Politics, and the Law   19
The Consensus View   20
Conflict, Power, and the Law   23
    Identifying Competing Social Groups   24
    Peacemaking   25
    The Feminist Approach   25
        Feminist Explanations of Crime Rates   26
        Battered Women and Crime   27
The Police and Crime   28
How Much Crime?   30
The Public's Interest in Criminal Events   32
    Crime News   33
        The Interest in Crime News   33
        The Content of Crime News   35
        The Sources of Crime News   36
    Crime Drama   37
    Talking about Crime   38

Crime in Rumour and Legend   39
Crime Myths   42
Summary   43

PART TWO   THE CRIMINAL EVENT

Chapter Two   The Criminal Event   49
Introduction   50
Crimes as Social Events   52
Offenders   55
   Offender Characteristics   55
   Offender Perceptions   57
Victims   61
   "Victimless" Crimes   61
   Victim Characteristics   61
   Victim Perceptions   63
Bystanders and Witnesses   64
Police   65
   Police Practice   65
   Police Involvement in Defining Criminal Events   66
The Setting of Criminal Events   68
   The Social Setting   68
   The Community Setting   69
   The Physical Setting   70
   Social Domains   71
Studying the Criminal Event   73
   Precursors   74
   Transactions   74
   The Aftermath   76
Summary   77

PART THREE   THEORIES

Chapter Three   Psychosocial Conditions and Criminal Motivations   83
Introduction   84
Explaining Offender Behaviour   86
Sociobiological Explanations of Criminal Motivation   87
   Genetics   87
   Constitution   89
   Diet   92

Intelligence and Crime *93*
    Neuropsychological Theory *93*
    Learning Disabilities *94*
  Psychopathology *95*
Social Conditions and Criminal Motivation *96*
  Frustrated Ambitions *97*
  Status Deprivation *99*
  Strain and Delinquency *100*
  Recent Versions of the Strain Argument *102*
    A General Strain Theory *102*
    Crime and the American Dream *103*
Culture and Criminal Motivation *103*
  Norm Violation *104*
  Differential Association *105*
  Subcultural Explanations of Criminal Motivations *108*
  Is Mainstream Culture Criminogenic? *111*
Summary *114*

Chapter Four   Offending, Social Control, and the Law 117
Introduction *118*
Social Ties and Conformity *118*
  Social Controls and the Individual *118*
    Containment Theory *119*
    Theory of the Bond *120*
    General Theory of Crime *121*
    Power Control Theory *122*
    Interactional Theory *122*
    Life Course Perspective *123*
  Social Controls and the Community *124*
The Power of Law: The Deterrence Doctrine *128*
  Specific and General Deterrence *128*
  Legal vs. Informal Sanctions *132*
  Situational Deterrence *133*
  Ambivalence about Crime and Deterrence Strategies *134*
Rational Choice Theories *135*
  Committing a Crime *136*
  The Criminal Career *137*
    The Concept of Career *137*
    The Career Criminal *140*
Summary *143*

Chapter Five   Opportunities, Lifestyles, and Situations   145

Introduction   *146*

Opportunity Theories and Victimization   *146*

    Lifestyle Exposure   *146*

    Routine Activities   *151*

Crime as Interactions   *156*

    Victim Precipitation   *156*

    The Situated Transaction   *158*

    The Significance of Interactional Issues   *161*

Summary   *162*

**Chapter Six   Crime's Aftermath: The Consequences of Criminal
                Events   165**

Introduction   *166*

How Much Does Crime Cost?   *166*

    Financial Consequences   *168*

    Physical Consequences   *169*

    Emotional Consequences   *170*

    Behavioural Consequences   *173*

    Coping with the Costs of Victimization   *175*

Offender Outcomes: Social Stigma and Labelling   *176*

Social Outcomes: Individual, Organizational, and Governmental
            Responses   *177*

    Public Fear of Crime   *177*

        What Is the Fear of Crime?   *178*

        Patterns in Fear   *180*

    Individual-Level Factors   *180*

        Gender   *180*

        Age   *181*

        Race and Income   *181*

    Environmental Factors   *182*

        The Community Setting   *182*

        The Information Environment   *184*

        Community Reactions   *185*

Claimsmaking   *188*

Extreme Reactions: The Moral Panic   *190*

Summary   *192*

PART FOUR   RESEARCH METHODS

Chapter Seven   Researching Criminal Events   *199*
Introduction   *200*
Observing Crime   *200*
   Direct Observation in Naturalistic Settings   *200*
   Experimental Observation   *202*
Reporting Crime   *204*
   The Crime Funnel   *204*
   Police Reports   *205*
   The Uniform Crime Reporting System   *207*
   Victim Reports   *211*
   Offender Reports   *216*
      Reports from Known Offenders   *216*
   Ethnographic Research   *218*
      Self-Report Studies   *218*
   The Limitations of Crime Reports   *220*
      What Type of Event?   *220*
      Whose Perspective?   *221*
   Measuring Women's Victimization   *224*
      Patterns of Female Victimization   *225*
      Domestic and Sexual Assault   *226*
      Recent Research Innovations   *229*
Crime Rates   *230*
   The Nature of Crime Rates   *230*
   Some Uses of Crime Rates   *231*
   Crime Rates as Measures of Risk   *233*
Summary   *236*

PART FIVE   DOMAINS OF CRIME

Chapter Eight   The Family and the Household   *241*
Introduction   *242*
The Family and the Household   *242*
Family Violence   *244*
   Precursors   *244*
      Characteristics of Families   *245*

Inequality in Family Relations   *246*

Isolation and Economic Stress   *247*

Transactions   *248*

Location and Timing of Family Violence   *250*

Patterns of Family Violence   *252*

The Aftermath   *252*

Short- and Long-Term Consequences of Family Violence   *252*

Family Violence and Delinquency   *254*

Crimes against the Household   *256*

Precursors   *256*

Transactions   *259*

Professional vs. Amateur Thieves   *259*

Risk, Ease of Entry, and Reward   *261*

The Aftermath   *263*

Summary   *266*

Chapter Nine   **Leisure**   *269*

Introduction   *270*

What Is Leisure?   *270*

Precursors   *271*

Leisure as a Corrupter   *271*

Leisure and Freedom from Social Control   *276*

Leisure Activities and Opportunities   *277*

Transactions   *278*

The Street   *278*

Young Males   *279*

Vandalism   *280*

Bars   *282*

Dating Violence   *282*

Tourism   *285*

The Aftermath   *286*

Summary   *289*

Chapter Ten   **Crime and Work**   *291*

Introduction   *292*

Crime, Employment, and Unemployment   *292*

Employment and Victimization   *293*

Unemployment and Offending   *293*

Victimization and Work   *296*

Individual and Occupational Characteristics   *297*

Precursors   *299*
Transactions   *302*
The Aftermath   *304*
Crime and Legitimate Work   *305*
What Is Occupational Crime?   *305*
Precursors   *307*
Transactions   *311*
The Aftermath   *312*
Enterprise versus Organized Crime   *313*
What Is Organized Crime?   *314*
Precursors   *319*
Transactions   *322*
The Aftermath   *324*
Summary   *325*

PART SIX   RESPONSES TO CRIME

Chapter Eleven   Summary and Review of Public Policy Responses to Crime   *331*

Introduction   *332*
Summary of Findings on the Criminal Event   *332*
Responding to Crime   *337*
The "Get-Tough" Approach   *337*
Public Health and Public Safety   *340*
Crime Prevention through Opportunity Reduction   *345*
Crime Prevention through Social Development   *351*
Community-Based Policing   *356*
Summary   *361*

References   *363*
Copyright Acknowledgments   *397*
Authors Index   *399*
Glossary/Subject Index   *409*

PREFACE

In this edition of *The Criminal Event*, we have sought to improve and expand on themes that appeared in the first edition. Underlying our approach is a commitment to the view that criminology can be taught in an integrative fashion, such that theories and data are presented in a way that involves more than a simple recitation of facts. The conventional approach to criminology provides definitions of crime, reviews the important theoretical debates, talks about measurement, suggests correlates of crime, and discusses the nature of societal reaction. While this style of course organization provides all of the material that an introductory student needs, such an approach is disjointed: like a story without a theme, it becomes a collection of seemingly unrelated anecdotes in which different researchers tell us how we should study what we study. Too often in such an approach, "sound bites" substitute for an integrated examination of the issues.

We believe that introductory criminology has long paid too much attention to the discrete elements of crime and ignored the complex and multifaceted nature of criminal events. In this book, we use the idea of the criminal event to provide the missing theme. This theme runs through our discussion of what motivates people to commit crime, of who suffers and how, and of what we should do about the problem of crime. This perspective allows us to examine the determinants of crime, as well as individual choice and opportunity, as part of a more complete explanation of criminal outcomes.

Further, we believe that we should look at crime in different contexts, since variations in situations and settings produce variations in the ways in which crime evolves. We have identified three domains of crime that guide our analysis of context: the family, leisure, and work. These domains include most daily behaviour and have been the prime areas of study in research on crime and its consequences.

The text that appears here, then, reflects our effort to achieve the objectives laid out above. We have been careful to include the major theories in our discussion. We have also made a concerted effort to include as much contemporary research on crime as possible. As Richard A. Wright has said, introductory criminology books often have failed to reflect the current state of the research. We have tried not to fall into the trap of simply repeating old truths but have sought confirmation of our points in current empirical studies.

In this edition, beyond updating crime statistics and research studies (including new example boxes), we have added material on a number of topics. Most notably, we have revamped the theory chapters, and have added a new chapter on crime's aftermath (Chapter 6). The book also contains new material on intelligence and crime, psychopathology, status deprivation, strain theory, containment theory, control theory, and interactional theory. In addition, we have added a section on the life course perspective and new material on situational deterrence and rational choice theories. We have also illustrated how this material pertains to crime policy and have updated our discussion of crime prevention strategies.

We believe that these changes have added more depth to the theoretical arguments made in the book and strengthen the explanation that ties these theories to the criminal event perspective.

To recap:

- Our use of an integrating theme—that of the criminal event—enables the reader to understand crime as more than simply a collection of loosely connected elements.
- Because it is important to study crime in different contexts, we have identified three domains of crime—family, leisure, and work—to guide our discussion of context.
- We give careful and detailed consideration to all of the major criminological theories.
- We use as much contemporary research as possible to inform our points of discussion.
- We summarize our discussion to point out how the criminal event perspective can be used in developing strategies for preventing crime.

New to this edition is a combined glossary and subject index. The terms defined in this section appear in bold type on first mention in the text. Also new to this edition are chapter previews and, at the end of each chapter, a series of questions for review and discussion.

Special thanks go to Charlotte Forbes at ITP Nelson. Charlotte has been a staunch supporter of this book from the beginning. She has been a strong ally and loyal friend, helping us through the minefield of the publishing business. Evan Turner did a great job putting all of the material together for the launch, and Bob Kohlmeier, once again, did a great job producing the final pages. Thanks go to Jim Leahy for copy editing the manuscript and to Hannah Scott for preparing the indexes. We greatly appreciate the work of the reviewers who took time to provide us with countless suggestions to help us improve certain parts of the text that needed more work. For their efforts on our behalf, we thank Larry R. Comeau, Sheridan College; Peter A. Eglin, Wilfrid Laurier University; Robert M. Gordon, Simon Fraser University; and Fiona M. Kay, University of British Columbia. We are grateful as well to our own criminology students as well as students and faculty at other colleges and universities who have used the book and have offered advice and criticism that have informed this revision. In this respect, special thanks are owed to Steve Baron, Margaret Beare, Brian Burtch, Larry Comeau, and Julian Tanner.

Les Kennedy would like to thank his colleagues and support staff at the University of Alberta for their support of this work. Specifically, he would like to thank Kerri Calvert, of the Sociology Information Centre, for her constant help in keeping him up-to-date. He would also like to thank graduate students, past and present, at the U of A who have provided him with constant intellectual challenges. In particular, thanks to Chris Andersen for his help in updating the crime statistics used here; Erin van Brunschot for her work on the Instructor's Manual; and Jonathan Alston for his contribution to the Web page.* Les would also like to thank Hannah Scott, Francis Donkor, and Michael Weinrath for their feedback on classroom experiences with the first edition, which has been useful in improving this version. He would also like to acknowledge the inspiration of Bill Meloff, a special friend. He will be missed by all. Of course, special thanks go to Ilona, Alexis, and Andrea for providing perspective as well as the moral support that is needed to complete a long, intensive job of writing.

Vince Sacco would like to thank his friends and colleagues in the Department of Sociology at Queen's University. As always, they provided support and encouragement. Kimberley Sanders and Joan Westenhaefer facilitated text preparation and helped to demystify electronic mail and the conflicting demands of various word processing applications. Finally, and as always, the biggest thank-you is owed to Tiia, Katherin, and Daniel, who help in more ways than they realize.

---

* Visit the ITP Nelson criminology Web site at criminology.nelson.com

PART ONE

INTRODUCTION

CHAPTER ONE

What Is Criminology? Defining and Constructing the Problem of Crime

WHAT'S IN CHAPTER ONE

In this chapter, we introduce criminology as a discipline and examine two major schools of thought: positivism and classicism. Classicists view the offender as rational, deterred by the threat of sanction or responsive to social control. Positivists argue that explanations of criminality—and hence the secret to crime cessation—are found in forces that cause criminal behaviour. We also explain what constitutes crime, focusing on the ideas of *actus reus* (the guilty act) and *mens rea* (the guilty mind). We explore, as well, the different views presented by consensus theory versus conflict theory. The former presupposes a commonly accepted definition of crime while the latter argues that criminal definitions are open to debate as they are often imposed by self-serving interest groups. In addition, we examine the role of the police and the media in defining the extent and pervasiveness of crime. Finally, we discuss myths about crime.

INTRODUCTION

We are confronted daily with many different accounts of crime events that occur in our neighbourhoods and cities, and across the country. These crimes include stabbings in back alleys; beatings of young kids by gangs whose only motivation is to steal distinctive clothing from the victims; major commercial scams in which lending agencies are accused of using illegal practices to defraud clients of their savings; and con games that target vulnerable people with get-rich-quick schemes. Through the media, public forums, and discussions with family and friends, we are confronted with the problem of making sense of these crime events, which on the surface appear quite different from one another.

It is the central contention of this book that there are consistent ways in which we can approach these and other crimes, ways that allow us to make sense of what happened and to put it in a broader context. While we may not always be able to understand why people do certain things, we can search for explanations of crime by examining such factors as circumstances and offender and victim characteristics. What factors led up to the act? Who else was involved? Where did the event take place? What did the police do? We also want to know what was done after the event occurred to deal with its consequences. What punishment was handed down to ensure that similar events did not happen again? While the examples presented above may seem to be unique social events, they share many characteristics that allow us to make sense of them as a singular category—that is, as criminal events.

In presenting an overview of explanations of crime, we will introduce the major theories of criminology as well as the research methods and data that are used to test hypotheses and identify trends in crime. We will also present findings from the considerable research literature, with particular emphasis on crime that occurs at home, during leisure, and at work, as well as the times when and places where most crimes occur. Because explanations of crime heavily influence views of how society should respond to it, it is important to understand what the current program responses are and how they can be brought into line to more effectively deal with crime.

Our approach to the study of crime is defined by the discipline of criminology, a school of inquiry that has gained in stature and credibility over the years. Strong traditions have developed within this school of thought, many of which are complementary, as we will see. Let us begin by looking at criminology as a discipline, as practised in Canada and elsewhere, before we review the various factors that influence the study of crime.

7

*What Is
Criminology?
Defining and
Constructing
the Problem
of Crime*

WHAT IS CRIMINOLOGY?

Criminology is a subject area that draws on a number of different disciplines as it seeks to clarify the nature of the criminal event. Through this interdisciplinary perspective, criminologists attempt to understand not only the motivations of the offender but also the nature of the circumstances leading up to the act and its consequences for the victim(s), for others in the community, and for society at large. Criminologists are also called on to provide insights into how we should respond to crime (for example, through changes in policing strategies or through the development of crime prevention programs). Finally, criminologists monitor the ways in which changes in the laws and their interpretation can affect how people behave in society and, in turn, how agents of social control respond to this behaviour.

The interdisciplinary nature of criminology means that people with quite different types of training contribute to the understanding of criminal events. Criminologists include historians, psychologists, political scientists, economists, legal scholars, and sociologists. For the most part, though, when criminology is taught outside of departments of criminology and criminal justice, it is treated as a subdiscipline of sociology. The fact that sociology has become the major focus of criminological training in North America can be explained by the tendency of sociologists to be more involved than researchers from other disciplines in the study of social problems. In addition, the major figures in the teaching of criminology have been sociologists by training, a fact reflected in the courses that are offered. The tendency in Europe, in contrast, is for criminologists to reside in law schools, which gives a more legal orientation to the research that is pursued there.

The interdisciplinary programs in criminology have been very successful in creating a focus for many people who are interested in the study of crime. For example, the strong emphasis in quantitative sociology on survey research has provided the impetus to accumulate important data through victimization surveys. Economic

WHAT IS CRIMINOLOGY?

Criminology

Criminology uses an interdisciplinary perspective to understand not only the motivations of the offender but also the nature of the circumstances leading up to the act and its consequences for the victim(s), for others in the community, and for the society at large. Criminologists study ways in which we should respond to crime through changes in policing strategies or through the development of crime prevention programs. In addition, criminologists pay close attention to the ways in which changes in the law and their interpretation can affect the ways in which people behave in society and, of course, the ways in which agents of social control respond to this behaviour.

perspectives, too, have made important contributions in the understanding of offender motivations.

There is a strong tradition of criminological research conducted in Canada, with criminologists working mainly in sociology and criminology departments across the country. The research interests of Canadian researchers cover the whole range of topics in the discipline, from the study of homicide (Silverman and Kennedy, 1993) to the investigation of the prevalence of violence against women (Johnson, 1996b) to corporate (Snider, 1993) and organized (Beare, 1996) crime. We draw on this research in the discussion that follows. We also introduce findings from research done in other parts of the world. The growth of modern criminology has been strongest in the United States, particularly as a result of federal funding for research in the 1970s and 1980s in response to the problems of large-scale social disorder in American cities. More recently, the U.S. government has spent large sums on the study of drug-related crime but less liberally in other areas of research. Still, relatively little money is spent on criminological research when compared with the amounts committed to other areas, such as medical or biophysical research. Recent interest in the study of violence and in the application of technology to the control of crime has attracted strong funding support, but this still lags significantly behind the sums allotted for scientific research. This disparity exists despite the large costs that some criminological research entails, particularly large-scale victimization surveys and longitudinal studies of offenders.

There is a great deal of interest in the study of crime in countries outside of North America. For example, many of these countries have become involved in large-scale victimization surveys as, for example, in Britain, where the British Crime Survey (Mirrlees-Black, Mayhew, and Percy, 1996) has been used in the extensive development of policing policy, community crime prevention programs, and offender programs. Again, we will draw on this work in this book.

Our presentation will be heavily influenced by recent thinking in criminology that places great significance on the routine nature of crime and maintains that individual lifestyles bring offenders and victims together in time and space to create crime opportunities. The crime that results creates consequences for all parties concerned, as a result of either police intervention or the actions of third parties.

CLASSICAL AND POSITIVIST VIEWS OF OFFENDERS

Studying the crime event as a consequence of routine does not mean that we ignore the importance of criminological thinking that has been developed over

9

What Is Criminology? Defining and Constructing the Problem of Crime

the centuries to explain offender motivations or the role of punishment in deterring crime. Criminological thought goes back to the ideas of Cesare Beccaria, who wrote in the late 1700s about the need to account for the psychological reality of the offender. The state, he argued, needs to use the fear of pain to control behaviour. Beccaria's view emphasized reform of the repressive and barbaric laws of eighteenth-century Europe, a period in which the administration of justice was arbitrary and abusive. The standing of the person in the community had a direct impact on the treatment that he or she could expect from the courts; justice therefore was relative rather than absolute.

According to Beccaria, the degree of punishment should be sufficient to outweigh the pleasure one derives from a criminal act (Martin, Mutchnik, and Austin, 1990: 8). It was Beccaria's views, together with those of Jeremy Bentham after him, that so heavily influenced modern thinking about deterrence and punishment. According to this **classical school** of thought, the "rational man" would act to avoid punishment—hence the importance of laws that were clear about both how one should act and what the costs of deviating from this lawful behaviour would be (Bohm, 1997).

Beccaria is better described as a social reformer than as a criminologist in the modern sense of that term. He was more interested in changes that would make the criminal justice system effective and fair than he was in explaining the causes of crime. Still, implicit in Beccaria's view is a model of what offenders are like and why they offend. For Beccaria, the offender's behaviour could be understood in terms of a principle of "hedonism." In short, the offender is seen as a kind of rational calculator who seeks to maximize pleasure and minimize pain. From this perspective, a person commits crime when the pleasure promised by the offence outweighs the pain that the law threatens.

The classical model of "rational man" led to a view that the law could be used as an instrument of control. This assumed, however, that men and women were not only free to act but also equal in their ability to do so. In the late 1800s, Cesare Lombroso's positivist views began to question this assumption. His basic belief was that human behaviour was *determined*, a view that stands in direct opposition to Beccaria's assumption that people have free will. For Lombroso, the individual's constitution predetermined responses to surroundings and was influential in creating deficiencies in human behaviour that led to criminality; thus, heredity was a principal cause of criminal tendencies (Martin, Mutchnik, and Austin, 1990: 29). These assumptions led Lombroso to argue for a perspective that emphasized the development of crime types.

For Lombroso, one important category was the "atavistic criminal." His use of the term *atavism* was meant to imply that such offenders were throwbacks to an earlier period in human evolution. In other words, their behaviour was less likely to conform to the demands of contemporary social life because they were related to a more primitive human condition. Lombroso believed that the physical signs of atavism could be described and measured in a scientific manner. Born criminals not only acted in a particular way but looked a particular way. The atavistic criminal might be expected to have ears of unusual size, fleshy lips, pouches in the cheeks, and a head of unusual size and shape (Vold and Bernard, 1986). Lombroso was not suggesting that such characteristics caused criminal behaviour in any simple sense, but rather that they served as visible indicators of the type of person who was likely to behave in this way.

Lombroso's ideas were very influential and even found their way into the popular culture of the period. For instance, the title character in Bram Stoker's novel *Dracula* (1975) is based on Lombroso's description of the atavistic criminal. However, despite their popularity, these ideas were largely discredited even during Lombroso's lifetime. Lombroso's lasting contribution is not the specific content of his theories but rather his more general approach to the problem of crime. Unlike the classical writers who preceded him, Lombroso did not see crime as a product of free will; instead, according to this **positivist school**, crime was something that could be understood in terms of causes and effects.

We should stress that the legacies of classical and positivist thought are alive and well in the context of contemporary criminology. However, they have taken researchers in somewhat different directions. The positivist tradition has come to be linked to theories of criminal motivation. As we will see in Chapter 3, these theories encourage us to ask questions about the kinds of factors that push or pull people into criminal conduct. In contrast, the classical legacy is linked to theories and research that emphasize the factors that constrain people from developing or acting on criminal motivations. As we will discuss in Chapter 4, when these constraints are weak, people have more freedom to do as they please—which sometimes means behaving criminally. As will become clear, these ideas are not necessarily contradictory in the modern criminological context. As Felson (1994: 22) observes, societies provide both temptations and controls, and "as any society generates more temptations and fewer controls, it invites a crime wave."

For all their differences, the various theories that fall roughly into these two schools of thought have in common a fixation on criminality

---

WHAT DOES IT MEAN?

Classical vs. Positivist

Classical criminology views the offender as rational, deterred by the threat of legal sanction and responsive to social control. Positivists argue that the explanations of criminality, and hence the secret to crime cessation, are found in forces outside of the offender that influence criminal conduct.

rather than crime; that is, they focus little attention on the dynamics of the criminal event itself, except as it relates to offender actions (for example, trying to explain why an individual would act in a particular way at a particular time). Only in recent years has the criminal event in its totality served as a focus of criminology (Gottfredson and Hirschi, 1990).

Following from this orientation, there has been an intensive investigation into the relationship between situational factors and individual lifestyles that allows us to consider simultaneously motivation and structural conditions in the environment, including the deterrent effects of possible detection and punishment. We have begun to understand more clearly what happens in crime events and to apply this knowledge as a basis for predicting certain outcomes. Using this approach, modern criminology has emerged with a more holistic view of the crime problem (Miethe and Meier, 1994).

DEFINING CRIME

CRIME AS LAWBREAKING

CRIME AND LAW

In Western society, **crime** is defined strictly as behaviour that breaks the law and is liable to public prosecution and punishment. In a fundamental way, terms like *crime, offender,* and *victim* are legal concepts. An **offender**, for instance, is someone who is recognized as having behaved in a way that contravenes the criminal law. Whether it is appropriate, however, to label an event participant as an offender, criminal, or lawbreaker may be debatable. Individuals who are judged to be offenders by the law may not see themselves in this way or be regarded as such by witnesses or even victims. To a considerable degree, criminal trials are organized, state-sponsored attempts to determine who should be considered an "offender."

Social events have meaning as criminal events, then, only in reference to law. As Nettler (1984: 32) states, "Crime is a word, not a deed," and to label something a crime is to invoke the moral evaluation of the behaviour that is embodied in the law. Thus, the law may be understood as a form of social control that evaluates the moral nature of the behaviour in question. When we describe an act as criminal, we imply that the act is disvalued. It is a form of wrongdoing that "good people" should avoid at the risk of punishment. One of the major functions of the law is to deter people from engaging in the behaviour that the law prohibits. The law comprises a set of written rules that are supported by state authority and accompanied by a standardized schedule of penalties.

11

What Is Criminology? Defining and Constructing the Problem of Crime

Even when there is a clear agreement that an offence has been committed, there may be disagreement about what type of offence it is and what to do about it. In a startling break from tradition, an Edmonton judge, in early 1992, decided to accept a charge of second-degree murder directed against a couple who had grievously assaulted their foster child. The judge ruled that, even though the child was not technically dead (parts of the child's brain stem were still functioning, and he continued to breathe spontaneously), sufficient evidence existed that the persistent vegetative state that resulted from the child's injuries should be incorporated into the legal definition of death. This judgment sparked a heated debate over what might be considered to be a fairly straightforward issue: the definition of life and death.

> ## WHAT IS IT?
>
> ### *Crime*
>
> In Western society, crime is defined strictly as behaviour that breaks the law and is liable to public prosecution and punishment. A criminal intention *(mens rea)* without the action *(actus reus)* is not a crime.

Subsequently, the charge was reduced to aggravated assault, and the couple was convicted. John Dosseter, a bioethics expert, commented on the reduced charge: "I don't think society is ready for such an important matter [changing the definition of life and death] to be decided in such a way in the courts. The matter needs more debate and I don't think a simple court decision is going to do it" (Moysa, 1992: A1). The public and lawmakers must debate changes in the law such that death would be recognized as something beyond the complete cessation of life.

In a similar way, the law is undergoing changes in how it defines actions such as murder. In a case that occurred in the United States, the owners of a business that extracted silver from photographic chemical were convicted of murder when it was revealed that they knowingly exposed their employees (some of whom died) to dangerous and ultimately fatal working conditions. As this case illustrates, one does not have to wield a knife or fire a gun to be labelled a murderer. That same case also exemplifies the difficulty of establishing motives. Did these managers intend to kill? Probably not. Did they know that what they did might result in death? The courts decided that they did and found them guilty of the consequences of their actions. These are considerations that arise in cases in which neglect or incompetence have deadly outcomes.

THE FOCUS ON OFFENDERS

In general, the law is more concerned with crime or criminal behaviour than with criminal events (Gould, 1989). In other words, the law focuses on what offenders do (rather than on other event elements) in deciding what a crime is or when a crime occurs. From a legal standpoint, crime is largely synonymous with the actions of the offender.

Criminologists often find it useful to distinguish between crime *mala in se* and crime *mala prohibita*. This distinction alerts us to the fact that not all crimes resonate to the same degree with popular morality. Crimes ***mala in se*** are crimes that are seen as wrong in and of themselves. They are acts that most people would see as wrong even if they were not against the law and that have been widely condemned both historically and cross-culturally. Murder, robbery, and other predatory crimes are examples of crimes *mala in se*. In contrast, some types of behaviours are not as widely or as consistently condemned. Crimes ***mala prohibita*** are acts that are wrong not in and of themselves but by prohibition. Alcohol consumption and certain sexual activities, for instance, are viewed as criminal only in some societies and only at some points in history.

Brantingham, Mu, and Verma (1995) note that, while Canada has over 40 000 different federal and provincial statutes and municipal bylaws, only those that are defined by federal law are technically crimes. The principal piece of Canadian criminal law is the Criminal Code of Canada, a federal piece of legislation that includes most but not all of the categories of offending we normally think of as crimes (Osborne, 1995).

CONTEXT

Regardless of whether an act violates a law, context is important in determining criminality. The fact that someone behaves in a way that *seems* to be inconsistent with the requirements of the law does not mean that he or she has committed a crime. To be criminal in a legal sense, an act must be intentional (Boyd, 1996). The mere physical act—known legally as the ***actus reus***—is not enough. There must also be a willful quality to the act—what the law refers to as ***mens rea*** (Nettler, 1984). Moreover, to be criminal, an act must be committed in the absence of a legally recognized defence or justification (Boyd, 1996). For example, while the law defines assaultive behaviour as a crime, a particular assaultive act may not be criminal if it was accidental (rather than intentional) or was committed in self-defence (and therefore legally justifiable).

INDIVIDUAL ACCOUNTABILITY

All criminal law derives from a model of behaviour that accounts for individual psychology. Individuals must employ judgment in controlling their acts so that accidents do not occur. A criminal intention (*mens rea*) without the action (*actus reus*) is not a crime. Since intent is part of the definition of crime, prose-

13

What Is Criminology? Defining and Constructing the Problem of Crime

cutors must establish such purpose in the perpetrator. They sometimes try to do this by constructing the motive (Nettler, 1984), asking, "Why would the person act as he or she did?" Establishing a motive does not establish guilt, however; intent and action together are required to obtain a criminal conviction.

Courts can also define the criteria used in judging guilt. The law traditionally has sought to hold able but negligent people accountable for their actions. To do this, it has included the concept of **constructive intent**. The penalties for doing damage through negligence are usually lighter than those for being deliberately criminal, yet the term *crime* applies to both. However, again, these interpretations evolve over time as contexts change. In 1990, the Supreme Court of Canada removed some responsibility as incorporated in the idea of constructive intent. Under the previous interpretation of the law, for example, carrying a weapon in a robbery in which a homicide occurred could lead to a verdict of guilty of murder even if the offender had no intention of killing anyone. The Court believed that this judgment of guilt violated the Charter of Rights and Freedoms. Now, if someone is killed during the course of another crime, this is not automatically considered to be a case of first-degree murder.

In some cases, individuals may commit acts that are beyond their control to prevent. This situation is covered by a judgment of competence, which may be restricted because of age, duress, self-defence, or insanity. With respect to age, all criminal behaviours of youths are handled not in the criminal justice system, but rather in the juvenile system. In Canada, children under 12 cannot be held responsible for their actions in the criminal sense. Children from 12 to 17 are held culpable for their actions but are judged separately from adults through the Young Offenders Act (YOA). Unlike the Juvenile Delinquents Act, which it replaced, the YOA is a body of criminal law that establishes a justice and corrections system separate and distinct from the adult system. It acknowledges that juveniles have special needs, require special legal protection, and should not be held as fully accountable as adults for violating the criminal law (Bala, 1991: 39).

Whereas the Juvenile Delinquents Act was based on a philosophy of *parens patiae* in which the state, acting as a kind of "superparent," was given wide latitude in dealing with the child, the YOA makes the rights and responsibilities of youth much more central issues (Corrado and Markwart, 1996). Recent notorious cases in which young offenders who committed serious crimes received light sentences under the YOA have resulted in changes to the act that allow prosecutors to waive individuals who have committed serious crimes to adult court and to extend sentences such that they are served past the statutory age limit of juvenile offenders. This is what occurred in a stabbing case in

15

What Is Criminology? Defining and Constructing the Problem of Crime

which a Calgary teenager was given a life sentence with no parole for ten years after attacking a 13-year-old (*Globe and Mail*, 1993: A3). Part of the sentence was to be served in juvenile detention until he reached 18, with the balance to be served in an adult institution.

Individuals operating under **duress** may also claim that they did not intend to commit a crime and therefore are not guilty of an offence. In these cases, it must be proved that some unlawful constraint of influence was used to force an individual to commit an act that he or she would otherwise not have committed (Rush, 1994). The idea that one is under duress when committing a crime is often difficult to prove. The degree of force used must be commensurate with the degree of harm the individual perceived was being directed his or her way. Duress, however, is never a defence against murder.

SELF-DEFENCE

Self-defence involves actions taken to protect oneself or one's property in the face of a threat involving reasonable force. These cases are not always straightforward, and our view of self-defence is evolving. Originally, the doctrine of self-defence held that the danger must be immediate and severe in order to justify criminal actions. More recently, in delineating situations in which self-defence claims may be made, the law has begun to recognize issues such as power differentials between victims and offenders and/or the presence of a long-term pattern of abuse and the fear that might be associated with it. An example of this can be found in the use of the "battered woman syndrome," in which a battered woman who killed her abuser when she had reasonable cause to think that her life might be in danger (regardless of whether she had actually been physically abused in the immediate incident) claims self-defence. Recently, the Supreme Court of Canada accepted the argument of self-defence in these cases.

INSANITY

When it comes to proving insanity, it is incumbent on the defence to prove a state of insanity; the prosecution is not required to prove sanity. Putting the onus on the defence has the effect of restricting the extent to which an individual can claim that a limited capacity to form intent resulted from mental breakdown.

LEGAL AND SOCIAL CONTROLS

The legal system plays an important role in managing criminal events. Legal definitions of crime may appear to be immutable, determined by clear-cut rules of evidence in establishing guilt or innocence, but in reality, this is not the case.

BOX 1.1   THE INSANITY DEFENCE IN CANADA

Being acquitted of a crime by reason of insanity is not a ticket to freedom.

Despite what the public may think, perhaps only one in 100 murderers is judged insane, says Dr. Herb Pascoe, a forensic psychiatrist at Alberta Hospital, Edmonton.

And for that small percentage, an insanity verdict can be a more severe punishment than serving a fixed jail sentence. Most jail terms have endings, but there are no guarantees of freedom for an individual judged insane.

Pascoe estimates that at any one time, there are 35 to 40 people in the province who have been acquitted of an offence by reason of insanity.

He optimistically predicts only one-third will leave hospital and remain out. Even for those, the road to recovery and release is arduous.

"You can expect one-third of the patients will do very well and gradually will work their way out of the hospital to resume a useful place in the community," says Pascoe. Another third will stay the same or their conditions will worsen, and the conditions of the last third will go up and down.

"For all the publicity insanity trials get, the number of acquittals is very, very small," he says. "About one out of every 100 murders results in an acquittal by reason of insanity.

"It's a small number but, of course, when it happens it's pretty gruesome, sadistic stuff."

The Criminal Code allows for an insanity verdict if the person, when he committed the offence, was "in a state of natural imbecility or (had) disease of the mind to an extent that (rendered) him incapable of appreciating the nature and quality of an act or omission or of knowing that an act or omission (was) wrong."

The code continues: "A person who has specific delusions, but is in other respects sane, shall not be acquitted on the ground of insanity unless the delusions caused him to believe in the existence of a state of things that, if it existed, would have justified or excused his act or omission."

Following an acquittal by reason of insanity, the person is remanded to Alberta Hospital on a lieutenant-governor's warrant.

He will be kept at the hospital until a review board, consisting of a Court of Queen's Bench justice, two psychiatrists, a lawyer and lay person, recommend the warrant be cancelled.

"We don't want to take chances," says Justice Neil Primrose, board chairman. "A person under certain circumstances could be dangerous.

"But generally, the rehabilitation and recovery of patients has been very good, in my experience."

17

What Is Criminology? Defining and Constructing the Problem of Crime

BOX 1.1   THE INSANITY DEFENCE IN CANADA   (CONT.)

"There are all sorts of safeguards and we are very conservative," says Pascoe. "Things do not happen in a hurry. If a patient makes good progress it will still be several years before he will be allowed out."

The review board meets twice a year in Edmonton and reviews all patients committed on a lieutenant-governor's warrant.

The members hear recommendations from attending psychiatrists, social workers and psychologists. Only the board has the power to recommend a patient be given certain liberties or freedoms, such as ground passes, weekends with family or special outings under strict supervision.

If a patient does exceedingly well, he may eventually be allowed to work during the day and live at the hospital at night.

If all goes well, the patient may eventually be given a conditional discharge on the warrant, and finally an absolute discharge.

Until that time patients can be brought back to hospital at any sign of trouble.

"Most of the patients here appear to be a lot more together than a member of the public would think," says Dr. Maggie Tweddle, a consultant forensic psychiatrist.

"But if they were so obviously crazy, they wouldn't be so dangerous.

"I wouldn't dare let some of these people out without the warrant for several years," says Tweddle. "We have a responsibility to the patient and to the community.

"We're treading a pretty narrow line between doing what is best for the patient and dealing with society. It's certainly a challenge."

SOURCE: Joanne Munro, "Insanity-Based Acquittal Rarely Route to Early Freedom," *Edmonton Journal*, September 6, 1983, p. B1. Reprinted by permission.

Legal responses can be and are heavily influenced by circumstance, public tolerance, and judicial discretion. Police and courts apply the law not only to fight crime and punish criminals but also to reduce social conflict. Any study of crime needs to account for behaviour that is disorderly or dangerous but not yet unlawful. Alternative or informal legal responses set the outside limits of criminality by redefining criminal justice system responses to misbehaviour.

Law is only one form of social control (Black, 1976). Social life is also regulated by informal expectations about how people should and should not behave. Whether we call these expectations etiquette, professionalism, or simply good taste, people evaluate the morality of each other's behaviour and respond accordingly through a variety of means. Gossip, ridicule, and ostracism are forms of social control that involve less formal social processes than do legal forms. When actions are classified as crimes, much more is implied than the mere condemnation of the behaviour. Calling an act a crime implies that the problem will be processed in a particular way and that specific state agencies will assume responsibility for solving it. In other words, to label a particular deed a crime is to confer "ownership" of the problem in question to the police, the courts, and other criminal justice agencies (Gilsinan, 1990).

If a problem is defined as one that involves an uninformed public acting on the basis of incomplete or incorrect information, then educational experts might be expected to provide a solution. If a problem is defined as one that results from some medical condition, then mental or physical health professionals will dominate efforts at problem amelioration. However, when behaviour is deemed criminal, the issue will likely be surrendered to law enforcement and crime prevention specialists. Evidently, these alternative views are associated with dramatically different consequences. As Gusfield (1989) notes, it makes a real difference whether we see social problems as involving people who are troubled or people who are troublesome.

CRIME AND MORALITY

The idea of crime starts with some conception of proper behaviour that is based on an accepted form of **morality**. Society sets out general rules detailing what is permissible or normative behaviour. Moral standards change whether we want them to or not, and accompanying the changes are variations in the content of crime. "The broad boundaries of offenses against property, person, and society remain fairly steady, but the criminal content within these boundaries varies" (Nettler, 1984: 2). What we define as normative behaviour is affected by our reactions to behaviour as morality evolves over time.

A related issue involves the forces that bring about changes in public beliefs about morality. A question posed by Jack Gibbs—"With what frequency must a type of act occur before it is considered a norm?" (1981: 14)—can be asked with reference to delinquent or criminal behaviour. Suppose that large parts of the society partake in what is considered to be criminal behaviour. Does the fact that the behaviour is widespread make it normative? Obviously, this depends on the degree of harm being done and on the willingness of the society to retaliate against this harm. For example, violence in the American "Old West" was commonplace during the settlement years. The behaviour of gunslingers appeared to be normative, but was it acceptable? Clearly, the strong demand by inhabitants of these settlements for law enforcement indicates that they wanted the violence to be curtailed. Criminologists must assess

19

*What Is
Criminology?
Defining and
Constructing
the Problem
of Crime*

how legal and moral definitions of crime coincide with the circumstances that people face, circumstances that evolve into events that demand enforcement and result in labelling individuals as criminal.

Our approach to the study of crime takes into account the issues related to its normalcy, particularly in our review of the impact that changes in law have on definitions of criminality. But the definitions that victims and offenders themselves bring to criminal situations (definitions that we measure in victimization surveys, reports on crime, action by public interest groups, and reports in the media) heavily influence how we react to and what we do about crime. The perspective that we offer in this book questions the recent tendency in positivist criminology to isolate one or two characteristics of individuals as a way of increasing our precision in predicting their criminal tendencies or identifying a "criminal type." We believe that this type of theory building is preclusive in that it sets up artificial borders around different aspects of crime and discourages criminologists from looking at the social bases of crime—that is, crime as it evolves out of social interaction and affects social structures.

The artificial boundaries placed around crime actually change through continuous negotiation of what constitutes criminal behaviour, both in the ways individuals respond to criminal behaviour and in the ways the criminal justice system tries to control it. While positivist approaches certainly simplify the number of elements we have to consider in our assessment of crime, they ignore the complexity of the criminal event—its precursors, the circumstances that prevail during the act, and its aftermath.

CRIME, POLITICS, AND THE LAW

Why are some kinds of criminal events aggressively prosecuted by the criminal justice system while others do not seem to arouse much indignation? How do some types of "crime problems" become the central concern of policymakers who talk about "the war on drugs" or the need for "zero tolerance" of family violence? Where do the laws that deem some types of events as criminal come from in the first place? Answering such questions requires a systematic study of the social processes that shape and constrain organized reaction to criminal events. Theoretical approaches to these issues help us to recognize that these reactions should be understood not only as the decisions of police officers, policymakers, or politicians but also as part of larger social processes that affect behaviour at the individual level.

Two theoretical explanations have been advanced to account for reactions to crime (Akers, 1994). One argues that these reactions emerge out of and reflect a social consensus about morality and about the need to respond to particular types of events in particular ways. The other view suggests that reactions to crime have more to do with power, conflict, and inequality than with social consensus.

At a very broad level, these approaches may be distinguished with respect to the ways in which they conceptualize the role of social interests (Bockman, 1991). According to consensus theorists, the members of a society have many interests in common, and their reactions to crime may be said to serve these collective interests. Laws are written and enforced to meet the needs of the majority. Deviation from these laws is generally accepted as reason for punishment. Conflict theorists, on the other hand, argue that in a complex society, social groups may pursue different interests, and that the degree of success with which they do so depends on how powerful they are. In this framework, reactions to crime can be understood as reflecting particular class, cultural, or other social interests rather than more broadly defined collective interests.

THE CONSENSUS VIEW

In the study of reactions to crime, the concept of social consensus is meant to alert us to the apparently broad-based agreement in society about what kinds of acts are serious crimes warranting direct and immediate intervention and what types are not. **Consensus theory**, which relates to our discussion of crime as an attack on social morality, is associated with a number of important scholars (Durkheim, 1964; Parsons, 1951; Pound, 1943). It suggests that, even in a complex, highly differentiated society like our own, people who differ from one another in terms of gender, age, ethnicity, and social class are likely to agree about certain basic moral standards.

Punishment is directed toward a commonly agreed-upon set of behaviours that offend social mores. We punish murderers more severely than we punish other criminals because of the general social consensus that murder is among the most serious infractions that a person can commit. We "criminalize," through the passage of laws, behaviours that are widely understood as threatening to our shared values, and we attach the most severe penalties to those crimes that offend our sense of collective morality most deeply.

The consensus view has gone so far as to assert that crime is functional, an idea that originated in the work of Emile Durkheim. According to the functional approach, without the contrast to "normal" behaviour that is provided by crime, we would have difficulty establishing acceptable and tolerable limits

21

What Is Criminology? Defining and Constructing the Problem of Crime

to human actions. Criminal definitions provide us with the boundaries of behaviour beyond which we should, and dare, not go. As Kennedy (1990) notes, these boundaries create the illusion that crime is an isolated phenomenon, unrelated to other types of social activity. Theories of crime are based on classifications of the social forms and factors associated with criminal behaviour (Cain and Kulscar, 1981–82: 386). The preclusive view of delinquent behaviour that results from placing artificial borders around crime discourages criminologists from addressing conflict that occurs beyond these borders—and that may motivate crime in the first place. From a functionalist perspective, there is no need to address the idea that the boundaries around crime may change as a result of changes in both individual and criminal justice system responses to criminal behaviour.

From the functionalist point of view, reactions to crime, as expressed in criminalization or punishment, make up one of the most basic ways in which our sense of collective morality is communicated. The moral indignation reflected in the passage of a law, the policy decision to increase the penalties for a given type of crime, and the punishment of an offender are all reminders of what binds us together as members of a society. Consistent with this view, a large body of public opinion research indicates that, by and large, our legal responses to crime reflect widespread social sentiments (Cullen, Link, and Polanzi, 1982; Goff and Nason-Clark, 1989; Hansel, 1987; Miethe, 1982; Rossi et al., 1974; Sigler and Johnson, 1986; Warr, 1989).

The consensus position and the research it has spawned have attracted much criticism. Most generally, opponents have argued that the consensus view oversimplifies the complex relationships among groups that pursue different interests with varying levels of resources. To measure consensus in a public opinion survey begs the question as to where the consensus comes from in the first place. It is one thing to argue that consensus spontaneously emerges from the collective will of the population. It is quite another to suggest that consensus results from the fact that some individuals have a vested interest in reacting to criminal events in a particular way and are able to convince the rest of the population that their world view is the right one. In either case, we might find that public opinion data reveal widespread agreement about the relative seriousness of different crimes.

WHAT DOES IT MEAN?

Consensus vs. Conflict

Social consensus is meant to alert us to the apparent broad-based agreement in society about what kinds of acts are serious crimes and deserving of direct and immediate intervention and what types are not. Conflict approaches argue that responses to crime must be seen as part of a larger struggle between groups who attempt to use the law, or legal control, in the pursuit of their interests.

Further, by assuming that crime is functional, we justify actions that are taken by the state to repress certain groups. The actions of the police and the judiciary become focused on the disadvantaged, on visible minorities, and on other groups that lack the resources to escape this kind of attention. Such criminalization is dysfunctional in that it exacts a human cost and at the same time devalues initiatives that attempt to deal with the problems faced by these groups in ways other than through law enforcement.

Sellin (1938) cautions that using an unqualified set of *legal* definitions as the basic units or elements of criminological inquiry violates a fundamental criterion of scientific inquiry. The scientist must be free to define his or her own terms in attempting to understand any phenomena, including the crime event. Accepting without qualification the definitions of crime and criminals as laid down in law renders criminological research theoretically invalid from the scientific point of view (Sellin, 1938: 24). What is necessary, claims Sellin, is an approach to crime in which the definitions of criminal behaviour can change and evolve depending on the nature of the interactions among individuals and between them and the agencies that administer control over social behaviour. The way in which we articulate the problem of crime can help us focus on its root causes. Adopting inflexible definitions of the criminal event will probably lead us to deal only with the symptoms of crime and not with the causes. However, we must know not just *what* these definitions entail but also *how* they are developed (Kennedy, 1990). Further, the negotiation of justice may be a reflection not only of what the agents of social control *can do* but also what they are *prepared to do* in attacking crime.

The definitions of crime through law, then, may be seen as unchangeable, determined by the rules of evidence in establishing guilt or innocence. Alternatively, law can be seen as defining the boundaries of unacceptable behaviours depending on circumstance, public tolerance, and judicial discretion. Agents of social control use the law not only to deter crime and punish criminals but also to reduce social conflict. Some behaviour that is not dealt with through the formal application of law may nevertheless be disorderly, threatening, or dangerous. Any study of crime needs to account for behaviour that has these characteristics but is not yet unlawful. Criminologists must also consider alternative responses, such as community-based mediation, that have developed as a means of dealing with this kind of behaviour. Even though they do not elicit any specific legal sanction, alternative or informal responses establish the outer limits of criminality by redefining criminal justice responses to misbehaviour.

23

*What Is
Criminology?
Defining and
Constructing
the Problem
of Crime*

BOX 1.2   DON'T SOME LAWS REFLECT CONSENSUS?

The view that laws emerge out of and reflect special interests seems to be contradicted by the commonsense observation that some laws, at least, appear to reflect the interests of everyone in society. For example, laws against murder, robbery, or sexual assault would seem to be in everyone's interest, not just those who have the most power.

However, the late British sociologist Steven Box (1981) argued that it is not really correct to say that the law prohibits murder, sexual assault, or robbery. Rather, it prohibits certain types of such behaviours while at the same time not prohibiting other behaviours that, while very similar, are likely to be committed by more powerful people.

With respect to murder, for instance, Box wrote that

> the criminal code defines only some types of killing as murder; it excludes, for example, deaths which result from negligence such as employers' failure to maintain safe working conditions in factories or mines … or deaths which result from government agencies' giving environmental health risks a low priority … or death resulting from drug manufactures' failure to conduct adequate research on new chemical compounds before conducting aggressive marketing campaigns. [Therefore,] criminal laws against murder, rape, robbery and assault do protect us all, but they do not protect the less powerful from being killed, sexually exploited, deprived of their property, or physically or psychologically damaged through the greed, apathy, negligence and the accountability of the relatively more powerful. (48–49)

CONFLICT, POWER, AND THE LAW

In contrast to the consensus view, **conflict theory** asserts that, even if a consensus exists about what constitutes a serious crime and what does not, the source of the consensus must be taken into consideration. Moreover, it is incorrect to maintain that this consensus is a spontaneous product of group life. As one critic of the consensus position has recently written, "Laws do not simply appear miraculously on our law books and do not reflect 'society's' values. Instead, the acts and people we call 'criminal' and our concern with crime at any given time reflect the activity of groups in this society seeking legal support for economic, ideological and status interest" (Sheley, 1991: 39). From this standpoint, definitions of crime must be seen as part of a larger struggle among groups attempting to use the law, or legal control, in the pursuit of their interests.

IDENTIFYING COMPETING SOCIAL GROUPS

There is little agreement among scholars as to what might constitute such competing groups in society. Marxian scholars, for instance, locate attempts to control the mechanisms for reacting to crime in the conflicts between social classes (Chambliss, 1986; Reiman, 1990). For these theorists, such conflicts are a central feature of capitalist societies. The powerful economic classes, which own property and industries, seek to expand and consolidate their control of the less powerful classes, which must sell their labour to the capitalist class in order to survive. The legal machinery provides one important means by which this may be accomplished (Schissel, 1992).

At the same time, Marxian scholars encourage us to recognize that industries that pollute the environment and victimize consumers are generally treated less harshly than the street criminal who robs a convenience store (Michalowski and Bohlander, 1976). This is because the criminalization or aggressive prosecution of these industry actions would not be consistent with capitalist interests. For the Marxian theorist, the fact that the average person might agree that the cold-blooded killer of a convenience store night clerk should be treated more harshly than the CEO of a corporation that sells defective—and potentially dangerous or even lethal—products does not demonstrate evidence of a spontaneous consensus about what types of crimes are more serious. It merely demonstrates the ability of powerful interests to manipulate the consciousness of the members of a capitalist society.

Other proponents of the conflict position favour a model of group relations that is more diffuse than the one embraced by the Marxians. Laws and other aspects of the legal machinery do not merely reflect class conflict but may involve a variety of other interests as well (Bernard, 1981; Gusfield, 1963; Jenkins, 1992; Turk, 1976). Conflicts arise between cultural, lifestyle, or ethnic groups, and the factors that propel groups to use the legal machinery in the service of their interests may be diverse. The conflicts in which social groups are involved are not necessarily fought on a level playing field. Groups differ in the degree to which they have access to resources that allow them to influence the outcome of the conflict. From this perspective, the machinery of legal control can be thought of as one such resource. Groups may wish to see laws passed in order to have their values officially recognized by society; or they may wish to see the law used to control a group they believe threatens their values or social position.

PEACEMAKING

25

*What Is
Criminology?
Defining and
Constructing
the Problem
of Crime*

In a recent interpretation of conflict theory, Quinney and Wildeman (1991) offer a perspective that emphasizes peace and social justice. They argue that many of the dilemmas and contradictions in mainstream ("bourgeois") criminology in the United States at the end of the twentieth century are the result of a theoretical chaos in the field. As Quinney and Wildeman see it, this chaos stems from the persistence of certain popular beliefs that dominate the thinking about crime. As originally outlined by Pepinsky and Jesilow (1984), these include the following:

- Crime is increasing.
- Most crime is committed by the poor.
- Some groups are more law-abiding than others.
- White-collar crime is nonviolent.
- Regulatory agencies prevent white-collar crime.
- Rich and poor people are equal before the law.
- Drug addiction causes crime.
- Laws make people behave themselves.

In Quinney and Wildeman's (1991) view, these beliefs fail to address the fundamental inequality in a society in which the power to control punishment, which lies in the hands of the state, dictates that certain groups will be unfairly treated by the criminal justice system. In this respect, criminalization is a means of imposing violence on the underclass.

Quinney and Wildeman encourage us to consider both alternative ways of responding to social ills and the broader issues that generate criminality, including social and economic disadvantage. Their solution is to offer a criminology of **peacemaking**, which involves reducing punishment/imprisonment and promoting programs that encourage treatment, rehabilitation, alternatives to prisons, mediation, and enhanced social justice. Peacemaking's nonviolent approach to crime reduction includes strategies of problem-oriented policing in which the emphasis is on *preventing* crime rather than *reacting to* crime in a punitive way (Quinney and Wildeman, 1991: 107).

THE FEMINIST APPROACH

The idea of peacemaking has found its way into feminist approaches to criminology (Simpson, 1989). In the **feminist** view, felicity and harmony are regarded as the highest values, and much emphasis is placed on the themes of caring, sharing, nurturing, and loving. According to Harris (1991):

This contrasts sharply [with] the orientation that values power and control above all else. Where the central goal is power, power conceived as "power over" or control, people and things are not viewed as ends in themselves but as instruments for the furtherance of power. Hierarchical institutions and structures are established both to clarify power rankings and to maintain them. The resulting stratifications create levels of superiority and inferiority, which carry differential status, legitimacy, and access to resources and other benefits. Such divisions and exclusions engender resentment and revolt in various forms, which then are used to justify greater control. (88)

A major part of the feminist effort, Harris suggests, involves attempts to identify and confront characteristics and values that are not conducive to the full realization of human potential. In addition, feminists reject negative values that are used to justify stereotyping and that work to support the groups in power. Consistent with the ideas offered in the criminology of peacemaking, the feminist view proposes that the emphasis on control (which is epitomized in incarceration) be replaced by an emphasis on strategies that address the serious disharmony in society. Undermining social inequalities and enhancing social interaction are ways in which the potential for violence and crime can be reduced.

FEMINIST EXPLANATIONS OF CRIME RATES

In addition to seeking to understand the overall causes of crime, feminists explore the basic issues related to female criminality, starting with why the female crime rate is so much lower than that for males. Naffine (1987) examines the different theoretical approaches that have dominated criminological thinking and finds them wanting in their explanation of female involvement (or noninvolvement) in crime.

Theories that Naffine characterizes as masculinity theories, as exemplified by the work of Silverman and Dinitz (1974), have argued that men and women differ in terms of the traits that create a propensity toward criminal behaviour. According to Naffine, these perspectives give rise to a basic but serious empirical problem. "Those who theorize the significance of masculinity for criminality (and femininity for conformity) have never managed to specify exactly what it is about masculinity and femininity which triggers this behaviour, let alone define these concepts in a consistent and convincing manner" (Naffine, 1987: 60).

Feminist criminologists argue that the reasons we have seen a limited growth in female crime over the past decades is not that women are more

27

What Is Criminology? Defining and Constructing the Problem of Crime

passive and conforming but rather that they are more interested than men are in seeking alternatives to confrontation and aggressive action. Female crime occurs not because women become more like men but rather because the structural supports that women require to maintain relationships or to achieve their goals either are not available or are being used against them. Feminists have called for a new view of social control, one that moves away from the notion of the "reasonable man," with its emphasis on decision making based on the male experience, and toward a perspective that encompasses the experiences of all individuals (Naffine, 1987: 1).

BATTERED WOMEN AND CRIME

The feminist reinterpretation of social control is consistent with the fact that, in the legal landscape, an increasing number of claimants are not only representing certain groups as victims but also negotiating to have offenders considered in a different light. A similar trend can be seen with respect to the cases of women who kill their husbands after suffering long-term physical abuse. What has confounded the courts in dealing with these cases is that often there is no evidence of self-defence at the time of the murder and, in many instances, the crime actually appears to have been premeditated. However, advocates argue that women charged with such crimes should not be judged solely on the evidence gathered on the scene. Rather, adjudication of the act should include consideration of the pattern of abuse that preceded it.

As stated previously, courts have come to accept as an acceptable defence the claim that ongoing violence directed against women creates a **battered woman syndrome**. This syndrome is characterized by a sense of helplessness whereby women come to believe that they can neither leave the abusive relationship nor effectively act to reduce the physical abuse; hence, violence is their only recourse. Striking back when the abuser is asleep or otherwise vulnerable makes the act appear premeditated.

> ### WHAT DOES IT MEAN?
>
> #### *Battered Woman Syndrome*
>
> This syndrome is characterized by a sense of helplessness, where women come to believe that they cannot leave an abusive relationship nor can they effectively act to reduce the violence.

Until fairly recently, women who killed their abusive partners in such circumstances were routinely convicted of manslaughter or murder and often were sentenced to long prison terms. In the late 1970s and early 1980s, however, courts began to allow expert witness testimony regarding the battered woman syndrome, and how the experience of long-term abuse might impart a sense of imminent personal danger (generally required in a self-defence plea) in a woman who killed an abusive partner (Gillespie, 1989). In many nations, unlike Canada, the battered woman syndrome defence is still not recognized as a special category of justification for the commission of a homicide, but the use of expert witness testimony in such cases continues to be allowed and to influence decisions regarding guilt or innocence.

THE POLICE AND CRIME

The discretionary aspects of policing strongly affect which events will be targeted and acted on. No group is more influential than the police in designating crime events.

When an event comes to their attention, the police may invoke a wide array of discretionary powers (for example, collecting evidence, investigating the claims of the victim[s], and arresting the offender or offenders). In short, the police have the power to "certify" an event as a crime by assessing the match between the event as they understand it and their working knowledge of what the law disallows.

How do the police encounter situations that they might designate as crimes? Attempts to answer this question have tended to emphasize the distinction between proactive and reactive policing services. Black (1970) notes that, in the case of **proactive policing**, the police become involved in incidents when their own investigative or patrol activities bring to their attention events that may be designated as crimes. Only about 10 percent of the cases in which the police are involved are the result of proactive policing. By contrast, in the case of **reactive policing**, the police become involved in criminal events when asked to do so by a member of the general public. Thus, it is important to understand the circumstances under which citizens request police intervention.

Surveys of crime victims have proven to be a valuable source of information in this regard. Most crimes that come to the attention of the police are reported by the crime victims themselves. People who reported crimes to the police were most likely to say they did so because they hoped to recover stolen property, because "the offence was a crime," or because they wished to prevent being further victimized by the offender. The 1993 **General Social Survey**

WHAT DOES IT MEAN?

Proactive vs. Reactive Policing

In proactive policing, the police become involved in incidents as a result of their own investigative or patrol activities, which bring events that may be designated as crimes to their attention. In reactive policing, the police become involved in criminal events when requested to do so by a member of the general public.

29

*What Is
Criminology?
Defining and
Constructing
the Problem
of Crime*

(GSS) showed that a substantial number of victimizations are not reported to law enforcement agencies. Among these, sexual assault is least likely to be reported (police officers were not informed of 90 percent of sexual assaults, while 68 percent of nonsexual assaults went unreported). The criminal event most likely to be reported during 1992 was break-and-enter, 68 percent of which were reported (Gartner and Doob, 1994).

The most common reasons for not reporting criminal victimization were: the incident was considered too minor to report (54 percent), victims felt that the police could not do anything about it (47 percent), or victims dealt with it another way (43 percent). Contrary to popular belief, victim surveys reveal that a fear of retaliation by the offender plays a relatively minor role in reporting decisions for most crimes. However, fear of revenge was given as a reason in 29 percent of sexual assaults and 19 percent of nonsexual assaults (Gartner and Doob, 1994).

Victims may have other reasons for not reporting crimes. For example, they may prefer not to report because they feel that the police cannot be of assistance to them or that the police are inefficient, ineffective, or biased. Further, victims may choose not to report because they perceive the crime to have been of a personal or private nature. For example, rates of reporting for stranger-perpetrated crimes are generally slightly higher than those for crimes perpetrated by someone known to the victim. Victims may themselves be involved in some form of criminal activity at the time of the incident and may therefore be reluctant to invite a police investigation (Block, 1974). In some instances, victims do not report crimes because they have at their disposal other means of dealing with the situation (Kennedy, 1988). For example, a teenage boy who has been assaulted by a peer may be more likely to seek retaliation through personal action than through police intervention.

Members of some social groups are somewhat more likely than members of other groups to report crime to the police, although differences in this regard are not particularly strong (Gottfredson and Gottfredson, 1988). Crimes involving female or elderly victims, for instance, have higher levels of reportability. This is perhaps because many women and many elderly have at their disposal fewer alternative resources for dealing with victimization and its consequences (Fattah and Sacco, 1989; Skogan, 1976). While people who view the criminal justice system negatively might be expected to be less likely to contact the police, the influence of such attitudes appears to be slight (Block, 1974; Gottfredson and Gottfredson, 1988).

In contrast, available data indicate that reporting decisions are strongly influenced by the characteristics of the criminal events themselves. The more serious the event, the greater the probability that it will be reported to the police. Thus, incidents that involve physical injury, significant property loss, or the use of a weapon, or that occur in or near the victim's residence, are more likely than incidents without these characteristics to be brought to the attention of the police (Block, 1974; Gottfredson and Gottfredson, 1988; Skogan, 1977).

These findings are consistent with the view that people report crimes to the police when there is good reason to do so but decline to report crimes when the costs of reporting outweigh any potential benefits. For victims of sexual assault or wife abuse, fear of retaliation or concerns about stigmatization or mistreatment by police negate the advantages associated with reporting. In general, reporting crime is best viewed as part of a rational decision-making process that takes account of the crime, the offender, the victim's resources, and the perceived limitations of police responsiveness (Gottfredson and Gottfredson, 1988).

How Much Crime?

Now that we have some sense of what constitutes crime and which factors may affect its reporting, what does this mean for the overall volume of crime that comes to the attention of the police? As can be seen in Figure 1.1, the overall rate of crime more than tripled between 1962 (the first year these crime statistics were calculated) and 1995. More specifically, violent crimes increased almost fivefold, while property crimes nearly tripled (Statistics Canada, 1995).

As Martin and Ogrodnik (1996) point out, however, in the years since 1991, there have been steady decreases in crime rates in Canada (3 percent in 1992, 5.3 percent in 1993, and 4.8 percent in 1994). Less research attention has been paid to explaining the reasons for these declines than for the three decades of growth in crime rates. Kennedy and Veitch (1997), in a detailed review of the crime rate drop in Edmonton from 1991 to 1994 (a 39 percent decline in property offences and a 32 percent drop in crimes against people), suggest that this has resulted due to a combination of factors. They argue that the drop in property crime has resulted from increases in private security measures and new crime prevention practices, including proactive community policing initiatives that seek to solve problems rather than simply reply to calls for service. Another new police initiative is to divert calls to community stations and to use more discretion in the handling of crime complaints (sometimes leading to solutions other than arrest to deal with problems such as minor assaults and other disorder crimes). The implications for community policing initiatives on crime trends will be more fully discussed in Chapter 11. Of interest here is the fact that,

Figure 1.1 Crime in Canada, 1962–1995

31

What Is Criminology? Defining and Constructing the Problem of Crime

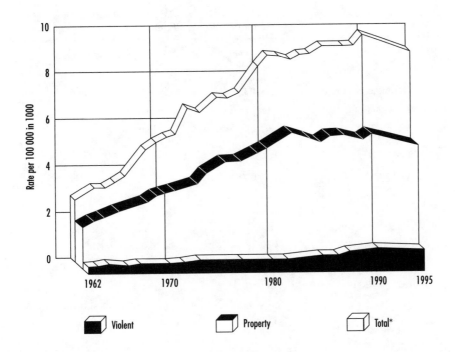

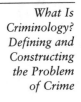

* Total excludes traffic and drug offences and federal statutes.

SOURCE: *Uniform Crime Reporting Survey,* Canadian Centre for Justice Statistics.

although the crime rate drops have not been as steep everywhere as they have been reported in Edmonton, the overall trend has been downward. This is likely due to the adoption of community policing initiatives nationwide. Future trends in crime rates are difficult to predict, but it would appear that we are on a downward course, as the programs that can be credited with bringing about this decline become more successful and widely adopted.

Table 1.1 provides a picture of major offences for 1995. Here we can see that property crimes far outnumbered violent crimes, which made up only about 11 percent of total crimes reported for 1995. Theft under $5000 was the crime most likely to occur, while homicide was the least likely to occur.

Crime rates in Canada also vary by geographic region. Historically, crime has increased as one moves from east to west in Canada, with the highest levels being in British Columbia (and the Yukon and Northwest Territories) and the lowest in the Maritimes (see Figure 1.2).

Table 1.1   Crime in Canada, 1995[1]

Offence Type	Number	Rate per 100 000 Population	% of Total
Violent crimes			
Homicide	586	2	
Attempted murder	932	3	
Sexual assaults	28 216	95	
Nonsexual assaults	230 167	777	
Robbery	30 273	102	
Abduction	1 040	4	
Total violent crimes	297 704	995	11.2
Property crimes			
Break and enter	390 726	1 320	
Motor vehicle theft	163 293	552	
Theft over $5000	41 194	139	
Theft under $5000	820 099	2 770	
Have stolen goods	31 128	105	
Fraud	104 052	351	
Total property crimes	1 550 492	5 237	58.5
Other Criminal Code	805 862	5 237	30.4
Total crime	2 651 058	8 954	

[1] Excludes traffic offences

SOURCE: Adapted from D. Hendrick (1996), "Canadian Crime Statistics, 1995," Statistics Canada, *Juristat,* Catalogue No. 85-002, Volume 16, Number 10.

Patterns and trends of crime are heavily influenced by changes in the population and by the socioeconomic forces that impinge on daily life. We will examine these factors in greater detail in later chapters.

THE PUBLIC'S INTEREST IN CRIMINAL EVENTS

The fact that violent crime still constitutes a small proportion of all crime events is at odds with the public perception about the extent and pervasiveness of this type of crime. Public attitudes toward crime are strongly influenced by

33

What Is Criminology? Defining and Constructing the Problem of Crime

Figure 1.2   Rates per 100 000 Population of Total Criminal Code Offences, Canada and the Provinces and Territories, 1991, 1995

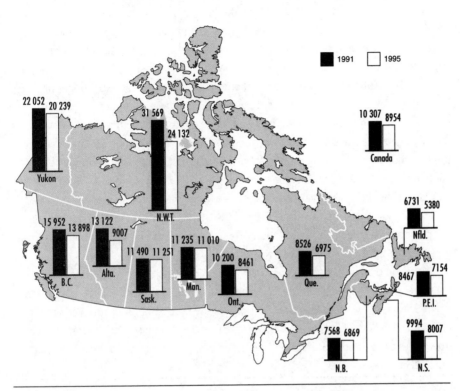

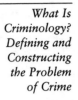

SOURCE: Statistics Canada.

the extensive treatment of this subject in the media. Of course, there is a widespread public fascination with the topic of crime. Lawbreaking figures prominently in what we see and hear in the mass media and in the conversations that we have with one another. What are these popular images of crime? Where do they come from? What implications do they have for the ways in which we think about and respond to crime?

CRIME NEWS

THE INTEREST IN CRIME NEWS

While there are differences across media types and across communities with respect to the amount of coverage that crime receives (Liska and Baccaglini, 1990), generally speaking crime is widely reported by all popular news media (Dominick, 1978; Ericson, Baranek, and Chan, 1991). Why is this? The simple answer may be that media audiences are interested in such stories, and

BOX 1.3   CRIME TOURS

The public ambivalence about crime manifests itself in various ways. Much of the popular culture that we find in television, books, and movies focuses on the sensational character of crime in society. While most members of the general public express concern about the problem of crime, it is an endless source of fascination.

This fascination has extended in recent years to the tourist experience. In many large American cities, visitors may take guided tours of famous local crime scenes. In Chicago, Untouchable Tours provides customers with a scenic view of the city's most famous gangland locations, including the Biograph Theater (where the FBI shot and killed bank robber John Dillinger) and the former headquarters of gangster Al Capone. A tour company in New York City offers the Sidewalks of New York tour, which allows paying guests to visit famous Manhattan murder scenes. Visitors to Hollywood can ride in a Cadillac hearse as they visit local sites, including the places where Janis Joplin and John Belushi overdosed on drugs and the home where mobster Bugsy Siegal was murdered.

Vacation planning is made easy by travel guides such as *Unauthorized America* ("a travel guide to the places the Chamber of Commerce won't tell you about") by Vince Staten, *New York Notorious* ("a borough-by-borough tour of the city's most famous crime scenes") by Paul Schwartzman and Rob Polner, and *Murder USA* ("a true-crime travel guide to the most notorious killing grounds in America") by Tom Philben.

SOURCE: "Crime Tours," *Crimebeat* (January 1992), pp. 29–31.

journalists therefore rely on crime news because it "sells" (Gordon and Heath, 1981). Some audience members may view crime news as an important source of information about the "facts" of crime, while others may be caught up in the dramatic and sometimes lurid nature of crime news.

Katz (1987) argues that audience fascination with crime news has little to do with a search for the truth about crime or with the dramatic qualities of crime reporting. Instead, he maintains, crime news allows audience members to work out their own positions on moral questions of a general yet also personal nature. For example, many crime stories deal with the competence or insensitivity of offenders. As Katz (1987) expresses it, we read accounts of "ingenious, vicious, and audacious crimes of deceptions that trick the close scrutiny of diligent customs inspectors, of the most bloody murders, of big heists in broad daylight" (50). Such stories demonstrate to the audience the nature and limits of human competence and human sensibility. They are of interest to the audience precisely because the dilemma of assessing personal

35

*What Is
Criminology?
Defining and
Constructing
the Problem
of Crime*

competence and maintaining one's own moral sensibility is routinely encountered in day-to-day life. For Katz (1987), reading crime news is a "ritual moral exercise [and, as such,] appears to serve a purpose similar to the morning shower, routine physical exercise and shaving" (72).

THE CONTENT OF CRIME NEWS

Studies on the content of **crime news** have yielded informative findings (Marsh, 1991). First, there appears to be little direct correspondence between the amount of *crime news* and the amount of *crime* (as measured, for instance, in official statistics). In other words, objectively measured trends in crime do not correspond closely with trends in the amount of crime news (Garofalo, 1981a; Katz, 1987). Second, the degree of media attention to crime depends on the type of offence. Violent, relatively infrequent crimes like homicide are emphasized, while property crimes, white-collar offences, and other nonviolent, frequently occurring crimes are underreported (Graber, 1980; Humphries, 1981; Randall, Lee-Sammons, and Hagner, 1988; Skogan and Maxfield, 1981). Third, crime news presents an exaggerated image of the proportion of offences that result in arrest (Sacco and Fair, 1988; Skogan and Maxfield, 1981); that is, the media portray police as far more effective than they really are. Fourth, media attention is focused on the early stages of criminal justice processing (detection and arrest); the later stages of legal processing are largely ignored (Hans, 1990).

Analyses of crime news also indicate that media coverage is notable not only for what it includes but also for what it excludes. Crime reporting is often criticized for ignoring the relationship between crime and broad social conditions. Jon Katz (1993) reports that gun murders have now become so common in large U.S. cities that major newspapers and networks tend to ignore them. Katz states that the readers of large dailies primarily reside in suburbs outside of the areas in which the violence is the greatest. As a result, only the most sensational of the violent crimes are reported, leaving the inner-city residents with no mainstream media to report on their most urgent problems.

Humphries (1981) suggests that while news reports associate criminal violence with youth, maleness, and minority membership, they ignore the historical view of how labour markets and related institutions shape employment opportunities and the size and composition of the pool of people vulnerable to arrest. This tendency to portray crime as perpetrated mainly by pathological individuals precludes alternative explanations. For instance, a report about a single mother accused or convicted of child abuse may describe her as "disturbed" and ignore the following questions: "Was the mother receiving welfare or was she unemployed? Was the child attending a day-care program or receiving any other social services? Had the mother been a victim of child abuse?" (Gorelick, 1989: 423).

The biased nature of media crime reporting is clearly illustrated in Voumvakis and Ericson's (1984) study on newspaper accounts of attacks against women. While the accounts covered in this study offer explanations for the "crime wave," they do so by emphasizing (1) the ways in which the victims' actions placed them at risk; (2) the need for a more coercive, and presumably more effective, response from the criminal justice system; and (3) offender pathology. Voumvakis and Ericson maintain that these terms of reference, although not necessarily unreasonable, are restrictive in that they rule out alternative interpretations, particularly those that link crimes against women to more general patterns of gender inequality. Reporting that emphasizes the need for more police, more punishment, and more vigilance by women does not allow for discussion of broader programs of social reform that might correct these inequalities. A more recent study by Stone (1993) of the ways in which the Toronto media treat the topic of violence against women shows that feminist viewpoints are most often absent from such reports.

THE SOURCES OF CRIME NEWS

Studies of news production practices emphasize the ways in which judgments of "newsworthiness" come to be applied to categories of events (Chibnall, 1977; Fishman, 1978). Such judgments reflect the ways journalists view their society, the work in which they are engaged, and the audiences they serve. Criminal events (especially violent ones) conform closely to the professional values of journalists for several reasons (Ericson, Baranek, and Chan, 1987).

First, such incidents have spatial and temporal characteristics that lend themselves easily to news production routines. Murders, thefts, and sexual assaults are discrete events that occur in the period between the publication of successive editions of a newspaper or between successive radio and television newscasts. Second, reports of criminal events are readily comprehensible to an audience and thus require little in the way of background information. In addition, because there is an almost limitless supply of crime news, the number of crime-related stories can be expanded or reduced depending on the needs of media decision makers and on the amount of space or time that must be filled on any given day (Warr, 1991). Finally, many crimes lend themselves to a dramatic narrative form that features the exploits of clearly defined "good guys" and "bad guys" (Ericson, 1991).

The reliance of news organizations on a continuous flow of crime news has led to the establishment of well-defined relationships between news organizations and those who are viewed as reliable and credible suppliers of such information (Gordon and Heath, 1981). The police are the principal source of

37

*What Is
Criminology?
Defining and
Constructing
the Problem
of Crime*

crime news, and the "police wire," press release, news conference, or beat reporter provides the link between the world of crime and the news media (Ericson, Baranek, and Chan, 1989). Because the police are able to supply a steady stream of stories that are "entertaining, dramatic, amusing and titillating" (Ericson, 1991: 207), journalists implicitly adopt a police perspective on the problem of crime (Fishman, 1981).

The police–journalist relationship is mutually beneficial (Katz, 1987). It allows journalists regular access to a valued news commodity and, through reference to the police as the official spokespersons on crime, it lends credibility, authority, and objectivity to media reporting. Correspondingly, the relationship allows police to present themselves as experts on crime and at the same time reaffirms police ownership of the problem of crime.

This exploration of the role that police sources play in the production of crime news helps to explain why interpersonal violent crimes such as homicide or robbery receive greater coverage than crimes by or against businesses (Ericson, 1991). First, the established source–journalist relationships that exist with respect to so-called common crimes generally do not exist in the case of business crime. Second, stories about business crime may be judged as less newsworthy because they are generally more complex, less dramatic, and often more difficult to personalize (Randall, Lee-Sammons, and Hagner, 1988).

CRIME DRAMA

Crime drama has been an important part of television since the medium's inception. From *Dragnet, The Untouchables,* and *Racket Squad* to *Homicide, NYPD Blue,* and *New York: Undercover,* each decade has witnessed countless lawyers, police detectives, and private investigators engaged in the prime-time pursuit of law and order. As in the case of crime news, television crime drama conforms closely to the stylistic and commercial requirements of the medium (Sumser, 1996). These programs rely heavily on dramatic conventions that emphasize suspense and violent action. The storytelling formula of crime shows typically provides a format in which these conventions can be conveniently maximized (Ericson, 1991; Sparks, 1992). As crimes are investigated, and as wrongdoers are pursued and ultimately brought to justice, opportunities abound for car chases, fistfights, and gunplay. It is rumoured that a television executive was once asked why so many of the programs on his network dealt with police officers and private detectives. He reportedly responded, "I suppose we could do a one-hour dramatic show about mail carriers. But just exactly what would we have them do every week?"

Because the essentially escapist nature of television crime drama is well recognized, no one really expects the world of crime portrayed in such programs to constitute a valid portrait of real-life crime and criminals. The images have more to do with the needs of the medium than with a desire to accurately map reality. Still, it is worth noting that crime in television drama, like crime in the news, tends to be disproportionately violent (Dominick, 1978). Additionally, television criminals are generally older than their real-life counterparts, with their age grouping more closely approximating that of the audience (Pandiani, 1978). Whereas crime data suggest that offenders are typically poor, television criminals are more likely to be affluent. Any suggestion of an association between crime and minority group membership is typically downplayed in crime dramas in order to avoid alienating a significant segment of the viewing audience, which would clearly not be in the best interests of a commercial medium. As a result of these influences, television criminals are typically "white materialists, motivated by greed and lasciviousness" (Newman, 1990: 263).

The distinction between television news and television drama is less clear than it once was (Cavender and Bond-Maupin, 1993; Hans, 1990; Newman, 1990). Programs such as *America's Most Wanted, Unsolved Mysteries,* and *Hard Copy* combine traditional news documentary techniques with the familiar narrative style of dramatic television. These program formats (sometimes labelled "info-tainment" or "reality television") have proliferated both because they have proven popular with audiences and because they are relatively inexpensive to produce. Crime, like other social problems, continues to be a source of both entertainment and income in the mass media (Gusfield, 1989).

The ongoing debate about violence in the media and its effects on audiences has recently intensified. Discussion of the issue in the United States Senate (in hearings chaired by Senator Paul Simon) has convinced many television officials that if they do not voluntarily do something about lessening the display of graphic violence in their shows, they are likely to face legislated standards. The effectiveness of the Simon hearings was reflected in the fact that all four American networks sent their presidents to testify as to the steps they had taken—including self-censorship—to address these problems. The issue has also been taken up by advocates (including the president of the United States) of the V chip, which allows consumers to censor violent programming automatically. Broadcasters, not surprisingly, have expressed concerns about the loss in audiences that would result from this technology.

TALKING ABOUT CRIME

People not only read crime news and watch crime shows on television but also talk about crime (Sasson, 1995). A major study of reactions to crime in three

39

*What Is
Criminology?
Defining and
Constructing
the Problem
of Crime*

major American cities found that people cited their friends and neighbours, rather than the mass media, as their principal sources of information about local crime conditions (Skogan and Maxfield, 1981). Nonetheless, talk about crime is frequently focused on events that have achieved a high degree of media notoriety. Heavy media coverage of serial killings, child abductions, or crimes committed by or against celebrities is likely to generate considerable public discussion. Much talk also centres on crime in the local environment. Residents of high-crime neighbourhoods tend to talk more about crime (Skogan and Maxfield, 1981); they are more likely to be personally acquainted with crime victims and thus to have more stories to tell about crime and its consequences.

In their study on fear of crime among the elderly, Kennedy and Silverman (1985) report the surprising finding that respondents who expressed high levels of fear also had higher levels of contact with family members than did other respondents. The continuous cautions that the elderly (particularly those who live on their own) receive from their families may have the paradoxical effect of exacerbating rather than calming their fears.

CRIME IN RUMOUR AND LEGEND

Sometimes talk about crime seems to bear only a very tenuous relationship to social reality. In 1956, news spread throughout Taipei that a number of children had been victims of slashings with what appeared to be razor blades or similar weapons (Jacobs, 1965). In 1944, many residents of Mattoon, Illinois, were reportedly the victims of a "phantom anaesthetist" who entered their homes and sprayed them with a paralyzing gas (Johnson, 1945). In 1969, stories spread through the city of Orléans, France, that Jewish dress-shop owners were kidnapping young women and selling them into the "white slave trade" (Morin, 1971). More recently, stories have appeared in many communities in North America about the threats posed to children by Halloween sadists, who poison or otherwise contaminate the "treats" they dispense to unsuspecting children (Best, 1990).

There was no real evidence to corroborate any of these stories. Their fanciful quality suggests a close kinship with sociological definitions of "rumour" (Rosnow, 1988; Rosnow and Fine, 1976). Like all rumours, they represent forms of **improvised news** that express anxieties and uncertainties about some aspect of social life (Shibutani, 1966). For example, Best (1990) argues that the spread of stories about Halloween sadists during the 1970s was a response to three forms of social strain that characterized the period. The first was an increasing public awareness of, and concern over, the vulnerability of children to child abuse and a range of other victimizing experiences. The second was the general increase in the fear of crime and in the threats posed to personal safety by anonymous strangers. The third was an increasing mistrust of persons outside of one's group. Best (1990: 143) characterizes the Halloween sadist as a symbolic expression of these three anxieties: "The sadist, like other dangers, attacks children—society's most vulnerable members; the sadist, like the stereotypical criminal, is an anonymous, unprovoked assailant; and the sadist, like other strangers, should be met with suspicion rather than trust."

Folklorists use the term **urban legend** to characterize many of the crime stories that travel along interpersonal channels of communication (Brunvand, 1981, 1984, 1986, 1989). Brunvand (1984: ix) describes these legends as "highly captivating and plausible, but mainly fictional oral narratives that are widely told as true stories." Urban legends are widely circulated and typically deal with attempted abductions in shopping malls or amusement parks, psychopaths who terrorize babysitters, the contamination of children's "lick-and-stick" tattoos with hallucinogenic drugs, and criminally insane killers who stalk couples on "lover's lane." While these stories vary in their details from place to place and over time, their moral substance has remarkable durability.

Wachs (1988) argues that urban folklore regarding crime has considerable entertainment value in that both the telling and the hearing of the stories may provide opportunities for dramatic and frequently humorous release. She further characterizes these stories as "cautionary tales" that advise listeners of the dangers of urban life and the need for constant vigilance.

Some kinds of urban legends are more newsworthy than others. Stories about bicycle thieves generally have less currency than stories about killers on the loose. Skogan and Maxfield (1981) found that, in the cities that they studied, neighbourhood talk about crime was largely dominated by stories about elderly or female victims.

While talk about corporate and white-collar criminals appears to be infrequent, it does exist (Kapferer, 1989). In recent years, for instance, stories have circulated that some major businesses are under the control of satanic cults (Brunvand, 1984) or are willfully contaminating food products (Kapferer, 1989). In the American context, folklorist Patricia Turner (1993) has undertaken research showing that in some inner-city African-American communities, rumours circulate which suggest that certain tobacco companies and fast-food outlets are run by genocidal, racist organizations.

Sometimes stories have very real consequences before it becomes evident that they are in fact hoaxes. In the summer of 1993, a media scare erupted over the "discovery" of hypodermic needles in Pepsi cans. All aspects of Pepsi's operations were scrutinized to determine how this could have happened. After much bad publicity, Pepsi was able to demonstrate that it is virtually impossible to insert a needle into a can during the high-speed canning processes employed in its plants. Subsequently, the story was exposed as a series of hoaxes, but not before serious damage had been done to Pepsi's image. Concerns have been raised not only about the serious consequences of such hoaxes but also about the media's role in sounding the alarm and perpetuating public doubts about a product.

41

What Is Criminology? Defining and Constructing the Problem of Crime

BOX 1.4 TERROR ON CAMPUS: AN URBAN LEGEND

Folklorist Jan Harold Brunvand (1993) describes an urban legend that circulated around university campuses in the American South and Midwest in 1988. According to rumours, a psychic had predicted on a television talk show that a mass murderer was going to terrorize campus residents on Halloween night.

From place to place, the specific details of the rumour changed. The talk show in question was variously named as *Oprah*, *Donahue*, and *Geraldo*, among others. The universities in question were variously named as Florida State, Purdue, Ohio Northern, and Slippery Rock.

According to the version of the story that circulated in Florida, a psychic on the *Oprah Winfrey Show* had predicted that a knife-wielding maniac, dressed as Little Bo Peep, was going to slash his way through a dormitory or sorority house. The story persisted despite statements from the show's producers that no such guest had appeared and no such prediction had been made. An elaboration of the story described proposed action by university officials to evacuate residences on Halloween, although such action was never considered. At Purdue, it was said that the prediction involved the deaths of twelve students living in an "X-shaped" dormitory.

According to Brunvand, rumours of this type frequently circulate around university campuses in the fall. Usually, the stories describe killings that will occur at a school, the name of which begins with a particular letter or which is situated near a particular configuration of mountains or rivers. In general, the target building is usually described as being of a particular shape and size or as having a particular type of name. Such stories have been circulating since at least 1968.

Brunvand states that, even though these stories lack a factual basis, some students are likely to react as though the stories are true. They may, for instance, move out of residence on Halloween night or barricade their doors.

Real-life mass murders on campus (such as those at the University of Montreal and Concordia) may lend to such stories an air of credibility.

Much of what we see on television or hear during late-night storytelling sessions can be described as crime myths (Kappeler, Blumberg, and Potter, 1993): distorted and misleading information that nevertheless is accepted as fact. For instance, many people believe these crime myths:

- The elderly face the highest risks of victimization of any group in society.
- Most crime is violent.
- Serial killers account for a substantial number of murders each year.
- Rates of victimization have risen dramatically in recent years.
- The risk of wife assault increases substantially on Super Bowl Sunday.

However, according to the best social scientific evidence, none of these statements is true.

According to Kappeler and colleagues (1993), crime myths serve several important social functions. First, they help us organize our views of crime and the criminal justice system within a ready-made framework that clearly identifies criminals, victims, and crimefighters. Second, these myths support and maintain established views about crime. Third, they help us fill in the gaps in knowledge that social science has not or cannot fill. Finally, these myths provide an outlet for emotional responses to crime and help to establish the channels by which emotions can be transformed into action.

The problem of drunk driving demonstrates the power of myths. As Walker (1994) argues, drunk driving, like many problems in criminology, has been subject to active mythmaking. According to Walker, myths associated with drunk driving include the following:

- *Drunk drivers are responsible for half of all traffic fatalities.* According to Walker, this claim originated in a 1968 U.S. Department of Transportation report, and subsequent analyses have shown the figure to be greatly exaggerated.
- *The traffic safety problem is getting worse.* In fact, Walker claims, the rate of traffic accidents and traffic fatalities has been steadily declining since the 1920s.
- *Everyone drives drunk from time to time.* Instead, Walker maintains, studies have shown that the drinking habits of close to 80 percent of the population are unlikely to cause them to drive drunk.
- *Drunk drivers "get off" easily.* On the contrary, Walker states, even before the great crackdown of the 1980s, conviction rates for drunk drivers were fairly high.

43

*What Is
Criminology?
Defining and
Constructing
the Problem
of Crime*

- *Drunk drivers tend to kill other drivers or pedestrians.* Actually, Walker asserts, over 90 percent of the people killed by drunk drivers are the drivers themselves or their passengers.

Because crime myths are so pervasive and so durable, they sometimes interfere with our ability to approach the subject matter of criminology in an open manner. However, in the chapters that follow, the gap that separates cultural myth from empirical reality will become increasingly evident.

■ ■ ■

SUMMARY

The study of crime is an interdisciplinary endeavour that draws on a variety of techniques in highlighting different aspects of the criminal event. While crime is, strictly speaking, the breaking of the law, we need to understand more than simply offender motivation in explaining how and why crime occurs. A number of factors influence the definition of criminal behaviour, including variations in legal interpretations, changing social morality, police actions, and (for various reasons) nonreporting of crime. Thus, we need to be sensitive to social as well as legal definitions of crime events.

In attempting to explain crime, criminologists generally adopt one of two perspectives. The first approach, classicism, views offenders as rational beings who weigh the benefits of criminal activity against the costs of apprehension. The second approach, positivism, looks instead at the offenders' behaviour as something determined by their constitution and/or social and economic conditions. In addition, crime can be defined as based on consensus or conflict of special interests. The emphasis in these approaches is on the motivation of offenders.

Crime statistics compiled by the police indicate that the volume of reported crime has increased dramatically over the last thirty years. Property crimes represent most of all reported crime, while violent crime makes up about 14 percent of the total.

Crime events as presented in the media and in public discussions frequently do not accurately represent the true nature of crime. Media treatment of crime often creates the impression that certain types of crime (for example, homicide or armed robbery) are more prevalent than is actually the case. Both media presentations and informal talk emphasize the more exotic and "exciting" types of crime; their depictions of criminal events are often more entertaining than informative.

■ ■ ■

QUESTIONS FOR REVIEW AND DISCUSSION

1. What is the difference between an action in which there is no intent to harm and one in which an individual has this intent?

2. How much crime is there? Discuss both the incidence and extent of crime in Canada.

3. Do people who have psychological problems always get off based on an insanity defence? If not, why not?

4. In what ways do your family and friends talk about crime? How does this influence your sense of how much crime there is? How does their discussion of crime compare with what you read in or hear through the media?

5. Is news reporting of crime accurate? Discuss the factors that may create distortions in the extent and incidence of crime.

PART TWO

THE CRIMINAL
EVENT

CHAPTER TWO

The Criminal Event

WHAT'S IN CHAPTER TWO

In this chapter, we introduce the concept of the "criminal event," explaining how crime takes place through the convergence of motivated offenders, victims, and others who may increase the chance of harm or who may act to deter criminal behaviour. We also detail the three stages of criminal events: precursors, transactions, and aftermath. Precursors relate to the way the law defines acceptable behaviour in society and the way people in the community define morality as well as to the various types of predisposing factors that bring offenders and victims together. These factors affect how individuals treat one another. The transaction involves the criminal act itself. Key considerations here include the offender's behaviour, the role of the victim, and the part that third parties, including the police, play in affecting the nature of the event. The aftermath refers to the consequences of the crime, including harm to the victim, punishment of the offender, and public reactions to crime.

INTRODUCTION

In this chapter, we will outline a framework for organizing our integrated approach to the analysis of crime and crime control. This framework emphasizes the study of crime as **criminal events** (Gould, 1989). As we have already pointed out, throughout most of the history of criminology, researchers have attempted to understand crime largely in terms of the actions of criminal offenders (Miethe and Meier, 1994). The simple implication of this approach is that crimes represent little more than the enactment of the will of people who are motivated to behave criminally. If this view is valid, the task of the criminologist is to try to explain why some people behave criminally, while the task of the police and other criminal justice agencies is to prevent offenders from behaving criminally or to capture and reform them after they have done so.

Although we cannot hope to understand crime in society without reference to the lawbreaker, it is also true, as noted previously, that there is much more to crime than the offender. Crimes also involve, in many cases, victims who resist their victimization and in so doing affect the course of action (Kleck and Sayles, 1990; Webb and Marshall, 1989; Ziegenhagen and Brosnan, 1985). Further, crimes may involve bystanders and witnesses whose presence can deter an offender or whose apparent tacit approval of the offender's actions can facilitate the commission of the crime (Shotland and Goodstein, 1984). Bystanders or victims may also summon the police, whose appearance at the scene may affect the response of offenders.

The criminal event cannot be separated from the physical and social settings in which it occurs (Miethe and Meier, 1994). Many forms of crime are intricately linked to the routine activities in which both victims and offenders engage as well as to the places in which these activities occur (Sherman, Gartin, and Buerger, 1989). More generally, criminal events involve the members of the public whose response to perceived increases in crime levels results in pressure on police to pursue more aggressively some categories of offenders. On an even broader scale, crimes involve the actions of lawmakers and the social groups to whom they are responsive. The concept of the criminal event encourages us to conceptualize crime in terms that encompass but also extend beyond the study of offenders. In other words, rather than being *individual* events, crimes are *social* events (Gould, 1989).

BOX 2.1   THE DIVERSE CHARACTER OF CRIMINAL EVENTS

CASE ONE

I'm on the seventh floor of a seven-story building, and there are steps to go to the roof, and there's nothing on the roof except tarpaper. For some obscure reason, people manage to get into the building. There's no intercom system, and there's just a buzzer. One night, the door buzzed, and we buzzed back because we had expected company. We go to the door and looked through the peephole. We see this body come up the steps, come off the elevator, and start looking around. So Rob [Karen's husband] stuck his head out of the door and said, "Get the hell out of here!" And the guy said, "If you come after me, I'm gonna knife you to death!" Rob quickly beat a fast retreat and shut the door. So we went and called the cops. In the meantime, the guy comes up the steps to the roof, and we hear shuffling around on the roof [group laughter]. So we go to the door again, and we're looking around the door—shuffle— [laughter]—and the guy comes down again to the seventh floor, and a light goes on when you push the elevator button. He pushed the button at the *exact* second that the cops hit the button. So you couldn't tell if someone downstairs was coming up. But you never saw anybody get such a *surprise in their entire life* when he's standing there to open the elevator door and there's these cops: *"All right, get outta here!"* [group laughter]. (cited in Wachs, 1988: 9–10)

CASE TWO

Buried in secret files of the Ford Motor Company lies evidence that big auto makers have put profits ahead of lives. Their lack of concern has caused thousands of people to die or be horribly disfigured in fiery car crashes. Undisclosed Ford tests have demonstrated that the big auto makers could have made safer automobiles by spending a few dollars more on each car. (Anderson and Whitten, 1976: B7)

CASE THREE

Another form of gaining extra money is "double dipping" whereby a practitioner can essentially claim two fees for the provision of one service. This form of abuse is exemplified by the salaried surgeon at a large city hospital who was billing the government health system for private patients he consulted with and operated on while working for the hospital. In effect, this surgeon was collecting extra income for the treatment given, a practice that almost doubled his salary. Health investigators who initially questioned the surgeon by phone on his billing patterns were astonished when the doctor confessed to "double dipping." He claimed that he was required to commit fraud because his hospital salary would not sustain his accustomed affluent lifestyle. RCMP

BOX 2.1   THE DIVERSE CHARACTER OF CRIMINAL EVENTS (CONT.)

because his hospital salary would not sustain his accustomed affluent lifestyle. RCMP investigation into the case stalled, however, when the surgeon's supervisor stated that permission had been given for "loose working arrangements" for the salaried position, enabling the surgeon to work whatever hours he chose at the hospital in addition to performing fee-for-service treatment. Despite the investigators' convictions that the supervisor was "covering up" for the surgeon, it was not possible to prove the case and the investigation had to be discontinued. (Wilson, Lincoln, and Chappell, 1986: 133)

CASE FOUR

I remember one particularly violent time. When we were first married. He was out drinking and he came home stinking drunk. I suppose I must have said something. Well, he took a fit. He started putting his fist through the walls. Finally, he just picked up the Christmas tree and threw it at me. (Gelles and Straus, 1988: 95)

CASE FIVE

The accused had been attending a party on a cold winter night. During the evening he started the car to warm the engine so the car would start when he was ready to go home. He did not intend to drive home, however, and had arranged for someone else to drive since he knew he was impaired. The police found him behind the wheel with the motor running. The Supreme Court affirmed the decision of the Court of Appeal which held the intent to drive the vehicle is not necessary for the offence. The court stated: "Care or control may be exercised where the accused performs some acts or series of acts involving the use of the car, its fittings or equipment ... whereby the car may be unintentionally set in motion creating the danger that the section is designed to prevent." (Barnhorst, Barnhorst, and Clarke, 1992: 236)

CRIMES AS SOCIAL EVENTS

To characterize crimes as "events" is to recognize them as incidents that occur at particular times and in particular places. Like any other type of social event—a dinner party, a corporate board meeting, or a car accident—criminal events are more likely to happen under specific circumstances and to involve specific types of people. This conceptualization of crime runs counter to our tendency to think about criminal events as merely the by-product of chance. We speak of the crime victim as having been "unlucky." We maintain that crimes occur because some people are "in the wrong place at the wrong time."

If such events are accidents, however, they are *systematic* accidents (Felson, 1987). Like many other surprises in life, criminal events are made more or less likely by the choices people make about how and where they spend their time, energy, and money.

The term *event* also conveys an *episodic* quality. Criminal events, like all forms of social events, have a beginning and an end. This is not to deny that the participants in the event may have had a prior association or, in the case of a homicide, for instance, that some form of conflict may have predated the event (Luckenbill, 1977). It is to suggest, however, that the criminal event has its own dimensions, which are both related to and distinct from what went on before it. In a similar way, we can speak of the aftermath of criminal events, in which other social processes are set in motion. Much of the daily business of the criminal justice system is relevant in this respect. Offenders are accused and tried, court dispositions are carried out, and victims must learn to cope with the pains of victimization (Lurigio and Resick, 1990). In addition, members of the public who learn about criminal events through mass media reports or conversations with neighbours may become more concerned about their personal safety or about the crime problem and its effect on society.

The *social* character of criminal events derives from the fact that they involve interactions between people. If the event has several offenders, these offenders interact with one another as well as with victims or bystanders. The police interact with these and other event participants. Even an act of vandalism involving a lone youthful offender and an unoccupied school building has social dimensions. A sticker on the door advising that the property is patrolled by security guards may encourage the offender to weigh the risks associated with the offence. Conversely, a run-down building with broken windows may be read by the offender as announcing that no one cares about the appearance of the property (Kelling and Coles, 1996). In either case, the offender reads and (using past experience as a guide) interprets the signs and then acts accordingly. The vandalism itself may be intended as a message to other youths or to unpopular teachers.

The behaviour of any one participant in the criminal event, then, intersects with and influences the behaviour of other participants. This interaction plays a key role in shaping the course of the event, determining the stages through which it proceeds and the extent to which it will be judged a serious one. In order to fully appreciate the complexity of criminal events, we must understand their behavioural and situational elements (Birkbeck and LaFree, 1993). A consideration of the principal participants in these events provides a useful starting point.

BOX 2.2 ABORIGINAL HOMICIDE EVENTS

Anthony Doob, Michelle G. Grossman, and Raymond P. Auger (1994) of the
University of Toronto have analyzed Aboriginal homicides in Ontario using data
from the Canadian Centre for Justice Statistics. Their analysis involved a study of
all homicides in Ontario between 1980 and 1990, comparing those that involved an
Aboriginal suspect or victim and those that did not. Some of their findings were:

- In Ontario (as in Canada as a whole), Aboriginal people are overrepresented as
  homicide victims and suspects.
- The rate for Aboriginal people living on reserves was roughly the same as the
  rate for those living off reserves.
- Both Aboriginal and non-Aboriginal people tended to be killed by members of
  their own cultural groups. In other words, homicide (like all forms of violent
  crime) is intra- rather than interracial.
- Compared with non-Aboriginal cases, Aboriginal victims were more likely to
  be male and to be killed in incidents that involve only one victim.
- Aboriginal suspects tended to be younger and were more likely to be female
  when compared with non-Aboriginal suspects.
- Male Aboriginal victims of homicide were more likely than victims who were
  not Aboriginal to be killed by a family member.
- Alcohol use (by both victims and offenders) was more likely in the case of
  Aboriginal than in the case of non-Aboriginal homicides.
- Incidents involving Aboriginal victims were more likely than incidents involv-
  ing other victims to occur after a nonviolent social encounter, an argument, or
  a fight that escalated.

Based on their findings, the authors conclude:

> Given that aboriginal homicides appear to be the unpremeditated conse-
> quences of the escalation of normal disputes between people who know
> one another, it appears unlikely that criminal justice interventions will
> have much impact on the rate of homicide. The social and economic
> conditions of deprivation in which aboriginal people live are similar on-
> and off-reserve. It is not surprising, therefore, that homicide rates are
> similar in these two settings. It is likely that elevated homicide rates will
> remain unless such conditions are changed.

OFFENDERS

OFFENDER CHARACTERISTICS

The accumulated body of criminological research indicates that particular social characteristics are associated with a higher likelihood of offender involvement in criminal events. For most categories of offences, offenders tend to be young, disadvantaged males. The relationship between age and offender status has been well documented through the use of a variety of data sources (Gottfredson and Hirschi, 1990; Hartnagel, 1996). Involvement in offending is highest among those in late adolescence and early adulthood. Property crime offending peaks at a somewhat earlier age than does violent offending (Flowers, 1989). Property crime arrests peak at age 16 and drop by one-half by age 20, while violent offending reaches a peak at around age 18 (U.S. Dept. of Justice, 1988). Crimes such as embezzlement, fraud, and gambling do not conform to this general trend in that they are characterized by higher levels of involvement somewhat later in the life cycle (Steffensmeier and Allan, 1995).

Offender status is also strongly related to gender (Campbell, 1990) (see Table 2.1). Data collected from 140 Canadian policing agencies in 1995 revealed that 87 percent of all offenders who were charged with violent crimes and 77 percent of those charged with property crimes were male, as shown in Table 2.2 (Hendrick, 1996). While the rate at which women are arrested has increased somewhat over the past thirty years, the offending rates of males continue to be higher than those for females in virtually every category of crime. Also noteworthy is the fact that most of the increase in women's offences during this period came in the category of property crime; the violent crime offence rates for females has remained fairly steady (Boritch, 1997: 30). Although recent evidence indicates that the gender gap in offending has been closing, much of the rhetoric about the "new female criminal" has overstated the case. The narrowing of the gender gap has occurred primarily with respect to nonviolent property crime, for which the gender differential has always been less extreme than for violent crime (Boritch, 1997: 37; Hartnagel, 1996). For most types of criminal events, offending is still very much a male activity.

For many so-called common varieties of crime, such as assault, burglary, robbery, and homicide, offending is associated with various measures of social and economic disadvantage (Flowers, 1989; Silverman and Nielsen, 1992). These differences emerge most clearly when the most serious forms of crime are examined (Harris, 1991). Arrest data reveal that offenders tend to be unemployed, temporarily employed, or employed in part-time, unskilled, or semiskilled jobs (Flowers, 1989). Offending is also associated with minority

Table 2.1   Profile of Incarcerated Offender Populations in Canada, 1994

Male			*Female*		
Profile	Number of Offenders[1]	%	Profile	Number of Offenders[1]	%
Age 20–34	7 269	53.6	Age 20–34	167	51.7
Single[2]	7 666	56.6	Single	185	57.3
Common law	3 923	29.0	Common law	58	18.0
Married	1 665	12.3	Married	43	13.3
Serving first penitentiary term	6 722	49.6	Serving first penitentiary term	240	74.3
Serving a sentence of less than six (6) years	7 241	53.4	Serving a sentence of less than six (6) years	200	61.9
Serving a sentence for:			Serving a sentence for:		
Murder	1 863	13.7	Murder	50	15.5
Schedule I offence[3]	8 401	62.0	Schedule I offence	153	47.4
Schedule II offence	963	7.1	Schedule II offence	68	21.1
Nonschedule offence	2 323	17.1	Nonschedule offence	52	16.1

1   Profile was based on an on-register male population of 13 550 and an on-register female population of 323.

2   Includes offenders who are separated, divorced, widowed, and not stated.

3   Schedule I offences include serious violent offences; Schedule II offences include serious drug offences. Nonschedule offences are offences that do not meet the criteria of Schedule I or Schedule II offences.

Race	*Male*		*Female*	
Caucasian	10 481	77.4	209	64.7
Aboriginal	1 668	12.3	58	18.0
Black	725	5.4	24	7.4
Asiatic	209	1.5	7	2.2
Other	303	2.2	8	2.5
Not stated	164	1.2	17	5.3
Total	13 550	100	323	100

SOURCE: Solicitor General of Canada, *Basic Facts about Corrections in Canada*, 1995.

Table 2.2 Persons Charged, by Gender (Selected Offences, Percent) 1995

	Male	*Female*
Offence Type		
Violent—Total	86	14
Homicide	87	13
Attempted murder	90	10
Sexual assaults	98	2
Nonsexual assaults	85	15
Robbery	89	11
Property—Total	77	23
Break and enter	93	7
Motor vehicle theft	92	8
Theft over $5000	82	18
Theft under $5000	68	32
Fraud	71	29

SOURCE: D. Hendrick (1996), "Canadian Crime Statistics, 1995," Statistics Canada, *Juristat,* Catalogue No. 85-002, Volume 16, Number 10: 5.

group membership. Such an association has been extensively documented with respect to African-Americans in the United States and Native people in Canada (Sampson, 1985; Silverman and Nielsen, 1992). Corporate crimes suggest a departure from this pattern in that offenders involved in such crimes tend to be "predominantly well-educated people with good jobs" (Snider, 1992: 320).

An emphasis on the social and demographic characteristics of individual offenders should not detract attention from the fact that, in the context of many criminal events, offending has collective dimensions. Most delinquent acts, for instance, are committed in groups rather than by individuals (Osgood et al., 1996; Tanner, 1996; Warr, 1996). Criminal events involving corporate offending or organized crime may involve several complex levels of organization (Snider, 1992). These differing levels of offender organization strongly affect the course of criminal events.

OFFENDER PERCEPTIONS

Those who are defined by others as offenders may not share this view of who they are or what their actions mean. Black (1983) argues that much of what is

BOX 2.3   FEMALE AND MALE SERIOUS OFFENDERS

Alex Loucks and Edward Zamble (1994) undertook a study to determine the similarities and differences in social background and criminal history among samples of female and male offenders. Over an eighteen-month period, 100 adult female inmates of the federal Prison for Women participated in the study. The study involved a detailed review of institutional files as well as structured interviews addressing a range of social and psychological issues. The authors compared the results of this study with an earlier, similar study of male offenders. Although the samples were not identical, and although analysis of the data is continuing, the authors of the study have been able to identify a number of interesting similarities and differences with respect to female and male offenders.

- Both the men and the women came from relatively disadvantaged backgrounds (15 percent of the women and 33 percent of the men). However, the authors note, the differences from national averages are not overwhelming. In addition, the samples represent the full range of Canadian society.
- It was also the case that both male and female offenders had difficult personal histories. For example, they had dropped out of school early, were not well trained for employment, and had high levels of unemployment and poor work histories.
- A substantial number of both the men and women spent the first years of their lives living with adults other than their parents.
- There was evidence of emotional maladjustment, including substance abuse and attempted suicide. The women prisoners, however, had much higher levels of depression. In terms of coping skills, the offenders could be described as "minimally effective."
- Most had substantial criminal records. On average, women had 10.8 previous convictions while men had 12.6.
- Overall, there was no evidence that the crimes that resulted in penitentiary terms for women were any less serious than the offences committed by male penitentiary inmates. While men were far more likely to be imprisoned for robbery, women were more likely to have been imprisoned for nonfatal assaults.
- The female offenders were only half as likely as the men to report at least moderate alcohol abuse and twice as likely to report at least moderate drug abuse.

regarded as crime by the criminal justice system is seen as something quite the opposite by those whom the criminal justice system labels as offenders. From the offender's viewpoint, crimes frequently have a moralistic basis. According to Black (1983), offending actually can serve as a form of social control when people use it to define and respond to behaviour they regard as having violated expectations of appropriate conduct.

Seen in this way, those who commit assaults, acts of vandalism, or even murder may be understood as individuals engaged in a quest for justice (Agnew, 1990; Katz, 1988). This position recognizes that those who are judged to be offenders frequently feel victimized by those against whom they offend. Studies of homicide have shown that the eventual victim is often the first event participant to brandish a weapon or to threaten deadly force (Luckenbill, 1977; Wolfgang, 1958). Similarly, in many cases of assault, offenders may feel that they are merely responding to verbal or physical transgressions on the part of others (Felson, Baccaglini, and Ribner, 1985; Luckenbill, 1984). The wife who shoots her husband after years or decades of abuse may question a justice system that categorizes her as the offender and her husband as the victim.

If asked to explain their actions, offenders typically offer two types of accounts: excuses and justifications (Scott and Lyman, 1968). With an **excuse**, an individual admits that a given act is wrong but denies responsibility for the act. With a **justification**, on the other hand, an individual accepts responsibility for the act but denies the immorality of the act. Such accounts provide distinct interpretations of offenders, their victims, and their offences.

A study of convicted rapists found that, while offenders admitted their offences, they denied that they were to blame for what had happened (Scully and Marolla, 1984). By offering excuses relating to the use of drugs, alcohol, or the persistence of "emotional problems," they attempted to disown their blameworthiness. In a similar way, police use of force against suspects may be excused by defining it as a natural outcome of the strong emotions that arise in the course of police work (Hunt, 1985). White-collar offenders might argue that their crimes are committed out of ignorance or an inattention to detail and, further, that they must be considered in the context of an otherwise law-abiding life. Even contract killers may offer rationalizations that mitigate personal blame. Levi (1981) maintains that organized-crime hit men deny responsibil-

HOW DO THEY DIFFER?

Excuses vs. Justifications

An excuse admits that a given act is wrong but denies responsibility for the act. A justification, on the other hand, accepts responsibility for the act but denies the immorality of the act.

ity by emphasizing the need to avoid the potentially fatal penalties that could result from their failure to fulfill a "contract."

Offenders may even claim that their crime has had positive effects. White-collar criminals, for example, might argue that their actions saved a failing business and thereby preserved much-needed jobs. They may also favourably compare their offences with those of "real" criminals like robbers or rapists (Benson, 1985). People who are guilty of workplace theft or income tax evasion might defend their actions by arguing that "everyone does it" and "the only real crime is getting caught."

Offender accounts may also make reference to the culpability of victims. The rapist may contend that the victim seduced him or that she said no but really meant yes (Scully and Marolla, 1984). While these justifications do not deny the accusation, they do deny the moral and legal interpretations that others attach to the behaviour. In the case of police violence, some types of people are defined by the police as legitimate targets of physical force because they are known "cop haters" or troublemakers (Hunt, 1985).

However, offender accounts may be driven by more than personal motivations. Frequently, they reflect pervasive cultural beliefs. The excuses and justifications articulated by the rapist, for instance, borrow from more general sexist beliefs in the blameworthiness of sexual assault victims. In addition, the cultural environment and the historical period partly determine the degree to which an offender account is viewed as plausible. In the late twentieth century, people tend to dismiss accounts that propose demonic possession as an excuse for crime, although such accounts would have been accepted in an earlier period. By contrast, the "culture" of large bureaucracies currently allows white-collar offenders to deny personal responsibility for their actions (Benson, 1985) but does so in a period in which public sentiment increasingly is that these individuals need to be held accountable for their actions (Snider, 1992).

Offender accounts also alert us to the fact that we apply the label of offender only with relative certainty. Most of us are unequivocal in our judgment of the man who hides in the bushes and sexually assaults a woman who happens by. Until recently, however, our feelings about labelling as rapists offenders who were intimately involved with their victims have been more ambivalent. Many people might argue that a husband who assaults a wife has somehow committed a less serious act than has a stranger who assaults another stranger (Bograd, 1988).

Our judgments about the suitability of an offender label may be further complicated by the social context in which the offending occurs. A homicide that results from a heated argument between drunken patrons of a bar may not seem as clear-cut as one that occurs in a more sedate environment. When we draw attention to the relationship between offender labels and offender characteristics, to the victim–offender relationship, or to the social setting, we are suggesting that the study of the offender is inseparable from the study of other dimensions of the criminal event.

VICTIMS

'VICTIMLESS' CRIMES

For many types of criminal events, it is useful to recognize a **victim** role. Victims include people whose purses are stolen, whose homes are broken into, or who are murdered in the course of the event. For other event categories, such as drug use or gambling offences, victims cannot be said to exist in any direct and immediate way, although many would argue that it is incorrect to consider such offences **victimless crimes** (Schur, 1965; Meier and Geis, 1997).

The degree to which the law should be applied to victimless crimes revolves around the issue of harm. While there is widespread support for legalizing various forms of vice, great concern persists as to the potential negative effects of doing so. The prevailing view is that victimless crimes are not victimless and need to be regulated through criminal law.

Proponents for removing the legal sanctions associated with victimless crimes argue that policing these acts represents an overreach of the law and that consenting adults should have the freedom to partake in certain activities. Further, criminalization tends to affect only the disadvantaged and others who cannot pursue these activities in private. Advocates of legalization argue as well that many of the problems associated with victimless crimes would be eliminated were these behaviours permitted in regulated (but legal) environments. From their perspective, it is not the behaviour itself but rather the fact that it has been driven underground that gives rise to the surrounding criminal subcultures.

VICTIM CHARACTERISTICS

Surveys of direct victims of crime demonstrate that involvement in criminal events as a victim, like the involvement as an offender, is not a random matter. In fact, many of the social characteristics associated with offending are also associated with victimization. For one thing, like offenders, the victims of crime tend to be young. According to a national study of crime victims, the Canadian General Social Survey (GSS), the highest rates of both violent and property (theft) crimes were experienced by people between the ages of 15 and 24. The violent crime victimization rates (assault) for young people, for example, were more than four times the rates of violent victimization for those between the ages of 45 and 54 (see Table 2.3). This finding is consistent with that of similar surveys done in the United States and elsewhere (Fattah, 1991). Despite much talk about a crime wave against the elderly, people over the age of 65 are least likely to be victims of crime (Fattah and Sacco, 1989). In fact, the 1993 GSS results indicate that those 65 years of age or over had rates too low to even be reliably calculated.

Surveys of crime victims also show that gender differences in risk of victimization vary by type of crime (Smith, 1987). The 1993 Canadian General

Table 2.3 Personal Victimization Rates of Males and Females per 1000 Population, by Victim Characteristics, Age 15+, Canada, 1993

Characteristics	*Male*	*Female*	*Total Population*
Overall Rate of Victimization	136	151	143
Evenings out (per month)			
<10 evening activities	37	84	66
10–19 activities	116	142	130
20–29 activities	102	156	129
30+ activities	232	258	243
Residence			
Urban	141	168	155
Rural	105	110	108
Age			
15–24	304	333	318
25–44	135	178	156
45–64	73	74	74
65+	—	—	—
Marital status			
Married, common law	85	85	85
Single	245	311	274
Separated or divorced	187	374	301

SOURCE: Rosemary Gartner and Anthony Doob (1994), "Trends in Criminal Victimization: 1988–1993," Statistics Canada, *Juristat*, Catalogue No. 85-002, Volume 14, Number 13.

Social Survey, for instance, revealed that while males experienced a robbery rate of 12 per 1000, women had a rate half that at 6 per 1000. In the case of assault, the results show that males had a rate of 68 per 1000 and that women had a rate of 66 per 1000. With respect to sexual assault, the rate for men was too low to be estimated reliably, while women reported a rate of 29 per 1000 (Gartner and Doob, 1994). Note, too, that several researchers question the extent to which surveys like the GSS accurately portray the levels of women's victimization, an issue we will return to in Chapter 7.

The link between social disadvantage and victimization is less clear-cut than in the case of offending, as it varies by the type of event (Cohen, Kluegel, and Land, 1981; Fattah, 1991). For serious crimes of violence, studies seem to generally support the conclusion that those who are poor or who are members of ethnic minority groups are more likely to become victims of crime (Mirlees-Black, Mayhew, and Percy, 1996; Zawitz et al., 1993). In Canada, Aboriginal people account for about 2 or 3 percent of the population but make up about 15 percent of murder victims (Silverman and Kennedy, 1993: 220). Our ability to more generally describe relationships involving crime and ethnicity is impaired, however, by the fact that such data are not collected in Canada, except in the case of homicide data.

With respect to some forms of household theft, and personal theft that does not involve contact between the offender and the victim, the risks of victimization are greater for higher-income groups (Laub, 1990; Sacco and Johnson, 1990).

VICTIM PERCEPTIONS

Like offenders, victims may be reluctant to define events in which they are involved as crimes. In some cases, even while the event is underway, it may feature ambiguous or unfamiliar elements that are not readily understood as criminal victimization. A study of mugging victims reported that many of those victimized did not immediately define the event as a predatory crime; some even thought the mugger was a neighbour in search of assistance or someone playing a joke (Lejeune and Alex, 1973).

Willingness to label an event a crime generally depends on the degree of coherence between the victim's definition of a "typical crime" and the characteristics of the event in question (Ruback, Greenberg, and Wescott, 1984). However, some types of crimes are inherently more ambiguous than others. The meaning of many forms of sexual victimization may be highly problematic with respect to the labels that victims assign to them. For instance, a study of ninety-four women who were sexually assaulted in a number of ways did not define the act as rape unless sexual intercourse was involved (Scheppele and Bart, 1983). Crime definitions are generally less ambiguous when the events contain elements that imply a high degree of legal seriousness (Agnew, 1985b).

The issue of family violence provides a particularly vivid illustration of the importance of victim definition processes. The reluctance of women to label as criminal or abusive violence occurring in the context of intimate relationships has been well documented (Ferraro and Johnson, 1983; Sedlak, 1988). As in the case of sexual assault, there has been (until recently) a firmly entrenched cultural tendency to blame women for their victimization in domestic relationships. If women remain in abusive relationships, they may be labelled "sick" or "masochistic" or they may be accused of "bringing it on themselves." If they attempt to flee the abuse or confront the abuser, they may find relatively few supports available (Johnson, 1996b). Moreover, such actions may increase rather than decrease the risk of future victimization. As parents, in-laws, and neighbours choose sides, many may blame the victim for breaking up the family and suggest that if she really loved her children she would have "made the best of it." These factors may discourage a woman from viewing herself as a victim, since acknowledging that one's mate is an abuser is the first and hardest step in reevaluating and changing one's life circumstances, a process that might entail violent retaliation by the abusive partner. A denial of the violent character of the victimization and the victimizer may allow the abused partner to tolerate conditions an outsider would think intolerable (Ferraro and Johnson, 1983).

BYSTANDERS AND WITNESSES

In many cases, criminal events involve individuals other than those who can be described as offenders or victims. **Bystanders** in many events are more than passive spectators. They may by their very presence deter an offender from committing a crime or they may prevent an event from escalating. Conversely, they may facilitate the offender's actions. For example, a young male who is insulted by someone in the presence of his peers may be naturally inclined to respond in an aggressive fashion or else be encouraged to do so by his peers.

Bystanders may also call the police or offer to act as witnesses (Shotland and Goodstein, 1984). What bystanders do, if anything, depends on several factors. Their actions may be influenced, for example, by their view of or relationship to the victim and/or offender (Steffensmeier and Steffensmeier, 1977), by their assessment of the personal costs associated with intervention, and by their confidence in their ability to intervene (Shotland and Goodstein, 1984).

Bystanders are also affected by what they perceive to be transpiring between victim and offender. According to Shotland and Straw (1976), bystanders are less likely to intervene in a violent assault perpetrated by a man against a woman if they perceive them to be married rather than strangers. In a highly publicized case that took place in New York City a number of years ago, a woman named Kitty Genovese was attacked by a man in the courtyard of a large apartment complex (Conklin, 1975). The attack continued for a long period of time, during which Genovese's screams for help went unanswered. She finally succumbed to the attack and died on the street. Although many people in the apartment block witnessed the attack, no one called the police, much less intervened. According to those who researched the event, the apartment dwellers had interpreted the attack as a quarrel between a married couple and, therefore, as a private affair. Similarly, Davis (1991) suggests that when people witness adults physically abusing children in public, their reluctance to intervene in a "private matter" outweighs their concern for the child's welfare.

Criminal events are frequently ambiguous from the standpoint of bystanders. We do not expect to witness a crime and may be so engrossed in our own activities that an event may be well underway before it comes to our attention (Hartman et al., 1972). By the time we make sense of the event and think of a response, it may be too late. The presence of several bystanders tends to reduce the likelihood that any one bystander will assist a victim, particularly if the bystanders are strangers to one another and do not share a common cultural frame of reference (Shotland, 1976). One bystander among many is required to accept only part of the responsibility for not acting; he or she may rationalize that somebody else would take action were something seriously wrong.

Bystanders may be asked to perform as witnesses. How valuable are eyewitness accounts in providing accurate depictions of the activities in a criminal event? The research suggests that these eyewitness accounts are quite inaccurate, with bystanders failing to remember even key characteristics of the offender or the event (Loftus, 1979).

POLICE

POLICE PRACTICE

Police involvement in criminal events may result from either proactive or reactive mobilization. As the police engage in routine patrol work, they may encounter individuals or situations they define as criminal. Proactive policing is not in any sense a random or arbitrary process. Rather, it is heavily influenced by police priorities, prevailing community concerns, available police resources, and the styles and traditions that characterize police work in given areas (Desroches, 1991). This is exemplified in the contemporary commitment by most Canadian police agencies to community-based or problem-oriented policing, discussed in Chapter 11. Ericson (1982) reports that police officers who are engaged in patrol activities use cues that structure their proactive work. For example, their attention may be attracted by individuals who appear in particular places at particular times of the day. Conversely, events that could be defined as crimes are not labelled as such because the police choose not to stop and question a suspect.

In his study of the policing of a heroin-using community, Stoddart (1996) reports that heroin users who act as police informants are less likely to be pursued by the police than are heroin users who are perceived as interfering with police work. This finding suggests that proactive police activity is influenced not only by what the police do but also by the visibility of the offender's behaviour. Stoddart argues that changes in the nature of the heroin-using community over time have increased the probability of arrest. Members of this community today are more apathetic than their predecessors about the fate of their colleagues and less attentive to the risks associated with illegal drug use. Such factors increase the visibility of the behaviour, thereby facilitating police intervention.

It is worth noting that the line between reactive and proactive police mobilization is frequently unclear (Ericson, 1982). Citizens may decide to mobilize the police reactively as a result of police-sponsored crime prevention campaigns that encourage them to do so. Conversely, widespread public concern about specific crime problems may influence police to adopt a proactive mobilization strategy. Desroches (1991) reports on a police investigation of sexual behaviour in public washrooms, known as "tearooms." While the fact that evidence was gathered through police surveillance techniques would appear to suggest a proactive police stance on the problem, Desroches indicates this police involvement was largely a response to requests from citizens or businesses for more aggressive enforcement.

POLICE INVOLVEMENT IN DEFINING CRIMINAL EVENTS

The type of mobilization, whether proactive or reactive, does not indicate how the police will intervene in a particular event. The actions taken by officers may depend on a variety of contingencies, including the characteristics of the incident, the behaviour of the participants, and the nature of the requests being made of the police (Bayley, 1986; Gottfredson and Gottfredson, 1988; Smith, 1987).

Police tend to respond most emphatically to (that is, treat officially) events that they perceive as conforming to legal definitions of serious crimes (Black, 1970; Gottfredson and Gottfredson, 1988; Gove, Hughes, and Geerkin, 1985). Also of importance in determining police response is the relationship between the victim and the offender. According to Black (1970), the more distant the relationship between victim and offender, the more likely the police are to regard the incident as criminal. This observation is consistent with the frequently cited tendency of police officers to process crimes "unofficially" when the disputants are family members (Bell, 1987).

The characteristics of victims and offenders have been shown to influence police decisions. In an American study of police responses to interpersonal violence, Smith (1987) found that police officers are less likely to employ legal solutions in situations that involve African-American or female victims. In contrast, Boritch (1992) reports that the criminal justice system deals more harshly with female offenders than male offenders, particularly those who deviate from accepted standards of feminine behaviour. Violence between males is more likely to result in arrest than is violence between a male and a female, which tends to be resolved through less formal means, such as the physical separation of the disputants. Police decision making may also be influenced by the demeanour and preferences of the event participants (Smith, 1987). Thus, the police are more likely to label an event as a crime when the complainant is deferential to them or requests that they take official action (Black, 1970; Gove, Hughes, and Geerkin, 1985).

Increasingly, however, police discretion in particularly sensitive areas, such as family violence, is being removed. In most jurisdictions, police officers are now required, through a **mandatory charge rule,** to make an arrest when they have physical evidence that an assault has taken place, even if the victim is reluctant for them to do so (Johnson, 1996a). This practice was established, in part, in response to Sherman and Berk's (1984) findings that arrest is the most effective way of deterring violence among intimates and that mediative techniques do not curtail repeat offences.

For some observers, removing police discretion means reducing the chances that police bias will influence decisions about the seriousness of certain violent acts. For others, it means depriving police of the opportunity to defuse situations before they become dangerous. Recent research indicates that arrest may actually heighten rather than lower the chance of violence in domestic situations (Sherman, 1992). It has also been argued that bringing individuals into an overburdened court system ill-equipped to handle their problems merely creates new problems.

THE SETTING OF CRIMINAL EVENTS

THE SOCIAL SETTING

Modernization of our society over the last century has shaped the nature of social disorder and crime in contemporary cities. Gurr (1980) has extensively studied the ways in which crime in Western societies has been shaped by four aspects of **modernization**: (1) industrialization, (2) urbanization, (3) the expansion of the state's powers and resources, and (4) the humanization of interpersonal relations. Collectively, these factors have created the pressures in modern society that have led to an unprecedented rise in crime. Further, because many of these factors are difficult to change, the range of options in dealing with the growth of crime were reduced.

Accompanying the increase in personal wealth in the late nineteenth and early twentieth centuries was a demand for the protection of private property. Moral crusades led to calls for the constraint of undesirable practices such as gambling and vagrancy. The response to demands for more social order included devising techniques of legal criminalization, uniformed policing, and incarceration (Gurr, 1980: 36). The development of formal structures led to a transformation from the use of local action in controlling deviant behaviour to the formalization of response through legal codes and uniform policing.

Gurr suggests that this formalization was accompanied by an increase in humanitarianism, in which emphasis was shifted from punishment to rehabilitation. In recent years, victims rather than offenders have increasingly become the focus of this humanitarianism, a situation that, paradoxically, has resulted in an increased demand for harsher penalties for actions (including family violence) that previously were not included in criminal categories.

According to Gurr, the fear of crime that stems from the disorder of fast-growing cities has resulted in increased calls for more police and for more efficient and effective courts. The view that we are moving away from the community as the major basis of social control in society is counterbalanced by evidence that the community still plays a crucial role in both generating and controlling deviance. On the one hand, then, the community has become less important as a forum of social control because the state has assumed responsibility for protecting the victim. On the other hand, the diversity of communities makes the imposition of a unitary state power difficult.

To suggest that a relationship exists between criminal events and the places in which these events occur is to imply that location involves something more than just happenstance. In other words, place matters. Something about particular types of locations increases—or decreases—the likelihood that criminal events will unfold. Any attempt to investigate these issues is plagued by the fact that particular types of places are intricately linked to particular types of activities. People who live in the centre of a major city may structure their activities differently from those who live on the suburban fringe. Those of us who do not live in the downtown core may occasionally journey there in search of "excitement," but for rest and relaxation we head for the countryside. We shop at malls, drink in taverns, perform occupational tasks at work, and read or study at the library. We might ask why some of these places host more criminal events than others. Is it because certain types of people tend to be attracted to these settings? Does the physical character of a place make criminal events more or less likely? Are the activities associated with a particular setting more or less likely to lead to criminal events? While these issues are discussed in greater detail in later chapters, it is useful at this point to review some of the empirical evidence about the locations of criminal events.

THE COMMUNITY SETTING

According to data collected by police and survey researchers, rates of many types of crimes tend to be higher in urban centres than in rural areas (Brantingham and Brantingham, 1984; Fischer, 1976). Data from the 1993 General Social Survey reveal that there were significant differences in rates of certain violent crimes for residents of urban and rural areas. For example, the rates of victimization for assault were 72 per 1000 for urban dwellers and 53 per 1000 for rural residents, while the rates of robbery were 9 per 1000 for urban dwellers and too low to calculate for rural residents. In contrast, rates of sexual assault did not substantially differ by area of residence. Urban residents were sexually assaulted at a rate of 18 per 1000 and rural residents were sexually assaulted at a rate of 14 per 1000. Similarly, total household victimization also differed by place of location. Urban residents reported having their households victimized at a rate of 222 per 1000 households, while rural residents experienced a rate of only 133 per 1000 households (Gartner and Doob, 1994).

In urban centres, the rates of crime vary across neighbourhoods (Roncek, 1981). While research into the factors that characterize high-crime neighbourhoods sometimes produces conflicting evidence (Brantingham and Brantingham, 1984), much of the data indicates that these areas are likely to be poor and densely populated and to have transient populations (Cater and Jones, 1989; Flowers, 1989; Roncek, 1981; Stark, 1987).

Even in cities or neighbourhoods characterized by high crime rates, most locations are crime-free. For example, while we may think of subway stations as dangerous places, data collected by Normandeau (1987) in Montreal reveals that most stations have relatively low rates of crime, with only a few accounting for most of the crimes that occur in the subway system. This point is more generally illustrated in Sherman, Gartin, and Buerger's (1989) study of the locations of requests for police assistance in the city of Minneapolis over a one-year period. This study revealed that relatively few "hot spots" accounted for the majority of service calls; specifically, only 3 percent of the locations in the city (addresses or street intersections) accounted for 50 percent of the 323 979 calls. With respect to predatory crimes, robberies occurred at 2.2 percent, rapes at 1.2 percent, and automobile thefts at 2.7 percent of these locations.

THE PHYSICAL SETTING

What are the characteristics of the locations of criminal events? With respect to some types of crimes, part of the answer may be found in the physical design of places or the creation of **defensible space** (Newman, 1972; Taylor and Harrell, 1996). In the case of a property crime, settings that offer concealment in the form of poor streetlighting, large bushes or shrubs, or hidden alleyways may make a target more attractive to an offender (Shotland and Goodstein, 1984). Similarly, a convenience store located near a vacant field may be more vulnerable to robbery than one that is located on a busy city street (Sherman, Gartin, and Buerger, 1989). Figure 2.1 shows data on the time and location of assault in 1993.

In a somewhat different way, patterns of family violence may be related to some elements of physical design. Violence between husbands and wives typically occurs in private settings. The growth of single-family homes not shared with boarders, lodgers, or servants—coupled with the widespread cultural understanding that the home is a private setting closed to neighbours, friends, or even other family members, except by invitation—helps ensure the concealment of such violence (Gelles and Straus, 1988). Within the home, not all locations are equally risky. According to Gelles and Straus (1988), violence most frequently occurs in the kitchen, followed by the living room and the bedroom, although the latter place tends to be the setting for the most violent confrontations. "A fight that erupts in the bedroom, in the early morning, constrains both parties. It is too late to stalk out of the home to a bar and too late to run

Figure 2.1   Location and Time of Assault Incidents, Percent Distribution, 1993

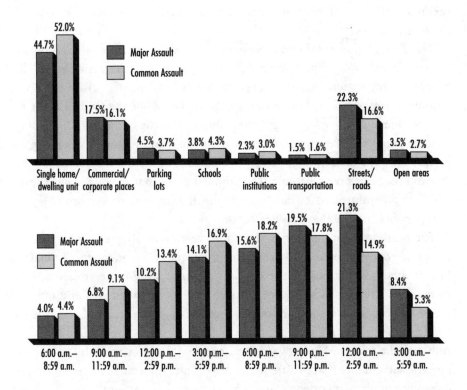

SOURCE: Incident-Based Uniform Crime Reporting Survey, Canadian Centre for Justice Statistics, 1993.

to a friend or a family member. The bed and the bedroom offer no protection and there are precious few places to flee or take cover" (Gelles and Straus, 1988: 94). By contrast, the bathroom is relatively free of spousal violence in part because such rooms are small, have locks, and are understood to be places of individual privacy.

SOCIAL DOMAINS

Social domains may be thought of as major spheres of life in which we invest most of our time and energy. In Chapters 8, 9, and 10, we focus on the three most important social domains—the family and household, leisure, and work. Each domain is distinguished by particular locations and patterns of activity (Lynch, 1987). People differ with respect to the amount of time they spend in each of these domains. For the elderly retired person, the social domain of the household may be of greatest importance. Children spend much of their time at home, but during the teenage years, involvement in this social domain declines while involvement in the workplace and in leisure activities outside the home increases.

These social domains differ, as well, in terms of their private or public character (Fischer, 1981). The household is the most private of settings, and the people we encounter there are generally better known to us than those we encounter at work or at leisure outside the home. While we tend to think of private domains as safer places than public domains, there is increasing concern about the prevalence of criminal actions that previously were seen as private acts. The definition of privacy is changing, as are the ways in which the law and the police treat privacy. The criminal event that may once have gone undetected or untreated in the "privacy" of the home is now more likely to attract public attention and police action.

The breakdown in the taboos about intervention in private lives reflects an increased concern about the harm done in violent events involving intimates. Private affairs in the business setting are also attracting more attention, and there is an increased awareness of the need to prosecute white-collar criminals whose socioeconomic status once put them beyond the reach of the law. In addition, the private policing of private space has become more commonplace. Although the relationship between private and public policing is still an uneasy one, the surveillance that private police offer is an important component in the deterrence of property offences and is impacting crime patterns, particularly in urban areas. Private police, however, are not subject to the same legal controls under which public police operate. For example, private security guards may evict individuals from shopping malls without any recourse to due process.

The distinctions we make among social domains may not apply with equal force to all individuals. Some people work out of their homes; others restrict their leisure activities to the household; still others may view the workplace as a leisure setting—a chance to gossip with co-workers. Despite these complications, the identification of distinct social domains helps us to clarify differences in patterns of criminal events.

The people we encounter in these social domains, the relationships we have with them, and the social activities that occur there strongly influence the kinds of criminal events that take place in a given social domain as well as the reactions to them. Victim surveys indicate that people who report that they frequently go out in the evening to bars also report higher rates of victimization (Gartner and Doob, 1994). Moreover, observations of barroom behaviour and police data suggest that taverns are the site of a disproportionate amount of crime (Engs and Hanson, 1994; Roncek and Pravatiner, 1989).

More generally, many types of criminal events develop in leisure settings. Much juvenile crime (including drug use, vandalism, and fighting) resembles leisure pursuits (Agnew and Peterson, 1989) and is most likely to occur when youths are engaged in unsupervised peer activities such as "hanging out" (Kennedy and Baron, 1993; Osgood et al., 1996). Many forms of sexual assault, especially "date rape," occur in leisure environments rather than in more structured environments (DeKeseredy and Kelly, 1993a; Johnson, 1996a). Similarly, homicides are most likely to occur when the participants are engaged in recreational pursuits in informal settings (Luckenbill, 1977).

Other types of criminal events are more closely related to nonleisure activities. For the organized criminal, crime is a form of work. For the white-collar or corporate criminal, the offending behaviour may represent little more than a simple extension of his or her legitimate business practices. In other cases, a person's employment may be related to the risk of criminal victimization (Block, Felson, and Block, 1984; Lindner and Koehler, 1992). For example, people who handle money, who work in an environment that is open to the general public, or who travel from one worksite to another are especially vulnerable to many forms of victimization (Collins, Cox, and Langan, 1987; Mayhew, Elliott, and Dowds, 1989). It is partially because of these factors that taxi drivers, police officers, and nurses experience relatively high rates of violence (Block, Felson, and Block, 1984). In still other cases, an *absence* of activity is related to the occurrence of criminal events. With respect to breaking and entering, for instance, households that are unoccupied for long periods of time are at greater risk of victimization than are households that have higher and more regular occupancy rates (Cohen and Cantor, 1981; Cromwell, Olson, and Avary, 1991; Waller and Okihiro, 1978).

STUDYING THE CRIMINAL EVENT

We have argued that, in studying **criminal events**, it is important to develop explanations that move beyond the motivations of offenders or the responses of victims. A more comprehensive view must consider (1) the **precursors** of the event, including the locational and situational factors that bring people together in time and space; (2) the **transactions** that indicate how the interactions among participants define the outcomes of their actions; and (3) the **aftermath** of the event, including the report to the police, their response, the harm done and the redress required, and the long-term consequences of the event in terms of public reactions and the changing of laws. Figure 2.2 shows a model of the criminal event and its key components.

As criminologists, we are interested in more than just the motivation of the offender or the actions of the victims that led up to the criminal act. These elements come together in a transaction that increases the likelihood that crime will take place. Understanding criminal events as deriving from predisposing conditions helps us to separate the social behaviour that is criminogenic from that which is not. Studying the precursors of criminal events also allows us to see that, depending on circumstance, behaviour that is defined or that evolves into criminality in one situation may not have the same consequences in other situations. The relationship between participants, the interpretation of the harmfulness of the acts, the anticipated responses to certain behaviour, the nature of the location—all may or may not combine to create a criminal outcome.

> ## HOW DO WE DEFINE IT?
>
> ### *The Criminal Event*
>
> The criminal event consists of its precursors, including the locational and situational factors that bring people together in time and space; the transaction, including how the interactions among participants define the outcomes of their actions; and the aftermath of the event, including the reporting to the police, their response, the harm done and the redress required, and the long-term consequences of the event in terms of public reactions and the changing of laws.

Of course, understanding preconditions will not necessarily allow us to predict criminal outcomes with greater accuracy. The difficulties of prediction are illustrated in the recent debate over the extent to which spousal homicide could have been anticipated on the basis of previous behaviours (Sherman et al., 1991). While the predictive capability of police is low with respect to spousal homicide, it is likely very high with respect to repeat interpersonal violence.

In determining the precursors of crime, we must reconstruct criminal events using information that may be distorted by faulty memories, rationalizations, and so on. But it is exactly this process that the courts use to establish guilt or innocence. In order to reflect legal as well as social reality, criminologists must incorporate a similar process in their approaches to crime.

TRANSACTIONS

When we study transactions, we move into an assessment of the circumstances, incidence, and frequency of certain types of crimes. As we will see in Chapter 7, different types of data sources (for example, Uniform Crime Reports, victim surveys, self-report studies) tell us about different aspects of the event, or at least provide different perspectives on such events.

Figure 2.2   Model of the Criminal Event

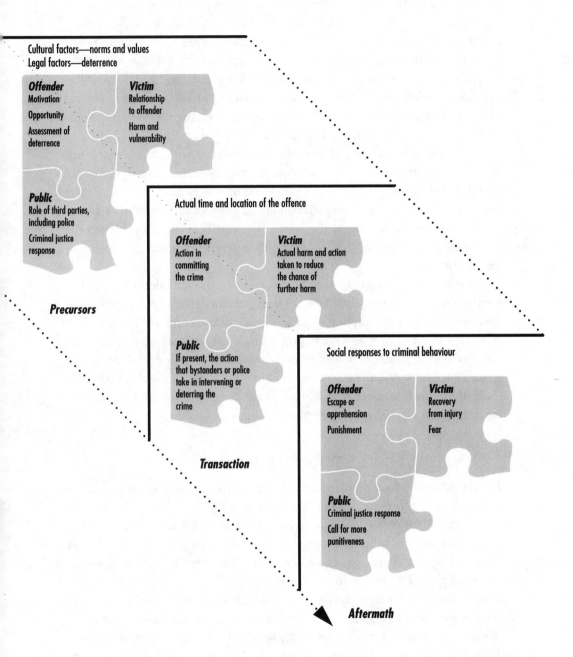

Cultural factors—norms and values
Legal factors—deterrence

Offender
Motivation

Opportunity

Assessment of
deterrence

Victim
Relationship
to offender

Harm and
vulnerability

Public
Role of third parties,
including police

Criminal justice
response

Precursors

Actual time and location of the offence

Offender
Action in
committing
the crime

Victim
Actual harm and action
taken to reduce
the chance of
further harm

Public
If present, the action
that bystanders or police
take in intervening or
deterring the
crime

Transaction

Social responses to criminal behaviour

Offender
Escape or
apprehension

Punishment

Victim
Recovery
from injury

Fear

Public
Criminal justice response

Call for more
punitiveness

Aftermath

We are interested in the particular groups that are affected by different types of crime. It is in this context that we are able to examine the changes in offender behaviour and the extent of victimization. We are particularly interested in viewing the criminal event not in isolation but, rather, as it relates to social events as well as to other criminal events. Discerning trends in these events helps us understand the extent to which we need to respond to them. We also want to understand how trends in crime patterns coincide with shifts in social and economic conditions, resources for policing, and so on. The explanations that these types of analysis provide throw light on the vulnerability of certain groups to social change and the extent to which legal intervention can work to deter or alter criminal behaviour.

Previously, we discussed the problems associated with defining (or not defining) certain events as criminal. Victims may not immediately appreciate that they have been subject to a crime, while offenders may rationalize their behaviour as something other than criminal. The strict definition of criminality derives from the actions of the police, who certify criminality through the enactment of legal process, either in naming an event as criminal or in arresting an offender.

But what about the events that do not come to the attention of the police but that we could nevertheless define as being criminal? This hidden dimension of crime has important implications for how we define criminal events, as well as for the processes by which the police target certain victims or offenders. Criminal events, then, are dynamic not only in terms of their responsiveness to interactional factors in the environment but also in terms of the claims that are made about them by interested parties. These claims are continuously changing in response to changing political and cultural values.

THE AFTERMATH

The extent to which we can develop an integrated perspective depends strongly on the types of information about criminal events to which we have access. We are concerned not only with the actual event but also with the reactions by the police, victims, and others. In considering the aftermath of an event, we are interested in the degree to which the victim has been harmed and in the resources needed to aid in his or her recovery. We are also concerned with whether the offender feels that he or she can repeat the offence with impunity. With respect to punishment, has there been sufficient certainty, severity, or celerity to deter a repeat occurrence? These questions frame a great deal of the discussion about how we are managing our crime problems. Lending focus to this debate are the responses to different types of crime. We need to understand that our responses to criminality are a function of our perspectives in interpreting the reasons for its occurrence; moreover, these reactions will influence the types of crime that we will experience in the future.

■ ■ ■

SUMMARY

Crime is, strictly speaking, the breaking of the law. But the laws and their interpretation are an embodiment of social morality. As such, they are subject to change, as is our understanding of criminal events. Crime is a social construct that varies according to definition and response by legal authorities. It is the job of criminologists to assess how legal and moral definitions of crime coincide with the circumstances that people face and then evolve into events that demand enforcement and result in labelling individuals criminals.

The criminal event is a social event. Like all other social events, it has a beginning and an end. Criminal events are social in that they involve interaction among human beings. The nature and form of this interaction shape the course of the event, determine the stages through which it proceeds, and define how serious it is judged to be in terms of harm done. Many different types of actors are involved in these events.

The most obvious participant is the offender. Offenders tend to be young, disadvantaged males. At the same time, however, we are witnessing a growth in family violence; the major offenders in these crimes frequently are older and better-off males. Further, women are increasingly becoming involved in property crimes.

Much attention has been directed at trying to understand the motivations, as well as the group pressures, that influence the behaviour of criminals. The study of offender perceptions provides an important source of information about the pressures that direct individuals to behave in certain ways. Offenders may choose to deal with their blameworthiness by rationalizing their crimes.

While the victims of crime, like offenders, tend, in general, to be young and male, other groups are heavily victimized in particular types of crime. Sexual assault and family violence are disproportionately directed against women. The nature of victims and their relationship to offenders, then, is very much a function of the type of event that has occurred and is governed by location and circumstance. Like offenders, victims may redefine the event as harmless or, at least, not criminal. Victim definitions can be very important in influencing the actions taken by criminal justice agencies in criminal events.

Bystanders and witnesses also play a role in defining and interpreting the social events that become crimes. They may defuse a violent situation or they may actually promote violence through their actions. While bystanders can be helpful in clarifying what actually occurred during a criminal event, their accounts often prove to be inaccurate.

The police play a major role in criminal events. They have the power to certify an event as a crime by assessing the match between the event as they have come to understand it and their knowledge of what the law disallows. In reactive policing, the police respond to reports from citizens, who may be either victims or bystanders. In proactive policing, certain groups or communities are targeted for police attention as a way of preventing criminal events.

With respect to intervention, the police are heavily influenced by their perceptions of what they can do to reduce crime. Police use a great deal of discretion in their work, discretion that can be used negatively to discriminate against certain groups. Police discretion in family violence cases is increasingly being removed.

The police operate through the administration of the law and, although they use some discretion in applying it, the legal structure outlines clear expectations vis-à-vis personal behaviour and the legal response to the breaking of these expectations. Law is a form of social control that defines individual actions on the basis of socially acceptable standards. Criminal events are social events and, as such, are governed by societal as well as legal tenets. Forms of control may also be socially based. Gossip, ridicule, and ostracism may combine with legal threats to discourage individuals from acting in a criminal manner.

One other important aspect of criminal events is the conditions under which they occur. The different dimensions of people's lives, ranging from family interaction and work to leisure-time activities, all invite different types of behaviour and offer circumstances that may or may not give rise to criminal events. A comprehensive view of the criminal event must consider three key components: precursors of the crime, the transaction itself, and the aftermath.

Criminal events, like all forms of social events, are complicated affairs. This chapter has discussed their basic dimensions and, in so doing, has raised questions about who participates in these events, when and where they occur, and why they elicit particular forms of societal reaction. In order to understand a criminal event, we need to understand how each of its elements combines and interacts. We cannot address the issue of sexual assault by reducing the problem to a single question—why do some men commit sexual assaults? Instead, we need to put this question in an appropriate context that also asks why some women are more likely than others to be victimized by sexual assault, when and where such assaults are most likely to occur, and why police, lawmakers, and members of the general public think about sexual assault as they do.

QUESTIONS FOR REVIEW AND DISCUSSION

1. How do offenders see their actions relative to their victims and to the situations they find themselves in?
2. What do we mean when we say that crime is a social event that takes place in time and space?
3. What role does the legal system play at each stage of the criminal event? Is it always the same agency that deals with the precursors, the transaction, and the aftermath?
4. When does a social event become a criminal event?
5. What does it mean when we say that a criminal event takes on the character of a transaction?

PART THREE

THEORIES

CHAPTER THREE

Psychosocial Conditions and Criminal Motivations

WHAT'S IN CHAPTER THREE

In this chapter, we will begin our review of the theories that have been used to explain crime. We focus on those explanations that deal with the question, Why are some people more inclined than others to behave in ways that violate the law? This involves an examination of offender motivation, including deficiencies in physiological or psychological makeup, propensities produced by troublesome social conditions, and problems that arise from the offender's commitment to cultural beliefs that condone criminal conduct.

What are criminological theories and why do we need them? In day-to-day conversation, we tend to use terms like *theory* or *theoretical* to describe something that may be interesting but is also irrelevant, unimportant, or impractical. We can dismiss what someone tells us with the retort, "While that may be true in theory, it doesn't have much to do with reality!" As students of criminology, however, we need to recognize that, far from being irrelevant, **theories** can be extremely useful and practical analytical tools.

WHAT ARE THEY?

Criminological Theories

Theories provide us with answers to questions about why crimes occur, why some types of people are more likely than others to be involved in crimes as offenders or as victims, why crimes are more likely to occur in certain places and at certain times, and why agencies of social control respond to crime as they do.

We can understand criminological theories as generalized explanations of criminal phenomena (Bohm, 1997). Our theories provide potential answers to questions about why crimes occur, why some types of people are more likely than others to be involved in crimes (as offenders or as victims), why crimes are more likely to occur in certain places and at certain times, and why agencies of social control respond to crime as they do. Of course, criminologists are not alone in seeking answers to these questions. Angry newspaper editorials may offer seemingly reasonable accounts of why crime rates are rising. On any given Sunday morning, television preachers explain crime and associated problems in terms of evil forces at large in the world. Crime victims may ask what they did that led to the victimization. While not always recognized as such, these accounts of why and how crimes occur represent a kind of theoretical thinking. However, we expect somewhat more from criminological theories than from so many of the "folk theories" that are part of our conventional wisdom.

First, **criminological theories** (at least of the type discussed in this book) are intended as general rather than specific explanations. Stated differently, we are usually not interested in why one particular offender committed one particular crime. Instead, theories should explain the patterns that characterize criminal phenomena in general. We want our theories to tell us, for example, why males are more likely than females to commit a violent offence, why the chances of victimization are reduced as people grow older, why big cities have higher rates of some kinds of crime than do small towns, or why crime rates shot up in the 1960s.

Second, we expect that our theories will be consistent with (and can therefore make sense out of) the *facts* of crime as revealed to us in the research process. The gross facts of crime, as we currently understand them, are consistent with a variety of different theoretical viewpoints. As a result, the evidence sometimes seems to support, at least partially, apparently competing views. Why, for instance, do we find higher rates of theft in bigger cities? Some sociologists have argued that large cities undermine the social controls that might discourage people from stealing (Wirth, 1938). Others have suggested that bigger cities are more likely to be home to the kinds of people (for example, young, unmarried males) who tend to steal no matter where they live (Gans, 1962). Alternatively, we might argue that the city provides a setting that accommodates an elaborate network of thieves, targets, and fences and thereby turns theft into a profitable and enduring activity (Fischer, 1975).

On the surface, each of these theories of crime and urban life might seem equally viable since each is consistent with the general pattern of empirical data. This implies that, in order to assess the relative value of these theories, we would need more detailed empirical knowledge about the relationship between crime and urban settings. As empirical data accumulated, we would hope to discover that one of the theoretical positions better accounted for the patterns we were observing.

This brings us to a third requirement of criminological theories. Like all forms of scientific theory, they should be falsifiable. That is, our theories must be stated in terms that allow them to be tested through research so that we can discover which theories provide false accounts of the phenomena being observed. A theory that cannot be rejected no matter what we discover is of little use to us.

We should emphasize that criminological theories are not merely intellectual abstractions with no real-life implications. On the contrary, theories may be highly practical, particularly when we use them as guides in our efforts to deal with crime as a social problem. Obviously, how we understand the causes of a problem has important consequences for what actions we take to resolve it.

Throughout its history, criminology has witnessed no shortage of attempts to theorize about crime. To the uninitiated, the choice of explanations can be bewildering as theories appear to contradict or at least compete with one another. Our review focuses on several types of theoretical questions. The first question concerns the behaviour of offenders, discussed in this chapter and in Chapter 4. Why are some people more inclined than others to behave in ways that violate the law?

In Chapter 5, we turn to another type of theoretical question. How do we understand the situations that allow offenders to act on their propensities? As we will see, an emphasis on situations and opportunities complements the more traditional motivational theories of crime. In Chapter 6, we examine theoretical explanations of what happens after a crime takes place.

EXPLAINING OFFENDER BEHAVIOUR

For many theorists, the explanation of crime boils down to one simple question that has spawned several complicated answers: Why do offenders do what they do? Criminologists traditionally have offered two general types of answers to this question. On the one hand, criminal behaviour can be understood as the product of unique factors that **motivate** lawbreaking. This approach derives from the positivist school of thought and seeks to discover the causes of criminal conduct. On the other hand, criminal behaviour can be understood as the product of **behavioural choices** that are freely and rationally made. This approach derives from the classical school of thought and sees as misguided the search for causes of criminal behaviour (causes referring to those factors that drive people to act in particular ways).

These perspectives differ in terms of the prominence they accord the role of **will** in human affairs. Theories that derive from the classical school conceptualize criminal behaviour as willful and purposeful. Theories that derive from the positivist school view will as a less significant characteristic of criminal behaviour and seek instead to understand how social and other factors compel, or at least encourage, criminal conduct. This chapter deals with those theories that reflect the positivist tradition; theories that reflect the classical tradition are discussed in the next chapter.

Three broad subthemes may be identified. The first views criminal motivation as resulting from deficiencies in the offender's physiological or psychological makeup. The second subtheme views offenders as a product of troublesome social conditions that propel them toward crime. According to the third subtheme, motivation arises from the offender's commitment to cultural beliefs that condone criminal conduct.

SOCIOBIOLOGICAL EXPLANATIONS OF CRIMINAL MOTIVATION

GENETICS

In recent years, there has been a renewed interest in the influence of **genetics** and physiology on the creation of criminal offenders. This school of thought argues that certain individuals are more likely to commit crimes due to faulty genetic programming. In arguing that a predisposition toward criminality exists in certain individuals, some researchers have used genetic explanations of behaviour (Mednick, Moffitt, and Stack, 1987) while others have focused on sociobiological or constitutional aspects of individuals (Wilson and Herrnstein, 1985). This predisposition may occur through intergenerational genetic defects or through a constitutional deficiency deriving from short time horizons (that is, the absence of long-term goals) or inadequate socialization in early childhood.

The genetic approach has been used in the effort to determine the importance of family ties or blood relations in the control of individual deportment. Violent crime, in particular, can be explained in terms of its connection with genetics. For instance, individuals with intimate family ties offer the same protection from harm as would animals to their blood connections, whereas individuals with less intimate ties (for example, adopted children) are more likely to be subject to violence from non-blood relations (for example, step-parents) (see Daly and Wilson, 1988).

Ellis (1982) provides a review of the major factors that are included in a genetic explanation of crime. Genes influence behaviour through the nervous system. In any particular group of behavioural events, there may be so much genetic similarity in individual nervous systems within the human species that any differences in behaviour cannot be explained by genetic variation but rather depend on forces outside the individual. This has led to a debate over the extent to which nature (genes) versus nurture (environment) influences human behaviour in general and criminality in particular. The effects of nature versus nurture have been studied in four different ways: (1) general pedigree studies, (2) twin studies, (3) karyotype studies, and (4) adoption studies.

As Ellis (1982) explains, **general pedigree studies** involve establishing the extent to which people who are related also behave similarly.

DO THEY EXIST?

Crime Genes

Until we can improve on methodological deficiencies, we have no real scientific basis for arguing for (or against) the existence of a "crime gene."

This approach is nonexperimental, however, because it is difficult to control the effects of common genetic background versus environmental influences. While family members share both genetic and environmental factors with their children, if parents and children are criminal it is likely due to these shared factors rather than some environmental factor they do not share. The evidence shows that 30–45 percent of individuals with criminal records had one or more parents with criminal records. But, knowing about "crime in the family" does not really enhance our ability to use genetics in explaining criminality because we are really unable to detach family biology from environmental factors (including family socialization).

The second type of nonexperimental design is the **twin study**. According to Ellis (1982), this design allows for a comparison between the two types of twinning that occur in humans. The most common twins are the result of two ova fertilized by two separate sperm. These dizygotic (DZ) twins share 50 percent of genetic programming. In contrast, if a single fertilized ovum splits very early in its development, monozygotic (MZ) twins who share 100 percent of genetic programming are formed. Twin studies show a higher level of concordance between MZ twins in their criminality than between DZ twins, leading some to conclude that the genetic commonalities are the key contributory factors. However, due to the strong similarity in their appearance, MZ twins elicit common responses from others more so than do DZ twins. This similarity in treatment, a factor in the socialization of MZ twins, may be more important in guiding their behaviour than the fact that they share genetic programming.

The third type of study discussed by Ellis (1982) involves genetic karyotypes. **Karyotype studies** compare the size, shape, and number of specific chromosomes in individuals. Some researchers report that among criminal males, the Y chromosome has a higher-than-expected probability of being larger than among noncriminals. In addition, research shows that some offenders have an unusual number of chromosomes, that is, a number other than the twenty-three pairs typical of humans. XYY karyotype males, while rare among the criminal population, are still more likely to appear in groups of persons convicted of or imprisoned for a crime than among control populations. However, the research in this area suffers from small samples and inconclusive explanations; the correlations that exist are not readily interpreted as causative factors linking these karyotype differences to criminality.

The fourth design is based on **adoption studies**. As Ellis (1982) points out, we can contrast the behaviour of near-birth adoptees (persons adopted by nonrelatives shortly after birth) to that of both their genetic and their adoptive parents. If the behaviour is due to genetics, adoptees should more closely resemble their genetic parents (whom they have never seen) than their adoptive parents. Properly executed adoption studies offer a powerful experimental design for isolating the effects of genetic factors from the influences of socialization and other environmental effects. For example, if some individuals exhibit criminal tendencies, and the birth parents but not the adoptive parents do likewise, it is assumed that this behaviour is due to genetic programming.

In the research to date, the efficacy of using *genotypes*—that is, genetic makeups—to identify likely candidates for criminal behaviour is not very well established. The most credible research is provided by adoption studies, but these have, in fact, reported fairly low concordance rates between the offending patterns of identical twins who have been separated at birth and raised with different families (Mednick, Moffitt, and Stack, 1987). In evaluating the relative importance of genetic structure and environmental influences, adoption studies report little evidence that genetic differences explain differences in criminality.

Walters and White (1989) summarize the problems of genetic-based research as follows:

> Genetic factors are undoubtedly correlated with various measures of criminality, but the large number of methodological flaws and limitations in the research should make one cautious in drawing any causal inferences at this point in time. Our review leads us to the inevitable conclusion that current genetic research on crime has been poorly designed, ambiguously reported, and exceedingly inadequate in addressing the relevant issues. (478)

Until these deficiencies are addressed, there is no real scientific basis for arguing for (or against) the existence of a **crime gene**.

CONSTITUTION

The biological approaches have also focused on the **constitutional structure** (including the body types and psychological propensities) of offenders. Having reviewed research by Garofolo (1914) on Italian convicts and studies by Sheldon (1940) on incarcerated juveniles, Wilson and Herrnstein (1985) conclude that one can detect certain physiological similarities among offenders. For example, short, muscular young males are the types most likely to appear in prison populations. According to Wilson and Herrnstein (1985), "The biological factors whose traces we see in faces, physiques, and correlation with behaviour of parents and siblings are predispositions towards crime that are expressed as psychological traits and activated by circumstance" (103).

BOX 3.1 BODY TYPE AND CRIMINAL BEHAVIOUR

In a famous study, researcher William Sheldon (1949) attempted to determine the relationship between physique and the tendency to engage in criminal behaviour. Sheldon used a method called *somatotyping* in order to categorize three basic types of body build—endomorphic, ectomorphic, and mesomorphic—each of which he argued was associated with a particular type of temperament.

As pictured in Figure 3.1, the body types represent extreme forms. Most individuals are a combination of all three types.

In comparing a sample of known delinquents with a control group of students, Sheldon maintained that delinquents were more likely to have mesomorphic physiques and the accompanying temperament, which emphasized risk-taking, adventure, and an interest in physical activity.

The difficulty with the constitutional approach is that knowing about **body type** doesn't tell us much about a person's propensity to act criminally; it tells us (and only if we believe the research) that some inmates happen to be short and muscular. Moreover, body typing ignores the fact that one of the most popular activities in men's prisons is weightlifting. It also fails to consider the fact that, in a violent encounter, the less muscular combatant will tend to lose the contest and end up in the hospital, while the more muscular participant will emerge as the victor and end up in prison. Further, this approach doesn't address other important factors related to crime, including the circumstances under which a motivated offender comes to participate in criminal activity.

In defending the constitutional approach to criminality, Wilson and Herrnstein (1985) borrow from classical criminology to argue that crime is a rational act based on a calculation of potential gain versus loss. Through this process, individuals weigh the possibilities that they will succeed in their endeavours. Individuals may discount potential costs through a process whereby immediate gratification becomes the paramount concern. This choice is not really a free choice, however, as it is predetermined by poor socialization and constitutional deficiencies. The short time horizons possessed by individuals with these deficiencies distort the way in which their decisions about benefits and costs are made. Such individuals will tend to involve themselves in criminal activity for short-term gain. According to Wilson and Herrnstein, they represent criminal types who need to be isolated and subjected to high levels of deterrence, thereby restricting their behaviour and reducing the likelihood of criminality. Thus, the state's role is to set up contingencies that will reduce the benefits and increase the costs of misbehaviour.

**Figure 3.1   Sheldon's Somatotypes in Relation to Physique and
Temperament**

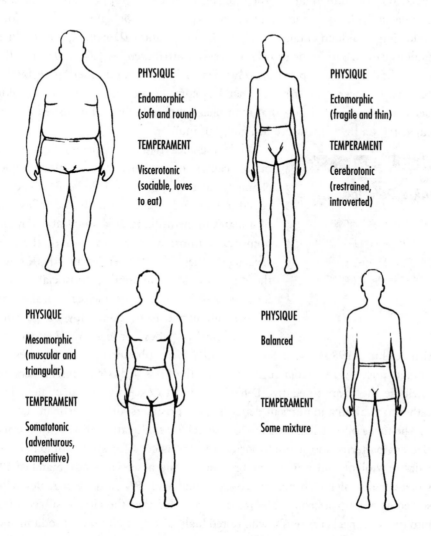

PHYSIQUE

Endomorphic
(soft and round)

TEMPERAMENT

Viscerotonic
(sociable, loves
to eat)

PHYSIQUE

Ectomorphic
(fragile and thin)

TEMPERAMENT

Cerebrotonic
(restrained,
introverted)

PHYSIQUE

Mesomorphic
(muscular and
triangular)

TEMPERAMENT

Somatotonic
(adventurous,
competitive)

PHYSIQUE

Balanced

TEMPERAMENT

Some mixture

SOURCE: Curt R. Bartol, *Criminal Behaviour: A Psychosocial Approach*, 3rd Ed. (Englewood Cliffs, NJ: Prentice-Hall, 1991).

The deterministic nature of constitutional theories firmly establishes them in a positivistic framework that maintains there is little offenders can do to change their propensities to act criminally. From this perspective, we need to reduce the likelihood of criminal activity by isolating individuals who are likely to be problem offenders.

Some researchers are interested in the degree to which **diet** can affect the behaviour of individuals. Strong scientific evidence supports the idea that certain individuals are more prone to hyperactivity or aggressive behaviour following a sudden intake of sugar (hypoglycemia) (Dorfman, 1984). In a famous case, a San Francisco city supervisor attributed his 1978 murder of the mayor and a fellow supervisor to his diet of Twinkies and other "junk food." His lawyers were able to use what has come to be known as the **Twinkie defence** to convince a jury that their client suffered from "diminished mental capacity" and was therefore not guilty of murder.

> ## WHAT IS IT?
>
> ### *The Twinkie Defence*
>
> An argument that, due to the overconsumption of junk food, a defendant experiences "diminished mental capacity" and is therefore not guilty of criminal behaviour.

While the idea that such dietary factors are major causes of violence seems questionable, changing dietary practices has been acknowledged to have a dramatic effect on the behaviour of inmates in institutions. In a study of detention homes in California, it was established that, by revising the diets of 276 juveniles, mostly through the reduction of sugar intake, antisocial behaviour declined by 48 percent, incidents of theft by 77 percent, incidents of assault by 82 percent, and refusal to obey orders by 55 percent (Kindelehrer, 1983: 143). Similar results were obtained when supplies of orange juice were increased, a finding that has led some researchers to attribute the former negative behaviours not to excessive sugar content but rather to vitamin and nutrient deficiencies in prisoners' diets (Dorfman, 1984).

The focus on nutrients has led to research on the relationship between **trace element** patterns and a predisposition to violence. One study compared 24 pairs of violent and nonviolent brothers, while a second study matched 96 violent males of mixed age and background with 96 nonviolent males who served as a control group. The research revealed that the violent subjects fell into two groups: (1) type A's, who tested high in copper and low in sodium and potassium and who were episodically violent, and (2) type B's, who were the reverse and who displayed consistently antisocial behaviour. As the type A pattern tended to fade with age, hair analysis (a procedure for tracking trace elements) could be used by parole boards to predict, on the basis of the mineral content in the subject's body, when episodic violence would likely cease (Dorfman, 1984: 46).

The applicability of these findings to offenders outside of institutions is impossible to determine. They do provide some interesting suggestions about how our lifestyle, particularly our diet, influences our actions. They do not tell us much about what situations elicit violence or about what social factors (for example, early childhood socialization, peer pressure, or fear of stigmatization) may play a role in deterring it.

The ingestion of substances other than food has attracted a great deal of attention in criminological analyses. Drugs, including alcohol, are present in many criminal events. The criminality that surrounds the illicit sale and purchase of drugs makes their use of interest to us. As with dietary factors, what is unclear is how important drugs are in providing an explanation for criminality. Their presence in criminal situations may be related but not central to the explanation of criminality. Many people use (and abuse) alcohol without becoming violent and attacking other people. Yet, as evidenced by the many bar fights that occur, alcohol sometimes appears to fuel violent attacks.

Explanations based on genetics, constitution, and diet can be summed up this way: If one accepts that crime is a cultural and social concept, defined through custom and law, it seems unlikely that such a thing as a "criminal type" or a "crime gene" exists whereby behaviour is preprogrammed to deviate from this social construct or, indeed, that certain people with particular body types or diet will generally offend. These explanations, while interesting, seem to be more useful for describing the conditions of incarcerated offenders and assisting in controlling their behaviour than in predicting the likelihood of criminality in the first place.

INTELLIGENCE AND CRIME

NEUROPSYCHOLOGICAL THEORY

There has been an upsurge in interest in the relationship between **IQ** and behaviour (see Murray and Herrnstein, 1994). It has long been recognized in criminological research that a correlation exists between IQ and delinquency, but, as Moffitt, Lynam, and Silva (1994) report, we do not know why or how low IQ influences antisocial behaviour. They argue that one way to approach this issue is to look beyond IQ by applying **neuropsychological theory,** according to which, people with identical IQ scores can have very different patterns of mental strengths and weaknesses. Moffitt and colleagues claim that IQ offers limited information about which of these strengths or weaknesses influences behaviour. The IQ test compresses an aggregate measure of abilities (notably verbal skills and spatial perception) into a single composite indicator of performance. Most neuropsychological test batteries include a standard IQ test, which measures verbal and spatial functions very accurately, but they also add more tests to cover functions such as memory, motor skills, and mental self-control. A battery of neuropsychological tests can reveal, for instance, that children with identical low IQ scores might suffer from different and relatively isolated problems such as impulsive judgment, weak language processing, poor memory, or inability to match visual information with motor actions. Each type of deficit could be more accurate than the overall IQ in predicting delinquency, but each would contribute to delinquency through a unique theoretical causal chain (Moffitt et al., 1994: 279).

LEARNING DISABILITIES

Addressing psychological dysfunction in terms of learning, Culliver and Sigler (1991) provide an extensive review of the relationship between learning disabilities and juvenile delinquency. **Learning disabilities** are defined as problems faced by children and youths with dyslexia, dysgraphia, aphasia, perceptual and motor deficits, poor intersensory integration, and minimal brain dysfunction. Although these disabilities are often difficult to detect, there is a strong belief that they are directly related to delinquent behaviour in youths.

Culliver and Sigler report that five hypotheses have been used to study this relationship. The *school failure hypothesis* argues that academic failure results from learning disabilities and that this failure becomes self-perpetuating. As a result of their frustration, students become more aggressive and are, in turn, labelled as troublesome. Through rejection from teachers and administrators, these youths withdraw from mainstream activities and become involved in inappropriate behaviour and, ultimately, delinquency. The *susceptibility hypothesis* contends that learning-disabled students have unique characteristics, such as impulsiveness, inability to anticipate future consequences, and irritability. In acting out their feelings, they are more likely to become delinquent. The *differential arrest hypothesis* posits that learning-disabled students are more likely to be apprehended by police because they are less able to conceal their activities than their non–learning-disabled peers. In addition, this hypothesis suggests that learning-disabled students cannot effectively interact with police due to poor social perception and to abrasiveness and are therefore more likely to be arrested. The *differential adjudication hypothesis* argues that delinquents with learning disabilities who are arrested and charged are more likely to be convicted of crimes due to their inability to cope with the process of criminal justice adjudication. "Moreover, learning disabled students are unable to vindicate their feelings and concerns regarding the criminal charges" (Culliver and Sigler, 1991: 125). Finally, according to the *differential disposition hypothesis*, learning-disabled delinquents face a higher chance of receiving harsher sentences than non–learning-disabled delinquents.

Culliver and Sigler report that while the potential link between learning disabilities and delinquency has generated much interest, research results "tend to create more confusion and uncertainty than fact upon which sound theories can be built and effective programs developed" (125). This same conclusion is reached by Cornwall and Bawden (1992) in their assessment of the link between reading disabilities and aggression. As Skaret and Wilgosh (1989) state, the problems with the research should lead us to deal with the effects of learning disabilities on delinquency in a different way. They suggest that, rather than struggle to provide definitive findings supporting a causal relationship, we should pay attention to the fact that adolescents with learning disabilities seem to be at relatively high risk for delinquency. "Sound remedial education practices, including counselling and other support systems will improve academic achievement and social skills, and *may, possibly*, lead to some reduced delinquent behaviour" (Skaret and Wilgosh, 1989: 121). This is the same prescription offered by Moffitt, Lynam, and Silva (1994) in their conclusions about the remedial effects of using psychoneurological testing in assessing propensity toward delinquency.

PSYCHOPATHOLOGY

Gottfredson and Hirschi (1990) focus on psychological dysfunction in their general theory of crime, which we will describe in more detail in Chapter 4. To them, the central aspect in criminal behaviour (or, in fact, any imprudent behaviour) is low self-control (Arneklev et al., 1993; Forde and Kennedy, 1997). This lack of self-control derives from ineffective childhood socialization and is manifested in personality characteristics that model the behavioural problems associated with learning disabilities or low IQ. Results of low self-control include impulsivity, preference for simple tasks, risk-seeking behaviour, high need for physical activities, self-centredness, and temper. Gottfredson and Hirschi (1990) theorize that these personality characteristics combine to lead certain individuals, when offered the opportunity, to commit crimes.

For the most heinous crimes, such as sexually motivated murders or serial murders, we often apply the label of **psychopath** to the perpetrator. According to Hickey (1991), however, the term *psychopath* is used to describe a potpourri of individuals determined by societal and medical standards to possess antisocial qualities or characteristics. He claims that the label of psychopath is used interchangeably with that of *sociopath*, and because of the generality of the term, the psychopath "often turns out to be exactly what we want him or her to be" (50).

Psychopaths are often described as aggressive, insensitive, charismatic, irresponsible, intelligent, dangerous, hedonistic, narcissistic, and antisocial. They are viewed as exceptional manipulators, capable of pretending to possess "normal" human emotions even while remorselessly carrying out their own personal agendas. They are outwardly normal but are known for their inability to maintain long-term commitment to people or programs.

Knowing that someone meets the criteria of psychopathology, however, is of little benefit in isolation from any other theoretical framework (Jeffery, 1990: 364). Jeffery suggests that we look at psychopaths in terms of a framework that emphasizes the functioning of the nervous system in times of threat. As Jeffery points out, psychopaths do not become anxious or fearful in the presence of punishment or danger because their autonomic nervous systems are not aroused by danger. Further, the inability of psychopaths to anticipate the consequences of their actions means that they make little attempt to avoid punishment or pain (Jeffery, 1990: 364).

People who fit this categorization are believed to be more dangerous than other criminals, maintaining a consistency in their criminal behaviour over their lifetime. Hickey (1991) reports that psychopaths are commonly found in institutions and constitute approximately 20–30 percent of prison populations. The dilemma for criminological researchers is that the indeterminacy of the psychopathology symptomology means that people can hide these tendencies while leading "normal" lives. We know about their tendencies only when they act out their antisocial fantasies. Often, it takes some time to uncover these individuals' acts, as shown by the long crime sprees of serial murderers. For example, John Wayne Gacy, "The Killer Clown," was considered a model citizen, often dressing up as Pogo the Clown to perform at children's parties and hospitals. When he was caught, the police found twenty-nine bodies in the crawl space and under the cement driveway of his house, while four other victims had been dropped into a nearby river. He was caught only after one of his intended victims escaped and reported him.

SOCIAL CONDITIONS AND CRIMINAL MOTIVATION

It has been argued that, in a variety of ways, the social conditions under which people live make it difficult for them to be law-abiding. From this perspective, criminal behaviour may be understood as the means by which people attempt to deal with the frustrations that characterize their lives and the problems that confront them.

People who aspire to achieve goals they cannot realistically attain may feel pressure to behave in a criminal fashion. Such pressure is most likely to be felt by those who occupy disadvantaged positions in the social structure. Perhaps the best-known version of this argument was articulated in the late 1930s by the sociologist Robert Merton, who sought to explain how particular forms of social organization create the strains that lead to nonconformity.

Using American society as an example, Merton (1938) argued that if everyone in the society is encouraged to pursue the goal of material success, those who do not have access to the legitimate means by which success is to be achieved will be frustrated by their lack of opportunity. Those at the bottom of the social hierarchy—the poor, ethnic minorities, or recent immigrants—do not have easy access to quality education, inheritance, or other means by which the American Dream might be realized. Since success is still important to them, they must find ways of adjusting to the social strain that society imposes on them. The adjustments in many cases may involve criminal conduct.

BOX 3.2   MERTON'S PARADIGM OF DEVIANT BEHAVIOUR

Robert Merton (1938) argued that nonconformist behaviour results when people find themselves in situations in which they are encouraged to pursue cultural goals that prevailing social arrangements do not allow them to achieve. While such individuals may have internalized these goals, they lack the legitimate means with which to achieve them. In such situations, individuals must adjust their behaviour to accommodate the gap between the goals and the means.

Merton identified five such adaptations in the goals–means relationship.

1. *Conformity.* Individuals who make this adaptation accept as legitimate both the goals and the means for achieving them. This is the adaptation that most people make.
2. *Innovation.* Innovation involves accepting the goals but rejecting the means of goal attainment. For example, the person who embezzles accepts material gain as a legitimate goal but rejects the culturally prescribed means for achieving it.
3. *Ritualism.* This adaptation involves accepting the means for achieving the goal but rejecting the goal itself. Individuals who engage in ritualism simply "go through the motions" without coming any closer to the goals they supposedly seek.

4. *Retreatism.* In the case of retreatism, there is a rejection of both the means and the goals. At least in terms of what the culture prescribes, those who opt for this adaptation may be described as dropouts.

5. *Rebellion.* Like retreatism, this form of adaptation involves rejecting both goals and means. Rebellion differs from retreatism in that it involves the substitution of other goals as well as other means by which they might be achieved.

Merton presented his five adaptations in schematic form as follows (where + means accept and − means reject).

	Goal	Means
Conformity	+	+
Innovation	+	−
Ritualism	−	+
Retreatism	−	−
Rebellion	−	−
	(+)	(+)

Merton's **anomie theory** proposed that frustration and alienation develop when individuals who aspire to the economic goals of society (including upward social mobility) are not provided the means with which to achieve these goals. That is, a gap exists between expectations and opportunity. In responding to the anomie that develops due to this gap, certain adaptations occur. One such adaptation involves the use of criminal means to achieve conventional goals such as wealth. Blau and Blau (1982) argue that it is not absolute but relative deprivation that results in frustration and a sense of personal injustice, which, in turn, leads to criminal activity.

Consider the gangster Al Capone. Arguably, the goals to which he aspired did not differ significantly from the goals pursued by "legitimate" business-people. Capone sought wealth, power, and celebrity. He differed from conventional entrepreneurs with respect to the means he employed to achieve these objectives, but not with respect to the objectives themselves. Seen in this way, the behaviour of gangsters, thieves, and other goal-oriented criminals is best understood as the product not of a pathological personality but of social arrangements that create a gulf between what people aspire to and what is actually available to them.

Frustrated ambition does not always manifest itself in individuals like Al Capone. It may come in more mundane forms. According to Messner (1989), criminality can be attributed to a number of factors, including race, income, and particularly unemployment. In contrast, Wilson (1983) has found that the research relating unemployment to crime is inconclusive. His explanations for criminality are consistent with the views of those who argue for frustrated ambition. His emphasis, though, is different. He claims that unemployed individuals may commit crime for any number of reasons and that it may not be the unemployment per se that causes criminality but rather the problems inherent in crime deterrence. Wilson also asserts that crime may cause unemployment. What is not evident, he argues, is whether "some people turn to crime because they are poor, some people may be poor because they have turned to crime and are not very good at it, and still other persons may have been made poor and criminal because of some common underlying factor" (126). In Wilson's view, the lower classes are less likely to be socialized to the ways of society and will thus have a greater tendency toward criminal behaviour. Support from the public for targeting these groups for policing and for deterrence resides in the fact that their numbers are disproportionately represented in crime statistics (as perpetrators) and in prison populations.

At the same time, some argue that the lower classes are overrepresented in prisons because (1) the police tend to discriminate against them, (2) much of the lower-class behaviour is public and therefore more likely to be open to sanction, and (3) the crimes of the poor receive more attention than the white-collar crimes of the rich (Reiman, 1990; Snider, 1992). Property crimes like embezzlement can have more detrimental effect on society than theft, breaking and entering, and other typical crimes of the poor. Notwithstanding this view, Wilson (1983: 39) believes the rise in crime is due not to poverty or racism per se but rather to a failure of individuals from the lower class to adopt behaviour that is more consistent with societal norms.

STATUS DEPRIVATION

Several years after the publication of Merton's work, Albert Cohen followed a similar line in his investigation of gang delinquency among working-class juveniles. For Cohen (1955), the source of much juvenile crime was rooted in the problems experienced by disadvantaged youths who aspired to middle-class status but who were judged inadequate by a school system that dispensed status rewards on the basis of middle-class criteria. In other words, children from a working-class background typically find that, because their socialization experiences have not prepared them to compete effectively for status within the classroom, they come up short when they are assessed by the school's **middle-class measuring rod**. According to Cohen, working-class youths may experience feelings of frustration and inadequacy when they confront middle-class expectations regarding punctuality, neatness, and the need to postpone gratification.

One reaction on the part of youths may be to reject the source of their problem, namely, the middle-class value system of the school. Delinquency may signal such a rejection, particularly if it celebrates standards that stand in direct opposition to those of the middle-class society. Delinquency that appears intended to offend members of conventional society rather than to achieve some specific goal may serve this purpose. For Cohen, much delinquency has an "in your face" quality precisely because it is meant to signify a rejection of middle-class values. Thus, Tanner (1996: 63) writes, while aggressive and destructive delinquency may appear senseless to others, to the delinquents themselves, "it is a powerful way of hitting back at a system that has done them no favours."

> ### WHAT DOES IT MEAN?
>
> ### *Middle-Class Measuring Rod*
>
> Working-class youth may experience feelings of frustration and inadequacy when they confront middle-class expectations regarding punctuality, neatness, and the need to postpone gratification.

STRAIN AND DELINQUENCY

Richard Cloward (1959) and Lloyd Ohlin (Cloward and Ohlin, 1960) borrowed heavily from the writings of Robert Merton to demonstrate that a comprehensive theory of delinquency must explain not only why juveniles engage in delinquency but also why they engage in one type of delinquency and not another.

Like Merton, Cloward and Ohlin (1960) argued that the motivation to delinquency could be located in the discrepancy between the goals to which lower-class youths aspire and those actually available to them. Cloward and Ohlin were also influenced by Merton's view that the legitimate means to goal attainment are socially structured such that not everyone in society finds the legitimate means to conventional goals equally available. For some people, the legitimate means of obtaining success goals, such as education or a good job, are out of reach, and it is precisely this lack of legitimate opportunity that creates the pressure to deviate in the first place. Cloward and Ohlin extended Merton's theory by arguing that it is important to recognize that illegitimate means are also structured. The opportunities to be criminal are no more evenly dispersed in society than are the legitimate means to achieve success goals. Building on this logic, Cloward and Ohlin theorized that the kind of delinquent a youth becomes depends on the kinds of opportunities he or she has to be delinquent.

Cloward and Ohlin (1960) used the term **illegitimate means** to encompass two major aspects of the delinquent opportunity structure. The first is the opportunity to learn a delinquent role. As Sutherland (1947) argued, learning how to be delinquent and why it is acceptable to be delinquent are necessary precursors to being delinquent. Second, the concept of illegitimate means implies the opportunity to actually play a delinquent role. An individual can become a member of a drug network or stolen-car ring only if such organizations exist in his or her social environment. For Cloward and Ohlin, then, a central theoretical problem was to understand how particular types of community organizations make particular types of delinquent opportunity structures possible. Their analysis identified three forms of delinquent opportunity structures, each of which was associated with particular types of social conditions.

The first form, the **criminal pattern**, is characterized by a rational delinquency oriented toward the pursuit of monetary objectives and exemplified by organized theft or the sale of drugs or other illicit goods or services. Delinquency of this type is most likely to emerge in lower-class neighbourhoods in which a stable adult criminal world exists and in which the criminal and conformist sectors of the community are highly integrated. When such integration exists, the "cop on the beat" is willing to look the other way and the "honest" storekeeper is occasionally willing to fence stolen goods. The presence of a stable adult criminal world provides a structure for recruitment and upward mobility for juveniles who view criminality in career terms.

While neighbourhoods that give rise to the criminal pattern may be described as socially organized, we expect a different pattern to emerge from neighbourhoods that are characterized by a high degree of social disorganization. Socially disorganized slums lack a stable adult criminal world and thus an established criminal structure. This situation may be doubly frustrating for neighbourhood youths who have already experienced the disparity between legitimate goals and legitimate opportunities. Moreover, as Shaw and McKay (1942) pointed out, these areas lack the social controls that work to contain the behavioural manifestations of this frustration. For these reasons, Cloward and Ohlin discerned in socially disorganized areas a **conflict pattern** of delinquency. The conflict pattern is characterized by gangs who express their frustration fighting over contested neighbourhood turf.

Finally, Cloward and Ohlin maintained, it is unwise to assume that everyone who engages in criminal or conflict opportunities will be successful. We are not all cut out to be drug dealers or gang warriors. Cloward and Ohlin use the term *double-failures* to describe people who are unable to succeed through either legitimate or illegitimate means. Double-failures tend to become involved in a **retreatist pattern** in which delinquency is organized around the consumption of drugs.

RECENT VERSIONS OF THE STRAIN ARGUMENT

A GENERAL STRAIN THEORY

While strain theory is no longer a dominant view in criminology, there has recently been a revival of interest in the perspective (Menard, 1995). Agnew (1992), for instance, has recently proposed a **general strain theory**, which extends the logic of the argument well beyond that originally proposed by Merton. According to Agnew, strain theory focuses on negative relationships with others. Negative relationships are those in which individuals are not treated the way they would like to be treated; such relationships promote anger, fear, and frustration, which may lead to delinquency.

With specific reference to juvenile offending, Agnew argues that there are three major types of strain. The first type results when we believe that others are preventing us or threatening to prevent us from achieving what we want to achieve. This type is most familiar because it is very similar to the type of strain described by Merton. The second type of strain results when we believe that others have removed or are threatening to remove what we already possess and what we value. This might include the loss of a boyfriend/girlfriend, a move out of one's neighbourhood, or the death of a parent. The third type of strain results when our relationships with others cause us to experience negative life events. These might include negative relationships with teachers, abuse by parents, or bullying by peers.

As individuals attempt to cope with the negative emotions that these relationships cause them to experience, they may explore delinquent solutions. Depending on the type of strain being experienced, drug use may be a means of escape, violence may be a way to get even, or theft may allow one to acquire material goods that are not otherwise available. Several tests of the revised general strain theory have provided empirical support for the argument and helped us to better understand the conditions under which strain and delinquency are related (Brezina, 1996; Paternoster and Mazzerole, 1994). Agnew and White (1992) found that the various types of strain had a significant effect on delinquency and that the effects were most important for adolescents who lacked self-efficacy and who had delinquent friends.

CRIME AND THE AMERICAN DREAM

103

*Psychosocial
Conditions
and Criminal
Motivations*

Even more recently, Messner and Rosenfeld (1997) have elaborated Merton's argument in order to provide an explanation of why the United States has such high rates of serious crime relative to other industrialized nations. Like Merton, they suggest that the root of the problem is the "American Dream," which they define as a commitment to the goal of material success that everyone in society pursues under conditions of open, individual competition. As a result of the widespread allegiance to the American Dream, many people adopt an "anything goes" mentality as they chase their personal goals.

According to Messner and Rosenfeld, the problems created by the American Dream are magnified because the economy and the lessons that it teaches dominate other social institutions, such as the family and the school. They note, for instance, how family activities and routines are required to conform to the schedules and rewards of the labour market and that, despite much rhetoric about "family values," it is the homeowner and not the homemaker who is admired and respected. In a similar way, the school is not a setting that produces model citizens but one that teaches competition for grades as students prepare for labour force participation.

This institutional balance of power, they argue, has two important consequences. First, it allows the competitive and individualistic message of the American Dream to diffuse to other settings. Second, because the lessons of the economy override the lessons taught in other institutional environments, the social control that we expect the school or the family to exert over criminal behaviour is undermined. Both conditions are conducive to high rates of crime. The applicability of this approach to Canadian studies of crime has suggested that Canadian society is able to protect those who fall out of the race for the "dream" through social assistance programs and strong community support, although, with changes in government policies, these may be falling away (Papadopoulos, 1997). The dominance of the competition model in defining success in Canadian society may lead us to parallel the American experience in promoting individual success, creating the possibility that elements of strain evident in parts of the U.S. population will appear in Canada, as well. What this means for the potential of rising crime rates remains unclear.

CULTURE AND CRIMINAL MOTIVATION

Another major approach locates the origins of criminal motivation in the cultural worlds to which offenders have exposure. The cultural milieu in which we are socialized provides us with our ideas about what is right and wrong, moral or immoral, appropriate or inappropriate. When our socialization is successful, we internalize these views and attempt to behave in ways that conform to the cultural standards that we have learned. It follows that, if we are exposed to beliefs and ideas that support behaviour that the law defines as criminal, we may be more likely to behave in criminal fashion.

As with theories that locate the sources of criminal motivation in the stress-inducing nature of social arrangements, cultural accounts present a "normalized" picture of the offender. In other words, offenders are not necessarily pathological; they merely have learned a particular set of cultural lessons. Their behaviour is normal within a particular cultural context.

NORM VIOLATION

As we pointed out in Chapter 1, crime finds its origins in **norm violation**, with norms defined as a set of culturally prescribed acceptable behaviours. Are there societies in which it is possible to find complete compliance with all norms? Is it possible to have a society that is free of norm violation? Over the years, utopian communities have been depicted in literature as constituting the earthly expression of a spiritually inspired way of life. B.F. Skinner (1948) raised the possibility of developing and applying social intervention programs, such as those based on social learning theories, to design societies in which individuals will not feel the need or the inclination to deviate. In Skinner's utopian world, the motivations, needs, and aspirations of individuals are conditioned through reinforcement schedules designed to promote prosocial, nondeviant behaviour. Skinner argued that, in societies in which individual interests and abilities are properly assessed and managed, there will be no need for norm violation; in other words, the individual's socialization, intended to promote his or her self-interest, will have been programmed to coincide with the collective interests of the community.

The argument against the notion that we can be free of norm violation comes from the idea, promoted by Durkheim (1964), Becker (1963), and others, that societies are always subject to norm violation due to their inevitable tendency to create outsiders and insiders. It is in the rejection of marginal individuals or outcasts that norms become defined in a way that justifies the exclusion of outsiders. Further, through this process, the legitimation of the norms for those who consider themselves insiders is reinforced by the application of sanctions against norm violators.

A key question, then, becomes, Is it true that as social morality declines, crime increases? The popular view is that much of our social fabric has been heavily rent by the rapid changes resulting from urbanization, modernization, and immigration. The breakdown of traditional communities and extended families has led to a crisis of confidence in our conventional institutions—the family, the schools, the church, and so forth. From this viewpoint, the reduction in the influence of these organizations and the increased individualization in society has diminished adherence to prosocial values. The increase in rates of divorce, unemployment, transience, and so on is accompanied by an increase in the levels of crime. The difficulty with the notion of a shared morality is that it centres on the adherence to traditional values. Rather than the loss of traditional values or the transition to a new set of norms, it is the social disorganization itself that contributes to criminality (Durkheim, 1964).

Addressing this issue in a somewhat different way, we can ask, Is there a **universal form of crime**? Cross-cultural studies have shown that, while most societies condemn murder and incest, they do not always treat these behaviours as criminal (Douglas and Waskler, 1982; Schur, 1979). Sometimes an informal mechanism exists whereby such deviation comes to be sanctioned through civil action or through the social processes of expulsion from the group or shaming (Horowitz, 1990).

> **DOES IT EXIST?**
>
> ### A Universal Form of Crime
>
> Beyond expulsion from the group and shaming, there are myriad variations in the ways in which behaviour comes to be sanctioned. These variations reflect different types of morality and lawmaking across societies.

As far as other types of behaviour are concerned, the myriad variations in the ways in which they come to be sanctioned reflect different types of morality and lawmaking across societies. Japan has been offered as a model of the kind of society that can attribute its low crime rate to certain cultural and social constraints. Yet one must approach this comparison with care, because a great deal of the behaviour in Japanese society that is dealt with informally would, in our society, probably end up being dealt with by the criminal courts. What we find across societies, then, is not always a difference in behaviour but rather a difference in the societal response to behaviour.

DIFFERENTIAL ASSOCIATION

Cultural approaches focus not only on norm violation as criminal behaviour but also on criminal behaviour that is normative. One of the early pioneers of this perspective was Edwin Sutherland, who in the 1930s proposed a cultural theory of crime that he called the **theory of differential association**. Contrary to the prevailing wisdom of his day, Sutherland (1947) maintained that crime is a learned behaviour. In the process of interacting with others, whose own views support criminal conduct, one person can learn to be criminal just as another can learn to be a mechanic, a stamp collector, or a lover of classical music. According to Sutherland, the differential rate at which people associate with the carriers of criminal values determines the differential rate at which they engage in criminal conduct.

For Sutherland, differential association involves two important types of learning. First, one must learn actual techniques of crime commission. In some cases, these techniques are very simple and do not differ markedly from law-abiding behaviour. For example, stealing a car when the owner has left the keys inside is not so different from driving one's own car. In other cases, specialized skills are required—for instance, stealing a locked car when the keys have not been left inside.

Sutherland emphasized that knowledge or technical skills alone are insufficient to explain criminal behaviour. Everyone has some idea of how to commit a wide variety of crimes. And yet, while most of us could figure out how to murder or assault someone, we refrain from committing such acts. In addition to technical knowledge, one must have exposure to the "specific direction of motives, drives, rationalizations and attitudes" (Sutherland, 1947: 6). Stated differently, to behave criminally, one must learn that crime is an acceptable type of behaviour.

Consistent with the principles of the theory of differential association, Desroches (1995) found that among the bank robbers he studied, almost one-half became involved in bank robbery as a result of their association with other offenders. Typically, he found, they learn their modus operandi from more experienced criminals who convince them that bank robbery is both fast and easy. Through this process of differential association, robbers learn not only how to rob a bank but also how to justify the crime and to view it as a low-risk offence.

These types of learning imply the existence of cultural knowledge and beliefs that promote criminality and to which only some of us have sustained exposure. Sutherland's approach has been particularly helpful in explaining why normally law-abiding individuals take up criminal activity in their work environments. According to Sutherland (1961), white-collar crime occurs because people have learned how to commit it and because they have learned from others that it is an acceptable form of behaviour.

BOX 3.3   THE TENETS OF DIFFERENTIAL ASSOCIATION THEORY

Edwin Sutherland was one of the few criminologists to formulate a theory in terms of an interrelated set of propositions. The following statements, from Traub and Little (1980), refer to the process by which a particular person comes to engage in criminal behaviour:

1. *Criminal behaviour is learned.* Negatively, this means that criminal behaviour is not inherited, as such.

2. *Criminal behaviour is learned in interaction with other persons in a process of communication.* This communication is verbal in many respects but includes also "the communication of gestures."

3. *The principal part of the learning of criminal behaviour occurs within intimate personal groups.* Negatively, this means that the impersonal agencies of communication, such as movies and newspapers, play a relatively unimportant part in the genesis of criminal behaviour.

4. *When criminal behaviour is learned, the learning includes (a) techniques of committing the crime, which are sometimes very complicated, sometimes very simple; (b) the specific direction of motives, drives, rationalizations, and attitudes.*

5. *The specific direction of motives and drives is learned from definitions of the legal codes as favourable or unfavourable.* In some societies an individual is surrounded by persons who invariably define the legal codes as rules to be observed, while in others he is surrounded by persons whose definitions are favourable to the violation of the legal codes.

6. *A person becomes delinquent because of an excess of definitions favourable to violation of law over definitions unfavourable to violation of law.* This is the principle of differential association. It refers to both criminal and anticriminal associations and has to do with counteracting forces. When persons become criminal, they do so because of contact with criminal patterns and also because of isolation from anticriminal patterns.

7. *The process of learning criminal behaviour by association with criminal and anticriminal patterns involves all of the mechanisms that are involved in any other learning.* Negatively, this means that the learning of criminal behaviour is not restricted to the process of imitation. A person who is seduced, for instance, learns criminal behaviour by association, but this process would not ordinarily be described as imitation.

BOX 3.3   THE TENETS OF DIFFERENTIAL ASSOCIATION THEORY (CONT.)

8. *While criminal behaviour is an expression of general needs and values, it is not explained by those general needs and values, since noncriminal behaviour is an expression of the same needs and values.* Thieves generally steal in order to secure money, but likewise honest labourers work in order to secure money. The attempts by many scholars to explain criminal behaviour by general drives and values, such as the happiness principle, striving for social status, the money motive, or frustration, have been, and must continue to be, futile, since they explain lawful behaviour as completely as they explain criminal behaviour.

SUBCULTURAL EXPLANATIONS OF CRIMINAL MOTIVATIONS

In complex, highly differentiated societies like our own, cultural "pockets" exist when groups of people are engaged in intensive interaction and confront common problems or share common interests. It is in this sense that we speak of subcultures of rap music fans, marathon runners, or the police. Because participants in these worlds are also participants in the larger culture shared by the rest of us, such **subcultures** are both part of and distinguishable from the larger culture. It can be argued that subcultural involvement promotes criminal behaviour when the subcultural values in question are inconsistent with the conformist values enshrined in law.

Earlier in this century, Thorsten Sellin (1938) suggested that the high rates of crime among immigrant groups can be understood with reference to the culture conflict that ethnic subcultures encounter. His view acknowledged that when people migrate from one country to another, they carry with them considerable cultural baggage. We recognize this fact when we visit a restaurant in Little Italy or attend a cultural festival in Chinatown. However, this cultural baggage may also include ways of acting that, although not considered criminal in the country of origin, are defined as such in the host country. By way of illustration, Sellin (1938) tells the story of a Sicilian father in New Jersey who "killed the sixteen-year-old seducer of his daughter, expressing surprise at his arrest since he had merely defended his family honour in a traditional way" (68).

Like Sellin, anthropologist Walter Miller (1958) attempted to understand how the cultural values of a particular group can increase the likelihood of

BOX 3.4   CRIME AND CULTURE

Many theories of crime encourage a view that crime rates are higher among recent immigrants. Thorsten Sellins's (1938) theory of culture conflict, for instance, focuses on the criminogenic character of the conflict between immigrant and host cultures. In a similar way, strain theories suggest that the social and economic problems faced by new immigrants may put them in conflict with the law. Moreover, it is part of the "popular wisdom" about the problem of crime that those who are new to Canada are a bigger source of trouble than those who were born here.

To what extent are these beliefs supported by the empirical evidence? In order to answer this question, Robert M. Gordon and Jacquelyn Nelson (1996) reviewed existing studies and analyzed data from the province of British Columbia. Contrary to popular understanding, they conclude that people from nonaboriginal, visible ethnic minorities are significantly underrepresented in the federal correctional system and in the youth and adult correctional systems of British Columbia. In fact, they found that there are only about half as many immigrants as one might expect, given their numbers in the general population.

One of the factors the authors identify as important in explaining this pattern is the character of much of the immigrant population. British Columbia, for instance, attracts a large number of Asian immigrants each year, many of whom are distinguished from earlier groups of immigrants by the presence of "protective factors" that ease adjustment. Among the most important of such factors are the legitimate financial resources that immigrants bring with them to this country. Many of the immigrants who have moved to British Columbia are investors, retired people, or entrepreneurs.

As the authors note, such findings complicate our understanding of the relationship between immigration, culture, and crime and require a critical reexamination of the theories that attempt to link these concepts.

---

criminal conduct. Miller studied lower-class life in a large eastern U.S. city in an effort to identify the distinct character of lower-class culture. He was particularly interested in the ways in which this subculture might relate to the delinquencies of lower-class male youths. Miller argued that life in the lower class was organized around six **focal concerns**:

1. *Trouble.* Life is a series of troublesome episodes: trouble with the police, with the welfare officer, with one's neighbours, and so on.

2. *Toughness.* "Machismo" is widely prized in lower-class areas as an interactional style.
3. *Smartness.* Not intellectual ability, but the ability to live by one's wits is valued.
4. *Excitement.* Life is best described as boring and monotonous, punctuated occasionally by thrill-seeking behaviour. Excitement might include bouts of drinking or fighting.
5. *Fate.* Life is largely seen in terms of good luck and bad luck.
6. *Autonomy.* There is a general desire to be free of the control of police, landlords, welfare workers, and others who might seek to regulate life.

WHAT DOES IT MEAN?

Subculture of Violence

A powerful cultural emphasis on social honour and the need to save face when a threat to one's honour occurs in a public setting means that a derogatory remark made about one's character may be seen as sufficient reason to engage in physical battle. To argue that violence, in this sense, is subcultural is to argue that it is "normative."

For Miller, these focal concerns are themselves problematic because they suggest a value orientation that is at odds with the legal code. People who live their lives in terms of these focal concerns are likely, sooner or later, to end up in trouble with the law. However, for Miller, the problem is aggravated by the fact that the type of slum areas that he describes are environments in which gangs of male adolescents are likely to form. In these gangs, he suggested, the focal concerns of the lower class are exaggerated as youths attempt to model what they understand to be adult behaviour. The result is a kind of over-conformity to a value scheme that promotes behaviour likely to invite legal sanction.

Other theorists have applied similar logic to explain patterns of homicide and assault. Noting that much interpersonal violence is concentrated socially (among young members of the urban underclass) or regionally (in, for instance, the U.S. South), they argue that offenders (and frequently their victims) may behave as they do because they are immersed in a **subculture of violence** (Felson et al., 1994; Rice and Goldman, 1994; Wolfgang and Ferracuti, 1967). This subcultural orientation, it is argued, requires that some kinds of transgressions be resolved in a violent fashion. The longstanding feud between the Hatfields and McCoys is a stereotypic example of the violent subculture.

Much assaultive violence seems to originate from what many would consider to be minor or trivial altercations. An exchange that begins with a stare, a jostle, or an insult may end with one of the parties seriously injured or dead. Such patterns only make sense, subcultural theorists maintain, when we recognize the underlying powerful cultural emphasis on social honour and the need to save face. Given this emphasis, a derogatory remark made in a public setting may be enough to provoke physical retaliation.

To argue that violence, in this sense, is subcultural is to argue that it is normative. In other words, the physical defence of one's honour is not merely what one *can* do but what one *must* do to retain the respect of other cultural participants. Because the violence is normative, the person who behaves violently is unlikely to feel a sense of shame or embarrassment for doing so.

We should note that, within the context of the subculture-of-violence argument, it is the particular cultural interpretation given to an affront to character, not the affront per se, that is the source of the violence. Precisely because the cultural environments differ, a sneer is less likely to provoke trouble in a university faculty club than it is in a lower-class bar.

A weakness of the subcultural approach is that it tends to infer rather than identify independently the difference between subcultural values and subcultural behaviours. Hagan (1985) argues further that there is little empirical evidence to suggest that groups adhere to deviant subcultures in which violence is considered an integral part of the group's functioning. Instead, the violence is more likely a consequence of situational factors such as opportunity and circumstance rather than a specific group goal.

Is Mainstream Culture Criminogenic?

Subcultural arguments generally proceed from the assumption that it is useful to distinguish between a subculture that somehow promotes criminality and a conformist mainstream culture that is reflected in criminal law. Yet not all theorists who have examined the relationship between crime and culture share this assumption. Some have attempted to argue that the so-called conformist culture may itself promote criminal behaviour.

For instance, an argument can be made that violence against women finds considerable support in broad patterns of cultural belief. For many feminist writers, sexual assault and wife abuse have less to do with the subcultural orientation of a deviant minority than with pervasive cultural representations of women in mass media entertainment or advertising. When "slasher" movies, television dramas, and sexually explicit, over-the-counter magazines and videos portray women as willing or deserving victims of violence, it is not surprising that the message will be picked up and acted on by some in the society.

In a similar vein, Coleman (1987) argues that the behaviour of white-collar and corporate criminals is, to an important degree, promoted by a **culture of**

competition that defines wealth and success as the central goals of human action. He argues that criminal action in the support of either profit margins and bottom lines or personal success clearly reflects the influence of pervasive cultural beliefs. "[The] fear of failure is the inevitable correlate of the demand for success, and together they provide a set of powerful symbolic structures that are central to the motivation of economic behaviour" (Coleman, 1987: 417).

One of the most influential statements concerning the relationship between criminal behaviour and mainstream culture was provided by David Matza and Gresham Sykes (1961). Their analysis of juvenile delinquency led them to conclude that much youthful crime is better said to reflect **subterranean values** rather than subcultural values. Subterranean values are not, as subcultural values are, part of the belief system of some identifiable criminal minority. Instead, they are values that are held by many in society, although they may be in conflict with other cherished values.

Matza and Sykes suggest that, while many researchers have identified such values as "disdain for work" and "search for kicks and thrills" as subcultural values of delinquency, considerable evidence indicates that these value orientations are much more widely held. Middle-class conformists and juvenile delinquents may express their disdain for work or search for kicks in very different ways, but the value orientations held by both groups appear to have much in common. Anyone who has seen *Pulp Fiction, Natural Born Killers,* or similar blockbuster movies would be hard-pressed to make the case that violence does not have a wide cultural appeal.

According to Matza and Sykes (1957), the rules of conventional society are rarely as inflexible as subcultural theories make them out to be. In fact, those who learn the lessons of mainstream culture understand that, while criminal behaviour is *usually* wrong, it is not *always* wrong. Conventional morality prohibits acting criminally, but it also provides us with reasons it is sometimes all right to do so. Matza and Sykes term these culturally derived justifications of criminal conduct **techniques of neutralization** and argue that, in a very real way, they make offending possible.

Matza and Sykes (1957) identify five such neutralization techniques that are used by juvenile offenders. First, by denying responsibility, offenders express their belief that their crimes result not from ill will but from circumstances and conditions beyond their control. Second, by denying injury, offenders claim that the crime does not in fact harm others. Third, by denying the victim, offenders accept responsibility for their actions and acknowledge the harmful consequences, but suggest that victims are to blame for what happens to them. Fourth, by condemning the condemners, offenders may counteract the negative evaluations that others make of them—that is, they reject those who reject them. Finally, by appealing to higher loyalties, offenders maintain that the actions in which they engage are necessary if obligations to family and peers are to be met.

The central point of the neutralization argument is that knowledge of techniques of neutralization precedes and makes possible involvement in criminal activity. From this perspective, people are able to break the law because they define the law as irrelevant to their own behaviour. Techniques of neutralization are acquired as one gains knowledge of the cultural environment to which one is exposed. Through this process of redefinition, individuals come to view criminal acts as acceptable, and this gives them the freedom to commit such acts. The redefinition of vandalism as a "harmless prank," of assault as "getting even," or of theft as "borrowing" removes the moral inhibitions that might normally prohibit these behaviours.

Subsequent research has been unable to unequivocally support Matza and Sykes's and claim that neutralization precedes rather than follows involvement in crime (Agnew and Peters, 1986; Hamlin, 1988). Some researchers have attempted to account for the complexities involved in neutralization processes by arguing that neutralization is a "hardening process" (Minor, 1981). In other words, over time, criminal behaviour and techniques of neutralization become mutually reinforcing, such that attempts at neutralization may both precede and follow criminal involvement. As a result, a commitment to both the behaviour and the cultural definition of the behaviour as acceptable intensifies. Thus,

> ## WHAT DOES IT MEAN?
>
> ### *Techniques of Neutralization*
>
> First, through *denial of responsibility*, offenders express their belief that their crimes result not from ill will, but from circumstances and conditions beyond their control. Second, through *denial of injury*, offenders reject any claim that the crime results in harm to others. Third, through *denial of the victim*, offenders accept responsibility for their actions and acknowledge the harmful consequences, but suggest that victims are to blame for what happens to them. Fourth, offenders may counteract the negative evaluations that others might make of them through *condemnation of the condemners*—that is, they reject those who reject them. Finally, through the *appeal to higher loyalties*, offenders maintain that the actions in which they engage are necessary if obligations to family and peers are to be met.

the employee who steals at work may define the pilfering as a legitimate substitute for unpaid overtime or, alternatively, as a harmless activity (given that the costs are covered by insurance). The behaviour that these definitions reinforce may also be self-reinforcing over time as the commitment to the act and the morality of stealing develop in a mutually supportive fashion.

■ ■ ■

SUMMARY

What causes some people to behave in a criminal fashion? is a question that reflects the influence of the positivist school of criminology, which views criminal behaviour as the product of causal forces working within or upon the offender. Sociobiologists have argued that the constitution of some individuals, programmed through their genetic structure, makes them more likely to commit crime. Wilson and Herrnstein claim that one can detect certain physiological similarities among offenders. In their view, offenders' constitutional deficiencies lead them to discount the costs of crime through a process whereby immediate gratification becomes a paramount concern. Such discounting can also be the consequence of physiological episodes brought about by problems with diet, drugs, alcohol, and so on.

A strong sociological tradition in criminology emphasizes social conditions as a major influence on motivations to offend. This perspective views criminal behaviour as the means by which people attempt to deal with the frustrations they face in day-to-day life. The frustrated ambitions of individuals who aspire to success goals but who lack the means to achieve them result in the anomie that leads to criminal innovation. According to Merton, criminogenic conditions reside in the gap between ambition and legitimate means.

This gap can widen as a result of the economic deprivation resulting from unemployment, particularly that which affects young people. Most crime is committed by individuals in the lower socioeconomic groups, and prisons are most likely to be filled with individuals from these groups. Some criminologists have argued, however, that this is the case not necessarily because these groups are more delinquent, but rather because they are easy targets for the police, who expend more effort on street crime than they do on white-collar crime.

The focus on frustration led criminologists to look at gang delinquency among working-class juveniles. For Cohen, much juvenile crime is rooted in the difficulties experienced by disadvantaged youths who aspire to middle-class status but are judged inadequate by a school system that assigns status rewards on the basis of middle-class criteria. Rejection of this value system, in Cohen's terms, may signal delinquency.

According to cultural theorists, the criminogenic conditions that influence individual behaviour emerge from the milieu in which offenders operate. There is not necessarily anything pathological about offenders; they merely may have learned a particular set of cultural lessons that, in their case, teaches them how to act criminally. Their behaviour, then, is normal within a particular cultural context and explicable given that they have been thrust outside of the normal operations of society. The same process that ostracizes offenders also serves to strengthen the bonds among insiders, as sanctions are applied against norm violators.

It is possible, then, to look at criminals as outsiders who are punished for failing to conform to the explicit norms of the dominant culture. It is also possible to look upon certain criminal behaviour as normative. Sutherland's differential association theory proposes that crime is learned behaviour. For Sutherland, the differential rates at which criminals associate with the carriers of criminal values determine the differential rates at which they engage in criminal conduct. This perspective allows us to account for the fact that certain cultural insiders, while adhering to the law in their personal lives, commit crimes in the context of their working lives.

The idea that there may be more than one set of values in society raises the possibility that mainstream culture is itself criminogenic. Matza and Sykes argue that those who learn the lessons of mainstream culture learn that criminal behaviour is usually, but not always, wrong. Some acts can be rationalized or neutralized with explanations that find their basis in the tenets of mainstream society.

■ ■ ■

QUESTIONS FOR REVIEW AND DISCUSSION

1. What types of diet are more likely to make people criminal? Is the link between poor diet and criminality a direct one?
2. Can you think of exceptions to the body-typing predictions for different crimes that are not likely to be committed by people with particular body shapes?
3. Why do you think we pay so much attention to explanations of violent behaviour that emphasize "psychopathology"?
4. How is crime learned from others?
5. Why do individuals need to neutralize their feelings about the victims of their crimes?

CHAPTER FOUR

Offending, Social Control, and the Law

WHAT'S IN CHAPTER FOUR

In this chapter, we will examine the ways in which informal and formal social controls influence criminal offending. Offenders may not require a distinct or unique motivation to commit crime. Rather, people may offend when social pressures that might prevent them from doing so are weak or absent. These pressures can derive from the influence of social bonds to others that restrict illegal behaviour. This control may extend beyond family and friends to the community. It is here, through informal sanctions, such as shame and guilt, and through the deterrence that develops through the application of the law, that individuals are precluded from criminal behaviour.

The theories discussed in the previous chapter, by and large, would seem to suggest that since criminal behaviour has unique characteristics, it requires unique motivations. However, by putting so much energy into trying to determine what unique types of social arrangements or cultural exposure drive crime, motivational theories risk losing sight of a basic question, namely, is motivation sufficient or necessary to explain offending? Just because individuals are moved or inclined to behave in a particular way, does this mean that they will? Motivational theories assume that it is the propensity, desire, or willingness to offend that separates offenders from nonoffenders.

Many theorists do not agree with this position, however. They argue that motivation to behave criminally is probably much more widespread than is actual criminal behaviour (Agnew, 1993). We can all think of occasions when lying, cheating, or stealing may have been the most effective way of achieving our goals. According to critics of motivational theories, what separates the offender from the nonoffender has less to do with the presence of motivation and more to do with the ability to act on this motivation. This position acknowledges that we are not always free to act in ways consistent with our motivations.

In this chapter, we examine approaches that focus on the ways in which informal and formal social controls influence criminal offending. The underlying significance of these perspectives is that criminal behaviour may not require a distinct or unique criminal motivation. Instead, people may offend when the social pressures that might prevent them from doing so are weak or absent. Thus, criminal behaviour is not so much the product of criminogenic forces as it is a rational choice made by individuals who feel no constraints about engaging in it. The emphasis on rationality, choice, and control reflects the legacy of the classical school of thought.

| **SOCIAL TIES AND CONFORMITY** |

SOCIAL CONTROLS AND THE INDIVIDUAL

It has been argued that **informal social controls** in the form of relationships that people share with others who support and promote the values of conformity are an important source of social control. Many theorists have argued, for instance, that the strength and quality of social ties that link juveniles to their (conformist) teachers, parents, and peers discourage involvement in delinquency. Strong ties to parents, for instance, make possible effective adult monitoring and supervision of juvenile leisure activity (Gottfredson and Hirschi, 1990; Wells and Rankin, 1988, 1991). Parent–child relationships characterized by caring, trust, and intimate communication offer support to adolescents who may be contemplating delinquent reactions to the problems that face them (Patterson and Dishion, 1985).

CONTAINMENT THEORY

The criminologist Walter Reckless (1967) developed **containment theory** in order to try to explain how, even in areas characterized by high rates of delinquency, many youths seem to be so law-abiding. Like many of the theorists discussed in the previous chapter, Reckless recognized that many factors can "pull" and "push" people into crime—for example, they can be pulled into crime by the attraction of what they see as "easy money," or pushed by the frustration resulting from blocked opportunity. However, what interested Reckless was the fact that many more youths seem to experience these motivational pushes and pulls than engage in delinquent conduct.

Using the logic of **control theory**, Reckless reasoned that youth are insulated from delinquency by **"inner"** and **"outer" containments** that constrain nonconformist behaviour. *Outer containments* are those aspects of the individual's social environment that help to ensure that delinquent behaviour does not occur. Most importantly, these might include the relationships with family members and the members of other primary groups. These groups set standards for individuals, teach and reinforce appropriate conduct, and provide a sense of belonging. *Inner containments* are those elements that are part of the individual's psychic makeup; for Reckless, these containments were the more important of the two. Inner containments represent the products of effective socialization and the successful internalization of rules regarding acceptable behaviour. The most important element of inner containment, according to Reckless, is self-concept. Within this perspective, a "good" self-concept implies an ability to tolerate frustration, a strong sense of responsibility, and a clear orientation toward future goals. Most importantly, the containment value of self-concept implies an ability to think of one's self as a "law-abiding person." Such a view of self may prove to be an effective buffer against pressures to deviate.

WHAT ARE THEY?

Inner and Outer Containments

Inner containments represent the products of effective socialization and the successful internalization of rules regarding acceptable behaviour. Outer containments are those aspects of the individual's social environment that help to ensure that delinquent behaviour does not occur.

The most influential statement of the relationship between social ties and social control is Travis Hirschi's **theory of the bond.** Hirschi (1969) argued that the causes of juvenile delinquency are not to be located in some type of unique delinquent motivation, but rather in the weakness of the **social bond** that links delinquent adults to the world of conformist others. Weak bonds allow individuals to formulate behavioural intentions that reflect narrow self-interest. Lying, cheating, and stealing are frequently the outcome.

For Hirschi, the bond to conformist society is composed of four distinct strands. The first strand, **attachment,** refers to the degree to which children are sensitive to the expectations of parents or teachers. Sensitivity to expectations means that the potential reactions of conformist others must be taken into account when delinquency is contemplated. If a youth cares about the views of parents or teachers, delinquency is defined as a less attractive option.

The second strand, **commitment,** refers to the amount of time and energy youths invest in a conventional activity such as obtaining good grades. The greater the investment, the less likely juveniles are to engage in behaviour that jeopardizes it.

The third strand, **involvement,** refers to participation in the world of conformity—jobs to be done, projects to be undertaken, goals to be achieved, and deadlines to be met. In short, involvement in the world of conformity leaves little time for involvement in delinquency. This strand reminds us of the old adage that "idle hands are the devil's workshop."

The fourth strand is **belief.** In Hirschi's view, one need not argue, as subcultural theorists do, that delinquents are committed to a set of distinctly delinquent values. Instead, one need only argue that juveniles differ in the extent to which they believe that the conformist values of parents, teachers, or others are worthy of respect.

Strong social bonds—defined by Hirschi as high levels of attachment, commitment, involvement, and belief—insulate youths against delinquent involvement. In order to explain why some youths are delinquent while others are not, we need to focus on the weakness of delinquents' bonds rather than on the factors that motivate them to behave in criminal fashion.

WHAT DOES IT INCLUDE?

Theory of the Bond

The first strand, *attachment,* refers to the degree to which children are sensitive to the expectations of parents or teachers. *Commitment,* the second strand, refers to the size of the investment of time and energy that a youth has made to a conventional activity such as getting good grades. The third strand, *involvement,* refers to participation in the world of conformity such that little time is left for delinquency. The fourth strand, *belief,* refers to the degree to which youths believe that the conformist values of parents and teachers are worthy of respect.

More recently, Travis Hirschi has elaborated his view of the relationship between social ties and delinquency and, in collaboration with Michael R. Gottfredson (1990), has proposed a **general theory of crime** applicable to all forms of crime including white-collar and organized crime. Unlike some other theorists, they argue that it is unnecessary to offer distinct explanations for distinct types of criminal conduct. This is because, despite their differences, crimes of many sorts may be defined as "acts of force or fraud undertaken in pursuit of self-interest" (Gottfredson and Hirschi, 1990: 15).

Moreover, they suggest that the acts we call crimes share many common elements:

- They provide immediate gratification of desires.
- They are exciting, risky, or thrilling.
- They provide few or meagre long-term benefits.
- They require little skill or planning.
- They result in pain or discomfort for the victim.

In short, they argue, crime as a type of activity appeals to people who are impulsive, short-sighted, physical, risk-taking, and nonverbal. As pointed out in Chapter 3, Gottfredson and Hirschi use the term *low self-control* to describe this propensity and maintain that people who are attracted to crime will also be attracted to other activities, such as drinking and driving (Keane, Maxim, and Teevan, 1996) and drug use (Sorenson and Brownfield, 1995), that share similar elements.

What are the sources of low self-control? For Gottfredson and Hirschi, it originates in child-rearing. Child-rearing that is effective in discouraging delinquency requires that parents (1) monitor their child's activity, (2) recognize deviant behaviour when it occurs, and (3) punish such behaviour when it does occur. Low self-control results when this process goes awry. Parents may not care what their children do, or, even if they are concerned, they may be unable to supervise their children effectively or to punish the offending behaviour.

For Gottfredson and Hirschi, low self-control is the key cause of criminality. As such, it explains why some people rather than others are likely to behave in criminal fashion. They recognize, however, the need to distinguish between criminality as a propensity and crime as a social event. Crimes occur when individuals with low self-control encounter situations and opportunities conducive to offending. Forde and Kennedy (1997) provide support for the importance of low self-control in explaining crime behaviour, but they find that this effect is indirect because it operates through situational factors, such as following risky lifestyles, that enhance the chance that individuals with low self-control will act in delinquent ways.

POWER CONTROL THEORY

Power control theory, which was developed by John Hagan, Ron Gillis, and John Simpson (Hagan, 1989; Hagan, Gillis, and Simpson, 1979, 1987, 1988), provides another example of the ways in which family relationships permit or discourage delinquency. Of central interest to these writers is the fact that males are much more delinquent than females. Hagan, Gillis, and Simpson attempt to explain this fact in terms of the differential ability of the family to control male and female children.

Consistent with the general social control argument, power control theory argues that social control is stratified within the family setting (Tibbets and Herz, 1996). In traditional patriarchal families, which accept a cultural claim to male dominance, girls are subject to greater control than boys. In addition, mothers are assigned a greater responsibility for the control of dependent children. Two important implications follow from this position. First, the informal social control processes in which family members are involved affect female more than male family members. Mothers are more likely to be the subjects and daughters are more likely to be the objects of this control. Second, as a result of these differences, male children are considerably freer than female children to engage in a wide range of risk-taking behaviour, some of which involves delinquency.

INTERACTIONAL THEORY

Terence Thornberry (1987; Thornberry et al., 1991) and colleagues have proposed an **interactional theory of delinquency** that has at its core assumptions derived from control theory. However, Thornberry attempts to link the logic of control theory to the insights derived from arguments stressing the role of cultural learning and peer influence. Like Hirschi, Thornberry argues that adolescents are at risk of engaging in delinquent behaviour when they have low levels of attachment to parents, of commitment to school, and of belief in conventional institutions and people. Thornberry emphasizes that the weakness of the ties to conventional others does not make delinquency inevitable although it does make it more likely.

Further, Thornberry argues, it is too simplistic to assume (as many theorists seem to do) that social ties to the world of conformity are unchanging. On the contrary, they may strengthen or weaken over time in response to changing circumstances. Most notably, while weak social bonds to parents or teachers may make delinquency possible, delinquency that has already occurred may further affect these relationships. Consider the example of a youth whose weak bond to parents contributes to his or her engagement in delinquent activities. When the parents learn about the delinquency, they may react by rejecting the youth or by subjecting him or her to severe punishment. Such reactions may further undermine the relationship between child and parents, thus making delinquency an even greater possibility. In terms of illuminating the criminal event, the real strength of Thornberry's argument is that it attempts to come to terms with the dynamic and fluid character of criminality.

LIFE COURSE PERSPECTIVE

Another version of social control that pays explicit attention to change over time is the **life course perspective** formulated by Robert Sampson and John Laub (1990; Laub and Sampson, 1993). These writers were interested in attempting to reconcile two contradictory sets of research findings. On the one hand, a body of research indicates that adult criminality is very strongly influenced by patterns of childhood behaviour (Wilson and Herrnstein, 1985). This research suggests that because people embark on criminal paths long before adulthood, the characteristics of adults' social roles (such as unemployment) are largely irrelevant as causes of crime. On the other hand, another body of research indicates that changes in people's lives (like getting or losing a job, or getting married or having children) affect the likelihood of involvement in crime. Sampson and Laub argue that because most criminological attention is focused on the study of teenagers, researchers have not really examined how the propensity to crime does in fact change or remain stable over the life course.

Their life course perspective makes an important distinction between "trajectories" and "transitions." *Trajectories* describe the pathways on which people are located or the directions in which their lives seem to be moving. *Transitions*, however, are specific life events—like a first job or a marriage or the birth of a child—that might or might not serve to alter the trajectories. For example, a juvenile who is actively involved with delinquent peers, who lives in an abusive home, and who is failing at school might be on a criminal trajectory. However, suppose in the later teen years, the individual begins a romantic relationship with someone who is nurturing and supportive, and the two decide to get married and raise a family. After the individual develops a deep commitment to the relationship and begins to plan for and think about the future, the involvement in crime is diminished. In the life course framework, we would see the marriage as a transition that altered the individual's criminal trajectory.

For Sampson and Laub, trajectories change when transitions alter the nature and number of social bonds that help to ensure conformity. However, they argue that it is not simply the occurrence of particular life events that is likely to bring these changes about. Rather, it is the "social investment" in the institutional relationship that dictates the salience of informal social control.

It is important to point out that the interpretative value of the life course perspective extends beyond the level of the individual. Macmillan (1995), for instance, has recently used life course theory to explain increase in rates of Canadian property crime over the last several decades. During this period, Macmillan argues, young people were likely to leave their parental homes earlier, to marry later, and to wait longer for parenthood. The implication with respect to life course theory is that young people (especially young males) were less likely to make those transitions that would have connected them to networks of informal social control. These changes may be said to have led to an increase in the pool of potential criminal offenders over the period. Macmillan's analysis shows that changes in rates of crime may be related to structural changes in the life course.

SOCIAL CONTROLS AND THE COMMUNITY

Other theorists have speculated about the roles played by informal social control at the level of the local community or the neighbourhood. According to Wirth (1938), the larger, the more densely populated, and the more heterogeneous a community, the more accentuated are the characteristics associated with urbanism, including isolation and social breakdown. Urbanism brings together individuals who have no sentimental or emotional ties to one another. From this emerges a spirit of competition, self-aggrandizement, and exploitation. To counteract this spirit, society reverts to formal controls.

People who are in frequent social contact with strangers and acquaintances also develop a reserve toward one another. The strong family and friendship ties necessary for intimate communities disappear in cities, and the result is higher levels of alienation, anomie, and delinquency. To prove the point, Wirth points out that crime rates in urban areas are higher than those in rural areas, where the informal social controls between intimates still operate.

If some urban neighbourhoods more effectively constrain the delinquent inclinations of youths, then we might be able to explain why some parts of the city have higher rates of delinquency than do others. Theoretical arguments of this type were originally proposed by Clifford Shaw and Henry McKay, two sociologists associated with the University of Chicago. Shaw and McKay (1942) were interested in trying to understand why some parts of the city of Chicago had consistently high rates of crime, delinquency, and other social problems. What intrigued them was the fact that rates of delinquency remained high even when the resident population, identified at any given point in time, moved out or died and were replaced by new groups of urban residents. In other words, regardless of changes in the ethnic or demographic mix of the population residing within an area, rates of delinquency were relatively constant. For Shaw and McKay, urban variations in rates of crime are associated with the social context of urban areas rather than with the specific characteristics of the populations who live there.

According to Shaw and McKay, high-crime areas are characterized by a high degree of **social disorganization**, which may be defined as an inability on the part of area residents to achieve their common values or solve their common problems (Kornhauser, 1978). Shaw and McKay argued that areas characterized by a high level of social disorganization tend to be economically disadvantaged, to have a high rate of population turnover, and to be racially and ethnically diverse. In such areas, the informal social controls that might be expected to constrain delinquency are ineffective. As predicted by Wirth (1938), local friendship networks are less likely to develop and the level of participation in formal or voluntary organizations is low. As a result, adults in these communities may be ineffective in their attempts to supervise or control teenage peer groups that are likely to become involved in delinquency (Sampson and Groves, 1989).

We see the logic of the social disorganization argument manifested in many forms of crime prevention that attempt to re-create a sense of community in high-crime neighbourhoods. Neighbourhood Watch and similar programs seek to increase the level of interaction among residents and at the same time encourage them to develop a sense of responsibility for their neighbours.

Fischer (1976) argues that the city is not as disorienting—and its inhabitants not as vulnerable to social breakdown—as Wirth maintained. He points out that urban environments actually provide more opportunities for social support than do rural areas and that the ties extend beyond the boundaries of neighbourhoods to stretch across the city.

According to Krohn, Lanza-Kaduce, and Akers (1984), Wirth's view of cities reflects the claim that deviant behaviour results from the weakening or severing of one or more of the social bonds (Hirschi, 1969). This perspective is consistent with the arguments put forward by control theorists. Fischer's portrayal of an integrated but highly diverse urban setting offers a different view, one that emphasizes that learning deviant behaviour results from (differential) association with people who provide models, definitions, and reinforcements for such behaviour (Krohn, Lanza-Kaduce, and Akers, 1984: 355).

Krohn, Lanza-Kaduce, and Akers speculate that the differences in explanation provided by Wirth and Fischer revolve around the quality of the primary relationships across communities. Wellman and Leighton (1979) argue that modern cities have replaced intimate, spatially bounded communities with "liberated" communities (that is, networks of friends and acquaintances who live outside of the individuals' neighbourhoods). Despite the view that the neighbourhood is not essential to social support, neighbourhoods that have a high degree of interaction are more likely to control crime informally through the residents' collective ability to respond to violations of the law and/or neighbourhood norms (Unger and Wandersman, 1985: 143). This informal control depends, however, on the neighbourhood having a consensus on values or norms, the ability to monitor behaviour, and a willingness to intervene when necessary. These characteristics are generally absent in those urban neighbourhoods where crime is high.

While interpersonal conflict is a pervasive and inevitable feature of social life (Kennedy, 1990), most conflicts are resolved in a peaceful fashion. We might avoid the conflicting parties, give in to the demands that they make, report them to the police, or sue them. Horowitz (1990) points out that the law does not respond to all grievances in the same way. A teenager who complains that his elderly neighbours have been playing their Zamfir records too loudly will probably receive a cooler reception from the police than the elderly neighbour who complains about the volume of the teenager's Marilyn Manson music. Similarly, argue conflict theorists, poor and minority communities are less effectively policed than are more middle-class neighbourhoods, and behaviour that would not be tolerated in higher-status areas is considered "normal" in areas characterized by greater social or economic disadvantage. These observations imply that teenagers or those who are socially disadvantaged may be more likely to engage in violent or other criminal forms of conflict expression. Where it is applied, the formal response through police intervention has been referred to as an "overreach" of the law, the implication being that a low tolerance is exhibited for behaviours that could be handled more effectively through informal sanctions (Morris and Hawkins, 1970).

The incidence of crime may also depend on interethnic and interracial relationships that develop in areas where groups with different backgrounds come together. The confusion and misunderstandings that arise from differences in family practice and cultural values can lead to tensions and conflicts, which can develop into criminal behaviour along the lines proposed by Sellin (1938). Research by Smith (1982) suggests that many people use ethnic stereotyping as a pragmatic means of managing the dangers of urban life. These informal strategies usually entail setting up social and physical distances in order to avoid potentially harmful encounters. The avoidance of certain areas is a common strategy for coping with crime in urban centres.

In addition, Suttles (1972) found that, particularly in ethnic communities, boundaries are set by public displays of territorial marking (for example, threatened gang fights). These boundaries indicate, through spatial mechanisms, "with whom it is safe to associate" (Suttles, 1972: 161). The marking of territory plays a role in reducing neighbourhood conflict by excluding those who are considered to be different or undesirable. Conflict with people outside of the neighbourhood takes on a symbolic character of protectiveness of the turf.

In disorganized areas, people are less likely to know their neighbours or to be interested in their welfare. The high level of cultural distance between different groups inhabiting the area and the rapid turnover of population mitigates against the development of a strong sense of community spirit. It is more difficult to monitor the behaviour of others in the neighbourhood when we do not recognize them and thus do not know whether they have a right to be there (Stark, 1987). Under such circumstances, we are not only less likely to fail to recognize people but also less likely to recognize their property; thus, stolen property that is carried around the neighbourhood by a stranger, or even by someone we know, is unlikely to be identified (Felson, 1986). In contrast, in small, tightly knit communities in which the residents know one another both culturally and personally, we expect that informal community control will operate more effectively.

Many of the social institutions that might be expected to control the behaviour of youthful offenders are also less effective in socially disorganized areas. Formal social controls in the form of churches and schools, for instance, may not enjoy a high level of community support, in which case their social control functions may be undermined (Stark, 1987). In well-integrated areas, we might expect that community organizations will form in response to the problem of local crime or delinquency. However, when the level of social disorganization is high, voluntary groups formed to address community problems are less likely to develop.

In a recent restatement of the social disorganization perspective, Bursik and Grasmick (1993) distinguish three types of social controls that are rendered less effective in areas characterized by high levels of social disorganization. The first type of control functions at the "private" level. These are the types of controls that are associated with the family, the friendship group, or other groups with which one has an intimate association. The second type is "parochial" control and represents the effects of broader patterns of interpersonal association. Such controls are exerted by local schools, stores, churches, or voluntary organizations. The third type is "public" or external control. This refers to the ability of the local community to mobilize sources of control that originate beyond its boundaries. Local communities will not be equally successful in their attempts to get the urban bureaucracy to allocate funds to neighbourhood projects or to get the police to take neighbourhood problems seriously.

Bursik and Grasmick argue that when such controls are operating, they discourage crime by discouraging both criminal motivation and the opportunities for crime. They also note that these controls do not emerge instantaneously. Instead, they emerge slowly as residents associate with one another and establish relationships over time. Factors that contribute to residential instability undermine the processes that lead to effective community controls and therefore make higher rates of crime and delinquency more likely.

THE POWER OF LAW: THE DETERRENCE DOCTRINE

SPECIFIC AND GENERAL DETERRENCE

Laws threaten penalties for their violation, and deterrence theories are concerned with the ways in which these threats are communicated to potential offenders. More specifically, deterrence theories attempt to determine how the reaction to the threat of penalties decreases the likelihood of offending. **Specific or special deterrence** refers to the ways in which individuals are deterred, through punishment, from offending or reoffending. For example, suppose you break into a house, are apprehended, and then are sentenced to prison for a period of time. If the prison term discourages you from committing another such crime, we might say that it is a special deterrent. According to the principle of **general deterrence**, individuals are deterred from breaking the law when they see others who have done so receive punishment. Thus, in our housebreaking example, friends who witness the punishment that you receive for having broken the law will desist from breaking and entering.

> ### WHAT DOES IT MEAN?
>
> ### *Specific vs. General Deterrence*
>
> Specific deterrence refers to the ways in which individuals are deterred from offending or reoffending by receiving punishment. In general deterrence, individuals who see offenders receiving punishment will be deterred from breaking the law themselves.

The success of specific and general deterrence is based on three properties of legal threats. The first such property is the **severity** of the penalty. Does the law threaten prison or a fine? Are offenders likely to be sentenced if they are caught, or are they likely to be released with a warning? The criminal code clearly states the punishment attached to each crime, and sentencing guidelines are set for judges to apply in the cases that come before them.

It is assumed that all individuals in society are aware of the law's prescriptions about punishment and are deterred in direct proportion to the escalating threat of this punishment. Thus, it should be widely understood that the most severe punishments are reserved for the most serious crimes. For example, the death penalty is reserved solely for the crime of homicide, and only for certain

---

BOX 4.1   THE PERCEPTION OF LEGAL AND OTHER THREATS

Arguments in support of deterrence assume that people will be discouraged from engaging in crime if they perceive as salient the threats of the criminal law. How do people perceive these threats? And how, in relative terms, do the risks of legal punishment compare with the risks of other misfortunes associated with illegal conduct?

A national study on drinking and driving provides some data that address these questions. The survey, which was sponsored by Health and Welfare Canada (1989), collected information about the beliefs, perceptions, and behaviour of approximately 10 000 Canadians in the ten provinces.

The survey revealed that more than one-third of Canadians aged 16 to 69 acted, the previous year, in at least one of several specific ways to avoid drinking and driving. Approximately one-half of these people said that they feared having an accident, while just over one-third said that they were afraid of getting caught by the police. Another 18 percent were afraid that they might lose their driver's licence or be jailed.

Respondents' reactions to the following hypothetical scenario further illustrate the nature of their perceptions:

A person goes to a bar after work to have a drink with friends, drinks enough to be impaired, and then drives five miles home.

In these circumstances, only a small proportion of Canadians (10 percent) think the chances are high that the police will stop the driver on the way home. However, more than a third (34 percent) believe the driver is highly likely to have an accident. The same people who think the impaired driver will *not* be stopped by police on the way home are the ones who are most likely to say they themselves have driven after drinking. However, those who think the chances are high that the impaired driver will have an accident are less likely to report drinking and driving themselves.

Having stopped the impaired driver, will the police lay a charge? Over half (54 percent) of Canadians feel this is highly probable. Not unexpectedly, a higher proportion of those who think the driver is unlikely to be charged also say they have driven after drinking. However, this group is also more likely to think that if the driver is charged, a drinking-and-driving conviction will follow.

Figure 4.1   Responses to Questions about a Hypothetical Drinking-and-Driving Situation,* Age 16 to 69, Canada, 1988

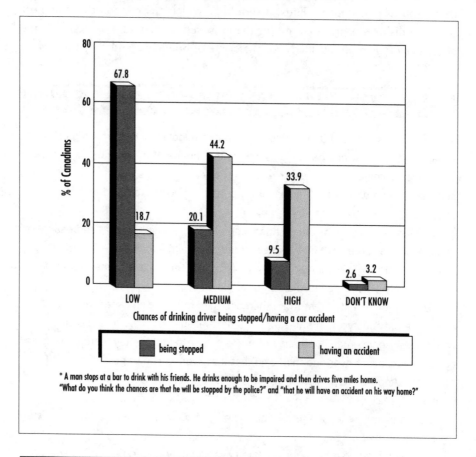

Chances of drinking driver being stopped/having a car accident

* A man stops at a bar to drink with his friends. He drinks enough to be impaired and then drives five miles home.
"What do you think the chances are that he will be stopped by the police?" and "that he will have an accident on his way home?"

SOURCE: Health and Welfare Canada, *National Survey on Driving and Drinking, 1988: Overview Report*. Reproduced with permission of the Ministry of Public Works and Government Services Canada, 1997.

severe types of homicide at that. Theft and other property crimes are punished less severely and, again, within the category of theft, harsher sentences are reserved for more serious crimes (generally measured according to the specific dollar value of the stolen property). Sentencing guidelines on both the provincial level and the federal level may change fairly often, presumably reflecting changes in our sense of the seriousness of various offences.

The second property of legal threats is the **certainty** of punishment. Regardless of what the law threatens, how likely is it that an offender will be apprehended and sentenced? Many research studies have argued that, with respect to possible deterrent effects, certainty is a more important characteristic of legal penalties than is severity. In other words, a high likelihood of being punished is more important than being punished in a specified manner.

Certainty of apprehension and conviction is clearly influenced by factors that relate to the reporting of crime. As we saw in Chapter 1, the majority of the crimes that are known to the police were brought to their attention by the public. For various reasons, however, many crimes go unreported. Further, many crimes that *are* reported remain unsolved. In both cases, the offender "gets away" with the crime. The rational offender calculates the certainty of risk and then acts on this calculation: when risk of apprehension and conviction is high, the crime is less likely to occur.

The third property of legal threats is the **celerity** (**swiftness**) of punishment (Clark, 1988). When justice is delayed, there may be a perception either that the punishment is unfair or that it will have a diminished impact on the offender. Concern has also been raised that delayed justice may unfairly stigmatize an individual who is in fact innocent. Court backlogs that lead to delays of a year or more in hearing cases have led some to argue that the cases should be dismissed without the determination of guilt or innocence. The message conveyed by such dismissals would be that the criminal justice system is unable to handle cases swiftly and that this circumstance casts doubts on the likelihood of them handling them at all.

It is worth noting that Mark Stafford and Mark Warr (1993) have recently called into question the distinction which most researchers make between general and specific deterrence. In short, they argue that the distinction is really a false one. To argue about general deterrence effects is to argue that those who form the audience have no direct knowledge of the punishment in question. However, some of those who learn about the punishment of others have committed the same kind of act for which the punishment is being meted out, although they themselves did not get caught. In other words, they have experience with "avoiding punishment." Similarly, in the case of research on specific deterrence, it is usually assumed that the punishment the individual experiences will affect the likelihood of subsequent offending. At the same time, the individual who is being punished may have knowledge of others who committed similar acts and didn't get caught. Thus, Stafford and Warr maintain, the distinction that is usually made between general and specific deterrence rests on a number of simplifying assumptions that distort empirical reality. Rather than speak of general and specific deterrent effects, they suggest, it makes more sense to speak of indirect and direct experience with punishment and punishment avoidance.

Some researchers suggest that, in emphasizing the importance of penalty characteristics, deterrence theories have adopted too narrow a view of how legal
threats discourage crime. Williams and Hawkins (1986) assert that the deterrent effects of legal sanctions may be supplemented by at least three types of
sanctions: (1) commitment costs, (2) attachment costs, and (3) stigma of arrest.

Commitment costs refer to the possibility that arrest may jeopardize
people's investments in some legitimate activity. The greater a person's investment in some conformist line of activity, the more he or she will be discouraged from offending by a belief that arrest might threaten that investment.
Commitment costs may include concerns about future employment or educational prospects. **Attachment costs** refer to the costs associated with the loss of
valued relationships with friends or family members. The belief that arrest will
weaken these ties may make arrest a fearsome prospect. Finally, the **stigma of
arrest** relates to the belief that apprehension by the police may harm one's
reputation. It is important to distinguish this fear that others will learn about
one's arrest from the fear that they will learn that one has committed the act.
Williams and Hawkins point out, for example, that less stigma generally is
associated with driving while impaired than with being arrested for this action.
In the case of homicide, however, the stigma associated with arrest for the act
may not be much greater than the stigma associated with the commission of
the act. In general, Williams and Hawkins argue that because attachment
costs, commitment costs, and the stigma of arrest are forms of informal social
control that are activated by formal controls, they should be viewed as part of
the deterrence process.

An illustration of how this mix of legal and informal sanctions can work is
provided by recent research on the contribution of arrest to the reduction of
repeat wife assault. Donald Dutton and his colleagues (1992) examined data
from Vancouver and Alberta that compared results from a general population
sample with those from a group of arrested and convicted wife assaulters who
were undergoing treatment in a court-mandated program. Respondents were
asked to express their views of the likelihood (certainty) of specific legal and
social sanctions, assuming they were to assault their wives. They were also
asked to judge the severity of the punishment that would follow such an
assault. Police arrest was among the legal sanctions offered. The social sanctions included police being called, the partner leaving the relationship, disapproval of friends and family, and loss of self-respect.

The arrested assaulters reported a greater degree of confidence than those in
the general samples that an arrest would occur if an assault took place.
Interestingly, the general and treatment samples had similar responses to the ques-

tion relating to the loss of self-respect. In terms of severity of punishment, the two samples were high with respect to all factors. Thus, deterrence appears to be a function not only of the arrest but also of the social consequence of the arrest.

To test this theory further, responses made by assaulters before they entered the treatment program were compared with those made at the end of the treatment about a year later. Not only was there an increase in the perceived severity of arrest and conviction, but it was accompanied by a substantial increase in the judgment of the perceived severity of losing one's partner or facing social disapproval. Disclosure of these events, which are often kept private, can "be a first step toward generating informal sanctions from friends and family toward the assaultive male and an empowering support network for the victim. Because arrest makes disclosure more likely, that informal side effect of arrest could serve to reduce recidivism" (Dutton et al., 1992: 124). Here we have a case of legal sanction (arrest) and informal sanction (social disapproval) working together to increase deterrence.

Arguments about the deterrent properties of legal sanctions do not assume that potential offenders are accurately informed about the risks they face. How accurate their perceptions are is itself an empirical question of considerable scope (Henshel and Silverman, 1975). We can suggest, however, that, in terms of whether an individual will offend, what the law actually threatens is less significant than what people *believe* the law threatens.

SITUATIONAL DETERRENCE

Criminologist Maurice Cusson (1993) has criticized deterrence theory and research for its failure to address the specific character of the situations in which crimes occur. A typical research project might ask respondents to indicate how likely it is that they will be apprehended if they attempt to steal a car. Too often, however, the context of the automobile theft is not specified. Obviously, how risky one perceives car theft to be depends greatly on the specific circumstances under which the theft is attempted. Although study respondents may make certain assumptions in order to provide an answer to the researcher's question, the answers may have little to do with the actual assessment of risks that an individual makes in any specific situation.

In addition, Cusson notes, while researchers ask survey subjects to calmly assess the risks of apprehension, this research ignores the emotional character of the deterrence process. Deterrence, he argues, is not about the cold and rational calculation of risks but about fear. A burglar who breaks into a house may rationally believe that the chances of getting caught are low but may panic when he hears a noise. Fear can override rational calculation and make the deterrence process look quite different in reality than it appears in theory. For these reasons, Cusson suggests the need to consider deterrence as a situational factor. **Situational deterrence** emphasizes the ways in which the offender's fear of apprehension is related to the specific circumstances of the criminal event.

According to Cusson, potential offenders face two types of danger in the precriminal situation. The first type is immediate: the robber worries that the victim may fight back or be armed while the burglar worries that a barking dog might bite. The second type of danger refers to subsequent harm that is signalled by some element in the precriminal situation. Thus, the television monitor in the convenience store about to be robbed does not threaten the robber directly but may eventually if it leads to the robber's apprehension.

Cusson notes that the risks facing offenders before or during the commission of the offence do not guarantee that the offender will be deterred. Offenders differ in terms of the level of courage that they can muster in particular situations and also in terms of their ability to manage the fear they do experience. In addition, some crimes (such as joyriding or vandalism) may be more attractive precisely because they involve an element of danger.

The value of Cusson's analysis is that it forces us to recognize that deterrence effects are not embodied solely in abstract legal threats but also in the risks that offenders understand themselves to be facing in the settings in which criminal events actually occur.

AMBIVALENCE ABOUT CRIME AND DETERRENCE STRATEGIES

Clearly, deterrence arguments figure quite prominently in many public policy debates. Despite the perception that there is widespread consensus over the need to crack down on crime, public attitudes toward crime and its prevention suggest a strong degree of **ambivalence**, which has many sources. First, the public is concerned that the law is not adequately enforced (Currie, 1985). Research suggests that the public feels that the law generally reflects their values (Tyler, 1990) and that they obey the law because they believe it to be right. At the same time, however, they are critical of the way in which justice is currently being dispensed. Many believe that the law favours the rich and the powerful and that the legal process is too slow. The system as a whole is seen as ineffective in deterring serious crime, particularly in terms of the punishment that is administered (Brillon, 1985; Baron and Hartnagel, 1996).

There is no consensus in the research literature, however, concerning the effectiveness of punishment in reducing criminal behaviour. Cook (1977) concludes from his review of the research on deterrent effects (including the impact of capital punishment on the eradication of violent crime) that little persuasive evidence has been produced concerning the size, or even the existence, of the deterrence mechanism. The lack of strong support in the research literature undermines proposals for strict punishment regimens, especially if they are contrary to our views of what is humane and just.

Second, as Braithwaite (1989) points out, confusion develops over what is perceived as a conflict between crime control and respect for civil liberties. Some express concern that too much informal social control impedes individual freedom—neighbours spying on neighbours can be a real threat to personal privacy. However, punishment delivered by formal agents without the shaming that comes from informal social sanctions is ineffective. If the risk of arrest is perceived as low and the severity of punishment minimal, individuals may still be prevented from committing a crime by the stigmatizing reactions of others for being involved in crime.

A third problem that contributes to ambivalence about crime is the lack of consensus over the viability of expensive and seemingly ineffective incarceration (Miller and Anderson, 1986). At the same time, we are uncomfortable with leaving reintegration to the community. Few communities are ready to receive criminals as they begin their transition to "normal" life. In fact, there have been recent efforts by some communities to actively block the return of released offenders, particularly those who were imprisoned for sex offences. While offenders need to be reintegrated into society and kept from reoffending, there is limited effort by communities to take this job over from formal agencies.

A fourth and final factor contributing to the ambivalence about crime is the general awe with which we regard it. While the reality of violent criminality is usually horrific, its depiction in the media is titillating, thrilling, and addictive. Promoting prosocial behaviour in a society in which criminals are often depicted as folk heroes is no easy task (Phelps, 1983). While Skipper (1985) suggests that the folk hero syndrome is on the decline, there still exists in our society a residual belief that the criminal should be admired for expressing some degree of resistance to convention.

RATIONAL CHOICE THEORIES

Like deterrence theories, rational choice theories view the offender in a way that suggests clear links with the classical tradition. However, **rational choice**

theories take a somewhat broader perspective than do deterrence theories. While these theories recognize the role that legal threats play in deterring offending, they argue that other factors such as the potential gains that might be derived from the commission of a crime and the ease with which it can be committed are also important.

The increasing popularity of rational choice theory can be seen at least in part as a product of the dissatisfaction of many criminologists with more traditional motivational theories (Fattah, 1993). Theories that emphasize strain or cultural learning, for instance, are seen as creating a false distinction between criminal and noncriminal activity. Rational choice theories argue that both types of behaviour seem to be oriented toward the same kinds of ends (for example, money, self-gratification); therefore, criminal behaviour may not require a unique motivation (Cornish and Clarke, 1986). In addition, traditional motivational theories really only explain why some people might be predisposed to commit crimes, not why or how crimes are committed. Because crimes are events that occur in specific places at specific times, motivational theories may be faulted for their inattention to the situational context of criminal events.

Rational choice theories focus on offenders' actions based on perceived benefits rather than on some precipitating social or psychological factors (Clarke and Felson, 1993; Nagin and Paternoster, 1993). Moreover, as offenders seek benefits and attempt to avoid losses, they make decisions and choices that can be understood as reflecting rational thought. Therefore, the rational choice theorist argues that, rather than study what broad social factors (strain or cultural values) might influence offending behaviour, it makes more sense to study how offenders make these decisions. There are actually two broad types of decisions that invite attention.

COMMITTING A CRIME

One type of decision relates to the commission of particular crimes. How do burglars decide in which neighbourhood they will look for targets? How do they decide which house to break into? How do they decide what to do if they see a window sticker indicating that the home is protected by an alarm system? The answers to such questions allow rational choice theorists to develop an understanding of criminal events and the role that offenders play in such events (Tunnell, 1992). Obviously, when compared with many traditional theories of motivation, rational choice theory is interested in the situational character of crime (Birkbeck and LaFree, 1993).

In attempting to answer questions about offenders' decisions, rational choice theories do not assume that offenders operate in purely rational fashion. Instead, offenders usually employ a "limited rationality." In other words, they may inaccurately perceive the benefits of committing a particular crime, lack the time to weigh the possible outcomes, or have access to limited information with which to make the decision.

Contrary to some of the other theories discussed in this and the previous chapter, rational choice theorists argue that because specific situational factors are so important and because offender decision making varies across situations, it makes little sense to try to develop a generic theory of crime. The choices that must be made when an offender is deciding whether to rob a convenience store will be very different from the choices that will be made if an offender is deciding whether to steal a car or defraud a bank (Clarke, 1992).

THE CRIMINAL CAREER

The other major issue of interest to rational choice theorists relates to the **criminal career**. How do offenders decide to get involved in crime? How and when do they decide to give up a life of crime? The notion that crime may be thought of in career terms is widely shared both inside and outside of criminological literature. The true-crime section of any bookstore usually carries several titles that detail the exploits of the "professional thief," "professional robber," or "contract killer." Such books promise a look into a world of crime that, at least superficially, seems to be organized in ways that reflect the occupational structure of the "legitimate" work world. In some fundamental sense, these offenders view crime as their job. They have acquired the technical skills they need to perform this job, and they derive their livelihood principally from successful job performance. Just how superficial are comparisons between crime and legitimate work? Does it make sense to conceptualize criminal involvement in career terms?

THE CONCEPT OF CAREER

A useful place to begin this discussion is with a brief consideration of the concept of "career" itself. In occupational terms, the concept of career denotes "the sequence of movements from one position to another in an occupational system made by any individual who works in that system" (Becker, 1963: 24). This definition is consistent with popular usage. We think of a work career as beginning at some specific point in time and continuing until death, retirement, or a voluntary or forced career change. Over the course of the career, we can identify movement through various stages (which, in the context of formal organizations, we call promotions). Each stage brings with it new responsibilities and additional rewards and provides the individual with the skills, knowledge, or experience he or she needs to advance to successive stages.

The relative success that characterizes career movement is dependent on several "career contingencies." The occupational system may, for instance, allow for little career advancement, or the individual may lack the training that would allow movement beyond a certain occupational level. Contingencies include any factors on which career success depends. Within the setting of a

---

BOX 4.2   ROBBERS AND ROBBERY

Robbery is probably the type of violent crime that most people associate with the "career criminal." Thomas Gabor of the University of Ottawa and Andre Normandeau of the University of Montreal undertook a major study of robbery, mainly in the area of Montreal and Quebec City (Gabor and Normandeau, 1989).

Part of the study involved detailed interviews with 39 convicted robbers, all but one of whom were serving sentences in the Montreal area. The study revealed the following:

- The offenders were male, and most were under 30 years of age, had no more than a secondary school education, and came from a blue-collar background.

- The self-reported criminality was far in excess of that reported in their files.

- The offenders were motivated to rob by the fact that robbery is a fast and direct way to obtain money compared with the less lucrative and more complicated acts of break and enter and fraud.

- Unemployment, the need for drugs, and criminal associates were among the precipitating factors.

- Most of the subjects began their careers committing other crimes, such as auto theft or break and enter, before advancing to robbery.

- Early success at armed robbery allows the offender to gain confidence and to develop and refine "professional skills."

- As they aged, several offenders experienced increasing fear of prison sentences—a change motivated in part by their negative experiences in previous periods of incarceration and by the knowledge that successive sentences were likely to be longer.

business or other organizational bureaucracy, a useful metaphor is a high-rise building. Each floor represents a career stage, and the career itself may be understood as the elevator that carries people upward or, in unfortunate cases, downward. Clearly, the career concept has more general applicability. Think of your college or university career as having begun when you started your postsecondary education. As your career takes you through several well-defined stages, your success will be judged in large part by the grades you receive. However, your success will depend on career contingencies such as the types of examinations used to judge performance, the restrictions placed on program enrollment, and your abilities as a student.

How valuable is the career concept in the study of crime? Although there is a long history of research and theory that attempts to link the study of offending to the study of careers (Letkemann, 1973; Miller, 1978), criminologists debate whether this is a worthwhile exercise. Some criminologists maintain that the career concept is useful in understanding the relative degree of involvement of offenders in criminal activity. From this point of view, every offender may be said to have a criminal career. The use of the term *career* in this context does not necessarily mean that crime provides the offender's major source of livelihood. The individual who commits only one crime early in adolescence may have a short career in contrast to the person who engages in serious crime throughout his or her life. By focusing on criminal careers, we are encouraged to ask why offenders' careers develop as they do. While the "criminal career" is not a theory in and of itself, it is seen as a useful way of organizing what we know about crime.

Moreover, it is argued, the career concept encourages us to ask questions we would not otherwise be prompted to ask (Blumstein, Cohen, and Farrington, 1988a, 1988b). The first has to do with entry into a criminal career, which is sometimes called "onset." Here we might ask what sorts of factors encourage movement into a criminal career. Or we might try to discover the ages at which people typically begin criminal careers. The second question has to do with the degree of career productivity, which, in the context of legitimate work, might be called the "level of success." During the duration of the career, how many crimes do offenders commit, and what contingencies affect the relative success of criminal careers? Finally, we might ask about what is called "desistance." How and why do offenders end their criminal careers?

Advocates of the career concept argue that, for theoretical reasons, it is important to distinguish questions about onset from questions about frequency and desistance, since factors that affect one aspect of the career may be unrelated to another (Blumstein, Cohen, and Farrington, 1988a). For instance, some of the apparently confusing findings about the relationship between crime and unemployment might become more comprehensible if we recognize that unemployment may not be related to onset, productivity, and desistance in the same ways. For example, the level of unemployment might not be expected to affect the onset of criminal careers that people typically begin in their teenage years, before they are eligible to enter the adult labour force. Once a criminal career has begun, the availability of legitimate work may affect the timing of desistance. An individual may abandon a criminal career if offered more profitable legitimate work. Conversely, although most people end their criminal careers before middle age, desistance may be delayed if the rate of unemployment decreases the likelihood of securing a legitimate job. In general, the career concept suggests that it may be misguided to try to find simple and direct effects between familiar criminogenic concepts and rates of crime. Factors such as employment may affect different career aspects in different ways; and a factor that is important at one point of a career may have no causal significance at a later point.

THE CAREER CRIMINAL

Perhaps the most interesting findings to emerge from the research on criminal careers are those that relate to "career criminals," that is, offenders who commit crimes at a very high rate. The extreme differences in the rates at which individuals offend were first documented in a cohort study undertaken by Wolfgang, Figlio, and Sellin (1972). The researchers attempted to examine the offending patterns of all males born in Philadelphia in 1945 for the period up to their eighteenth birthdays in 1963. The study identified 627 career criminals who, while they constituted only 6 percent of the original cohort and 18 percent of the delinquents, were responsible for more than half of all the crime engaged in by cohort members. More importantly, perhaps, these career criminals were responsible for 71 percent of the murders, 73 percent of the rapes, and 82 percent of the robberies.

> **WHAT ARE THEY?**
>
> *Career Criminals*
>
> Career criminals are offenders who commit crimes at a very high rate.

Later studies support the view that small numbers of offenders account for large numbers of crime. A longitudinal study in England, known as the Cambridge Study of Delinquent Development, found that about 6 percent of a sample of 411 boys accounted for about 50 percent of all criminal convictions (Farrington, 1989). In a study by the Rand Corporation of offenders in California, Michigan, and Texas prisons, the most active 10 percent of all inmates who had committed robbery reported committing at least 58 robberies per year, while the most active 10 percent of burglars reported committing 187 or more burglaries per year (Chaiken and Chaiken, 1982).

However, contrary to what we might expect, this research also shows that offenders whose careers are characterized by high rates of offending seldom specialize in only one type of crime (Visher, 1991); instead, they tend to commit a variety of violent and property crimes (Kempf, 1987). The research into career criminals also shows that there is general stability in levels of offence seriousness over the course of a career. It does not appear, for instance, that the longer offenders offend, the more likely they are to move from one type of crime to another type that requires more technical skill or knowledge.

These findings regarding levels of offence seriousness and the tendency of so-called career criminals not to specialize in particular types of crimes have

---

BOX 4.3   THE CHARACTERISTICS OF ABORIGINAL RECIDIVISTS

James Bonta, Stan Lipinski, and Michael Martin (1992) have examined the problem of recidivism (reoffending) among Aboriginal offenders. They note that Aboriginal offenders are clearly overrepresented in the Canadian prison system. In 1991, 12 percent of admissions to federal penitentiaries and 19 percent of those sentenced to provincial custody were Aboriginal, even though Aboriginal peoples make up less than 3 percent of the Canadian population.

Using information from a federal database, the authors analyzed information on 282 male Aboriginal offenders. The average age of the offenders at the time of their federal incarceration was 26.7 years. Only 8 percent were first offenders and 16 percent were being incarcerated for the first time. Eighty of the inmates reported being of Métis origin, 13 were Inuit, and the remainder were status or nonstatus Aboriginals.

Property-related crimes were the most frequent reasons for incarceration. Nearly a third of the inmates had committed break and enter and 26.2 percent had committed other property crimes. Person-related crimes were committed by 31.6 percent of the inmates. The average sentence length was 41.8 months.

The overall recidivism rate for the sample was 66 percent. The researchers began their analysis by examining thirty variables they thought might be related to recidivism. More sophisticated analyses suggested that of that number, only three were of statistical importance. These included: prior incarceration, an offence of break and enter, and age of first conviction. In general, such "criminal history variables" are also related to recidivism among non-Aboriginal populations.

led some criminologists to be very critical of the career approach to offending. Gottfredson and Hirschi (1986, 1988, 1990) question whether there is anything of value to be gained from examining criminal careers. The concept of a career, they argue, usually assumes some notion of specialization and career progress; and yet, the available evidence undermines the validity of such assumptions.

Gottfredson and Hirschi also contend that it is fruitless to search for the unique factors that explain desistance from criminal careers since all offenders—irrespective of the types of offences in which they engage or the rates at which they engage in them—become less productive as they age. To argue that different factors explain different career elements is also misleading, according to Gottfredson and Hirschi, since most of the factors in which career researchers are interested (such as unemployment) are only weakly related to crime. For these authors, the tendency to engage in crime is highly stable for all offenders and is related to a low level of self-control.

In a somewhat different way, Luckenbill and Best (1981) also question the value of the career concept as a way of understanding crime and other types of nonconformity. They maintain that the analogy between legitimate and deviant careers is very limited, in large part because legitimate careers must be understood in the context of organizational settings while criminal careers emerge in much less structured settings. Criminal careers are not formed in response to institutional requirements that "spell out the career's positions, pathways for mobility, and rewards, while authorities enforce these rules and ensure the career's security" (Luckenbill and Best, 1981: 197). By contrast, those who are involved in deviant careers are not able to draw on such institutional resources. Moreover, they risk the possibility of social control sanctions and exploitation by deviant associates, and their rewards from deviance are uncertain. Luckenbill and Best (1981) express the differences between legitimate and deviant careers as follows:

> Riding escalators between floors may be an effective metaphor for respectable organizational careers, but it fails to capture the character of deviant careers. A more appropriate image is a walk in the woods. Here some people take the pathways marked by their predecessors, while others strike out on their own. Some walk slowly, exploring before moving further, but others run, caught up in the action. Some have a destination in mind and proceed purposefully; others view the trip as an experience and enjoy it for its own sake. Even those intent on reaching a destination may stray from the path; they may try a shortcut or they may lose sight of

a familiar landmark, get lost and find it necessary to backtrack. Without a rigid organizational structure, deviant careers can develop in many different ways. (201)

While the debate about the value of the career approach to understanding criminality is unresolved (Dechenes, 1990; Gibbons, 1988; Greenberg, 1992; Langan, 1983), comparisons between the legitimate and the illegitimate worlds of work are particularly illuminating with respect to particular types of crime. One such type is known as "enterprise crime," which is discussed in Chapter 10.

■ ■ ■

SUMMARY

Critics of motivation theories argue that many people contemplate breaking the law but do not. Formal and informal social controls may prevent them from acting in rational but criminal ways. Hirschi argues that delinquency emerges when controls diminish through the weakening of the social bonds that link adolescents to conformist others. Strong social bonds, which are based on high levels of attachment, commitment, involvement, and belief and which are built into the socialization that individuals experience at home and at school, insulate youths from delinquent involvement. These bonds are subject to pressure from changes in the ways in which families function. They are also influenced by the degree of social disorganization experienced in communities, disorganization that can lead to weakening social ties and increased levels of criminality.

The purpose of deterrence strategies is to communicate to individuals the threat that punishment will follow delinquent acts. If the law is not imposed in a quick, certain, and severe way, deterrence does not result. But deterrence depends on many factors, including the fear of punishment, the perception of risk, and so on. It has been suggested that what the law actually threatens is less relevant to the decision to offend than what people believe it threatens. Perceptions of deterrence are also affected by the widespread public ambivalence concerning the likelihood and efficacy of punishment.

Some criminals may be looked upon as making rational choices to be involved in crime, weighing the benefits of crime involvement against the costs of apprehension. This may mean that certain individuals are more likely to live a life of crime. Career criminals follow a path toward heavy involvement in crime. Even if they are not actually following crime as a career, there is evidence that a small number of individuals commit a disproportionate amount of crime.

■ ■ ■

1. What factors do you think would help to strengthen the social bonds between parents and children? Which ones weaken these bonds?

2. How effective are various legal and informal sanctions in deterring crime? Is the threat of jail the only form of punishment that is effective in stopping crime?

3. If crime is so profitable, why don't we all commit crimes?

4. If most crime is committed by a small number of people, why can't we simply focus on that small group and make sure that they are constrained from acting in criminal ways?

5. What is likely to stop a "career criminal" from continuing his or her life of crime?

CHAPTER FIVE

Opportunities, Lifestyles, and Situations

WHAT'S IN CHAPTER FIVE

In this chapter, we will focus on the role that opportunities, lifestyles, and situations play in the commission of crimes. Some criminologists have argued that criminal activity is dictated not only by the presence of motivated offenders but also by the array of opportunities that are afforded them to commit crime. These opportunities may come from lifestyles or "routine activities" that follow delinquent patterns. Risky lifestyles may end in higher levels of victimization, as well. When these crimes happen, they may be viewed as "situated transactions" that occur in a particular time and place.

INTRODUCTION

The fact that offenders are ready and willing to engage in criminal conduct, either because of their personalities, background, or views of the law, does not in and of itself explain the occurrence of criminal events. Potential offenders must encounter opportunities that allow these criminal inclinations to be given expression. This is no less true of crime than of anything else. An inclination to learn the saxophone, go to graduate school, or become a skydiver does not ensure that these things will happen. In such cases, as in the case of criminal events, it is useful to consider how opportunities allow individuals to act on their inclinations. It is important, as well, that we understand what transpires when offenders and opportunities meet. How do offenders offend and how are victims victimized? This chapter explores how contemporary criminologists theorize about these and related questions.

OPPORTUNITY THEORIES AND VICTIMIZATION

LIFESTYLE EXPOSURE

As discussed in Chapter 3, Cloward and Ohlin's analysis of criminal behaviour extended the range of relevant theoretical questions beyond the search for motivational factors. Their theory alerts us to the fact that it is not enough to explain why people might be motivated to break the law, since answers to this question generally do not explain why some laws and not others end up being broken. It is also necessary to understand how criminal inclinations are channelled by the opportunities to be criminal to which people have access.

Since the late 1970s, the study of criminal opportunities has been dominated by researchers interested in the study of victimization events. Known as **lifestyle exposure** or **routine activities theories**, these explanations focus on how variations in levels of crime from place to place or over time are related to variations in the opportunities to commit crime rather than to variations in the numbers of people who are motivated to commit crimes or who feel that they will be rewarded by this action.

The lifestyle exposure theory of criminal victimization was formally developed by Michael Hindelang, Michael Gottfredson, and James Garofalo in their 1978 book, *Victims of Personal Crime*. Their theory, which was grounded in the data of victimization surveys, sought to explain what it is about being male, young, single, or poor that increases the chances of being victimized.

Table 5.1   Location of Violent Victimizations, Age 15+, 1993

Location	Sexual Assaults	Robberies/Attempted Robberies	Assaults
percent occurring in:			
Victim's home	30	—	31
Other residence	17	—	5
Restaurant, bar	17	—	10
Commercial	24	—	24
Public place—other	—	57	27
Not stated	—	—	—

SOURCE: R. Gartner and A. Doob (1994), "Trends in Criminal Victimization: 1988–1993," Statistics Canada, *Juristat*, Catalogue No. 85-002, Volume 14, Number 13.

The linchpin of their argument is the concept of lifestyle. In general terms, *lifestyle* refers to the patterned ways in which people distribute their time and energies across a range of activities. We have no trouble recognizing that the lifestyle of a teenage male differs quite markedly from the lifestyle of an elderly female. Such differences relate to how and where time is spent, with whom one associates, and what type of leisure pursuits one enjoys. These lifestyle differences are not merely a matter of personal choice; they also reflect the social roles one is required to play and the various types of social constraints to which one is subject.

Where and how people spend their time is related to their risk of victimization. While the number of evening activities in which people engage outside the home increases their chances of becoming a crime victim (although it is evident that the home is also a location of a fair amount of violent crime), research suggests that crimes are more likely to occur in some places and in the course of some activities than in others. This is illustrated by data presented in Table 5.1.

Hindelang, Gottfredson, and Garofalo (1978: 251–64) offer the following eight propositions about victimization that summarize the link between lifestyle and key demographic variables such as age, sex, marital status, family income, and race:

1. The more time individuals spend in public places (especially at night), the more likely they are to be victimized.
2. Following certain lifestyles makes individuals more likely to frequent public places.

3. The interactions that individuals maintain tend to be with persons who share their lifestyles.
4. The probability that individuals will be victims increases according to the extent to which victims and offenders belong to the same demographic categories.
5. The proportion of time individuals spend in places where there is a large number of non-family members varies according to lifestyle.
6. The chances that individuals will be victims of crime (particularly theft) increase in conjunction with the amount of time they spend among non-family members.
7. Differences in lifestyles relate to individuals' ability to isolate themselves from those with offender characteristics.
8. Variations in lifestyles influence the convenience, desirability, and ease of victimizing individuals.

BOX 5.1   MULTIPLE VICTIMIZATION

Studies of crime victims not only tell us that some people are more likely than others to be victimized; they also tell us that those who have been victimized once are more likely to be victimized again. In other words, for crime victims, the chances of being victimized by the same or another type of crime are higher than they are for those who have not been victimized. This is illustrated by data collected in the 1982 Canadian Urban Victimization Survey. The survey investigated 60 000 Canadians' experiences with crime in 1981.

The first set of data below relates to "repeat victimization"—that is, the risk that a person who has been victimized by a particular type of crime will be victimized by that crime one or more additional times. For each of the personal crimes (as well as for the household crimes), the chances of becoming a victim again are greater than those of becoming a victim in the first place. Thus, the chances that victims of personal theft will be victimized again are almost twice as high as the risk of initially becoming a victim of personal theft (115 per 1000 vs. 63 per 1000). The risks of repeat victimization are even more dramatic for the other offences.

The second set of data relates to the probabilities of being victimized again, but by a different type of crime. While approximately 6 percent of all respondents were victims of personal theft (i.e., 63 per 1000), about 17 percent of assault victims, 19 percent of robbery victims, and 23 percent of sexual assault victims were victims of personal theft.

BOX 5.1 MULTIPLE VICTIMIZATION (CONT.)

Such data seem to suggest that some people may engage in lifestyles or patterns of routine activities that make them particularly prone to crime. It appears from research done elsewhere that factors that seem to be linked to single victimization (e.g., evening activities outside of the home or alcohol consumption) are also closely related to multiple victimization (Lasley and Rosenbaum, 1988).

Table 5.2 Likelihood of Repeat Victimization of Personal Offences

	Seven Cities	
Type of Personal Incident	Victimization Rate per 1000 Persons 16 and Older	Rate per 1000 Persons Victimized More Than Once by This Offence
Theft of personal property	63	115
Assault	53	212
Robbery	10	90
Sexual assault	3	105*

* The actual count was low; therefore caution should be exercised when interpreting this rate.

Likelihood of Cross-Crime Victimization of Personal Offences

Rates per 1000 Population 16 and Older

		Persons Also Victimized by:			
Type of Personal Incident	All Persons 16 and Older	Theft of Personal Property	Assault	Robbery	Sexual Assault
Theft of personal property	63	—	167	194	231
Assault	53	140	—	307	234
Robbery	10	31	58	—	77*
Sexual assault	3	13	15	30*	—

* The actual count was low; therefore caution should be exercised when interpreting this rate.

SOURCE: Solicitor General of Canada, *Canadian Urban Victimization Survey Bulletin 10: Multiple Victimization.* Ottawa: Ministry Secretariat, 1988. Reproduced with permission of the Ministry of Public Works and Government Services Canada, 1997.

Rates of personal victimization are relatively high for young minority males because these individuals tend to associate with people who are likely to offend (that is, other young minority males) and because they tend to frequent places (for example, bars) where offending often occurs. An elderly female, by contrast, is likely to associate with other elderly females (whose level of offending is very low) and to avoid high-risk settings. Lifestyle, in a sense, structures victimization opportunities. In explaining empirical variations in levels of personal crime, Hindelang and colleagues advance these opportunity structures, not offender motivation, as a central theoretical issue.

BOX 5.2 WARNING: SMOKING MAY BE HAZARDOUS TO YOUR HEALTH

Opportunity theories of victimization attempt to understand how particular elements of lifestyle increase exposure to the risk of criminal victimization. Several studies have shown that as alcohol consumption or the frequency of visiting bars increases, so does the risk of becoming a victim. Perhaps somewhat less obviously, University of California researcher Ichiro Tanioka (1986) has published evidence suggesting that victimization rates are higher for smokers.

The data for Tanioka's study came from the 1978 and 1983 American General Social Surveys. Among the questions asked of respondents were had they ever been "punched or beaten by another person" and did they smoke. Because the tendency to become a crime victim and the tendency to smoke are related to other social characteristics, Tanioka included in the analysis measures of age, sex, marital status, urban residence, employment status, and frequency of bar attendance.

The analysis revealed that, independent of the effects of the other variables included in the study, smoking had a significant effect on the risk of assault. Overall, 32.3 percent of smokers had experienced an assault, compared with 17 percent of nonsmokers. However, the relationship is even stronger for single females aged 18–49, among whom 43.5 percent were victimized, compared with 20.0 percent of nonsmokers.

This is not to suggest that smoking is a *cause* of victimization in any simple sense. What is more likely is that a measure of smoking indexes certain other lifestyle preferences (unmeasured in the survey) that are more directly related to victimization risk.

Cohen and Felson (1979) note that traditional motivational theories in criminology are unable to explain the dramatic increase in many forms of crime that occurred in Western nations in the post–World War II period. Many of the explanatory factors (for example, poverty, unemployment, size of inner-city population) indicated trends suggesting that crime rates should have been falling during this period rather than climbing. How, then, could the problem of rising crime rates be reconceptualized?

According to Cohen and Felson, the presence of a motivated offender is only one component necessary to the completion of assaults, sexual assaults, homicides, breaking and enterings, or other "direct-contact predatory violations." For such crimes to occur, two other conditions must be met. First, there must be a "suitable target"

WHAT DOES IT INCLUDE?
Routine Activities Theory
First, there must be a motivated offender. A suitable target against which the criminal motivation may be directed must also be available. Third, there must be an absence of capable guardianship.

against which the criminal motivation can be directed (for example, homes to break into, people to assault, and goods to steal). Second, there must be an "absence of capable guardianship," meaning that the motivated offender must meet the suitable target in the absence of anything (or anyone) that might prevent the crime from occurring.

Cohen and Felson suggest that variations in levels of crime are determined not only by the numbers of people willing to commit crimes but also by the numbers of suitable targets and by the levels of guardianship that are routinely exercised over these targets. Even if the numbers of suitable targets and the levels of guardianship remain unchanged, higher crime rates can be expected if the tempos and rhythms of social life affect the rate at which motivated offenders encounter suitable targets in the absence of capable guardianship. For Cohen and Felson, illegal activities must be understood as behaviours that depend on, and feed off, the "routine activities" of the population. "Although the fox finds each hare one by one, the fox population varies with the hare population upon which it feeds" (Felson, 1987: 914). As the structure of the routine activities changes, so does the frequency at which crimes occur.

How do these insights inform our theoretical understanding of why crime rates changed as they did after World War II? Cohen and Felson argue that changes in patterns of routine activities substantially altered levels of target suitability and guardianship and the rates at which these elements and motivated offenders came together in time and space. This period witnessed a broad shift in the locus of routine activities. In increasingly large numbers, women whose lives had revolved around the household entered or returned to the paid labour force or school. In addition, vacation periods became longer and travel became cheaper, so that holidays were more likely to be spent away from home. Even the frequency with which people dined at restaurants increased and gave rise to a booming fast-food industry. At the same time, divorce rates increased and people who were single were waiting longer before getting married. Both changes pointed to a significant rise in the number of smaller, single-person households and further contributed to the likelihood that leisure interests previously pursued at home would now be pursued elsewhere, among non-family members.

Not coincidentally, this period also witnessed "a revolution in small durable product design" (Cohen and Felson, 1979: 500). A general increase in the standard of living combined with technological advancement to produce a wide range of lightweight, durable consumer goods. Demand for tape recorders, television sets, and stereo equipment increased, as it later did for products like personal computers, CD players, and VCRs (Felson, 1994).

These changes, according to Cohen and Felson, exerted a profound impact on the rates of direct-contact predatory crimes. Through their effects on target suitability and guardianship levels, they provided greater criminal opportunities and pushed crime rates upward. The shift in routine activities away from the home exposed increasingly large numbers of people to criminal dangers from which they previously had been insulated. Moreover, in greater numbers, they left their homes unoccupied for increasing periods of time and thus deprived of capable guardianship. At the same time that guardianship was being lowered, homes were being stocked with larger numbers of highly desirable durable consumer goods that were easy to steal, carry, and sell or use. As guardianship declined, target suitability increased. One need not agonize over the question of criminal motivation, Cohen and Felson conclude, in order to understand an increase in crime over the period.

Newman (1972) borrows from the ideas of opportunity theory in arguing that the most effective way to reduce crime is to redesign public and private spaces in such a way that opportunities for crime are removed. The "defensible space" concept proposes that one can "harden" targets by installing locks or by improving surveillance, such that the criminal is deterred from committing the crime, either for fear of detection or simply because the target has been made inaccessible. The operators of 7-Eleven convenience stores redesigned

BOX 5.3 OPPORTUNITY AND MOTOR VEHICLE THEFT

Three-quarters of motor vehicle thefts and vandalism in Canada occur between 6 p.m. and 8 a.m. (Morrison, 1996). In 1993, the most common techniques for gaining access to motor vehicles were through the use of keys (43 percent) (keys may have been stolen, duplicated, or left in the vehicle) and by disabling the ignition lock cylinder (42 percent). In 10 percent of the thefts, the perpetrators focused on the vehicle steering lock, while a tow truck was used to illegally remove vehicles in 1 percent of the cases. For the remainder (3 percent), the vehicles were pushed or hot wired. The most likely location for motor vehicle crimes were parking lots. In over three-quarters of the cases, the stolen car was used for joyriding and was usually abandoned shortly after its disappearance.

Table 5.3   Motor-Vehicle Crimes[1] by Location of Incident, 1993

Location of Incident	Theft of Motor Vehicle	Theft from Motor Vehicle	Motor Vehicle Vandalism
Total number	24 113	138 911	82 459
Residential[2]	21%	16%	14%
Parking lots[3]	52%	48%	47%
Streets, roads, highways[4]	27%	34%	37%
Other	1%	2%	2%
Unknown	—	1%	1%
Total motor vehicle violations	100%	100%	100%
Average dollar value of thefts[5]	$5 351	$912	...
Average dollar value of damages[5]	$1 201	$302	$538

figures not appropriate or not applicable

[1] A single criminal incident may contain multiple motor vehicle violations. Percentages may not add to 100 due to rounding.

[2] Includes single homes, apartment units, and commerical residences.

[3] Includes commercial and public parking lots.

[4] Includes open areas, schools, public institutions, and public transportation.

[5] Average dollar stolen/damaged calculated on the number of known incidents. Total excludes incidents where the dollar value was unknown.

SOURCE: Uniform Crime Reporting Survey, Canadian Centre for Justice Statistics, Statistics Canada, 1993.

their premises under the direction of Ray D. Johnson, who had served twenty-five years for robbery and burglary in the California state penitentiary system. The insights provided by a former perpetrator led to a design that removed the chance of concealment:

> To allow clear sightlines from the street into the store, they moved cash registers up front and removed all advertising from the front windows. They also put bright floodlights outside the entrance, forcing potential robbers to perform where any passerby could look in and see.
>
> They also installed special cash drawers that make it impossible to get at more than $10 every two minutes. This gives the would-be robber the choice of getting away with very little cash, waiting "onstage" to make the payoff worthwhile or simply going elsewhere. (Krupat and Kubzansky, 1987: 60)

The incidence of robberies in the redesigned 7-Eleven stores was 30 percent lower than that in the stores that had not been redesigned.

In a similar vein, Sherman, Gartin, and Buerger (1989) identify high-crime areas known as **hot spots**. These places may be public (taverns) or private (households that are frequently reported for family disturbances). The authors' prescription is to minimize or eliminate the crime at these hot spots by increasing police surveillance or by removing them altogether. The idea that crime will be deterred through defensible space or through targeting hot spots supports the theory that offenders are motivated by opportunity. However, removing these opportunities will not necessarily reduce the desire to commit a crime—it may simply displace it to some other location. For example, police spend a great deal of time moving street prostitutes from certain areas only to have them reappear in other parts of town.

Over the past several years, a large body of research has grown up around the questions raised by opportunity theories of victimization (Cohen, Kluegel, and Land, 1981; Kennedy and Forde, 1990; Maxfield, 1987; Miethe, Stafford, and Long, 1987; Rodgers and Roberts, 1995; Rountree and Land, 1996; Skogan and Maxfield, 1981). Some writers, such as Terance Miethe and Robert Meier (1994) have attempted to refine and modify the theoretical approach to the study of victimization opportunity.

Miethe and Meier have proposed what they call a "structural-choice model of victimization." Building on the work of earlier writers (Cohen, Kluegel, and Land, 1981), they maintain that opportunity theories highlight the importance of four factors: the physical proximity to a pool of motivated offenders, exposure to high-risk environments, target attractiveness, and the absence of guardianship. However, they argue that current theories of victimization opportunity suggest two propositions. The first is that routine activities or lifestyles create a structure of criminal opportunity by enhancing the contact between potential offenders and potential victims. The second proposition is that the subjective value of a person or of property, and the level of guardianship exerted over person or property, determines which targets are chosen for victimization. Thus, their model implies that while patterns of routine activities expose some people or property to greater risks, the selection of specific targets will depend on the rewards and risks associated with one target rather than another. For Miethe and Meier, then, proximity and exposure are considered "structural" factors because they predispose people to differing levels of risk. Target attractiveness and guardianship, on the other hand, are best viewed as "choice" components because they determine which targets are selected, in contexts characterized by particular levels of risk.

In a very basic way, the ideas generated by opportunity theory and research have reoriented criminologists' thinking about the causes of crime. Opportunity theories have provided an additional piece to the puzzle as to why and where criminal events occur. A major limitation of these theories is that they have tended to pay little attention to the role of the offender or to the relationship between offender and victim. Rather, it has been assumed that probabilities of offending can be worked out on the basis of a set of conditions relating to opportunities.

The view of the offender that is generally considered most consistent with opportunity theories of victimization derives from the classical school of criminology, as discussed in Chapter 4. In one sense, opportunity theories reflect key assumptions of the social control and deterrence arguments. The suggestion that crimes are less likely to occur when capable guardianship is present is consistent with such arguments. In a related way, opportunity theories are perfectly compatible with rational choice theories of the offender (Clarke and Felson, 1993; Nagin and Paternoster, 1993). Offenders are assumed to make rational decisions about criminal action based on the offending opportunities that the environment presents to them.

Some writers (Osgood et al., 1996; Riley, 1987) have argued that offending (like victimization) can itself be understood as a function of routine activities. Thus, the routine activities in which people engage increase or decrease the likelihood that they will find themselves in situations that encourage or allow offending behaviour. Osgood and his colleagues argue that, for a range of criminal and deviant behaviour, situations conducive to offending are particularly prevalent when routine activities frequently place people in unstructured social activities with peers that occur in the absence of authority figures. The lack of structure leaves time available for deviance. In addition, when peers are present, various types of crime and deviance are not only more easy to accomplish, they are also more rewarding. Finally, the absence of an authority figure (such as a parent or a teacher) means that it is less likely that anyone will assume the responsibility for the social control of the offending behaviour.

CRIME AS INTERACTIONS

An important theoretical question in the study of criminal situations relates to the manner in which these events unfold over time. They are set in motion by offenders who are inclined to make use of available criminal opportunities. In order to explain why they follow a particular course of action, it is necessary to raise questions about the specific behavioural choices that offenders, victims, and others make in the situational contexts in which they find themselves. In particular, it is important to understand how the choices that each participant makes influence the choices made by others. Victims and offenders act and react, and in so doing, they exert mutual influence. Stated differently, crimes have an interactional character: what any one participant does depends on what others do. Although interactional dynamics have not attracted as much attention as issues like offender motivation, a general appreciation of how criminologists attempt to understand these interactions is necessary.

VICTIM PRECIPITATION

One of the concepts most frequently employed in the study of crime dynamics is that of **victim precipitation**, according to which the opportunity for crime is created by some action of the victim. In an early and influential study of 588 criminal homicides in the city of Philadelphia, the sociologist Marvin Wolfgang (1958) reported that, in about one-quarter of these cases, the victims could be said to have precipitated their own murder. In such cases, Wolfgang noted, it was the eventual victim who, frequently under the influence of alcohol, was the first to brandish a weapon or to threaten deadly force. The eventual offender, fearing for his or her own safety, either intentionally or unintentionally reacted to the threat in a way that proved fatal for the victim. In a stereotypical case, an altercation between two individuals at a bar escalates to the point at which one of the parties produces a gun or a knife or a broken bottle and says to the other party, "I'm

WHAT DOES IT MEAN?

Victim Precipitation

This occurs when the opportunity for crime is created by some action of the victim.

going to kill you." The other party responds with haste and force, and suddenly the person who uttered the threat is lying dead on the barroom floor.

The concept of victim precipitation encourages us to understand the outcome of a crime situation as the joint product of the behaviours of the offender and the victim rather than simply in terms of the offender's motivation. In the case of the barroom encounter, the killing can be said to result not from the killer's actions but from the killer–killed interaction. It is important to point out that what people might *intend* their words or their actions to mean in cases of this type is much less important than *how they are interpreted* by others engaged in the interaction. The person who brandishes a broken beer bottle and threatens death to a disputant may be expressing mere bravado rather than serious intent to harm the other party. To the disputant, however, whose judgment is clouded by alcohol and who believes the threat to be real, other interpretations of the situation are well out of reach. With respect to such cases, we have little trouble understanding the explanatory value of the concept of victim precipitation. The homicide would probably not have occurred, we can conclude, if the victim had not initially behaved in an aggressive fashion; thus, the victim was an active contributor to his or her own violent demise.

Problematic from a theoretical standpoint is the degree to which the explanatory logic of victim precipitation is generalizable to other types of events. Is it reasonable, for instance, to argue that crimes such as robbery, theft, or sexual assault can also be victim precipitated? In these types of events, does it make sense to argue that victims actively contribute to their own victimization?

Amir (1971) concluded from a study of over 600 rape cases in the city of Philadelphia that about one case in five was victim precipitated. Amir classified rapes as victim precipitated if the victim "actually, or so it was deemed, agreed to sexual relations but retracted before the actual act or did not react strongly enough when the suggestion was made to the offender" (266).

While we might be inclined to agree that victims who initially threaten their offenders in some sense precipitate a homicide, we would not agree that victims who initially consent to sexual relations precipitate rape if they subsequently change their minds. For one thing, the assumption in the latter case seems to be that the female rather than the male is responsible for the level of male sexual arousal and that if that arousal is not satisfied, the female must bear the violent consequences. In addition, it seems to imply that a subsequent decision not to engage in sex, when there has been some initial agreement to do so, is appropriately understood as precipitous of violence. Finally, homicide and sexual assault differ in a fundamental way that is obscured by the haphazard application of the concept of victim precipitation. The types of homicides described by Wolfgang involve events in which victims threaten their offenders with deadly force and are repaid in kind. In the cases of rape described by Amir, the victim is not behaving in a threatening or aggressive fashion, and the violence exhibited by the offender cannot be understood as "payment in kind."

Amir's study illustrates a serious concern that many people have with the concept of victim precipitation—that it is difficult to separate the moral dimensions of the concept from its explanatory dimensions. The claim that victims precipitate victimization seems uncomfortably close to the suggestion that victims should be blamed for their victimization. For many criminologists, victim blaming should be avoided at all costs (Timmer and Norman, 1984). At the same time, most people can express some degree of empathy for the battered wife who, after years of being subjected to violence, kills her abusive husband. To call a killing of this type victim precipitated does not usually elicit a charge of victim blaming.

For some criminologists, the solution is to recognize that crude attempts to sort crimes into precipitated and unprecipitated categories are doomed to failure. Victims and offenders may contribute to the unfolding of a criminal event in a variety of ways, and thus a broader taxonomy of victim and offender roles is necessary (Fattah, 1991; Karmen, 1996). Another solution involves recognizing that, in many cases, it is not appropriate to speak of victim or offender roles, since doing so minimizes our understanding of the ways in which the circumstances of events themselves determine who shall bear what label. In other words, there is a need to move beyond the study of victim precipitation to "the full round of interaction," which involves not only the eventual victims and offenders but also other event participants (Luckenbill, 1984).

WHAT DOES IT MEAN?

Situated Transaction

This refers to a process of interaction involving two or more individuals that lasts as long as they find themselves in one another's presence. If we are to understand criminal events as situated transactions, we need to emphasize the study of what goes on between the participants rather than what any one of them does.

THE SITUATED TRANSACTION

Goffman (1963) defines a **situated transaction** as a process of interaction that involves two or more individuals. If we are to understand criminal events as situated transactions, we need to emphasize the study of what goes on between the participants rather than what any one of them does. According to Goffman (1959), human behaviour is acted out as though part of a theatrical performance. What's important in the interaction is the impression that the actor gives to others. Based on this impression, which generally involves the playing out of a particular role in specific situations, individuals extract information about others in the interaction. When enough information is obtained for each individual to define the situation to his or her satisfaction, the roles can be properly acted out (Martin, Mutchnik, and Austin, 1990: 332). With these definitions in hand, individuals are able to sustain and complete a number of transactions throughout their daily lives. These transactions do not always have positive outcomes, however.

Luckenbill (1977) utilized an approach that draws on symbolic interactionism in his analysis of seventy homicides that occurred in California. Like other researchers, Luckenbill reported that these murders tended to occur in informal settings and generally involved people who knew each other. What distinguishes his approach, however, is his view of homicide as a product of the situated transaction rather than as a product of the behaviour of individual participants. For Luckenbill, situated transactions should be viewed as

---

BOX 5.4   STAGES IN THE SITUATED TRANSACTION

David Luckenbill has argued that homicide can be understood as a situated transaction. It is a "transaction" in that "an offender, victim and possibly an audience engage in an interchange which leaves the victim dead" and it is "situated" in that the "participants interact in a common physical territory" (1977: 196). Based on an analysis of seventy homicide events in a California county, Luckenbill argued that these incidents typically move through six stages:

- *Stage 1:* The opening move in the transaction is an action undertaken by the (eventual) victim and defined by the (eventual) offender as an offence to "face." For example, the victim says, "Get lost" or "What are you staring at?"
- *Stage 2:* The offender interprets the victim's words or actions as personally offensive.
- *Stage 3:* The offender makes an opening move in salvaging "face" or protecting "honour"—in short, the offender retaliates verbally or physically.
- *Stage 4:* The victim responds in an aggressive manner, and the actions suggest a working agreement that the situation is one suited to violent resolution. By cheering or heckling, onlookers may encourage the movement toward violence. They may also block a convenient exit for one or both parties or prevent others from breaking up the fight.
- *Stage 5:* There is a physical interchange, typically brief and precise.
- *Stage 6:* The brief battle is over, and at this point the offender flees or remains at the scene, either voluntarily or as a result of force applied by bystanders.

"character contests" in which efforts on the part of the disputants to "save face" result in deadly combat.

This perspective on criminal events is not meant to imply that situated transactions are restricted to one type of crime. The kinds of transactions that result in acquaintance rapes differ from those that result in homicides. Even in the case of homicides, important differences characterize the nature of the situated transaction (Williams and Flewelling, 1988). For example, it is incorrect to argue that the victims of mass murderers or serial killers are combatants who are committed to battle. (This is not to deny, however, that these crimes, too, have situational dynamics.)

In many cases, the complexities of transactions blur in our minds whatever a priori distinctions we might wish to make between victims and offenders. How useful is it for us to say that individuals are of a certain "criminal type" when we know that their behaviour can be affected to such a large extent by the situations they face and the roles they believe they must play in completing the transaction? It is the course of action that, to a large degree, determines the identity of the eventual victim and offender. We do not (as we do in cases of victim precipitation) look to the victim for the causes of the violence, but rather to the victim–offender exchange. With respect to the homicides described by Luckenbill, it should be clear that, up until the moment of battle, either party might have pulled out of the exchange or responded differently, resulting in quite different consequences. Questions about who should have done what (and when) to prevent the violence are likely to elicit more than one answer from interested observers. Baron (1997) in his study of street youth confirms this view of the importance of transactions in determining who is the victim and who is the offender. He reports that the more violent the altercations street youths participate in (as offenders), the greater their risk for violent victimization:

> It is likely that the capricious nature of these confrontations leaves partici-
> pants vulnerable to serious injury. It also appears that youths who are
> violent offenders are at risk for retributive victimization. On the street,
> past violations are subject to "evening up" tactics that often leave victims
> needing medical attention. (68)

According to Sampson and Lauritsen (1990), the difficulties in identifying offender and victim in many criminal events derive from the fact that the likelihood of victimization increases with the frequency of one's contact or association with members of demographic groups that contain a disproportionate share of offenders. In this matrix, the dynamics of the situation, using

Luckenbill's approach, make it likely that victims and offenders will be drawn from the same group, a view consistent with Hindelang, Gottfredson, and Garofalo's (1978) proposal that those with common lifestyles are more likely to be victimized by one another.

THE SIGNIFICANCE OF INTERACTIONAL ISSUES

The research on victim–offender interactions challenges many of the stereotypes that are inherent in other theoretical approaches. With respect to motivational theories, for instance, we are sometimes led to argue that crimes occur only because criminals are determined to commit them. Theories that focus only on opportunity, if not carefully interpreted, seem to suggest that crimes occur because motivated offenders find the opportunities to translate their inclinations into action.

In contrast, interactional theories suggest that more than motivation and opportunity are needed to understand why and how crime occurs. Crimes are the outcome of social exchanges between people who find themselves in specific circumstances and must make quick decisions about how they should respond to each other's behaviour (Felson and Messner, 1996). A robbery does not occur merely because an offender with an inclination to rob encounters an opportunity conducive to robbery. The potential victim may resist in ways that turn a potential robbery into an attempted murder. The potential victim of an attempted breaking and entering may "overreact" by killing the offender. Victims of property crimes contribute to the interaction through the steps they take—or don't take—to protect their property; their actions, or lack thereof, send a message to the potential offender about the risks of trying to steal the property. Victims are not, therefore, merely passive objects of an offender's predatory desires; nor are they necessarily active contributors to their own victimization. They are, however, key event participants whose actions shape and constrain event outcomes.

Similar comments apply to other participants. The study of homicide by Luckenbill, for instance, revealed that the role of bystanders in situated transactions should not be minimized. He found that the presence of bystanders and the actions they took shaped the course of the transaction. In the early stages, they sometimes increased the likelihood of mortal battle by encouraging the offender to interpret an offensive remark as requiring a firm response, while in the later stages, they sometimes supplied a weapon or blocked the exit of the potential victim. Of course, just as bystanders may facilitate the occurrence of a crime, they may also prevent crimes or transform one type of crime into another. A bystander who has the presence of mind to call "911" on witnessing an assault or who is familiar with cardiopulmonary resuscitation (CPR) may prevent an assault from becoming a murder.

■ ■ ■

SUMMARY

The pressure to behave in a criminal fashion is not sufficient to explain why people commit one type of crime and not another. Using a routine activities approach, researchers explain variations in levels of crime across places and over time based less on variations in the numbers of individuals motivated to commit crime than on variations in the opportunities to commit crime. The concept of opportunities revolves around the notion that some individuals have certain lifestyles or follow certain routines that make them vulnerable to criminal victimization. This lifestyle exposure, coupled with the presence of motivated offenders and the absence of capable guardians, makes becoming a victim of crime more likely. Changing routines, hardening targets through architectural change, and attacking hot spots (places where crime is most prevalent) all entail removing the opportunity to commit crime.

When crimes do occur, they take on a dynamic character that involves choices by offenders, victims, and others, all of which affect the outcome. Crimes can thus be said to have an interactional character: what any one participant does depends on what others do. An important consideration in this equation is the role played by the victim, who, together with the offender and other main players, comes to be involved in what is called a situated transaction. In such transactions, the characteristics of the individuals involved in an interaction come to define the direction that a crime will take. In the early stages of these interactions, it is often difficult to predict the eventual victim and offender. It is the actions that occur that more clearly define these roles. Depending on the actions of third parties, harm and guilt are clearly worked out only after the fact.

Interactional approaches suggest, then, that crimes are the outcome of social exchanges between people who find themselves in specific circumstances and who must make quick decisions about how they should respond to one another's behaviour. Their responses determine the outcomes. These outcomes are not always predictable in that they can be affected by many factors in the situation. Interactional approaches help us to determine the effectiveness of various strategies that are used by victims or police in deterring or preventing crime.

Questions for Review and Discussion

1. Why do you think that young males are more likely to live risky lifestyles than any other group?

2. What do you think will be the major change in future lifestyles that will make individuals in society more vulnerable to crime? Less vulnerable?

3. Are there steps that can be taken to reduce the likelihood that individuals who confront each other in interaction will escalate this dispute to violence?

4. The police play an important role as third parties in defining behaviour as criminal or noncriminal. What are the pluses and minuses of police using more discretion in deciding what should be treated criminally and what should be treated as a dispute that can be solved by the disputants themselves?

5. Are we likely to see a drop in crime as young people who follow risky routines become older and less likely to be involved in these types of behaviour?

CHAPTER SIX

Crime's Aftermath: The Consequences of Criminal Events

WHAT'S IN CHAPTER SIX

In this chapter, we will review the theories that deal with the aftermath of the criminal event. This includes a review of the costs of victimization, the labelling of offenders, and the consequences for the public including enhanced fear of crime. We will examine, in addition, the extreme forms of reaction to crime—moral panics—whereby the public responds intensely to the threat of criminal acts. These reactions have an important effect on the ways in which we come to define the crime problem through the action of claimsmakers in setting out our agenda for responding to criminal events.

| INTRODUCTION |

This chapter is concerned with what happens in the aftermath of the criminal event. The issues, theories, and research discussed remind us that, for analytical purposes, it makes little sense to say that criminal events end when the thief flees the scene or when the victim of homicide falls to the floor. The ways in which event participants and the rest of us respond to the event are as much a part of the event as the commission of the crime itself.

Several of the questions addressed in this chapter relate to the experiences of offenders and victims. How do offenders who are apprehended contend with the criminal status accorded them? What sorts of costs does crime present to victims? How do victims cope with these losses, and why do some manage better than others?

Our interest must not be confined to event participants, however. Criminal events elicit responses from many individuals and groups in society. As we will see, the **fear of crime** is regarded as a pervasive problem—particularly in large urban areas. Obviously, the aftermath of criminal events must be seen, to some extent, as an outcome of the event transaction as well as the wider social context within which these events occur. The level of injury experienced by a victim of violence, for instance, will be related to decisions made by the victim to resist an offender and decisions by the offender to actively overcome that resistance (Kleck and Sayles, 1990; Ziegenhagen and Brosnan, 1985). A "random" murder that is given sensationalist treatment by the mass media will elicit more public fear than a murder involving drinking partners (Liska and Baccaglini, 1990). And an offender who is caught selling illegal drugs when society is in a state of panic about drug crimes can expect less sympathy than an offender who is apprehended during a period when the level of concern is lower.

| HOW MUCH DOES CRIME COST? |

Any attempt to discuss the consequences crimes have for victims or the ways in which they attempt to cope with these effects is beset by some rather serious research problems. Perhaps the most notable can be termed the "specification problem" (Fattah and Sacco, 1989). In short, it is not always clear how we are to determine what should and what should not be considered an effect of crime.

167

*Crime's
Aftermath:
The
Consequences
of Criminal
Events*

| BOX 6.1 | THE COST OF VICTIMIZATION |

Paul Brantingham and Stephen Easton (1996) have attempted to calculate the total cost of crime victimization by taking into account direct and indirect costs to victims. These include monetary loss, productivity losses at work, hospitalization, and losses from income forgone by homicide victims. In addition, they include an estimate of the cost of the suffering and loss of productivity associated with such crimes as assault, rape, and murder, in addition to the cost of social services used by victims. They estimate that the monetary loss from property crime in 1993 was $4 billion; the direct incidental monetary losses from violent crime were $105 million; hospitalization costs were $68 million; loss of income forgone by murder victims was $526 million—for a total in all categories of $4.7 billion (this number is based only on crimes known to police). They calculate the total cost of crime victimization as $12.1 billion. These numbers do not include the costs of police, private security, courts, and corrections, which they estimate (conservatively) to be $12 billion.

Of course, specification is not always a problem. With respect to financial loss, it is obvious that the economic costs sustained when someone steals a purse from a victim equals the replacement price of the purse and its contents. But suppose the victim reacts to the theft by deciding to install deadbolt locks and to take taxis rather than walk to evening destinations. Suppose as well that she decides that instead of carrying cash she will write cheques for her purchases in the future. Should the costs of the locks, the taxi fares, and chequing charges be considered an economic cost of the crime? The nature of the problem becomes even more apparent when we recognize that financial losses are perhaps the easiest to calculate, given that there is a convenient standard of measurement.

With respect to physical injury, if a victim sustains a broken bone, the injury clearly should be considered a consequence of the crime. But if stress resulting from the crime aggravates a preexisting health condition, is it correct to say that the incident resulted in physical harm even though there are no apparent physical injuries? The problems with efforts to assess the costs of crime for victims emerge logically from the types of research methods that are used. Most typically, information about victimization outcomes, like other information about victims, comes from victim surveys or from specialized samples of crime victims.

Two general strategies can be used to investigate the ways in which victims are affected by crime. First, survey respondents can be asked directly about the losses that they experienced. These questions, like all questions that ask people to report on past events, are subject to errors as a result of faulty memory, dishonesty, and misunderstanding (Skogan, 1986). Usually, these questions focus on the most obvious losses to the victim, such as injury or stolen or damaged goods. While these questions are useful, they focus attention only on what happens during or immediately after the event but reveal little about what happens to the victim over the longer term. In the case of victimization surveys (like the Canadian General Social Survey, which is described more fully in the next chapter), respondents are asked about victimization events that occurred during some specified period (typically a year or six months) preceding the survey; therefore, our knowledge about problems that emerge later is minimal.

Respondents might also be asked about how they changed or limited their behaviour in response to the victimization. These questions require that respondents not only recall accurately when their behaviour changed but also understand the causes of their behaviour. However, criminologist Gwynne Nettler (1984) warns that research of this type is likely to confuse the causes of action with the reasons people give for their actions.

A second research strategy is to allow the researcher rather than the survey respondents to make judgments about the effects of the victimization experience. For instance, suppose we are interested in trying to determine whether the victim's involvement in a criminal event increased feelings of anger. Rather than ask victims directly if they are angry about the experience, we might compare victims and nonvictims in terms of the responses they give to more general questions about feelings of anger. If we discover that victims are more angry than nonvictims, we might conclude that the victimization experience is responsible for some of the difference. While this is standard social scientific practice, the results may not be clear since we probably asked the questions about victimization and about feelings of anger in the same interview. As a result, it is impossible to determine what is the cause and what is the effect. While it is reasonable to argue that victimization results in feelings of anger, it may be just as reasonable to argue that people who have an angry demeanour are more likely to become victims of crime.

The costs of crime for victims are generally considered to fall under four major categories: financial, physical, emotional, and behavioural.

FINANCIAL CONSEQUENCES

As stated, financial costs are among the most obvious costs associated with victimization. As with all types of costs, these may be direct or indirect. The

169

*Crime's
Aftermath:
The
Consequences
of Criminal
Events*

direct costs involve the value of the property stolen or damaged as well as any costs associated with medical care. Indirect financial costs may reflect lost work time, child care costs, or expensive lifestyle changes.

Results from the 1988 General Social Survey (Sacco and Johnson, 1990) indicate that two-thirds (64 percent) of all incidents and 93 percent of property victimizations resulted in financial loss to victims. When accounting for the extent of the loss, Sacco and Johnson report that approximately one-third of all incidents (32 percent) and one-half (47 percent) of the property incidents resulted in losses of under $200; only 8 percent of the total and 12 percent of property incidents resulted in losses of $1000 or more. The likelihood that the victims would recover their stolen property was rather slight, discounting the repayment that comes from insurance claims. In 86 percent of the incidents involving theft, victims indicated that nothing had been recovered. In only 7 percent of the cases did victims report that all of the property had been returned to them. In another 7 percent of the cases, victims were able to recover a portion of their lost property.

PHYSICAL CONSEQUENCES

Sacco and Johnson looked at the physical consequences of victimization reported in the 1988 General Social Survey. They found that for the vast majority of incidents (79 percent) victims reported that they experienced no difficulty in carrying out their main activities for all or most of the day after the victimization had taken place. If respondents reported impairment of any kind, 7 percent reported that it lasted for only one day while another 7 percent said that it was for longer than one day. Further, females were twice as likely as males to indicate activity limitations.

For those victims involved in incidents in which they were attacked, 15 percent reported that they sought medical attention. Of these, the majority visited a hospital, although mostly on an out-patient basis (Sacco and Johnson, 1990: 99).

A 1993 survey of violence against Canadian women (the methodology of which is discussed in the next chapter) provides more recent and more detailed information about the physical consequences of female victimization. According to Johnson's (1996b) survey of 12 300 women, 45 percent of those who reported being victims of wife assault and 22 percent of those who reported being victims of violent sexual assault stated that they had sustained physical injuries. In 1 in 5 cases of wife assault and 1 in 20 cases of violent sexual assault, the victims reported that they had sought and received medical care. According to Johnson, the injuries most frequently reported by assaulted women were bruises, followed by cuts, scratches and burns, and fractured and broken bones. Fifteen percent of women who said that their partners had been violent toward them during pregnancy suffered miscarriages or other internal injuries as a result of the attack. Fifteen percent of the women who suffered violent sexual attack also suffered internal injuries.

Data collected in the National Crime Victimization Survey (NCVS) in the United States provide further insights into the physical consequences of victimization. The analysis of NCVS data collected between 1973 and 1991 indicates that of those who were injured as a result of violent crime (84 percent received bruises, cuts, scratches, or other minor injuries), 1 in 6 received serious injuries (Zawitz et al., 1993). Among those who were victimized by violent crime between 1973 and 1991, 1 percent received gunshot wounds, 4 percent received knife wounds, and 7 percent suffered broken bones or had teeth knocked out.

While victimization studies are quite useful in telling us about the direct injuries incurred from criminal victimization, they tell us relatively little about longer-term effects. Although not evident in surveys of this sort, the injuries that result from physical encounters can lead to a worsening of existing health problems, and when mobility is restricted, the victim may be less able or even unable to exercise or to meet nutritional requirements.

EMOTIONAL CONSEQUENCES

Victims can experience a variety of emotional reactions to crime, from mild to extreme. These reactions may include shock, mistrust, sleeplessness, anger, stress, depression, and a diminished capacity to enjoy life events (Burt and Katz, 1985; Mayhew, Maung, and Mirrlees-Black, 1993). Victims may also express a sense of guilt because they blame themselves for what has happened (Mayhew et al., 1993). Table 6.1 describes the frequencies of various kinds of emotional effects reported by victims who responded to the 1993 Canadian Violence Against Women Survey.

One of the most significant effects that has been associated with victimization is an increase in fear of crime (Desroches, 1995; Johnson, 1996a; Keane, 1995; Skogan, 1987). Serious crimes, especially crimes of violence, may result in a **vulnerability conversion** (Lejeune and Alex, 1973) as victims develop a sudden understanding that they are more susceptible to the dangers of life than they thought. Figure 6.1, which employs data from the 1993 Violence Against Women Survey, shows how levels of fear differ by type of victimization

Janoff-Bulman and Frieze (1983) maintain that serious criminal victimization is stressful in large part because it is unusual and, unlike more routine stressors, it does not trigger well-developed coping mechanisms. Such events,

Table 6.1 Emotional Effects of Intimate Violence

171

Crime's
Aftermath:
The
Consequences
of Criminal
Events

Emotional Effect	Spouses	Victimization by: Dates and Boyfriends	Strangers
		percent	
Anger	30	31	32
More cautious/less trusting	18	32	36
Fear	21	27	31
Lowered self-esteem	18	12	7
Shame/guilt	10	11	9
Problems relating to men	10	16	6
Depression/anxiety	14	6	4
Upset/confusion/frustration	4	4	5
Shock/disbelief/disgust	3	4	5
Increased self-reliance	10	2	3
Other*	13	6	3
No emotional effects	13	9	12

* Includes sleeping problems, hurt, disappointment.

SOURCE: H. Johnson, *Dangerous Domains* (Toronto: Nelson Canada, 1996), p. 203.

they argue, make evident people's "psychological baggage" and suggest a need to question not only their assumptions of invulnerability but also other assumptions that underlie their day-to-day existence.

One such assumption is that "the world is meaningful." Most of us prefer to go through life believing that things happen for a reason, that good things happen to good people and that bad things happen to bad people. In general, it is comforting to think that, all things considered, the world makes sense. We can hold these beliefs because we also believe that we can exercise a certain amount of control over what happens to us. A serious, random act of crime, however, can challenge this assumption. In the aftermath of such an event, the world appears to make less sense—we have become victims of misfortune even though we may have tried hard to keep ourselves safe.

Criminal victimization may also undermine an individual's positive self-concept. Victims may develop feelings of weakness and helplessness and believe that they could have done more than they did to prevent themselves

Figure 6.1   Fear of Victimization

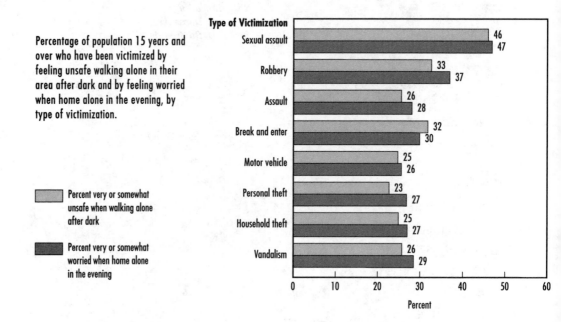

Percentage of population 15 years and over who have been victimized by feeling unsafe walking alone in their area after dark and by feeling worried when home alone in the evening, by type of victimization.

SOURCE: V.F. Sacco (1995), "Fear and Personal Safety," Statistics Canada, *Juristat*, Catalogue No. 85-002, Volume 15, Number 9: 9.

from being victimized. Traditionally, society has reinforced this view by holding victims responsible for what has happened to them.

It is not only violent interpersonal crimes that have emotional consequences. Burglary is one type of crime against property that can invite a strong response (Hough, 1985; Smith and Hill, 1991), in part because it can be viewed as a crime with the potential for violence. Even though victims are typically away from home when the offence occurs, they are forced to contemplate what might have happened had they been at home. In addition, because a burglary could threaten violence against other members of the household, each member of the household may feel concern not only for his or her own personal safety but also for the well-being of other family members. Finally, because burglary is a crime that represents an invasion of privacy and, in many cases, involves theft of or damage to objects that might have sentimental value, the emotional response may be severe (Hough, 1985).

Ironically, it has often been argued that victims' psychological distress can be magnified by social and criminal justice agencies charged with the respon-

173

*Crime's
Aftermath:
The
Consequences
of Criminal
Events*

sibility of helping victims (Rosenbaum, 1987). In particular, the police have sometimes been accused of failing to provide victims with the emotional support they require and often expect (Carter, 1985; Skogan and Wycoff, 1987). Victims may feel that the police are not doing enough to help them or to recover stolen property. When property is recovered, they may wonder why it is not returned to them more promptly.

To some extent, victim discontent with the police reflects the routine nature of police work. Some victims of even minor crimes expect a rapid response when they telephone the police. For the dispatcher overwhelmed by calls for service, however, a minor crime may be assigned very low priority. As a result, the victim feels let down by the police. In a similar way, victims who know with certainty that they have been victimized might expect that the police officer who arrives on the scene will accept their version of the story at face value and then engage in hot pursuit of the offender. For the police officer, the situation may be more ambiguous, and it may be necessary to ask questions before sense can be made of the event. In addition, the officer's experience suggests that "hot pursuit" is pointless because the offender is unlikely to be found in this way—if at all.

In general, much of the research on emotional reactions to victimization seems to indicate that when symptoms occur, they are likely to erode slowly over time (Burt and Katz, 1985; Hough, 1985). However, some evidence also suggests that symptoms sometimes persist or even reemerge months after the incident (Sales, Baum, and Shore, 1984). Such findings imply that the recovery process may not be as linear as is sometimes believed.

BEHAVIOURAL CONSEQUENCES

Some of the behavioural effects that result from victimization are directly related to physical injuries or economic losses. Victims may need to take time off from work, for instance, because medical care is required or because property must be repaired or replaced. In the 1988 General Social Survey, victims were asked whether or not they found it necessary to stay in bed all or part of a day. Only 10 percent of those involved in violent incidents reported that this was a consequence of their victimization (Sacco and Johnson, 1990: 99).

Victims exhibit a variety of behavioural reactions to crime, many of which are intended to make them safer. A common response is **avoidance behaviour**, by which victims seek to distance themselves from the kinds of people or situations they perceive as dangerous (DuBow, McCabe, and Kaplan, 1979). In extreme cases, this may involve changing residences or neighbourhoods (Burt and Katz, 1985). Victims might also try to increase home protection by installing new locks or an alarm system or personal protection through the purchase of a gun or enrollment in a self-defence course. An important irony revealed in research is that, while victims often engage in these behaviours, they may be less likely than others to believe that they are safer because they do so (Lurigio, 1987).

Victims also seek help from others. Data from the 1993 General Social Survey revealed that 27 percent of the victims of violence talked to someone about their victimization (Kong and Rodgers, 1995). This may have included a family member, a friend, a victim-helping agency, or someone else. However, women were about four times more likely than men (41 percent versus 11 percent) to look to someone for support. As we saw in Chapter 1, a common (although less common than many think) response is to contact the police. Victims appear most likely to do this when they see some practical or tangible reason to do so. However, even before they contact the police, victims often contact friends or family members in order to ask their opinions about what should be done. The victim might be unsure, in some cases, whether the event is in fact a crime or whether it is serious enough to warrant police intervention. These friends or family members can help clarify matters by reminding the victim of standards against which the event can be judged (Ruback, Greenberg, and Wescott, 1984).

This information-seeking behaviour has two important implications. First, it helps to explain why, according to some research, victims often wait well over an hour after an incident before notifying the police (Greenberg, Ruback, and Wescott, 1982). Second, it demonstrates that the victim's decision is not necessarily an individual one but rather reflects the social influence of others to whom the victim has access immediately following the crime (Ruback et al., 1984).

Over the longer term, victims might engage in some form of collective participation (DuBow et al., 1979). The most obvious form of such participation might be membership in some community crime prevention group such as **Neighbourhood Watch** (Rosenbaum, 1988). Alternatively, victims may get involved in one of the many generic or more specialized victims' groups that have proliferated in recent decades (Weed, 1995).

A common reaction is to tell others the story of the crime (Wachs, 1988). Lejeune and Alex (1973) reported that this was a near-universal tendency in their sample of mugging victims. They observed as well that the interest of the victim in telling the story seems to be matched by an interest on the part of others in hearing it. Telling the story of one's victimization might have important therapeutic value. When others react in supportive ways or tell similar stories, the victim may find it easier to make sense of the event and to put it into some broader perspective.

175

*Crime's
Aftermath:
The
Consequences
of Criminal
Events*

The behavioural reactions of victims can be easily overstated because most people are familiar with someone who has responded to crime in perhaps an extreme manner. However, in general, most victims do not seem to react to the crime by making major or basic lifestyle changes (Hindelang, Gottfredson, and Garofalo, 1978). Because our lifestyles are a product of our family responsibilities and occupational commitments, they are not changed easily.

Although there is a tendency in the criminological literature to think about such changes as **costs of victimization** that limit behaviour, there may be some benefits. As Skogan (1987) states, when people change their behaviour in other circumstances in response to negative experiences, we call this "learning." To the degree that such changes do make people less vulnerable without dramatically affecting the quality of life, they may be beneficial.

COPING WITH THE COSTS OF VICTIMIZATION

Victims differ in their ability to cope with the costs of criminal victimization due to a number of factors (Resick, 1987; Sales, Baum, and Shore, 1984; Skogan, 1987). Victims who are isolated from supportive others may find it more difficult to manage the stresses associated with crime than those whose families and friends are able to lend emotional or practical assistance. People with more economic resources may find it less difficult to absorb economic losses or to replace stolen or damaged property. Also important are prior psychological functioning and previous victim history. Individuals who are already suffering from depression may respond to criminal victimization more negatively, as might those who have already been victimized by crime.

One way in which victims attempt to cope with the costs of victimization is by engaging in a reevaluation of the event (Taylor, Wood, and Lichtman, 1983). In so doing, victims redefine the situation to make it less threatening to their self-esteem or to their future plans. In short, victims are being attentive to various cultural adages that advise us to "look on the bright side." Taylor and colleagues suggest that victims achieve this end through a series of evaluative strategies. They may, for instance, compare themselves with less fortunate others. Provided one chooses the criteria for comparison carefully, one can always find examples of people who have lost more or suffered more. Alternatively, despite suffering or loss, victims might try to discover some way in which the event was beneficial. In this respect, the victim might say, "I sure learned my lesson" or "I won't ever get myself into that situation again."

Agnew (1985b) suggests that this process resembles the neutralization process that Matza and Sykes (1961) described in their explanation of why offenders commit crime. However, rather than convincing themselves, as offenders do, that a particular criminal act is not really wrong, victims try to convince themselves that particular acts of victimization are not really harmful. Victims may, for instance, invoke a "denial of injury" in order to minimize the harm caused. Or they may articulate a "denial of responsibility" to minimize the guilt or shame that accompanies self-blame. These neutralizations, claims Agnew, allow victims to avoid feelings of fear or other negative emotions that sometimes accompany criminal victimization.

OFFENDER OUTCOMES: SOCIAL STIGMA AND LABELLING

In a simple way, a victim's loss is often an offender's gain. Losing cash or property in a theft or losing a physical encounter can translate into wins for the offender. Of course, the offender risks apprehension and punishment, but as we have seen in previous chapters, these risks are often slight. Proponents of punishment or rehabilitation contend that if offenders are apprehended, the criminal justice system may play an important role in discouraging further offending. A school of thought known as **labelling theory** proposes a markedly different view of how the frustration created by particular forms of social arrangements may motivate criminal behaviour (Becker, 1963; Gibbs, 1966; Kitsuse, 1962; Rubington and Weinberg, 1987). Labelling theorists maintain that the social response to minor and sporadic criminal acts may create conditions that increase the likelihood of more serious patterns of criminality.

Labelling theorists place great emphasis on the ways in which the responses of the police and the criminal justice system to people identified as offenders create problems for those who must bear the label of "criminal." Such a label can be understood as a form of stigma that makes it difficult for those on whom it has been imposed to lead normal lives. The person who is labelled a criminal, thief, delinquent, or troublemaker may find it difficult to obtain employment or to maintain friendships with others, who tend to react to the powerful emotional content of the

WHAT IS IT?

Labelling

A label can be understood as a form of stigma that makes it difficult for those on whom it has been imposed to lead normal lives. The person who is labelled a criminal, thief, delinquent, or troublemaker may find it difficult to obtain employment or to maintain friendships with others, who tend to react to the powerful emotional content of the label. People who have been labelled may be frustrated by their personal circumstances, or they may view as hypocritical the response of those who condemn their conduct. Increasingly, legitimate associations may become less available, and illegitimate associations more so.

177

*Crime's
Aftermath:
The
Consequences
of Criminal
Events*

label. People who have been labelled may be frustrated by their personal circumstances, or they may view as hypocritical the response of those who condemn their conduct. Increasingly, legitimate associations may become less available, and illegitimate associations more so.

Labelling theorists argue that the effects of societal reactions have important implications for the ways in which labelled people see themselves. Feedback that consistently provides the message that one is a disreputable person may eventually lead to acceptance of that definition. The effect of these labelling processes, then, may be to create a criminal self-identity, that is, **secondary deviance** (Lemert, 1951). The problems created by the labelling process increase the likelihood that the labelled person will develop a stable pattern of criminal behaviour. What labelling theory describes to us is a kind of self-fulfilling prophecy in that people who are treated as though they are beyond redemption will come to act as if they are. Thus, while the police and other criminal justice agencies intend to reduce involvement in crime, they very often have the opposite effect.

Criminologists have criticized the labelling approach for redirecting attention from the individual onto the agencies of social control and for failing to develop a body of supporting empirical evidence (Gove, 1975; Sagarin, 1975; Wellford, 1975).

SOCIAL OUTCOMES: INDIVIDUAL, ORGANIZATIONAL, AND GOVERNMENTAL RESPONSES

Crimes have implications not only for those who are directly involved but also for others who have only secondhand knowledge of these events. The ways in which members of the general public, government officials, and various private interests respond to crime invite criminological investigation.

PUBLIC FEAR OF CRIME

Since the early 1970s, researchers have been interested in the study of public reactions to crime. Much of this research has been organized around the study of the fear of crime. While surveys suggest that serious crime is a statistically rare event, the fear of becoming the victim of such a crime is much more pervasive. The notion that fear of crime may have become as serious a problem as crime itself has been taken up by journalists, and the media have covered the issue extensively in recent years.

Despite the fact that the term **fear of crime** is widely used in the popular and social scientific literature, there is relatively little agreement regarding its meaning; both *fear* and *crime* are complicated terms. Common usage of the term *fear* suggests an emotional or physiological reaction. We recognize that we are afraid when our mouths are dry, our hearts begin to pump, and the blood drains out of our faces. This, however, is not the way in which the term is typically employed by criminologists who do research in this area. After all, criminologists rarely have access to people when they are actually afraid (Mirrlees-Black, Mayhew, and Percy, 1996).

Most research on the fear of crime comes from surveys (often victimization surveys) in which members of the public are asked about their beliefs or perceptions regarding crime. As a result, fear is usually treated as an attitude or a perception rather than as an emotion. In addition, we most often treat fear as a personal rather than an altruistic matter in that we ask people about their worries regarding their own safety or the safety of their property. Warr (1991) argues, however, that people often are fearful not for their own safety but for the safety of other family members. Parents, for instance, may express less fear if asked about their own safety but more fear if asked about the safety of their children.

Skogan (1993) argues that the research literature indicates at least four distinct meanings of fear. The first meaning, *concern,* focuses on the extent to which people understand crime to be a serious problem in their communities. Concern is a judgment that people make about the frequency and seriousness of crime in the local environment. Using this definition, it is possible for a person to be concerned about crime without being personally fearful (Furstenberg, 1971).

A second definition of fear emphasizes *risk.* Research that uses this type of definition employs questions asking respondents how likely they think it is that they will become victims of crime at some point in the future. While this definition does not include an explicit emotional dimension, the assumption is that people who perceive their chances of being a victim of crime to be high will be more afraid.

Third, fear may be understood in terms of a *threat.* This definition stresses the potential for harm that people believe crime holds for them. Respondents to surveys are frequently asked, for instance, "How safe do you feel walking alone in

WHAT IS IT?

Fear of Crime

Fear is usually treated as an attitude or a perception rather than as an emotion. In addition, we most often treat fear as a personal rather than an altruistic matter in that we ask people about their worries regarding their own safety or the safety of their property. However, people often are fearful not for their own safety but for the safety of other family members.

179

*Crime's
Aftermath:
The
Consequences
of Criminal
Events*

your neighbourhood at night? Would you say that you feel very safe, reasonably safe, somewhat unsafe, or very unsafe?" Questions of this sort ask people how likely they think it is that they would be harmed if they were to expose themselves to risk.

Finally, fear may be defined in terms of *behaviour*. People may be asked not how they feel about their safety or how likely they think they are to be subject to harm, but about what they do (or say they do) in response to crime. Respondents may be asked, for example, whether they engage in "avoidance behaviour" or about the other precautions they take to protect themselves from crime.

It is not only the concept of fear but also the concept of crime that is problematic in this research. While it is rarely stated explicitly, the kinds of crime to which reference is made are those of a direct predatory nature. Respondents are usually asked about how much they worry about crimes like robbery or burglary or about their feelings of safety on neighbourhood streets. They are less frequently asked about how much they fear corporate crimes or violence in the family (Warr and Stafford, 1983).

Table 6.2 Fear of Crime, by Sex and Age, 1993 Canadian General Social Survey

| | Feelings of Safety Walking Alone in Neighbourhood after Dark | | | | |
	Very Safe	Reasonably Safe	Total Unsafe	Somewhat Unsafe	Very Unsafe
			percent		
Males					
15–24 years	50	43	7	5	1
25–44	51	40	9	6	3
45–64	47	42	11	7	4
65+	38	37	19	9	10
Females					
15–24 years	14	45	40	26	14
25–44	17	44	38	25	14
45–64	17	40	41	21	20
65+	13	22	58	19	38

SOURCE: R. Gartner and A.N. Doob (1994), "Trends in Criminal Victimization: 1988–1993," Statistics Canada, *Juristat*, Catalogue No. 85-002, Volume 14, Number 13.

Respondents to the 1993 Canadian General Social Survey were asked, among other questions, to indicate how safe they feel walking alone in their own neighbourhoods after dark. The survey revealed that, overall, 27 percent of Canadians did not feel safe (Gartner and Doob, 1994). A more detailed analysis of responses to this question can be found in Table 6.2.

PATTERNS IN FEAR

The term *public fear of crime* encourages the view that fear is a problem evenly shared by all members of society. As in the case of other social problems, however, the burden of fear falls more heavily on the shoulders of some than others. We can identify two broad sets of factors that have been shown to be related to differences in the fear of crime. One set of factors suggests characteristics of individuals, and the other involves the characteristics of their social environments.

Both sets of factors are important to a comprehensive understanding of fear of crime. The individual-level factors—gender, age, and socioeconomic or minority status—are often interpreted as measures of social and physical vulnerability. They explain why some people (women, the aged, the poor, racial minorities) might feel they are particularly susceptible to criminal victimization or less able to cope with the consequences of any victimization that does occur. In contrast, the environmental factors can be understood as describing dangers in the environment itself. When crime rates are higher, when public order is tenuous, and when people learn about local crime by talking to friends and neighbours, they define their environments as less safe.

INDIVIDUAL-LEVEL FACTORS

GENDER

Of all the factors that have been shown to be related to fear of crime, the strongest effects are associated with gender. Overall, women are much more likely to express anxiety about crime than are men (Johnson, 1996b; LaGrange and Ferraro, 1989; Skogan and Maxfield, 1981). For one thing, women are more likely both to be and to perceive themselves as smaller than and less physically capable than the typical male offender (Gordon and Riger, 1989). These physical differences are, of course, reinforced by the traditional gender-role socialization that encourages females to think of themselves as vulnerable to a variety of forms of danger and discourages the development of assertive methods for dealing with threatening behaviour (Sacco, 1990).

Another important factor explaining the higher levels of fear among women is the specific fear of rape (Gordon and Riger, 1989; Johnson, 1996b).

181

*Crime's
Aftermath:
The
Consequences
of Criminal
Events*

Although men are unlikely to express concern about the possibility of sexual victimization, this crime seems to be at the core of much of the concern that women express for their personal safety. Warr (1985) argues that, compared with many other crimes, women see rape as both serious in its consequences and frequent in its occurrence. This tendency to estimate the risks of rape as relatively high and the consequences as relatively severe has a significant impact on women's fear.

In addition, claims Warr, rape can be thought of as a "perceptually contemporaneous offense." In other words, it is a crime that can occur not only as an isolated act but also in connection with other crimes such as robbery or burglary. For women, the association of these crimes with sexual danger makes them even more fear-provoking.

AGE

It is widely believed that fear of crime is a particular problem for the elderly. Several studies do show that despite their lower victimization rates, older people express greater concern for their personal safety (Baldassare, 1986; Garofalo, 1981b; Skogan and Maxfield, 1981; Yin, 1980). The high level of fear has come to be regarded as reflecting reality by journalists, policymakers, and many social scientists (Cook and Skogan, 1990; Fattah and Sacco, 1989).

Arguments about the high level of fear among the elderly suggest important parallels with the case of women. Older people, it can be argued, possess lower levels of physical efficacy and fewer physical resources with which to cope with the threat of crime or the consequences of victimization (Yin, 1980).

Despite the popularity of the claim regarding high levels of fear among the elderly, it has been challenged by many researchers (Moeller, 1989; St. John and Heald-Moore, 1996; Yin, 1982). LaGrange and Ferraro (1987) argue that researchers who have found that fear increases in old age tend to measure fear by asking questions about feelings of safety while on the street alone at night. They maintain that while older people are more likely to give answers indicating anxiety about their personal safety, this question really has nothing to do with the day-to-day lives of most older people. For a variety of reasons relating to health, finances, and general lifestyle, older people do not typically find themselves walking alone on the street at night. This means that the answers are more hypothetical than descriptive of the everyday realities of the elderly.

RACE AND INCOME

Personal safety is a greater problem for low-income individuals and for visible minority groups (Baumer, 1978; Skogan and Maxfield, 1981; Will and McGrath, 1995). While the differences are not as great as in the case of gender, they are significant. Two factors might be advanced to explain these relationships. First, income and race are indicators of access to resources. Economic and racial minorities may be less able to take taxis, install alarm systems, or take other measures that might make them feel safer. Second, in many cities, there are very clear patterns of racial and economic segregation, and many neighbourhoods with large numbers of low-income or minority residents are also neighbourhoods with very high rates of crime. This means that measures of race and income, at the individual level, are related to fear because they are "proxy" measures for neighbourhood of residence.

ENVIRONMENTAL FACTORS

We are more likely to feel anxious about our personal safety in some settings than others. Warr (1990) has shown that people are more afraid of crime when they are alone, when they are in a novel setting, and when it is dark. Other research has shown that people are more likely to feel safe in settings that are open to observation, that would not allow a potential offender opportunities for concealment, and that would not block an escape or exit if they wished to make one (Fisher and Nasar, 1995). An awareness of environmental factors alerts us to the fact that fear is not just a sociopsychological characteristic that some people have and other people do not have but also a response to the social contexts in which we find ourselves.

THE COMMUNITY SETTING

In general, the fear of crime is a more significant problem in big cities than in small towns (Baumer, 1978; Garofalo, 1981b; Moeller, 1989). The simple explanation for this is that big cities have higher crime rates, and the greater fear of urbanites is a rational response to the reality of big-city crime.

While this is probably true, it is not necessarily the whole story. The urban sociologist Claude Fischer (1981) has suggested that fear is a more significant problem in cities because the "public world of city life" routinely presents residents with situations that increase their feelings of insecurity. As we travel through urban public places, we are likely to encounter people who are strangers not only in the personal sense but also in a cultural sense. Because cities are hotbeds of lifestyle innovation, Fischer argues, we always run the risk of finding ourselves on the street, in an elevator, or on a subway platform with people whose style of dress or public behaviour strikes us as weird or threatening. While many of the strangers we encounter are not criminals or delinquents, our unfamiliarity with groups whose lifestyles differ dramatically from our own may undermine our sense of security in cities.

183

*Crime's
Aftermath:
The
Consequences
of Criminal
Events*

Within communities, levels of fear vary from one neighbourhood to another. Again, some of the difference is due to differences in crime rates (Miethe and Lee, 1984). Residents who live in neighbourhoods where the levels of crime are higher are more likely to be concerned about their personal safety and the safety of their property than are people who live in neighbourhoods with lower crime rates.

However, levels of neighbourhood fear are also affected by what some writers have called "social disorder" or **incivility** (Baumer, 1978; Bursik and Grasmick, 1993; LaGrange, Ferraro, and Supancic, 1992; Skogan, 1990b). These terms refer to those low-level breaches of the social order that, while not strictly criminal, in many cases seem to be related to a sense of unease. Incivilities are usually considered to be of two types. Physical incivilities include conditions such as abandoned buildings, unkempt residences, and strewn trash and litter. Social incivilities include public drinking or drug use, panhandlers, and groups of noisy youths. In a study of reactions to disorder in forty neighbourhoods, Skogan (1990b) found that although disorder tends to be a problem where crime is also a problem, its effects on levels of fear supplement the effects exerted by the local crime rate.

BOX 6.2   COMMUNITY DISORDER

Researchers such as R. LaGrange and colleagues (1992) and Wesley Skogan (1990b) argue that public concern about disorder is usually gauged by asking survey respondents to indicate how serious a problem they perceive each of several different types of problems to be in their own neighbourhoods. The types of disorders about which people are typically asked include the following:

- trash and litter lying around
- dogs barking loudly or being a nuisance
- inconsiderate or disruptive behaviour
- graffiti on sidewalks and walls
- vacant houses and unkept lots
- unsupervised youths
- noisy neighbours
- people drunk or high on drugs in public
- abandoned car parts lying around
- kids or adults trespassing in people's yards

Why does social disorder promote fear of crime? A dominant interpretation stresses the role that disorder plays in signalling to people the breakdown of local social controls. People may read signs of incivility as indicating that in this neighbourhood people don't care very much about themselves or their community. In effect, the message is that neighbourhoods that can tolerate conditions like these can also tolerate more serious threats to person or property (Kelling and Coles, 1996).

WHAT ARE THEY?

Incivilities

Incivilities include physical conditions, such as abandoned buildings, unkempt residences, and strewn trash and litter, and social conditions, such as public drinking or drug use, panhandlers, and groups of noisy youth.

THE INFORMATION ENVIRONMENT

Fear of crime is a reaction to what we experience as well as what we see and hear. However, since fear is more pervasive than crime itself, it makes sense to ask what role various information sources play in the promotion of crime-related anxieties.

It seems reasonable to argue that the mass media must be an important factor in promoting fear of crime. After all, as we saw in Chapter 1, crime figures prominently in both news and entertainment media, and Canadians are avid consumers of mass media.

Despite the apparent logic of this argument, researchers have had trouble documenting the existence of a clear and unambiguous relationship between people's media diets and their fear of crime (Cumberbatch and Beardsworth, 1976; Doob and MacDonald, 1976; Heath and Gilbert, 1996; Sacco, 1995; Skogan and Maxfield, 1981). Some of the problem relates to limitations of the research. For instance, it is not always easy to determine what people learn from the mass media and what they learn from other sources (Doob, 1982). This is because most of us not only watch television news or read newspapers but also talk to friends or neighbours about what we hear and read.

Even when these limitations are taken into account, however, the effects of media on fear of crime are not as strong as we might expect them to be. It is, after all, too simplistic to argue that people respond in a predetermined way to media messages about crime. Individuals approach the media with their own predispositions, personal histories, and beliefs about media credibility, all of which affect their interpretations of the information they receive (O'Keefe, 1984; Schlesinger et al., 1992).

Although we are heavy consumers of media content, what we learn does not necessarily have much relevance to our judgments about our personal safety. Rather, we seem to learn these kinds of lessons far more effectively from other sources. The relevant research indicates the news about crime that moves through interpersonal channels in the form of gossip and rumour may be more likely to induce fear than the news that comes to us in broadcast or print form (Baumer, 1978; Bursik and Grasmick, 1993; Skogan and Maxfield, 1981). When we learn about crime by talking to our neighbours, for instance, we learn about victims of whom we might have some personal knowledge. In these cases, we cannot dismiss what we hear by telling ourselves that the victims are nameless and faceless and that they live somewhere else.

In comparison, the average crime story that we read about in the newspaper is stripped of much of its emotional content and is likely to involve victims who are much more anonymous. Moreover, the typical media crime story provides us with so little information about victims, offenders, or the circumstances of the crime that we learn relatively little that will help us assess the risks in our neighbourhoods, our workplaces, or anywhere else our daily routines take us (Gordon and Riger, 1989). Most crime news is "nonlocal" in character and thus not relevant to the judgments we need to make about the threats we face in local environments. Consistent with this view is the finding reported by some researchers that news coverage is likely to affect fear when the media give prominent treatment to random violent crimes that occur locally (Heath and Gilbert, 1996; Liska and Baccaglini, 1990).

COMMUNITY REACTIONS

How do individuals' reactions to crime have implications for the communities in which they live? Theorists have provided two general answers to this question. The first, derived from the writings of the famous French sociologist Emile Durkheim, suggests that public reactions to crime can make important contributions to the cohesion and stability of social life: "Crime brings together upright consciences and concentrates them. We have only to notice what happens, particularly in a small town, when some moral scandal has just been committed. [People] stop each other on the street, they visit each other, they seek to come together to talk of the event and to wax indignant in common" (Durkheim, 1933: 102).

From this view, crime is thought to shock our sentiments and reaffirm our commitment to the common values that the crime violates. Our communal opposition to crime unites us. We might speak out against crime, be more vigilant in the exercise of informal social control, join a concerned citizens' group, or support the toughening of laws intended to control crime. The overall effect described by this view is one of social integration and a strengthening of social control whereby crime rates may decline or at least stabilize.

In sharp contrast, others have suggested that because crime generates fear, it is more likely to drive people apart than to bring them together (Conklin, 1975; DiIulio, 1989). John Conklin argues that when people are less afraid of crime, they are more likely to trust others and to think positively about their communities and less likely to restrict their activities and reduce their social interaction with other community members. In contrast, when levels of fear are high, people are more likely to stay home at night and less likely to get to know or to be interested in their neighbours. Some might even be tempted to flee the community for a safer haven. Overall, then, crime does not build communities up as the Durkheimian model contends, but rather undermines communities by weakening interpersonal ties.

This view implies that public reactions to crime weaken informal social controls. When the streets are empty and neighbours cease to care what happens to one another, potential offenders may feel freer to take advantage of criminal opportunities.

Research evidence supports both points of view. In general, however, arguments about the ways in which crime drives people apart seem to have more empirical validity than arguments about the ways in which it brings them together (Skogan, 1981, 1990b). We should note, too, that the two arguments are not necessarily inconsistent with each other. Using data collected in six Atlanta neighbourhoods, for instance, Gates and Rohe (1987) distinguished three types of reactions to crime: avoidance, protection, and collective action.

BOX 6.3   CAN CRIME CAUSE CRIME?

Some researchers have argued that public reactions to rising crime rates can amplify subsequent crime rate increases. The central mechanism in this process is the breakdown of informal social control at the community level. Lynne Goodstein and Lance Shotland (1982) have described the processes by which crime rates spiral upward as follows.

The cycle begins with actual increases in the crime rate or with the occurrence of one or several particularly noteworthy crimes. Such crimes might include an unsolved murder or a series of sexual assaults for which an offender has not been apprehended.

In the next stage, information about these crimes and the threats that they pose to other members of the community is disseminated widely. People learn via the mass media or rumour networks that crimes are increasing and/or even they might be at risk.

BOX 6.3   CAN CRIME CAUSE CRIME? (CONT.)

As the information circulates, people begin to fear for their safety. This fear causes them to withdraw from community life. They stay home at night rather than go out and report that their enjoyment of the community has declined.

As people withdraw from the community, the delicate web of social relations begins to break down, as do the various informal social controls that regulate conduct. Thus, as the streets become less populated, they are subject to less control because citizen surveillance of them is reduced.

As the levels of community control decline, the levels of crime may be expected to rise; and as the levels of crime continue to rise, the cycle begins to repeat itself.

Goodstein and Shotland's argument is consistent with the theoretical view that crime is made more likely by the absence of controls that check it. As the authors note, empirical evidence supports each of the individual linkages just described. What is less clear, however, is the validity of the overall model, which has not been rigorously tested in its entirety.

They found that each type of reaction was related to a different combination of factors. Avoidance behaviour (avoiding places or people in the neighbourhood) was found to be related to local crime rates and the fear of crime. Protective behaviour (such as taking a self-defence course or obtaining a gun or watchdog) was more closely related to levels of neighbouring and the amount of control that respondents felt they could exert in the local area. Finally, collective reactions (such as involvement in local crime prevention efforts) were related to both sets of factors.

In an interesting reanalysis of this issue, Liska and Warner (1991) used the routine activities theory of Cohen and Felson (1979) to suggest why elements of both arguments are useful. In short, they contend that the Durkheimian view is correct in claiming that the effect of public reactions to crime is to reassert social controls in ways that stabilize crime rates or push them down. However, their view of the process by which this happens is closer to the position taken by Conklin than the one advanced by Durkheim.

As discussed in the previous chapter, the routine activities theory emphasizes the role that opportunities play in the commission of crime. Social patterns that separate people from their property and from their family members increase the opportunities for crime. Liska and Warner agree that public reactions to predatory crimes (like robbery) keep people at home and away from strangers. While this reduces their sense of community, it also allows them to exert greater guardianship over their persons and property. As this happens, opportunities for crime are decreased and greater control of crime is achieved.

CLAIMSMAKING

Fear can enhance the public's concerns about crime. How they react may be determined by the actions of the special-interest groups that lobby for attention to be paid to these concerns. Some writers refer to the processes by which laws are passed or legal reforms are initiated as claimsmaking (Best, 1995; Spector and Kitsuse, 1977). In the **claimsmaking** process, groups offer assertions about the existence of some problem that requires a policy solution. They then attempt to gain public support for these claims and to attract the attention of public officials and the mass media. Becker (1963) describes the claimsmaker as a "moral entrepreneur" who is best exemplified by the crusading reformer. According to Becker, there is "some evil which profoundly disturbs" these reformers, who believe that "nothing can be right in the world until rules are made to correct it" (147–48).

In the early stages, the claims may reflect a narrow set of relatively private interests (Pfuhl, 1986; Ross and Staines, 1972). Claimsmakers may regard themselves as representing those who have been victimized by some condition or who feel directly threatened by it (Weeks et al., 1986). However, claims may also be issued by agencies seeking to expand their mandates or by professional groups seeking to enhance their status. Researchers have suggested, for instance, that the pressure for the passage of computer crime laws has largely resulted from the crusading efforts of computer crime "experts" who, in publicizing the issue, were able to gain recognition for themselves and their work (Hollinger and Lanza-Kaduce, 1988).

Best (1990) asserts that, with regards to legislative and other policymaking bodies, claimsmakers may be described as being either insiders or outsiders. Insiders include political lobbyists,

WHAT DOES IT MEAN?

Claimsmaker

The claimsmaker is a "moral entrepreneur," best exemplified by the crusading reformer, who believes that rules must be formulated to combat the evil in the world.

189

*Crime's
Aftermath:
The
Consequences
of Criminal
Events*

representatives of powerful professional organizations, and members of government, all of whom have relatively direct access to those who make public policy. By contrast, outsiders have no such direct access and must rely to a greater extent on taking their message directly to the general public. In so doing, outsiders hope to enlist members in their cause.

Spector and Kitsuse (1977) offer a four-stage model of the claimsmaking process. In stage 1, groups attempt to argue that some condition is harmful and that public action (perhaps the passage of new laws) is necessary. In stage 2, the problem is recognized by some official agency; the result may be an official investigation (for example, a royal commission). Stage 3 is characterized by the reemergence of claims and demands, either by the original group or by others who express dissatisfaction with the official response to the problem. Stage 4 involves a rejection by claimsmakers of the official response (or lack of response) to the problem. Spector and Kitsuse acknowledge that this "natural history" model may not precisely describe all efforts to mobilize the public response to crime or other social problems. The manner in which any specific claimsmaking process unfolds will depend on several factors, two of which require particular attention.

The first involves the amount of opposition that claimsmakers encounter in their attempts to convince the public and policymakers that a particular type of remedy is necessary. In other words, some kinds of claimsmaking are more adversarial than others. Issues that do not have this adversarial quality are sometimes referred to as **valence issues**. Child abuse, crimes against the elderly, and computer crime are valence issues in that most people would readily agree that they are problems requiring public intervention. By contrast, efforts by claimsmakers to organize public support for interventions directed against abortion or pornography are frequently met by resistance or by counterdefinitions of what the problem really is (Ross and Staines, 1972).

A second factor affecting the fate of claimsmaking is the wider social context in which this process unfolds. Prevailing social values and beliefs may at any time facilitate or hinder claimsmaking. Based on an analysis of a large number of case studies of criminalization, Hagan (1980) argues that successful claimsmakers are usually able to make effective appeals to dominant cultural values. For example, it has been argued that the social problem of crime against the elderly emerged in the 1970s because there existed a "ripe issue climate" in which rising crime, the needs of crime victims, and the needs of the elderly were already seen as important problems.

While criminalization is clearly a form of claimsmaking, the passage of a law is not always enough to satisfy the claimsmakers. Much contemporary claimsmaking about crime is directed toward changing the ways in which behaviour that has already been criminalized is treated within the criminal justice system. The recognition in recent years of crimes against women, victims' rights, impaired driving, and crimes against the elderly as problems requiring more vigorous enforcement or innovative approaches attests to the validity of this observation.

In general, an understanding of responses to crime as the product of claims-making, conflict, and power (rather than of social consensus) alerts us to the biases of these responses. Such arguments cast serious doubt on the value of approaches that characterize the law as a neutral arbiter that can be understood without reference to the societies that produced it.

EXTREME REACTIONS: THE MORAL PANIC

In general, public reactions to crime can be characterized as subtle and routine (Hindelang et al., 1978). Typically, crime dominates neither our personal nor our public agendas. Sometimes, however, the media, the government, and members of the general public respond to crime in a much more intense fashion. The sociologist Stanley Cohen (1972) used the term **moral panic** to describe these kinds of episodes. Goode and Ben-Yehuda (1994) explain:

> During the moral panic, the behaviour of some members of a society is thought to be so problematic to others, the evil they do, or are thought to do is felt to be so wounding to the substance and fabric of the body social that serious steps must be taken to control the behaviour, punish the perpetrators and repair the damage. The threat this evil presumably poses is felt to represent a crisis for that society: something must be done about it and something must be done now; if steps are not taken immediately, or soon, we will suffer even graver consequences. The sentiment generated or stirred up by this threat can be referred to as a kind of fever; it can be characterized by heightened emotion, fear, dread, anxiety, hostility and a strong feeling of righteousness. (31)

According to Goode and Ben-Yehuda, moral panics can be recognized by several distinguishing characteristics:

- a heightened concern over some behaviour or the group that is thought to be responsible for it
- an increase in hostility toward the individuals in question
- a substantial or widespread consensus regarding the seriousness and the nature of the problem

- a public reaction that seems to be out of proportion to the size of the problem
- a volatile character such that panics emerge and subside rather suddenly

In recent years, we have witnessed several episodes that could be described in these terms. The social response to illegal drugs (Reinarman and Levine, 1989), serial killers (Jenkins, 1994), and child abduction (Best, 1988) provide illustrations of this concept.

One clear example of moral panic that has attracted the attention of several researchers is the satanic crime scare that emerged as a visible public issue in the 1980s (Richardson, Best, and Bromley, 1991; Victor, 1993). Late in the decade, it was argued on several fronts that North America was in the midst of a serious crime wave resulting from the conspiratorial actions of thousands of satanic cult members. The allegations included claims about the molestation of children in daycare centres, the satanic involvement of serial killers such as the "Son of Sam," the use of fantasy role-playing games to recruit teen satanists, graveyard desecrations, the covert actions of business leaders active in satanic worship, and police and government cover-ups of evidence that could expose the conspiracy (Richardson et al., 1991; Jenkins, 1992; Jenkins and Meier-Katkin, 1992; Victor, 1993).

> ## WHAT IS IT?
>
> ### *Moral Panic*
>
> "During the moral panic, the behaviour of some members of a society is thought to be so problematic to others, the evil they do, or are thought to do is felt to be so wounding to the substance and fabric of the body social that serious steps must be taken to control the behaviour, punish the perpetrators and repair the damage." (Goode and Ben-Yehuda, 1994)

The claims were promoted in several ways by several groups. The bizarre and sensationalist nature of the claims made them an attractive topic for afternoon talk shows and other "tabloid television" programs as well as for "legitimate" news organizations. A watershed event in this respect was the 1988 broadcast of a U.S. television special on satanic crime, hosted by Geraldo Rivera. The media fascination with these allegations was reinforced by a developing therapeutic community that claimed to have uncovered clinical evidence of the effects of satanic abuse and that promised effective treatment. In addition, many police departments developed units to fight occult crime, and the policing of satanic activity became a new law enforcement specialization (Hicks, 1991).

Careful analyses of these claims have shown that they lack substance (Bromley, 1991). Supporting "evidence" was at best ambiguous and at worst nonexistent. Moreover, the claims frequently defied logic and strained credibility.

Still, the overriding belief that satanists often pose as "respectable" members of society allowed those caught up in the panic to discount critics—because, of course, they could be satanic conspirators as well.

According to Jenkins and Meier-Katkin (1992), the roots of the satanic crime issue can be located in the political concerns of the fundamentalist religious right. They argue that the issue was framed and promoted in a way that reflected the concerns of Christian fundamentalists at a time when this movement was undergoing a rapid expansion.

More generally, Goode and Ben-Yehuda (1994) maintain that three types of theories have been used to explain the development of moral panics. The first, the *grassroots model,* views these panics as originating in the mood of the general public. The concern that is expressed by mass media or politicians is seen as a reaction to public sentiment rather than as a cause of it.

A second theory, the *elite-engineered model,* argues that moral panics represent the deliberate attempt on the part of the economic or political elite to promote public concern about some issue that does not involve their interests. In this way, the moral panic is seen as a form of consciousness manipulation that diverts attention away from the real social problems, solution of which might undermine elite interests.

The third approach, which is also the most commonly used perspective in the study of moral panics, is *interest-group theory.* Unlike the elite-engineered model, this perspective does not see the power or resources that create moral panics as narrowly concentrated in the hands of a small group. Instead, power is understood as more diffuse and more pluralistic. The implication is that moral panics may be set in motion by the actions of politicians, crusading journalists, or professional associations.

Goode and Ben-Yehuda argue that while the elite-engineered model does not seem to explain most moral panics, the other two perspectives are of greater value—particularly when they are used in combination. This is because the grassroots model allows us to see what fears and concerns are available as the raw materials for moral panics, and the interest-group model allows us to understand how these raw materials are intensified and mobilized.

■ ■ ■

SUMMARY

The costs of victimization include financial, physical, emotional, and behavioural consequences, and the ability to adjust depends on a number of factors. Victims who are alone may find it more difficult to manage the stresses associated with crime than will those whose families and friends are able to lend emotional or practical assistance. People with more economic resources may

193

*Crime's
Aftermath:
The
Consequences
of Criminal
Events*

find it less difficult to absorb economic losses or to replace stolen or damaged property. Also important are prior psychological functioning and previous victim history. Individuals who are already suffering from depression may respond to criminal victimization more negatively, as might those who have already been victimized by crime.

A further consequence of criminality is the social stigma attached to the offender. Labelling theorists emphasize the ways in which the responses of the police and the criminal justice system to people identified as offenders create problems for those who must bear the label of "criminal." Such a label can be understood as a form of stigma that makes it difficult for those people to lead normal lives. An individual who is labelled a criminal, thief, delinquent, or troublemaker may find it difficult to obtain employment or to maintain friendships with others, who tend to react to the powerful emotional content of the label. People who have been labelled may be frustrated by their personal circumstances, or they may view as hypocritical the response of those who condemn their conduct. Increasingly, legitimate associations may become less available and illegitimate associations more so. Feedback that consistently provides the message that one is disreputable may eventually cause that person to accept that definition. The effect of these labelling processes, then, may be to create a criminal self-identity, or secondary deviance. The problems created by the labelling process increase the likelihood that the labelled person will develop a stable pattern of criminal behaviour.

Fear of crime may also increase in the aftermath of crime. The research literature indicates at least four distinct meanings of fear. First, fear may mean "concern," a judgment that people make about the frequency and seriousness of crime in the local environment without necessarily being personally fearful. Second, fear may be equated with "risk," or how likely people think it is that they will become victims of crime at some point in the future. Third, fear may be understood as "threat," stressing the potential for harm that people believe crime holds for them. Finally, fear may be defined as "behaviour," such that the focus is on what people do (or say they do) in response to crime, including avoidance behaviour or other precautions taken to protect themselves from crime.

In response to the costs of victimization and the rise in fear, the public discussion of crime may be fuelled by special-interest groups pushing for increased police and criminal justice system interventions. These "claimsmakers" seek to get certain issues and problems on the forefront of the public agenda. Moral panic represents an extreme response, whereby there is an intense reaction to crime problems and strident calls for action, even in cases where the crimes being committed are few in number and not widely threatening to the public.

■ ■ ■

QUESTIONS FOR REVIEW AND DISCUSSION

1. Are there ways in which we can properly compensate crime victims for their losses? Should the offenders be involved in this process?

2. Can we use the label of offender in a positive way to help us rehabilitate offenders back into the community, or is it the case that once people offend they cannot be expected to behave normally again?

3. Is the fear of crime a realistic assessment of the risk of crime or a reflection of an overreaction to crime?

4. Do you agree that people should not change their behaviour in response to their fear of crime? Does not changing behaviour raise their chances of being victims, or does it keep the chances of victimization the same?

5. Can you identify different moral panics that have occurred and explain what the reactions to these panics have been?

PART FOUR

RESEARCH
METHODS

CHAPTER SEVEN

Researching Criminal Events

WHAT'S IN CHAPTER SEVEN

In this chapter, we discuss the major types of information about crime to which criminologists have access. Our discussion includes not only a description of these data sources but also a critical evaluation of their various advantages and disadvantages. We begin by addressing two very general types of crime information—observations and reports. We then discuss specific sources of crime data, including police, victim, and offender reports. We conclude with a discussion of crime rates.

INTRODUCTION

In the previous chapters, we detailed some of the major ways in which modern criminologists think about and attempt to explain criminal events. In so doing, we raised several significant questions about why particular types of events occur, when and where they occur, why they unfold as they do, and why some people are more likely than others to be involved in events, either as offenders or victims. This chapter takes up a related issue: How are the questions raised by criminological theory to be answered?

In assessing the validity of dominant explanations of criminal events, criminologists do not rely on idle speculation. Rather, they seek to determine the extent to which these explanations are consistent with the empirical evidence that describes these events. In other words, they have more confidence in a given theory if it is able to organize and make sense of the **"facts of crime"** as revealed by research data. This means, of course, that we need to concern ourselves with the quality of crime data. We begin by addressing two very general types of crime information: observations and reports.

OBSERVING CRIME

DIRECT OBSERVATION IN NATURALISTIC SETTINGS

At first glance, the study of criminal events might seem a relatively straightforward matter. If researchers wish to investigate criminal events, why do they not just position themselves so as to observe these events directly?

Observation could be accomplished in several ways. The researcher might (1) covertly observe a setting in which criminal events are known to occur with some frequency; (2) attempt to gain access to police or private security surveillance videotapes in order to monitor the action in a high-crime setting (Surette, 1992); (3) associate with people who engage in offending behaviour in order to observe their actions and the actions of those with whom they interact; or (4) obtain permission from the local police to join patrol officers for tours of duty on city streets (Black and Reiss, 1967; Ericson, 1982; Ferraro, 1989).

Although such methods of learning about crime events would seem to have an obvious advantage in that they allow researchers direct access to the types of information in which they

HOW ARE THEY USED?

Observations vs. Reports

Without question, most criminological research proceeds through the use of reports rather than observations.

are interested, they have serious limitations. First, they may not be very efficient because, statistically speaking, crimes are relatively rare events (O'Brien, 1986). Even if one conscientiously observes a high-crime setting, criminal events will occur only infrequently. Similarly, even if one associates with chronic offenders, it will become obvious that much of their time is spent in crime-free activity. Thus, researchers would have to expend a considerable amount of time and energy to amass a sufficient number of observations to allow something meaningful to be said about offenders or offending.

A second problem with direct observation is that criminal behaviour is usually secretive behaviour. Therefore, those who are engaged in such conduct generally will do whatever they can to ensure that external observers (including criminologists) will not have as good a view as they might like.

A third problem relates to the ethics of this method of data gathering. We should be concerned about the legal and moral obligations of the researcher who observes a crime in progress. We also should be leery of modes of data collection that involve researchers covertly observing people who are going about their business or misrepresenting their real purposes to people who take them into their confidence.

Finally, the data yielded by these methods of direct observation are limited with respect to the types of questions they can address. In general, while they may allow us to observe criminal events, they do not necessarily tell us much about why the events occur where they do or why some people are more likely than others to be event participants. For example, systematic observation of a high-crime subway platform might provide an opportunity to witness a number of minor thefts or assaults. However, such observations will not tell us how this subway platform differs from others where the crime rate is much lower. Similarly, observations (by whatever means) of juvenile misconduct tell us very little about why some juveniles engage in law-violating behaviour while others do not. And while police ride-alongs might increase the researcher's exposure to particular types of events, they do so in a way that is subject to numerous limitations. As we have mentioned in previous chapters, the police generally become involved in criminal events after receiving requests from citizens for police assistance. Thus, while police ride-alongs may do much to increase our understanding of the role of police in criminal events, they do relatively little to facilitate our direct observations of what transpires before police assistance is sought.

In sum, observation alone generally does not tell us much about how offenders, victims, or other event participants perceive their own actions or the actions of others. We cannot glean from observation why the offenders act as they do, how they perceive their victims, why they are willing to risk punishment, or what they believe the rewards of their actions to be. Answers to such questions can only be inferred from observing the event.

EXPERIMENTAL OBSERVATION

A second observational approach involves the use of **experimentation.** Rather than wait for things to happen, the researcher interested in exploring some aspects of criminal events arranges for them to happen. Experimentation allows for controlled observation of behaviour. Also, by varying experimental conditions, researchers can study the relationship between different conditions and event outcomes (Steffensmeier and Terry, 1973).

For example, Shotland and Straw (1976) designed an experiment intended to shed light on how bystanders respond when a man attacks a woman. Subjects in the experiment were told that they were taking part in an "attitude study." Each subject was directed to a separate room where a questionnaire was to be completed. Shortly after beginning work, the subject heard a loud verbal argument between a man and a woman in the hallway. After approximately fifteen seconds of heated discussion, the man physically attacked the woman, violently shaking her while she struggled, resisting and screaming. The screams were loud, piercing shrieks, interspersed with pleas to "get away from me" (Shotland and Straw, 1976: 991). What the experimental subjects did not know was that the assailant and the victim were drama students who were confederates of the researchers. Shotland and Straw's study revealed that subjects were more likely to intervene when they believed that the attack involved strangers rather than a married couple.

Tracy and Fox (1989) designed an experiment investigating automobile insurance fraud, a type of white-collar crime that does not frequently come to the attention of law enforcement officials. The researchers were interested in discovering whether automobile repair shops tend to give higher estimates for body work on insured vehicles. In order to investigate this issue, drivers who were confederates of the researchers presented assigned cars to randomly selected body shops across the state of Massachusetts. The analysis, which took the amount of damage and several other variables into account, revealed that, on average, estimates for insured vehicles were 32.5 percent higher than estimates for uninsured vehicles, a difference that the researcher concluded was unrelated to the extent of the damage, the sex of the driver, or the location of the body shop.

As these examples illustrate, experiments may provide a valuable means for answering some types of questions about criminal events. Still, experiments present some major problems, and their use by criminologists has been limited.

Most of the experimental work has not focused on what many consider to be the vital roles in criminal events: offender and victim. Instead, as in the case of the Shotland and Straw study, experiments have been used to study the reactions of witnesses or bystanders to contrived situations (Farrington et al., 1993; Frinell, Dahlstrom, and Johnson, 1980; Shotland and Goodstein, 1984).

Experiments that seek to entice people into criminal conduct or that feign the victimization of unsuspecting experimental subjects pose obvious ethical dilemmas. In some circumstances, such experiments place not only the study subjects but also the researchers or their confederates at risk of physical or emotional harm.

Field experiments can also be used to assess the impact that criminal justice programs have in reducing the incidence of crime. Two well-known studies are the Kansas City patrol study conducted by Kelling and colleagues (1974) and the Minneapolis domestic violence experiment administered by Sherman and Berk (1984). Both studies involved predetermining the police intervention that would take place in different targeted areas of the city and then assessing its impact on crime.

Kelling divided Kansas City into sectors and, with the cooperation of the chief of police, allocated different types of patrol strategies to each sector. As part of the research design, Kelling tried to ensure that similar types of neighbourhoods received different patrol tactics. The police then adopted three strategies: high-visibility patrol, low levels of patrol, and standard patrol levels. In analyzing the results, Kelling and his associates discovered that police patrol strategies had little effect on crime rates or fear of crime in the targeted areas. The areas that received high levels of police patrol were perceived as no more safe than those receiving lower levels. There was also little difference in the measured levels of crime.

Sherman and Berk's study was also based on a field experiment design. Its purpose was to reveal whether differences in how the police treat wife assaulters are associated with differences in the likelihood that these assaulters will reoffend. The study was restricted to cases of "simple" assault (assaults without serious injury). Each time the officers involved in the experiment encountered such a case, they were to follow experimenters' instructions, which involved a "random" choice among three forms of case processing: arrest, advice (which could include informal mediation), and an order to the suspect to leave the premises for eight hours. The behaviour of the suspect was tracked for six months after the incident in order to determine if different forms of treatment resulted in different levels of reoffending. The researchers concluded that arrested suspects are less likely to engage in subsequent violence against their partners.

Interestingly, in replications of Sherman and Berk's study attempting to fine-tune the original methodology, several studies yielded results opposite to those reported by Sherman and Berk, particularly that arrest led to higher levels of subsequent domestic violence among the unemployed than among the employed. Sherman (1992) attributes the discrepancy in findings to the increased precision of the testing that was used in the replications and to the differences in the demographic characteristics of the cities that were studied. He argues that it is exactly this ability to replicate and refine findings that makes the experimental approach so valuable as a means of guiding policy decisions using social science research.

While field experiments have indeed influenced policing strategies and shaped our understanding of crime incidence, they require a great deal of cooperation from the police. Concerns have also been raised about the ethics of shifting police resources as part of a research design, which may end up endangering people. Experimenters might attempt to deal with safety or ethical issues by developing experiments that do not involve engagement in real criminal events but that approximate processes that are common to these events. Such an approach characterizes much of the research into the effect of violence in the media on behaviour. Typically, the researcher exposes experimental subjects to a film or video depicting violence and then observes whether they behave in an aggressive fashion afterward. With children, the measure of aggression may involve aggressive play; with adults, it may involve the willingness of test subjects to behave punitively toward a confederate of the experimenter (Bandura, Ross, and Ross, 1963; Malamuth, 1983).

While such field experiments may pose no real danger to those who participate in them, critics charge that, because the experimental situations are artificial, they tell us very little about real-life criminals (Surette, 1992). The essence of this charge is that there is a huge difference between the willingness to behave "violently" in an experiment—when such violence is encouraged and does no real harm to anyone—and the types of criminal violence that concern the criminal justice system and so many members of the general public.

REPORTING CRIME

THE CRIME FUNNEL

The data most frequently used by criminologists interested in the study of criminal events come not from direct observation but from the reports of those who have direct knowledge of the event, principally the police, victims, and offenders. Criminal justice system agencies besides the police, such as courts and prisons, can be important sources of information about criminal events. After all, such agencies are in the "crime business" and keep records of people who are arrested, cases that go to trial, and the number of people incarcerated.

If our interest centres on the criminal event, the data made available by the various criminal agencies differ in terms of their value. In part, this is because different agencies have different needs and therefore do not all collect the same type of information. Of equal importance is the fact that criminal justice agencies are connected to one another in a "volume-reducing system" (Reiss, 1986a). In other words, there is a high level of attrition as cases travel through the various stages of the criminal justice system. Not all criminal events that come to the attention of the police result in an arrest, not all arrests result in a trial, and not all trials result in a conviction. Some writers have described this attrition process as a **"crime funnel"** (Silverman, Teevan, and Sacco, 1996). For example, according to government estimates (Canada, 1982), in the early 1980s:

- about 60 percent of all break and enter incidents were reported to the police;
- 10 percent of all break and enter incidents eventually resulted in someone being charged with the crime (17 percent of all of those reported to the police);
- 5.8 percent of all break and enter incidents resulted in a conviction (60 percent of those incidents that resulted in a charge).

In a similar vein, Dutton (1987) argues that, as cases of wife assault move through the criminal justice system, a "winnowing process" occurs. In his study, he found the probability of wife assault being detected by the justice system is about 6.5 percent. Once detected, the probability of arrest is about 21.2 percent. Given these contingencies, offenders in cases of wife assault he studied had only a 0.38 percent chance of being punished by the courts.

POLICE REPORTS

For the purpose of studying criminal events, the data contained in police records are quantitatively and qualitatively superior to those maintained by the courts or correctional agencies. In a quantitative sense, police data encompass a larger number of criminal events. In a qualitative sense, police data are not directly subject to the various sorting procedures whereby cases may later be processed out of the system in a nonrandom manner.

Police crime data are based on criminal events about which police have knowledge. You will recall, however, that any measure of "crimes known to the police" cannot be expected to be synonymous with all crimes that occur, because many crimes, especially less serious ones, are not reported to the police. The data discussed in Chapter 1 indicate that as much as 50 percent of the crime reported by victims to survey interviewers is not reported to the police. You will also recall that proactive policing results in the discovery of relatively few crimes. Thus, the types and numbers of crimes about which the police have knowledge depend primarily on the reporting behaviour of members of the general public.

Further, not all of the criminal events that come to the attention of the police become part of the official record. In research done in Edmonton, Kennedy and Veitch (1997) found that the overwhelming number of calls (both 911 and complaint line) to the Edmonton Police Service (EPS) led to congestion in the communication centre. In 1991, the number of calls to the centre, combining both 911 (serious injury accidents, alarms, and in-progress criminal occurrences) and the complaint line (nonemergency), peaked at 485 309. Over 100 000 callers hung up before getting a response, as it took 81 seconds to answer a nonemergency call. As Kennedy and Veitch suggest, it is possible that the actual number of crime occurrences was higher than reported as complainants got frustrated due to their inability to get through to the communication centre and simply gave up in their attempts to report these crimes. Through changes in access, particularly by directing complaints to four new divisional stations and twelve community stations, in 1994 the EPS was able to lower the average speed of answer of calls to 55 seconds and the number of abandoned calls to 50 000.

Getting through to the police does not guarantee that a crime will be recorded. A call from a citizen who reports a crime to the police may not lead to a car being dispatched, and no subsequent action may be taken (Gilsinan, 1989). Even when the police do show up at the scene, they may decide to treat the matter unofficially or as something other than a crime.

Some types of event characteristics increase the likelihood that a crime will be recorded (Gove, Hughes, and Geerken, 1985). Events with elements that suggest a high degree of legal seriousness are more likely to be recorded as crimes (Gottfredson and Gottfredson, 1988). In addition, when strong physical evidence or compelling testimony indicates that a crime has occurred, the event is more likely to enter the official record. An event is also more likely to be treated as a crime when the person who makes the complaint to the police urges that official action be taken (Black, 1971).

Recording rates relate not only to the characteristics of the event but also to the characteristics of the policing agency. Specifically, highly professional police departments are more likely to officially record crimes (Gove, Hughes, and Geerken, 1985), in part because these departments tend to make greater use of crime data in developing departmental priorities and deploying resources. Highly professional departments also rely to a greater extent on existing official records in the processing of citizen complaints, which means that there is a stronger incentive at all departmental levels to "write up" a larger number of police–citizen interactions (Skogan, 1977).

The descriptions of events that are officially labelled as crimes by an investigating officer may undergo significant changes as they move through the internal bureaucracy of the police department. As information travels from the line officer through the communications section to the records division, offences may be shifted from one category to another, downgraded, or ignored (Skogan, 1977). Thus, the amount of crime recorded by the police department is affected by the internal organization of the department and by the bureaucratic procedures by which information is processed (McClearly, Nienstedt, and Erven, 1982).

A study undertaken by the Canadian Centre for Justice Statistics (CCJS) (1990a) attempted to determine the extent to which differences between Edmonton and Calgary crime levels could be accounted for by differences in record-keeping practices. Although the city of Edmonton has traditionally had a higher rate of crime than Calgary, the difference has never been adequately explained with reference to those types of factors that are usually said to be associated with higher crime rates (e.g., high levels of unemployment or interprovincial migration). The CCJS study focused on the internal processing of information as a possible explanation. It revealed that information loss in the stages between the original call to the policing agency and the records section was greater in Calgary than in Edmonton. About 80 percent of the cases in Calgary reached the records section, compared with about 94 percent of those in Edmonton. To some degree then, the higher crime rate in Edmonton in the late 1980s is attributable to differences in the manner in which agency data were collected.

THE UNIFORM CRIME REPORTING SYSTEM

In Canada and the United States police crime data are collected and processed as part of what is known as a **Uniform Crime Reporting (UCR) system.** The Canadian UCR has been in existence since 1961 and was developed as a result of the joint efforts of Statistics Canada and the Canadian Association of Chiefs of Police. The stated objective of the UCR is to provide police departments with a consistent set of procedures for the collection of information relevant to crimes that come to the attention of the police.

Practically speaking, the UCR is a survey in which police departments across the country report crime information, in a standardized way, to the federal statistical agency (Statistics Canada), which collates the information and makes it available to interested data users, including government departments, criminologists, politicians, and the mass media. Since 1982, the Canadian Centre for Justice Statistics, a division of Statistics Canada, has had responsibility for collecting information from the police departments, which regularly respond to the survey.

In effect, there are really two UCR surveys (Grainger, 1996). One is the original UCR survey, which collects "aggregate" information from police departments on a monthly basis. For the last several years, however, a "revised" UCR survey has been under way, intended to correct many of the data deficiencies that characterized the original survey (Grainger, 1996; Silverman et al., 1996). These problems included the following:

WHAT IS IT?

Uniform Crime Reports

In Canada and the United States police crime data are collected and processed as part of what is known as a Uniform Crime Reporting (UCR) system. The stated objective of the UCR is to provide police departments with a consistent set of procedures for the collection of information relevant to crimes that come to the attention of the police.

---

1. The UCR counting rules required that, except in the case of homicide, offences that were completed and offences that were merely attempted were counted in the same category. In terms of the amount of harm done, there is usually a substantial difference between crimes completed and crimes attempted; but as aggregate counts, such measures obscure these differences.

2. When more than one legal violation occurred in the context of a single event, the UCR rules required that only the most serious act (defined in legal terms) be counted. In those situations in which an offender commits several crimes in the context of a single event, this counting rule undercounts the number of crimes.

3. The UCR system required that different counting rules be used in the case of personal crimes than in the case of property crimes. For personal crimes, the rules necessitated counting one crime for each victim. For property crime, the rule required that one crime be counted for each "separate and distinct incident." For example, in an incident where several privately owned vehicles parked in one block are all spray-painted with what appears to be the same spray can, it is concluded that one incident occurred and therefore one offence (of willful damage) is recorded (Statistics Canada, 1985: 17).

More basic problems related to the *types* of information that were collected as well as the *form* in which the data were presented. Until recently, the data collected in conjunction with the UCR survey were restricted to a few items. These included the type of offence (as defined by the Criminal Code), the number of offences reported, and the number of offences that were "unfounded." Offences are unfounded when, on the basis of a preliminary investigation, a judgment is made that the crime reported to occur did not occur. The number of "unfounded" crimes is subtracted from the number of crimes reported to yield a count of "actual offences."

The UCR survey also reported some limited information about the persons charged with the offence—whether they were male or female and whether they were adults or young offenders—and the "clearance status" of the incident. Clearance status refers to a judgment made by the police as to whether or not they can identify at least one of the offenders involved in the offence. If such a person is formally charged with the crime, then the offence is "cleared by charge." If, however, circumstances do not allow a charge to be made, the police count the incident as "cleared otherwise." This might happen, for instance, if a victim refuses to sign a complaint or if the offender dies before he or she can be charged.

Table 7.1 presents representative crime data for the calendar year 1995. The table suggests that the offences differ quite markedly in their associated clearance rates. Of the crimes described, homicide has the highest rate in part because murders frequently involve offenders and victims who know each other. It is also clear from the table that when crimes are committed against property, such as break and enter and vandalism, offenders are identified and thus crimes are cleared with greater difficulty.

Problems with the form of data collection and presentation in the UCR surveys related to the fact that, before the recent revisions, the UCR system required police departments to submit "aggregate totals" for each offence category. These aggregate totals represented summaries of police activity for each UCR category for the month for which the report was made. For example, in a given month, a police department might report that 100 assaults occurred, and that 90 assaults had been "cleared by charge." However, because these numbers represent summaries of police activity for the month, they do not necessarily have anything to do with each other. Many of the assaults that were cleared by charge may have been committed during the previous month. Similarly, some portion of the males or females who were reported to have been charged during the month may actually have committed their crimes during previous months.

Table 7.1   Offences Known to the Police Cleared by Arrest, 1995

Type of Crime	Number Reported	Percent Cleared by Arrest
Violent crime	294 704	73.7
Homicide	586	85.0
Sexual assault	28 216	68.8
Nonsexual assault	230 167	79.9
Robbery	30 273	31.5
Property crime	1 550 492	22.6
Breaking and entering	390 726	16.1
Theft over $5000	41 194	16.6
Theft $5000 and under	820 099	20.0
Motor vehicle theft	163 293	13.4
Total Criminal Code*	2 651 058	34.3

* Excludes traffic.

SOURCE: 1995 Uniform Crime Reports.

Such problems have undermined the quality and limited the usefulness of UCR data, and it is largely for these reasons that in 1988 the Canadian Centre for Justice Statistics and the police community began to phase in a revised UCR survey (Grainger, 1996). Importantly, these revisions make available a wide array of information that was not previously available. For instance, the revised survey collects information relating to the location of the incident, the use of weapons, and the value of stolen property.

The new UCR also collects more detailed information about the characteristics of accused persons, and, unlike the previous UCR, gathers data about the victims of violent crime. This information not only describes the basic social characteristics of offenders and victims (such as gender and age) but also their relationship and their use of alcohol or drugs (Grainger, 1996).

Equally important, the new UCR has changed from an aggregate to an "incident-based" reporting system. This means that data relating to offenders, victims, and criminal events are compiled on an incident-by-incident basis rather than as summaries, as was previously the case. As a result, the various kinds of information collected by the police are not collated as monthly totals but can be linked together in the context of particular incidents or criminal events.

As of 1995, the revised UCR survey began collecting data from 140 policing agencies in six provinces, representing 46 percent of the national volume of Criminal Code violations (Hendrick, 1996).

Because of these changes, UCR data will be much more informative in the future than in the past. Many of the problems that plagued the earlier system will be minimized. Most importantly, because the kinds of information collected by the survey have been expanded and because the system is incident-based, it will be possible to use UCR data to address a wide array of questions that could not be addressed previously. These include questions about the characteristics of victims of crime, the location of criminal events, the differences between stranger and intimate violence, and the relationship between weapon use and level of injury.

While revisions to the UCR will greatly enhance the quality of police data about criminal events, these new procedures leave unaddressed many other questions about those crimes that never come to the attention of the police in the first place.

VICTIM REPORTS

Reports from victims of crimes are a second major source of information about criminal events. Victims may be asked to describe what transpired during the event, how they reacted, whether the police were summoned, and what costs, of a physical or psychological nature, they may have sustained as a result of the incident. Data from victims of crime are usually collected in the context of a **victimization survey**. These are large-scale studies that ask randomly sampled members of some larger population about their experiences with crime. To date, four major victimization surveys have been undertaken in Canada. The first, known as the Canadian Urban Victimization Survey (CUVS), was undertaken in 1982 in seven major Canadian urban areas (Solicitor General, 1983). The second and third major studies, both part of the Canadian General Social Survey (GSS), were national surveys conducted in 1988 (Sacco and Johnson, 1990) and 1993 (Gartner and Doob, 1994). It is intended that the GSS victimization survey will be regularly undertaken at five-year intervals. A fourth major study, the Violence Against Women Survey (VAWS), was undertaken in 1993; at present, plans are not in place to repeat the study in the future (Johnson, 1996b; Johnson and Sacco, 1995).

Because criminal victimization is a statistically rare event, such surveys require a large number of interviews in order to yield a sufficient number of cases for analysis (O'Brien, 1985). The CUVS gathered data from approximately 60 000 urban Canadians, the GSS employs a sample of about 10 000, and the VAWS had a sample of over 12 000. Because of the large sample sizes, victimization surveys are very expensive research projects (Strike, 1995).

In order to increase the efficiency of the undertaking, it is common in victimization research to conduct the interviews by telephone. In such cases, researchers may use sampling procedures to generate a sample of telephone numbers to be called. Such procedures restrict data collection to households with working telephones. This may not be as serious a bias as it might at first appear as households without telephones account for less than 3 percent of the target population (Sacco and Johnson, 1990).

> **WHAT ARE THEY?**
>
> ### Victimization Surveys
>
> Victimization surveys are large-scale stud-ies that ask randomly sampled members of some larger population about their experiences with crime.

In the typical victimization survey, respondents are asked about a range of crimes against the person (such as sexual assault, assault, robbery, and personal theft) and against property (break and enter, theft of household property, or vandalism). Since these studies focus explicitly on victimization, they are usually restricted to the study of crimes that involve a direct victim. Special topic surveys, like the Violence Against Women Survey, may restrict even further the range of victimization experiences about which respondents are asked.

Victimization interviews usually consist of two parts. First, all respondents (whether they have been victims of crime or not) are asked questions from a "screening questionnaire." Some of these questions gather basic information on the gender, age, and other social and demographic characteristics of the respondents. Other questions ask respondents about their fear of crime or their attitudes toward the criminal justice system. More importantly, the screening

---

> **BOX 7.1   RESULTS FROM THE VIOLENCE AGAINST WOMEN
> SURVEY—ASSAULT BY STRANGERS**

Stranger assault is the stereotypical urban crime and provides the basis of much of the concern for personal safety, especially among women. How common is stranger assault, and are all women equally at risk? The 1993 Violence Against Women Survey provides data that speak to these questions.

In the twelve-month period before the survey, 3 percent of women aged 18 or over (317 000) had experienced sexual assault by a stranger, and a further 1 per-cent experienced assaults that did not contain a sexual element. When women were asked about assaults that had occurred since the age of 16, over 2 million (19 percent) said that they had been sexually assaulted and close to 800 000 said that they had been physically assaulted by a stranger at least once.

| BOX 7.1 | RESULTS FROM THE VIOLENCE AGAINST WOMEN SURVEY—ASSAULT BY STRANGERS (CONT.) |

The survey revealed that younger women (between the ages of 18 and 24) were more than twice as likely to have been sexually or physically assaulted than women aged 25 to 34. Consistent with other victimization surveys, the rates for older women were lower still.

In regional terms, women living in British Columbia, Alberta, and Ontario were more likely than those living in other provinces to have been assaulted by a stranger. In British Columbia, 26 percent of women reported being sexually assaulted and 11 percent reported being physically assaulted since the age of 16. In contrast, Newfoundland had the lowest rates of both sexual assault (12 percent) and physical assault (3 percent).

According to the study, most assaults occurred in some type of public area. Sexual assaults most often took place on the street (20 percent), at bars or dances (15 percent), or in public buildings (13 percent). Twelve percent of assaults took place in the home of someone other than the victim, and 7 percent occurred in the victim's own home.

---

questionnaire is used to identify those respondents who experienced one or more of the types of victimization that are of interest to the researchers.

After asking respondents whether they have been victimized, it is usual to ask victims a detailed series of questions about the victimization incident. Questions of this type make up the second major part of the interview. Victims may be asked questions about the location and circumstances of the crime or their relationship to the offender. They may also be asked about the financial losses they sustained or about the level of physical injury. Information may also be gathered about whether or not the victim reported the crime to the police or took any other action in the aftermath of the victimization episode.

As valuable as they are, data from victimization surveys, like the UCR data, have been subject to methodological criticisms (Miethe and Meier, 1994; Skogan, 1986). Chief among these are the following:

- Certain crimes are thought to be undercounted (for example, domestic violence offences).
- Undercounting may result because people forget things that happened to them, a phenomenon especially likely if the crime was a relatively minor one or, perhaps worse, if the individual is particularly accustomed to being victimized.

BOX 7.2   GENERAL SOCIAL SURVEY VICTIMIZATION SCREEN QUESTIONS

Section C: Criminal Victimization Screening Section

C1. The next few questions ask about some things which may have happened to you during the past 12 months. Please include acts commited by both family and non-family members.

	Yes	How many times?	No
C2. During the past 12 months, did anyone deliberately damage or destroy any property belonging to your or anyone in your household (such as a window or a fence)?	Yes ^{01} ○▸	⌊⌊⌋	No ^{02}○
C3. (Excluding those incidents already mentioned,) during the past 12 months ...			
(a) did anyone take or try to take something from you by force or threat of force?	Yes ^{03} ○▸	⌊⌊⌋	No ^{04}○
(b) (Other than the incidents already mentioned,) did anyone illegally break into or attempt to break into your residence or any other building on your property?	Yes ^{05} ○▸	⌊⌊⌋	No ^{06}○
C4. (Other than the incidents already mentioned,) was anything of yours stolen during the past 12 months from ...			
(a) the things usually kept outside your home, such as yard furniture?	Yes ^{07} ○▸	⌊⌊⌋	No ^{08} ○
(b) your place of work, from school or from a public place, such as a restaurant?	Yes ^{09} ○▸	⌊⌊⌋	No ^{10} ○
(c) a hotel, vacation home, cottage, car, truck or while travelling?	Yes ^{11} ○▸	⌊⌊⌋	No ^{12}○
C5. During the past 12 months, did you or anyone in your household own a motor vehicle such as a car, truck, motorcycle, etc?			
Yes ....^{7} ○			
No ....^{8} ○▸ Go to C7			
C6. (Other than incidents already mentioned)...			
(a) did anyone steal or try to steal one of these vehicles or a part of one of them, such as a battery, hubcap or radio?	Yes ^{13} ○▸	⌊⌊⌋	No ^{14}○
(b) did anyone deleberately damage one of these vehicles, such as slashing tires?	Yes ^{15} ○▸	⌊⌊⌋	No ^{16}○
C7. (Exluding the incidents already mentioned,) during the past 12 months, did anyone steal or try to steal anything else that belonged to you?	Yes ^{17} ○▸	⌊⌊⌋	No ^{18} ○

**BOX 7.2   GENERAL SOCIAL SURVEY VICTIMIZATION SCREEN
QUESTIONS (CONT.)**

Section C: Criminal Victimization Screening Section (cont.)

	Yes	How many times?	No
C8. Now I'm going to ask yo a question about being attacked. An attack can be anything from being hit, slapped, pushed or grabbed, to being shot or beaten. Please remember to include acts commited by family and non-family.			
(a) (Excluding the incidents already mentioned,) were you attacked by anyone at all?	Yes [19] ○▸	⌴⌴	No [20] ○
(b) (Other than the incidents already mentioned,) did anyone threaten to hit or attack you, or threaten you with a weapon?	Yes [21] ○▸	⌴⌴	No [22] ○
C9. Excluding incidents already mentioned,) during the past 12 months, has anyone forced you or attempted to force you into any sexual activity when you did not want to, by threatening you, holding you down or hurting you in some way? Remember this includes acts by family and non-family and that all information provided is strictly confidental.	Yes [23] ○▸	⌴⌴	No [24] ○
C10. (Apart from what you have told me,) during the past 12 months, has anyone ever touched you against your will in any sexual way? By this I mean anything from unwanted touching or grabbing, to kissing or fondling.	Yes [25] ○▸	⌴⌴	No [26] ○
C11. Were there any other crimes which happened to you during the past 12 months, which may or may not have been reported to the police?	Yes [27] ○▸	⌴⌴	No [28] ○
C12. *INTERVIEWER: Total the number of incidents reported in C2 to C11 and enter*	TOTAL ▸ ⌴⌴		
C13. *INTERVIEWER: Complete the number of accident and crime incident reports, as given by total boxes on pages 4 and 7.*			

SOURCE: Statistics Canada (1994), *The 1993 General Social Survey—Cycle 8 Personal Risk.*

- People may forget or misrepresent the time frame of their experiences and report crimes that are actually outside of the time reference of the study, hence inflating incidence rates.
- Respondents may lie to please the interviewer (that is, respondents may fabricate crimes in order to provide data).

In general, claims about the value of victim reports of crime derive from several assumed advantages of the research approach. First, it is frequently argued that because victimization surveys collect information directly from victims of crime, they can tell us about crimes that have not been reported to the police (Fattah, 1991). In so doing, victimization surveys provide a more valid estimate of the actual crime rate.

Second, because victimization surveys use samples drawn from the general population, data are collected from both victims and nonvictims over a given period. This allows researchers to compare the two groups and to analyze which social and demographic groups face the greatest risks of victimization as well as how these risks are affected by particular kinds of lifestyle behaviours such as drinking alcohol or living alone. These data can inform the development of theoretical models that link victim involvement in criminal events to factors of this type (Hindelang, Gottfredson, and Garafalo, 1978; Laub, 1987). These models were discussed in Chapter 5.

Finally, victimization survey approaches permit an investigation of the consequences of victimization and the ways victims cope with these consequences. These data shed light on the types of questions raised in Chapter 6.

OFFENDER REPORTS

Interviews with offenders can give us important insights into their behaviour, attitudes, and motivations. We might learn why they commit certain types of offences, how they feel about their victims, and how they assess their risk of being apprehended by the criminal justice system (Bennett and Wright, 1984).

REPORTS FROM KNOWN OFFENDERS

Perhaps the most obvious form of offender report makes use of data gathered from a sample of known offenders such as prison inmates or those who have been convicted of an offence and are awaiting sentence (Baunach, 1990). Surveys of this type can shed light on a range of subjects, including the use of weapons by offenders (Wright and Rossi, 1986) and the characteristics of offenders' victims (Innes and Greenfeld, 1990). Understanding such subjects gives us useful insights into how offenders regard their own actions as well as those of other event participants.

BOX 7.3   RACE AND CRIME STATISTICS

Should crime statistics include information about the race/ethnicity of victims or offenders? This question has formed the basis of a heated debate among politicians, media commentators, and academics in recent years. While such data are gathered in other nations (such as the United States), the Canadian UCR surveys do not routinely gather this information.

University of Ottawa criminologist Thomas Gabor (1994b) has argued that such statistics should be collected and refutes the three main arguments against their use:

1. *Publishing race-based crime statistics will increase friction between various racial or ethnic communities and justify harassment of minorities by the police.* Gabor argues that ethnic urban tension has arisen and developed in the absence of such information rather than because of it. In fact, he suggests, stereotyping and racial misunderstanding are more likely to occur when public debate is not informed by systematically collected information on the problem. In short, he maintains, it is better to discuss these issues up-front than to have large segments of the population brood about the threats they feel other groups present to them.

2. *Crime statistics on race or ethnicity will distort the true contribution to crime of different racial/ethnic groups due to discriminatory practices by the criminal justice system and the misclassification of the race or ethnicity of suspects by criminal justice personnel.* Gabor notes that other forms of data collection (e.g., victimization surveys or self-report studies) can be used to correct the biases of officially collected information.

3. *Collecting statistics on a suspect's race or ethnicity is a waste of justice system resources because these factors are not related to crime, and, even if they were, they leave us with few policy options.* Gabor argues that it is foolish to dismiss the possibility of a link between ethnicity and crime before such data are even gathered. Such data might help identify communities toward which intensive prevention efforts may be directed. Besides, there are many kinds of data about victims and offenders currently collected that describe victim or offender characteristics, for example, age and gender.

Given the difficulties involved in defining race and ethnicity, Gabor contends that it would be more useful to gather information about "national origin" than about race or ethnic membership per se. In this way, anyone born in Canada would be classified as a Canadian irrespective of ethnicity. For others, the country of origin or nationality would be recorded.

One major concern with surveys of known offenders relates to the generalizability of the findings (Flowers, 1989). Given that many offenders are not captured and that many of those who are captured are not convicted or sentenced, what we learn in interviews with convicted offenders may not be representative of the larger offender population.

ETHNOGRAPHIC RESEARCH

Ethnographic research provides another means by which information can be gathered from known offenders. As a research strategy, ethnography moves beyond the use of a structured interview as the researcher attempts to not only speak with but also directly observe and interact with the people being studied (Wright and Bennett, 1990). The researcher gathers offender accounts by informally participating in and developing some intimate knowledge of the social world of the offender.

This approach rests on the assumption that formal interviews with offenders yield very limited research data. Researchers may find it very difficult to gain access to members of "outlaw" motorcycle gangs (Wolf, 1991), organized-crime groups, and professional thieves through conventional means (Ianni and Reuss-Ianni, 1972; Wolf, 1991). However, if researchers are able to cultivate informal relationships with offenders, they may be able to penetrate their social world and thereby learn much that would be invisible to an outside researcher. Ethnographic studies of street gangs (Baron, 1989; Kennedy and Baron, 1993), violent criminals (Fleisher, 1995), or male prostitutes (Calhoun and Weaver, 1996) provide insights that could not be gleaned in police statistics or victim surveys. Chambliss (1975), a proponent of this method of urban ethnography, argues that the data on organized crime and professional theft as well as other presumably difficult-to-study events are much more available than we usually think. "All we really have to do is get out of our offices and onto the streets. The data are there; the problem is that too often the sociologist is not" (39).

WHAT IS IT?

Self-Report Study

Instead of being asked about their involvement in criminal events as victims, respondents are asked about their involvement as offenders. Like the victimization survey, the self-report study is intended to uncover crimes that have not been reported to the police (as well as to elucidate those that have).

SELF-REPORT STUDIES

Self-report studies predate victimization surveys, having become popular during the 1950s and 1960s. Like victimization surveys, **self-report studies** gather data from the members of some large population. However, instead of being asked about their involvement as victims in criminal events, respondents are asked about their involvement as offenders. Like victimization surveys, self-report studies are intended to uncover crimes that have not been reported to the police (as well as to elucidate those that have). Also like victimization surveys, self-report studies allow the sample to be

---

BOX 7.4   MEASURING SELF-REPORTED COMPUTER CRIME

How adequate are the data of official agencies, victim surveys, or self-report offender surveys in revealing the causes of computer crime? In theory, at least, each approach should be as applicable to the study of computer crime as it is to any other type of crime. However, our experience with these data sources is not so extensive as to allow definitive judgments to be made about their relative value.

Official data relating to computer crime seem to share many of the same problems with data relating to more traditional offending (Taber, 1980). The more routine problems of victim nonreporting and selective enforcement, however, are complicated by uncertainties about how computer crime should be defined (Bequai, 1987). The literature also indicates that researchers who attempt to survey organizations that are victimized by computer crime face serious difficulties with respect to sampling and data access.

While researchers have made only very limited use of self-report offending surveys, Sacco and Zureik (1990) provide some indication of how such a survey might proceed. These researchers undertook a survey of anonymous student respondents who were enrolled in computing courses at a medium-sized Canadian university. Respondents were asked to complete a twenty-two-page questionnaire that dealt with a variety of computing behaviours, attitudes, and perceptions. A total of 202 questionnaires were distributed in class to students who were enrolled in courses required for a major in computing science and other applied science disciplines. The sample spanned the usual four years of undergraduate instruction. Slightly more than 50 percent (105) of the participating students completed and returned the questionnaire.

In one section of the questionnaire, respondents were asked to indicate whether, during the previous year, they had engaged in any of five specific types of computer misbehaviour. The most frequently reported behaviour was the unauthorized copying of copyrighted material for personal use (62 percent). The least frequently reported behaviour was the unauthorized use of a program that was the property of a time-share system (5 percent). Equal portions (15 percent) reported that they had rummaged through discarded printout "for interesting program listings" or had used an unauthorized password. Twenty-nine percent indicated that they had used a program in such a way that they avoided being charged for its use.

broken up into respondents who have and who have not been involved in criminal events over a specified period. This allows the researcher to compare offenders and nonoffenders in terms of social and lifestyle characteristics that might be useful in testing explanations of criminality.

Self-report research has most frequently been used in the study of juvenile crime, although there is nothing in the approach that prevents it from being applied to the study of adults (Laub, 1987) or to "nontraditional" offences such as computer crime (Sacco and Zureik, 1990). The emphasis on juveniles has largely been a matter of convenience in that juveniles, in the context of the school classroom, represent a captive audience for the researcher (Chilton, 1991). Once a sample of respondents has been selected, the data about self-reported delinquency are collected in one of two ways (O'Brien, 1985). Some researchers use a questionnaire that includes a checklist of delinquent acts. Subjects are asked to indicate whether they have committed each of the acts and, if so, how frequently, over a given period. Alternatively, researchers may ask respondents about their delinquent conduct in face-to-face interviews. Each approach has its advantages. The questionnaire makes it easier to assure the respondent's anonymity. The interview, however, allows for more detailed questioning about the circumstances surrounding the delinquent conduct (Gold, 1970).

THE LIMITATIONS OF CRIME REPORTS

Much of what we know about criminal events is based on the reports provided by offenders, victims, and the police. In addressing the limitations of these data, two issues require consideration: (1) the type of event that is captured by each method of data collection, and (2) the perspective brought to bear on those events that are captured.

WHAT TYPE OF EVENT?

Each of the methods that we have discussed in this section is somewhat restricted in terms of the kinds of criminal events it illuminates. Victimization surveys usually ask respondents only about those events that have a direct and immediate victim (Reiss, 1986b). Because they are household surveys, they tend to exclude crimes that victimize businesses or the wider community (for example, vandalism of public property). Victimization surveys also exclude victims to whom access is limited, including children, the homeless, and residents of psychiatric or other institutions (Weis, 1989).

Self-report studies have been used primarily to obtain information about the "common delinquencies" of youth. They have been criticized for excluding the more serious, but less frequently occurring, types of delinquency (such as extreme forms of violence) while emphasizing nonserious forms of behaviour (such as "cutting classes" or "disobeying parents") (Braithwaite, 1981; Elliott and Ageton, 1980; Gove, Hughes, and Geerken, 1985; Hindelang, Hirschi, and Weis, 1981). When students in criminology classes are asked to demonstrate with a show of hands whether they have committed any of the "crimes" listed in the self-report questionnaires, a large number always respond in the affirmative. Even political leaders have admitted to experimenting with marijuana as youths. While a loose interpretation of these data, then, can make it seem that everyone is a criminal, such data give much substance to the idea that criminal offending (even of the more serious variety) is far more common than official statistics would lead us to believe and that distinctions between "offenders" and "everyone else" are only made with great difficulty (Gabor, 1994a).

The police reports that form the basis of the UCR are in some ways the most comprehensive data source. Unlike victimization surveys, the UCR includes crimes without direct victims, as well as crimes committed against businesses, the community, and those individuals who are unlikely to appear in surveys (Reiss, 1986b). A limitation of the UCR system is that the data it collects are based only on those crimes that the police know about.

WHOSE PERSPECTIVE?

The issue of perspective is central to any attempt to make proper use of crime report data. Each method offers a limited perspective since it elicits information from only some types of event participants. As we saw in Chapter 2, event participants' understanding of criminal events may differ quite markedly. We expect, therefore, that their reports will reflect these differences.

Victimization data rely on victims' perceptions of criminal events. As such, their quality is subject to whatever distortions, intentional or unintentional, characterize these perceptions. The accuracy of respondents' reports also is subject to numerous compromises. For example, respondents may fail to disclose experiences in which the researcher is interested (Skogan, 1986). If someone is victimized during the course of an illegal activity, he or she may not want to tell the researcher about it. If the event is of minor significance, it may be forgotten by the time of the interview; this may be a

> ### WHAT DOES IT MEAN?
>
> #### *Telescoping*
>
> Crimes that the victim regards as significant life events may be brought forward in time so that the respondent reports them as having occurred during the reference period when they actually occurred at an earlier point in time. Telescoping is most likely to be a problem in the study of serious violent crimes.

particular problem when the reference period about which the respondent is asked is very long. The opposite problem involves what is called **telescoping** (Skogan, 1986). In this case, crimes the victim regards as significant life events may be reported as having occurred during the reference period when, in fact, they actually occurred at an earlier point in time. Telescoping is most likely to be a problem in the study of serious violent crimes.

In many cases of serious victimization, the victim may be discouraged from reporting the event to a researcher. This may be true, for instance, in cases of family violence when the victim feels ashamed or embarrassed or believes that reporting the event may put him or her at risk. This may be a particular problem with sexual assaults or crimes involving strangers.

Victims' perspectives are limited in other ways as well. If respondents cannot or do not define an event as a crime, they are unlikely to tell a researcher about it (Block and Block, 1984). In some cases, people may be victimized but not realize it—many forms of fraud are intended to accomplish precisely this outcome. Similarly, if a purse is stolen but the victim believes that she has lost it, she will not report it to a researcher who asks her a question about theft. Much of the criminal harm that is perpetrated by corporations and governments is not readily apparent, even to those who are directly affected; as a result, victims may have no idea that they have been victimized (Walklate, 1989).

Respondents are also likely to differ in their views as to what level of violation constitutes a crime (Gove, Hughes, and Geerkan, 1985). Some studies show, for instance, that the reporting of assault victimization is more likely among highly educated people. Such a finding is most reasonably interpreted in terms of class differences in the definition of injury or in the willingness to tolerate violence rather than in terms of the greater threats of criminal violence faced by more highly educated respondents (Skogan, 1990a).

Self-report studies allow us to understand criminal events from the perspective of the offender. Yet offenders who have the most to hide may be least willing to participate in the research (O'Brien, 1985). Moreover, some offenders may exaggerate their wrongdoing (perhaps as a show of bravado), while others may be reluctant to admit to involvement in criminal activity (Wright and Bennett, 1990). When the latter do report, they may be more willing to admit to trivial rather than serious offences (Jupp, 1989).

In the case of the UCR system, the organizational perspective of policing agencies determines the rules for data collection. Administrative or political pressure may dictate that the policing of certain kinds of criminal events (for example, impaired driving) be emphasized over others (for example, "soft" drug use) (Jackson, 1990; O'Brien, 1985; Schneider and Wieresma, 1990).

Police practices, public tolerance for particular kinds of behaviour, and the needs of the agency for particular kinds of data all influence the ways in which data are collected (Savitz, 1978).

Reiss (1986a) argues that the perspective implicit in police data offers a distinct advantage over self-report and victimization data. Whereas the latter two data sources reflect the view of highly self-interested parties, police data allow for a more balanced picture. Police reports of criminal events are based on a wider variety of information sources, including victims, offenders, bystanders, and witnesses. In addition, police data normally are collected closer in time to the actual event than is the case with victim or offender surveys. As a result, police data are less likely to be influenced by the selective effects of memory.

In a similar vein, Gove, Hughes, and Geerken (1985) suggest that, in comparison with other data sources, official statistics provide more rigorous criteria for the definition of criminal events. They argue that victimization surveys give us only the victim's perspective, which is insufficient in determining whether a crime has in fact occurred. In order to make this judgment, we also need to know the offender's intention, the circumstances surrounding the event, and the condition of the victim (Mayhew, Elliot, and Dowds, 1989).

Criminal events that are recorded in official statistics have passed through two filters. First, they have been judged sufficiently serious to be worth reporting to the police. Second, they have been certified by the police as serious events deserving of criminal justice intervention. According to Gove, Hughes, and Geerken (1985), the reports contained in the UCR provide a good indicator of "the extent to which citizens feel injured, frightened, and financially hurt by a criminal act" (489).

These different perspectives have very important implications for how criminal events are understood. If, for example, an individual gets into a fistfight with a drinking companion, the event might be understood differently within the context of different data collection systems. If the individual is asked in a victimization survey whether anyone has hit him or threatened to hit him, and he responds honestly, he is likely to be counted as a victim. If he is asked in a self-report survey whether he has hit anyone, and he answers honestly, he is likely to be counted as an offender. If the police are summoned, they may, because of the circumstances and the relationship between the parties, screen the event out so that it never enters the official record.

We do not necessarily expect reports from different event participants to tell us the same things. Victimization surveys and UCR data may disagree because they employ different criteria in determining the types of events that are to be included (Blumstein, Cohen, and Rosenfeld, 1992; Gove, Hughes, and

Geerken, 1985; Menard and Covey, 1988; O'Brien, 1986). Thus, if researchers undertook a victimization survey in a given community and then compared the survey rates with the UCR rates for that same community, several sources of variation would be apparent. While the UCR measures would encompass crimes committed against businesses, institutionalized persons, and individuals who do not have a permanent residence, the victim survey would probably omit such crimes. The UCR rates would include crimes committed within the policing jurisdiction, irrespective of victims' place of residence. Thus, the UCR might include crimes committed against tourists who were visiting the community as well as crimes against commuters who work in the community but live elsewhere. By contrast, the victimization study, because it usually involves a household survey, would restrict attention to crimes committed against community residents, regardless of whether the crime occurred in the local community or elsewhere.

Similarly, the descriptions of offenders that emerge from police reports of crimes serious enough to have passed through citizen and police filters cannot be expected to concur with offender profiles that emerge from self-report studies that focus on nonserious delinquency (Hindelang, Hirschi, and Weis, 1981; West and Farrington, 1977).

Although for decades criminologists have engaged in an intense debate about the relative value of specific crime measures, clearly no single data source is sufficient to answer all of the questions we might have about crime events (Jackson, 1990; Menard and Covey, 1988). Because our data sources tell us different things, it does not really make sense to think about one data source as *better* than another. While subsequent chapters will make extensive use of data derived from these sources, it is important that these data always be approached cautiously and critically, as the discussion of the measurement of women's victimization illustrates.

MEASURING WOMEN'S VICTIMIZATION

Is it men or women who face the greatest risks of criminal victimization? The answer to this question depends on which crimes we wish to focus attention on, as well as which data sources we wish to use to investigate the issue. According the 1995 (revised) UCR, about one-half of the victims of violence were female (Hendrick, 1996). Not surprisingly, females accounted for most of the sexual assault victims (85 percent) and more than one-half of the level 1 (less serious) assaults (53 percent). However, males were more likely to be victims of homicide (67 percent) and robbery (61 percent). Men were also more likely to be the victims of the more serious level 2 and level 3 assaults (65 percent and 79 percent respectively).

Data from the 1993 General Social Survey indicate that while the rate of robbery is twice as great for men as for women (12 incidents per 1000 versus 6 incidents per 1000), the rates of theft of personal property and assault are largely comparable. In the case of sexual assault, the rate for women is 29 incidents per 1000 population, while for men the rate is too low to be estimated in a reliable fashion.

Such findings have implications that seem to extend well beyond a narrow concern with crime measurement on the part of academic researchers. They strongly influence the ways in which the public agenda is formulated, and they tend to legitimize the activities of some but not other social problems claims-makers. Feminist social critics who attempt to raise public awareness of the problem of crime against women are frequently opposed by those who claim that women's fear of victimization is not rooted in reality, but rather suggests a nonrational reaction to a world that threatens men more than it does women (Fekete, 1994). In response, some feminist researchers have generated research findings that provide estimates of female victimization that are wildly at odds with the data yielded by more traditional measures (Gilbert, 1991).

PATTERNS OF FEMALE VICTIMIZATION

These observations point to a need to understand the patterns of female victimization revealed by the UCR and by victimization surveys. The logical starting point in such an exercise is to determine areas of agreement across methodological approaches to women's victimization. Two such patterns are consistently reported by the advocates of both traditional and more critical research approaches (DeKeseredy and Hinch, 1991; Gartner and McCarthy, 1996). The first pattern concerns the fact that women are more likely than men to be victimized by people they know or with whom they have some ongoing relationship. The second, related pattern suggests that women have a greater tendency than men to be victimized in private (most notably the home) rather than public settings.

These patterns are clearly exemplified by gender differences in homicide victimization. Women are more likely than men to be killed in their own homes and are more likely to die at the hands of someone who is related to them. In 1995, for instance, 76 percent of female homicide victims were killed in a private residence, compared with 56 percent of male victims (Fedorowycz, 1996). Moreover, 60 percent of female victims, compared with 24 percent of male victims, were murdered by spouses or family members.

The two types of assault that we most closely associate with the victimization of women—domestic assault and sexual assault—also illustrate the private and intimate character of female victimization. In order to understand why official data and victimization surveys portray female victimization as they do, we need to assess how adequately these measures investigate crimes that are committed in private places and that involve offenders and victims who are in intimate relationships.

As we have discussed, many women who are abused in the context of marital relationships do not define what is happening to them as criminal (Kantor and Straus, 1987). Several cultural factors encourage these women to view such incidents as normal and to blame themselves for the violence (Ferraro and Johnson, 1983). Even the fact that a woman phones the police to report an attack by a spouse does not necessarily mean that she defines the event in criminal terms; her action may have less to do with "reporting a crime" than with trying to obtain immediate assistance in order to prevent injury. And even if women do define such events as crimes, they may choose not to phone the police for a variety of reasons (Kantor and Straus, 1987). They may perceive that taking such action places them at greater risk, or they may be concerned that the police or other criminal justice agents will not take them seriously.

As we have seen, the appearance of the police at the scene of a domestic violence incident does not always mean that the event will be counted as a crime. If there is no clear evidence of physical harm, the police may engage in mediation by attempting to cool the parties down, listening to their respective accounts, or issuing stern warnings (Bell, 1987; Kantor and Straus, 1987). The victim may be given information or advice or referrals rather than treated like a complainant in a criminal matter.

In many domestic disputes, the law may be viewed by the police as a means for dealing with the disorderly situation that confronts them rather than as a means for addressing the problem of wife assault (Gondolf and McFerron, 1989). The consequence of this is that, in many cases, no legal action is taken, because the situation is not seen as warranting a legal response. Even those cases that do involve a legal resolution do not necessarily require that official note be taken of the fact that a woman has been victimized. In conducting research in Newfoundland, O'Grady (1989) discovered that many instances of domestic violence were legally recorded not as assaults but as "weapons" or "drunk and disorderly in the home" offences.

As we pointed out in Chapter 1, many jurisdictions have attempted to reduce the use of police discretion in the handling of domestic assaults by passing laws that make arrest mandatory in these cases. However, such laws do not completely remove the discretionary decision making in which police engage. In one jurisdiction, police arrested an abuser in only 18 percent of the cases in which arrest was possible, despite the existence of a presumptive arrest law (Ferraro, 1989).

Victims of sexual assault, like victims of domestic violence, may be reluctant to apply a criminal label if the offender is an acquaintance. Using U.S. national victimization data, Lizotte (1985) reports that factors that make a strong case for prosecution are closely related to women's reporting decisions regarding rape. Thus, women are less likely to report an incident to the police when they are unmarried, when the offender is not a stranger, and when the offender has a right to be in the location in which the offence occurs. As a

BOX 7.5   THE CONFLICT TACTICS SCALE

Q35. No matter how well a couple get along, there are times when they disagree, get annoyed with the other person, or just have spats or fights because they're in a bad mood or tired or for some other reason. They also use many different ways of trying to settle their differences. I'm going to read some things that you and your (spouse/partner) might do when you have an argument. I would like you to tell me how many times (Once, Twice, 3–5 times, 6–10 times, 11–20 times, or more than 20 times) in the past 12 months you (READ ITEM).

Q36. Thinking back over the last 12 months you've been together, was there ever an occasion when (your spouse/partner) (READ ITEM)? Tell me how often (he/she) ...

Q37. (IF EITHER "NEVER" OR "DON'T KNOW" ON ITEM FOR BOTH Q35 AND Q36, ASK Q37 FOR THAT ITEM) Has it *ever* happened?

Q35. Respondent In Past Year	Q36. You	Spouse	Q37.
	1—Once	1—Once	
	2—Twice	2—Twice	
	3—3–5 Times	3—3–5 Times	
	4—6–10 Times	4—6–10 Times	
	5—11–20 Times	5—11–20 Times	
	6—More than 20	6—More than 20	1—Yes
	0—Never	0—Never	0—No
	(don't read)	(don't read)	
A. Discussed an issue calmly	1 2 3 4 5 6 0	1 2 3 4 5 6 0	1 0
B. Got information to back up your/his/her/ side of things	1 2 3 4 5 6 0	1 2 3 4 5 6 0	1 0

	BOX 7.5	THE CONFLICT TACTICS SCALE (CONT.)		
C.	Brought in, or tried to bring in, someone to help settle things	1 2 3 4 5 6 0	1 2 3 4 5 6 0	1 0
D.	Insulted or swore at him/her/you	1 2 3 4 5 6 0	1 2 3 4 5 6 0	1 0
E.	Sulked or refused to talk about an issue	1 2 3 4 5 6 0	1 2 3 4 5 6 0	1 0
F.	Stomped out of the room or house or yard	1 2 3 4 5 6 0	1 2 3 4 5 6 0	1 0
G.	Cried	1 2 3 4 5 6 0	1 2 3 4 5 6 0	1 0
H.	Did or said something to spite him/her/you	1 2 3 4 5 6 0	1 2 3 4 5 6 0	1 0
I.	Threatened to hit or throw something at him/her/you	1 2 3 4 5 6 0	1 2 3 4 5 6 0	1 0
J.	Threw or smashed or hit or kicked something	1 2 3 4 5 6 0	1 2 3 4 5 6 0	1 0
K.	Threw something at him/her/you	1 2 3 4 5 6 0	1 2 3 4 5 6 0	1 0
L.	Pushed, grabbed, or shoved him/her/you	1 2 3 4 5 6 0	1 2 3 4 5 6 0	1 0
M.	Slapped him/her/you	1 2 3 4 5 6 0	1 2 3 4 5 6 0	1 0
N.	Kicked, bit, or hit him/her/you with a fist	1 2 3 4 5 6 0	1 2 3 4 5 6 0	1 0
O.	Hit or tried to hit him/her/you with something	1 2 3 4 5 6 0	1 2 3 4 5 6 0	1 0
P.	Beat him/her/you up	1 2 3 4 5 6 0	1 2 3 4 5 6 0	1 0
Q.	Choked him/her/you	1 2 3 4 5 6 0	1 2 3 4 5 6 0	1 0
R.	Threatened him/her/you with a knife or gun	1 2 3 4 5 6 0	1 2 3 4 5 6 0	1 0
S.	Used a knife or fired a gun	1 2 3 4 5 6 0	1 2 3 4 5 6 0	1 0

SOURCE: Reprinted by permission of Transaction Publishers. *Physical Violence in American Families: Risk Factors and Adaptations to Violence in 8,145 Families*, by Murray A. Straus and Richard J. Gelles, 1990 / Copyright © 1997 by Transaction Publishers. All rights reserved.

result, the UCR measures sexual assaults for which the legal evidence is relatively clear but that are not necessarily typical of women's sexual victimization.

While it is often claimed that victimization surveys broaden the search for incidents of women's victimization, this technique also clearly excludes many types of events. Most notably, these studies undercount crimes that involve intimates—precisely the types of crimes that disproportionately victimize women. Moreover, victimization surveys usually ignore victimization in the form of obscene phone calls, exhibitionism, and sexual harassment in the workplace (Gillespie and Leffler, 1987; Hanmer and Saunders, 1984; Junger, 1987; Stanko, 1985).

RECENT RESEARCH INNOVATIONS

Several recent research innovations reflect attempts to provide a more valid assessment of women's victimization. Much research in the area of family violence, for instance, has made use of measures based on something other than traditional legal categories. The most frequently used measure, developed by Murray Straus and Richard Gelles, is known as the **Conflict Tactics Scale (CTS)**. CTS items are ranked in order of increasing seriousness. Items A–J describe nonviolent means of conflict resolution (such as use of verbal skills), while items J–S describe the kinds of violent acts that constitute wife abuse. In order to investigate such abuse, husbands or wives may be asked how frequently they or their partners use each of these strategies in conflict situations. In one sense, the CTS may be understood as an approach that combines victimization and self-report measures.

Although the CTS has been widely used, it has been criticized for ignoring both the consequences and the context of violent behaviour (DeKeseredy and Hinch, 1991). For example, the scale is unable to distinguish between a situation in which a husband offensively strikes his wife, causing serious physical injury, and a situation in which a wife defensively strikes her husband and causes no injury.

The previously mentioned Violence Against Women Survey represents one of the most ambitious and sophisticated attempts to investigate the problem of violence against women (Johnson, 1996a; Johnson and Sacco, 1995). As the survey included only female respondents, it does not allow us to compare directly the experiences of men and women. Still, it represents an attempt to focus on the specific problem of male violence against women in a way that takes account of the limitations that have hampered many previous efforts.

As stated, a total of 12 300 women 18 years of age and over across the ten provinces were interviewed for the survey. Respondents were selected using random-digit dialling techniques and were interviewed over the telephone. The design and implementation of the survey methodology reflected extensive consultations with government officials, academics, and women's groups directly involved in the problem of violence against women. Careful testing of survey questions, multiple measures, selection and training of interviewers, and lifetime victimization rates were all incorporated into the design of the survey (Johnson, 1996b). In particular the survey design was particularly sensitive to the ethical and safety problems created when those who are being interviewed may still live with their victimizers. The survey has yielded a wealth of valuable data and has become the model for similar surveys in the United States and elsewhere.

Obviously, claims about the low rates of crime experienced by women must be assessed with extreme caution. This is not because the research is done in a careless or unsophisticated fashion, but because all research approaches are subject to inherent limitations.

CRIME RATES

The form in which we most frequently encounter reports of criminal events is the crime rate, a measure that is widely used in criminology. Although journalists and politicians, among others, frequently issue declarations about rates of crime, we are seldom encouraged to think critically about what crime rate measures really are.

THE NATURE OF CRIME RATES

What are **crime rates**? As defined by Nettler (1984), "a rate compares events during a specified time against some base of other events, conditions or people. It takes the form $(m/P)k$, where m is a measure of some occurrence, P is a population count (or tally of some other condition of interest), and k is a constant" (47).

As this definition suggests, computing crime rates is a fairly straightforward matter. First, we develop some estimate of the numerator (m)—some count of criminal events. We have already discussed the major forms of such counts—crimes recorded by the police or reported in victimization surveys or self-report studies. Next, we select a measure of the denominator (P). This is generally thought of as a measure of the population that is exposed to the events, or is at risk of being involved in the events, as offenders or victims (Reiss, 1986a). Finally, the number we obtain when we divide the number of criminal events (m) by the measure of exposure or risk (P) is multiplied by

BOX 7.6   CALCULATING CRIME RATES

In order to calculate a crime rate, three quantities are required. The first is a count of the number of crimes. In the expression $(m/P)k$, this is the quantity m. Based on data collected in the 1993 General Social Survey, it has been estimated that, in 1992, there were 3.1 million crimes against persons in Canada involving victims 15 years and older.

Next, we need a measure of the population that could have been involved in these crimes as victims or offenders. In the expression $(m/P)k$, the measure of the at-risk population is P. Based on census data, we estimate the 1992 population of Canadians over the age of 15 to be 22 282 340.

Finally, in the expression $(m/P)k$, we need a constant, k, which will allow us to express the number of crimes that occur per k members of the population.

Putting all of the above together, we can calculate the rate of violent incidents per 1000 Canadians over the age of 15 as follows:

$$\frac{3\ 100\ 000}{22\ 282\ 340} \times 1000 = 139$$

some constant (k), so that the rate can be expressed per k units of exposure. The selection of the constant is largely arbitrary, but rates are traditionally expressed per 1000 or per 100 000 units of exposure.

SOME USES OF CRIME RATES

In criminology, we will make extensive use of crime rates in our investigation of criminal event patterns. By analyzing these rates, we can assess the value of particular theoretical arguments about how and why these events occur. Crime rates are also used by noncriminologists for a variety of other purposes. One of the most popular is as a "social barometer" that indexes the quality of life (Bottomley and Pease, 1986). Thus, just as the gross national product is employed as an indicator of our collective economic well-being, crime rates are frequently read as indicators of our social well-being (Waller, 1982).

At a personal level, we may factor information about crime rates into our decisions about whether we will buy a home in a particular neighbourhood, vacation in a particular locale, or allow our children to attend a particular school.

Crime rates also are used to assess the effectiveness of community-based crime prevention programs such as Neighbourhood Watch and Operation

| | BOX 7.7 ANNUAL AND LIFETIME VICTIMIZATION |

Annual victimization rates are important measures in that they tell us how many people (or how many households in a particular area) have been victimized by crime. Often, we use these rates to estimate our own risks of victimization. As an alternative measure, we can calculate lifetime chances of victimization. Using these rates, we ask, "What are my chances of experiencing this kind of victimization during my lifetime?"

Using a variety of U.S. data sources, Michael R. Rand was able to estimate the lifetime risks of homicide victimization as well as other forms of criminal and noncriminal misfortune (see Table 7.2).

Table 7.2   Annual and Lifetime Chances of Various Criminal and Noncriminal Events

Event	Annual Chance	Lifetime Chance
Homicide	1 in 10 200	1 in 151.0
Violent crime	1 in 32	1 in 1.2
Rape (females only)	1 in 714	1 in 12.5
Robbery	1 in 179	1 in 3.3
Assault	1 in 40	1 in 1.4
Personal theft	1 in 16	1 in 1.0
Accidental death	1 in 2681	1 in 38
Heart disease death	1 in 338	1 in 4.0

SOURCE: M.R. Rand, "Life Chances of Becoming a Victim of Homicide." In C.R. Block and R.L. Block (eds.), *Questions and Answers in Lethal and Non-Lethal Violence: Proceedings of the Second Annual Workshop of the Homicide Research Working Group* (Washington, DC: U.S. Department of Justice, 1993).

Identification as well as a large number of other criminal justice interventions (Gabor 1990b). And, as we have discussed, changes in crime rates are frequently used to evaluate the quality of police services.

Claimsmaking activities often include organized efforts to produce and publicize crime rate data that are said to document the issues to which the claimsmakers wish to draw attention (Best, 1988; Bottomley and Coleman, 1981). According to Gilbert (1991), such efforts "embody less an effort at scientific understanding than an attempt to persuade the public that a problem is vastly larger than is commonly recognized" (63). Best (1988) and Hotaling and Finkelhor (1990) have written about how "advocacy numbers" have been used in defining the problem of missing children. They suggest that "guesstimates" of the number of children abducted by strangers have greatly overestimated the prevalence of the problem. Best maintains that the use of crime data for political purposes generally proceeds from three basic assumptions: (1) big numbers are better than small numbers, (2) official numbers are better than unofficial numbers, and (3) big official numbers are best of all. As a result, data collection agencies, official or otherwise, may experience more pressure to keep numbers high than to keep them accurate (Reuter, 1984a).

Crime rates provide an important standard by which we are able to compare the relative extent of crime incidence across jurisdictions and across groups. In this context, they have been offered as a way of measuring individual risk of crime victimization.

CRIME RATES AS MEASURES OF RISK

In most of the cases just described, we are interested in crime rate measures because we interpret them as measures of risk. When we are told that the homicide rate per 100 000 people is four times higher in the United States than in Canada, for example, we are led to understand that, when the differences in population sizes are taken into account, the risk of homicide is much greater south of the border than north of it. Similarly, when we are told that the neighbourhood to which we are thinking of moving has a much higher crime rate than the neighbourhood in which we currently live, we may want to reconsider our decision.

How adequate are crime rates as measures of risk? Our answer to this question depends on how much confidence we have in the numbers that are used in the calculation of the crime rate. We have already discussed the many problems that confound our tallies of criminal events (that is, the numerator m of the crime rate equation). However, we also should be concerned about crime rate denominators (P).

In selecting a crime rate denominator, the usual practice is to use the total population residing within the jurisdiction in which the count of events has taken place. Such measures are usually referred to as **"crude" crime rates** because they provide only a very general assessment of the level of risk (Silverman, Teevan, and Sacco, 1996). They do not take account of the demographic characteristics of the population or the empirical fact that different segments of the population are involved in criminal events with different levels of frequency. This problem is sometimes countered through the use of a denominator that better reflects the population at risk. In **age-specific crime**

rates, the base number for calculating the rate might include only those individuals aged 18–24. However, the difficulties inherent in determining a number that accurately reflects particular subpopulations sometimes leaves such rates open to charges of inaccuracy.

HOW DO THEY DIFFER?

Crude vs. Age-Specific Crime Rates

In selecting a crime rate denominator, the usual practice is to use the total population residing within the jurisdiction in which the count of events has taken place. Such measures are usually referred to as "crude" crime rates. Age-specific crime rates use a denominator that better reflects the population at risk, such as individuals aged 18–24.

Nonetheless, we can reasonably argue that a more refined measure would take account of the differential risks faced by distinct segments of the population. Thus, since most of the crimes counted in crime and victimization rates involve young males, it may make more sense to standardize the level of risk in terms of the proportion of young males in the population rather than in terms of the total population. This is because a shift in the size of this segment of the population will exert a more significant effect on the overall rate than will shifts in other segments of the population, for instance, elderly women.

Not only the demographic composition but also the location of communities may be relevant to an understanding of crime rates (Gibbs and Erikson, 1976; Stafford and Gibbs, 1980). The concept of **ecological position** refers to geographic and economic relationships that link the community for which the rate is being calculated to nearby communities. Given their responsibility to patrol specific neighbourhoods, the police have always been interested in ecological factors. However, until recently, they have not had the ability to do a quick and detailed analysis that considers not only changes in crime rates across neighbourhoods but also other factors that may change, such as age composition. With the development of high-powered computers and large-scale data-processing packages that offer analysis on a geographic basis, the police now have the resources to do ecological analyses quickly, thereby enhancing their ability to respond to changes in neighbourhoods.

Ecological analyses are relevant in explaining why two communities may have populations of similar size and demographic composition but differing crime rates. Community A, for example, may be a considerable distance from neighbouring communities such that the residents of these other communities do not commute to Community A, either for employment or for recreational purposes. In other words, the members of the neighbouring communities are not regularly available as offenders or victims in Community A. When the official crime rate of Community A is calculated in terms of the population residing within Community A, most of the at-risk population will be taken into account.

By contrast, Community B may be a "central city" within a larger metropolitan area. Members of neighbouring communities may travel to and spend most of their working days in Community B. In addition, residents of these satellite communities may regularly attend cultural events or shop in the central city. If the residents of the satellite communities commit crimes or are victimized as they visit Community B, these crimes may be counted in the official crime rate of the central city. However, because these individuals are not residents of Community B, they are not counted in the denominator. If we fail to account for the differences in the ecological positions of Community A and Community B, we may be at a loss to explain why the latter community has a generally higher crime rate.

A study by the Canadian Centre for Justice Statistics (1990a), which was mentioned earlier in this chapter, suggests that some of the variation in the crime rates of Edmonton and Calgary may be attributable to differences in ecological position. While the city of Calgary has no significant suburban population, approximately 100 000 people reside in suburbs surrounding the city of Edmonton. When the rates of the two communities were recalculated on the basis of the metropolitan area rather than on the basis of city populations, the total Criminal Code rate for Edmonton decreased by 8.2 percent, while the corresponding decrease in Calgary was only 0.43 percent.

At a more basic level, we can reasonably ask whether population measures are adequate indicators of risk in the calculation of crime rates. Population measures give some indication of the numbers of people who expose themselves to risks (of offending or victimization), but they do not tell us about the frequency with which this exposure takes place. Populations may differ not only with respect to demographic structure but also with respect to members' potential for victimization. For example, a community in which people regularly spend a great deal of time engaged in evening activities outside the home may have a very different rate for some types of crimes than a community in which most people stay at home most of the time. The risky lifestyles that characterize the former community make its members more vulnerable to victimization (Kennedy and Forde, 1990).

For these reasons, many sociologists have argued in recent years that we need to measure risk more directly (Balkin, 1979; Fattah and Sacco, 1989; Lindquist and Duke, 1982; Stafford and Galle, 1984). For instance, it has been suggested that the elderly may have lower rates of victimization because their level of exposure to victimization risk is lower; if their victimization rates were to be adjusted for differential exposure, they might more closely approximate those of younger people (Lindquist and Duke, 1982). Efforts to examine such hypotheses have met with only limited success (Clarke et al., 1985; Fattah and

Sacco, 1989). Any comprehensive investigation of these issues must await considerable refinement in how the concept of "exposure" is defined for research purposes.

Finally, in a very different way, Hackler and Don (1990) argue that police crime rates might be made more useful if explicit account is taken of the fact that the recording of some crimes (e.g., assault) involves considerably more discretion (screening) than does the recording of other crimes (e.g., robberies). They argue that more useful information about provincial differences in rates of violence might be obtained by dividing the official assault rate by the official robbery rate in order to produce a "recording index." This index takes account of the police practices that record crime selectively and in doing so provides a "better indicator of actual criminal behaviour" (Hackler and Don, 1990: 262).

■ ■ ■

SUMMARY

Research data are indispensable to the understanding of criminal events. They allow for the testing of theoretical ideas, they help us chart the dimensions of criminal events for policy purposes, and they provide us with indicators of the quality of life. While data about criminal events may derive from many different sources, they tend to be generated by one of two basic investigative strategies: observations and reports.

Criminal events may be directly observed either in naturalistic settings or in the context of field or laboratory experimentation. While much can be learned about criminal events by waiting for them to happen (as in the former case) or by making them happen (as in the latter case), most contemporary research depends on information revealed by reports about crime.

The most widely used of such reports come from those who are most active in criminal events: police, victims, and offenders. The data collected by the police through the Uniform Crime Reporting system describe a wide range of crimes and provide a continuous national record. Recent revisions to the UCR survey are likely to increase the value of these data for both academic and policy purposes. The major limitation of these data relates to the fact that any police-based information system can tell us only about crimes that come to the attention of the police in the first place. A significant number of crimes that the police do not learn about are not included in the UCR system.

Surveys of victims and offenders are intended to illuminate those crimes that are not recorded by the police. Despite the valuable information they provide, these surveys are subject to all of the problems that characterize any type of survey. Victims and offenders are not always as accessible as we would like them to be, and we cannot always be sure that they will not, intentionally or unintentionally, distort the truth in response to questions about their involvement in criminal events.

The problems associated with these major sources of crime data—police, victim, and offender reports—do not suggest a lack of knowledge or awareness on the part of those who collect the data. Rather, they alert us to the fact that any attempt to investigate complex social phenomena is fraught with inherent difficulties. The ways in which crime data construct our statistical images of crimes against women illustrate this fact.

We have also seen that no single data source is likely to answer all of the questions that we have about criminal events. Our major data sources tell us quite different things, because they are likely to capture different types of events and to bring different perspectives to bear on these events. For this reason, it is unproductive to engage in endless debates about the superiority of one data source over another. To a considerable extent, the usefulness of any data source depends on how well it helps us to address particular questions.

We should not dismiss crime data just because our data sources are flawed and less comprehensive than we would like. A great deal can be learned from a judicious use of crime data. Although we know that our data are problematic, in many cases we also know *how* they are problematic. Frequently, the errors that characterize our efforts at data collection are not random, but systematic; knowing the sources and consequences of these systematic errors makes data more valuable than they might otherwise be.

■ ■ ■

QUESTIONS FOR REVIEW AND DISCUSSION

1. How useful are crime rates as a measure of our "quality of life"?
2. The UCR crime data often figure prominently in press reports of crime trends. What does the informed news consumer need to know about these rates?
3. What types of data collection problems do victimization studies and offender self-report studies share in common?
4. What are some of the more important ethical problems confronting criminological researchers?
5. Why is it too simplistic to claim that victimization surveys or self-report studies of offending are "better" than the UCR?
6. Do the major forms of crime measurement support or dispute the popular notion that there are "lies, damned lies, and statistics"?

PART FIVE

DOMAINS OF CRIME

CHAPTER EIGHT

The Family and the Household

WHAT'S IN CHAPTER EIGHT

In this chapter, we focus on crime in the family and the household. Our interest in criminal events in this domain centres on two substantive issues. The first issue is family violence. How do we make sense of the ways in which family members victimize each other? The second issue is crime against the household. Many types of property crime can be understood as crimes in which the household unit is the victim.

INTRODUCTION

In Part Three, we presented the different theoretical perspectives that criminologists have used to explain criminal behaviour and the evolution of criminal events. Part Five focuses on the ways in which criminal events cluster in particular social domains. Chapters 9 and 10 are concerned with the leisure and work domains. In this chapter, we analyze the domain of the family and the household.

In these chapters, we present crime events in an integrated fashion, reviewing what we know from current research about offenders, victims, the circumstances under which these events occur, and so on. As we proceed, we will alert you to the relevant theories that best explain the aspect of the event that we are examining. Some theories, particularly those that focus on motivation, work better in providing a framework for precursors. The transactions are generally best understood from opportunity perspectives, while the aftermath can be analyzed using insights drawn from theories about reactions to crime.

Throughout these chapters, we encourage you to think about the research findings being discussed using the theories that we have reviewed. The theories provide us with a road map to guide us through the details of research findings, helping us to identify commonalities in social behaviour and to provide an understanding of the complexities of social interaction. We begin with a description of the family and household domain.

THE FAMILY AND THE HOUSEHOLD

The concept of family has several different meanings in the literature of social science. A narrow definition might view the family as "husband and wife, with or without never-married children of any age, living at home, or a lone parent with or without one or more never-married children at home" (Deveraux, 1990: 33). Broader definitions, however, suggest that the concept of family includes any adult–child grouping (e.g., with lesbian or gay parents), and all intimate cohabiting or consciously committed support groups, including childless couples, communes, or networks of friends (Luxton, 1988).

In general, we understand the **family** as comprising any relatively enduring pattern of social relationships through which domestic life is organized (Miller, 1990). Customarily, the family is distinguished from other intimate groupings in that relationships are based on kinship. However, what we consider to be a family is as much a matter of cultural definition as social organization. For instance, our cultural view of the family as a unit of procreation leads many people to define a family in which the father is absent as a "broken" home (Wells and Rankin, 1986).

The **household** is generally understood as comprising the social and physical setting within which family life is organized. Many surveys (such as those used in the census) lead us to equate families with households, but in doing so, they may distort the empirical reality of family relations. Family relations in many cases extend beyond any particular household. Husbands and wives who are separated, for instance, usually maintain separate households, although (perhaps because of dependent children) family relations may be sustained.

It is clear from a wealth of demographic data that family relations have changed a great deal in recent years. For example:

- People are waiting longer to marry. In 1990, the average age of first marriage for both brides and bridegrooms was a full three years higher than it had been two decades earlier. In 1990, the average age for the first-time husband was 27.9 years, and for the first-time wife it was 26.0 years (LaNovara, 1994).
- Couples are living longer and living better after their children leave than ever before (Gauthier, 1994).
- Participation of women in the labour force has increased dramatically over the last several years. In 1991, 68 percent of mothers with children at home were in the labour force, up from 52 percent in 1981 (Logan and Belliveau, 1995).
- Families have grown smaller over the last two decades. The average number of people per family in 1991 was 3.1, compared with 3.7 in 1971 (LaNovara, 1994).
- The proportion of people living in common-law relationships has increased significantly (McDaniel, 1994).
- Increasingly large numbers of elderly people are living alone.
- Between 1966 and 1991, the proportion of lone-parent families rose from 8 percent to 13 percent of all families (Oderkirck and Lockhead, 1994); most of these families (over 80 percent) are headed by women.
- In 1990, 17 percent of first marriages ended in divorce, compared with only 11 percent in 1984 (McDaniel, 1994).

The Canadian family, then, is changing. We are witnessing a move away from the conventional single-family unit to variations that include single parents, multiple singles, and lone individuals. These varying structures make social relations within families different from what we would have expected in the past. In addition, as growing numbers of households have come to be occupied by the elderly, this group's dependence on their children is increasing.

Reflecting the change in family social relations are the significant changes that the physical setting of households has undergone (Hasell and Peatross, 1990). In the layout of the typical suburban home, formal dining rooms have been replaced by family rooms or TV rooms. Master bedrooms have increased in size and have walk-in closets and attached bathrooms, both of which make it easier for couples rather than individuals to get ready for work in the morning. Similarly, kitchens are larger so that adults in a hurry can jointly engage in meal preparation. All such changes have important implications for the types of criminal events that occur in the family domain, as well as for the rate at which they occur.

FAMILY VIOLENCE

The cultural tendency to idealize the family as the most intimate and nurturing of social groups traditionally has discouraged research into the extent to which violence is a part of family life (Miller, 1990). Consequently, the recognition of **family violence** as a social problem has occurred only very gradually, and in distinct stages, consistent with the evolution of claimsmaking, which we reviewed in Chapter 6. In the 1960s, the problem of child abuse emerged as a policy and research issue (Best, 1990; Nelson, 1984; Pfohl, 1977). In the 1970s, wife abuse moved onto the agendas of researchers and criminal justice professionals (Loseke, 1989; Tierney, 1982). In the 1980s, elder abuse came to be recognized as a form of family violence requiring attention (Leroux and Petrunik, 1990). Criminologists have begun to research and theorize about other forms of family violence as well, including sibling violence (Pagelow, 1989) and adolescent violence toward parents (Agnew and Huguley, 1989).

Until recently, it was widely believed that the police could do little about the problem of violence within the family. However, revelations about the pervasiveness of family violence have focused on the structure and dynamics of family life and on the need for involvement by criminal justice and other social agencies.

PRECURSORS

Any discussion of the preconditions of family violence must begin with a critical look at the social organization of family life, which may be said to contain within it the seeds out of which violent episodes grow.

Interpersonal conflict theory has been used to shed light on how families run into the kinds of problems that lead to interpersonal violence. The following proposals draw on the insights provided by Gelles and Straus (1988).

First, family life provides the social setting for omnipresent conflict. Family members spend a great deal of time with one another, and their interactions cut across a wide number of dimensions, ranging from decisions about how money will be spent to who will spend it; from where vacations will be spent to how to pay for them; from who will prepare dinner to what that dinner will consist of. The frequency of those interactions, coupled with their often intense nature, sets the stage for conflict. In addition, because the family is a heterogeneous social grouping—including within it males and females and people of different ages—it also provides the context for the playing out of gender or generational conflicts that have societal origins. Because family members usually know one another well, they are aware of each other's weaknesses and vulnerabilities. Such intimate knowledge facilitates the escalation of conflicts into violent exchanges.

Second, family life is private life. What happens between family members frequently takes place behind closed doors. The private character of family life reflects a consensus view that families are different from other social groupings. The privacy of the family has structured the ways in which the police and the courts have responded to intrafamily violence. Neighbours, friends, or co-workers may not know about violence that occurs between family members, and even if they do know about it, they may regard it as none of their business. Moreover, the view that violence in the home is a family matter may be shared by the victims of violence. All such factors reinforce the low visibility of violent conflict in the home and suggest the extent to which it is immune to many of the informal social controls that regulate such behaviour among nonintimates. Those who take a feminist perspective argue that concerns for the privacy of the home simply shield the abuser from the sanctions of the criminal justice system. Such concerns, they argue, reflect a bias toward maintaining power relationships in families that favour men while ignoring the injustices perpetrated against women.

Third, cultural attitudes toward family violence are highly ambivalent. In the family, unlike in the workplace or other more formal settings, physical violence continues to be tolerated. This is most evident with respect to the spanking of children (Davis, 1994). A majority of parents believe that under certain conditions, it is perfectly appropriate for one family member to use physical force against another family member. This is not to suggest that spanking is necessarily abusive (although it well may be), but rather that rules about violence in the home differ from rules about violence in other social domains. Nor does the tolerance of physical violence extend to dependent children alone. In the recent past, violent behaviour by husbands against wives was tolerated in much the same way as parental violence toward children currently is viewed. Most people still continue to regard violence among siblings as normal and natural and, despite obvious physical consequences, not really a form of violence at all.

Fourth, the family is a hierarchical institution. This means that some family members have more power than others. Obviously, parents are more powerful than children. As power control theory would predict, in traditional patriarchal family structures, which are characterized by the presence of an adult male authority figure, the husband is assumed to have the right to make decisions that are binding on other family members (Hagan, Gillis, and Simpson, 1985). Such authority relations, which are recognized by law, create a situation that allows those with more power to behave with relative impunity toward those who have less power. In addition, the widespread support for existing authority relations allows those with power to believe that they have a right to expect compliance from those who are less powerful. Violence may be understood as one effective way in which such compliance is gained.

INEQUALITY IN FAMILY RELATIONS

As we have said, consensus views of the family have been challenged by those who see that the inequality in family relations renders some people more vulnerable than others to intrafamily violence. Our tendency to categorize the major forms of family violence as "wife assault," "child abuse," and "elder abuse" reflects this fact. The consequences of this "hierarchy of family violence" rest most heavily on the shoulders of women, who have historically been economically dependent on men (Davis, 1988). Not surprisingly, as both children and adults, females face greater risks of violence in the family than do males. Victimization surveys typically show that women comprise between 80 and 90 percent of victims of spousal violence (Harlow, 1991; Klaus and Rand, 1984). According to data from the seven-city Canadian Urban Victimization Survey, for instance, women were the victims in 77 percent of family-related assaults, 90 percent of assaults between spouses, 80 percent of assaults between ex-spouses, and 55 percent of assaults involving other relatives (Solicitor General of Canada, 1985).

According to Fedorowycz (1996), spousal homicides account for about 1 in every 6 homicides. Of the total number of spousal homicides, women account for about three-quarters of the victims. Women are about six times more likely to be killed by a spouse than by a stranger. Moreover, in 1995, 6 in 10 incidents of spousal homicide involved a history of domestic violence known to the police.

Studies that use the Conflict Tactics Scale, which we introduced in Chapter 7, have presented findings suggesting that, in the context of the family, women are as violent as men. This has led some observers to argue that we need to focus attention on the "battered husband" as well as the battered wife (Steinmetz, 1977–78). However, these studies provide counts of violent acts that do not clarify the context, motives, or consequences associated with the violence (DeKeseredy and Hinch, 1991; Johnson, 1996b). As Saunders (1989) notes, by most measures of victimization—who initiates the violence, who uses violence offensively rather than defensively, and who is injured most—there is little question that women are more frequently victimized.

In the case of children, patterns of violence also reflect patterns of inequality and dependency. Family assaults—by both parents and siblings—are alarmingly common for all children. Recent data from Statistics Canada indicate that 37 percent of violent incidents against children were perpetrated by family members, usually parents (Johnson, 1995). As Rodgers and Kong (1996) report, according the 1993 revised UCR survey, the majority of child victims of physical assault (66 percent) were in the 11–17 age group. However, an opposite pattern appears in cases of child sexual assault, in which a slight majority of victims (56 percent) were 10 and under. Very young children are also more likely to be killed by a family member than are older children. The homicide statistics show that between 1981 and 1992 the largest percentage of children killed by a family member (48 percent) were under 3 (Rodgers and Kong, 1996: 120). Likewise, children are much more likely to be abducted by family members (33 percent) than by strangers or non-family members (Johnson, 1995). Another form of abuse that reflects hierarchy and dependency relationships is elder abuse, the victims of which may be infirm and reliant on a spouse or adult/child caregiver for the basic necessities of life (Pillemer and Finkelhor, 1988; Quinn and Tomita, 1986; but see Pillemer, 1985).

ISOLATION AND ECONOMIC STRESS

Conflict, privacy, ambivalent attitudes about violence, and inequality are not the only factors that contribute to the occurrence of violence in the family. When families are isolated from the wider community of kin, friends, and neighbours, the negative effects of privacy may be increased (Straus, 1990b). Under such conditions, those who behave violently may become increasingly insensitive to prevailing community standards regarding appropriate conduct. Further, they and their victims may lose or find less accessible the social supports that could be crucial in ending or preventing violence or in mediating the conflicts that lead to violence.

Conditions of economic stress may also contribute to violent conduct. The Violence Against Women Survey, as well as several other studies, has shown that low income is related to wife assault (Johnson, 1996b). As strain theories would predict, a husband or father who is out of work may use violence to compensate for the feelings of inadequacy that the perceived failure to play the breadwinner role may promote (Frieze and Browne, 1989). This interpretation is consistent with the widely reported finding that rates of family violence are generally higher among lower-income groups (Klaus and Rand, 1984; Schwartz, 1988; Steinmetz, 1986; Straus and Smith, 1990). Strain may also arise from noneconomic sources such as illness or the death of a loved one. In the case of child abuse or elder abuse, strain may originate from the demands of the caregiving experience itself (Fattah and Sacco, 1989).

TRANSACTIONS

How frequent are violent events within the family? For reasons discussed in Chapter 7, traditional victimization surveys typically provide low estimates of levels of family violence. However, the Canadian Violence Against Women Survey (VAWS) reported that 29 percent of women 18 years of age or over who had ever been married had experienced some type of marital violence; 15 percent of those were with a current partner, and 48 percent were with a previous partner. Similarly, a moderate percentage of women also reported "severe" husband-to-wife violence: 11 percent said they had been kicked, bit, or hit with a fist; 6 percent said they had been hit with an object; 9 percent said they had been beaten up; 7 percent said they had been choked; 5 percent said they had been threatened with a gun or had a knife used on them; and 8 percent said they had been sexually assaulted (Rodgers and Kong, 1996).

Other studies that have used the Conflict Tactics Scale provide estimates of wife assault that suggest the problem is far from uncommon. A survey of Alberta couples by Kennedy and Dutton (1989) found that the rate of wife abuse was 11.2 percent overall and that the rate of severe abuse was 2.3 percent. In the city of Calgary, Brinkerhoff and Lupri (1988) found the overall rate to be 25 percent and the rate of severe abuse to be 11 percent. Smith (1988) reports that among married or cohabiting women in Toronto in 1987, the rate of overall abuse was approximately 14 percent and the rate of severe abuse about 5 percent. These figures suggest levels of violence that are comparable to those revealed by American researchers. A national survey of U.S. couples found that in 1985, 1 out of 8 husbands carried out one or more

Table 8.1   Husband-to-Wife Violence in Canada, 1993

Violent Act	Marital Partnerships					
	All Partners		Current Partners		Previous Partners	
	(000s)	%	(000s)	%	(000s)	%
Total[1]	2652	29	1020	15	1781	48
Threatened to hit her with something	1688	19	461	7	1292	35
Threw something that could hurt her	1018	11	237	4	804	21
Pushed, grabbed, or shoved	2221	25	819	12	1500	40
Slapped	1359	15	295	4	1103	30
Kicked, bit, or hit her with his fist	955	11	154	2	819	22
Hit her with something that could hurt her	508	6	80	1	434	12
Beat her up	794	9	94	1	716	19
Choked her	607	7	76	1	540	14
Threatened or used a gun or knife	417	5	44	1	379	10
Sexual assault	729	8	108	2	629	17

[1] Figures will not add up to totals because of multiple responses.

SOURCE: K. Rodgers and R. Kong, "Crimes against Women and Children in the Family." In L. Kennedy and V. Sacco (eds.), *Crime Counts: A Criminal Event Analysis*, pp. 115–32 (Scarborough, ON: Nelson Canada, 1996).

violent acts against their partners and more than 3 out of every 100 women were severely assaulted by their partners (Straus and Gelles, 1990a). Sometimes these conflicts can have more serious consequences. Silverman and Kennedy (1993) report that approximately 40 percent of all homicides that occurred in Canada over the last 30 years involved family members. Further, Wilson, Daly, and Wright (1993) report that the probability that a registered-married woman would be killed by her spouse is nine times the chance that she would be killed by a stranger.

When we look at the prevalence of abuse, we find high numbers of victims. Smith (1988) found that in Toronto the number of women who reported ever having been abused was greater than 36 percent. It is, of course, true that such numbers, as high as they are, underestimate the amount of violence that occurs between husbands and wives. Respondents may have no more reason to report such events to survey interviewers than they have to report them to the police.

We know less about violence against children than about violence between spouses but there is reason to believe that such violence is widespread. While we know that the rate of child homicide is about 2 1/2 times lower than the rate for adults, there is a lack of information about other forms of violence toward children (Johnson, 1995). As discussed, part of the problem in generating such data concerns the widespread attitude that—in the case of children—some types of violence, such as spanking, are permissible.

Data collected by American researchers are instructive in this respect. Straus and Gelles (1990) report that in surveys conducted in 1975 and 1985, over 90 percent of parents said they had hit their children. Further, with respect to severe violence (which includes hitting the child with an object), the rates are quite high; 11 out of every 100 parents reported hitting a child in a way that probably fits most people's definition of abuse. These results are consistent with those of a Toronto study by Lenton (1990), who states that relatively mild forms of violence are common and "even the most severe actions are not infrequent" (169). During the survey year, 12 percent of mothers and 15 percent of fathers reported that they had beaten their children.

Research on violent events involving elderly victims is still in its early stages, although one national survey has been undertaken by Podnieks (1990). The study investigated the incidence of several types of abuse among a representative national sample of noninstitutionalized elderly Canadians. Podnieks found that the overall rate of abuse was 40 per 1000 elderly people, a figure that translates into approximately 100 000 elderly people. However, most types of abuse revealed by the survey were nonviolent in nature. Using a modified form of the Conflict Tactics Scale, the study revealed the rate of violent victimization of elderly people by family members or other intimates to be 5 per 1000.

LOCATION AND TIMING OF FAMILY VIOLENCE

The location and timing of violent events in general reflect the importance of the precursors discussed previously. Most violent events involving family members occur in the home. Typically, spousal homicides occur in private residences (most usually the home of the victim) (Gartner and McCarthy, 1996). The reason for this pattern is fairly obvious: the home is where family members are most likely to confront each other and where privacy allows these events to develop.

Intrafamily violence is most likely to erupt in the evening or late at night. Arguments that begin in the early evening may turn violent if they are unresolved as the night wears on (Gelles and Straus, 1988). The late-night and early-morning hours bring with them a reduction in the options available through which the matter could be resolved without violence. It is too late to call a family member or to leave the house in order to visit a friend. Stressful events that fuel tensions or challenge parental or patriarchal authority increase the likelihood of a violent episode involving children. Despite the attention paid to the physical mistreatment of very young children, it appears that much violence is directed against teenage children, whose various forms of adolescent rebellion may be viewed as requiring strict physical discipline (Pagelow, 1989).

On some occasions, the factors that contribute to the likelihood of a violent event come into sharp relief. Gelles and Straus (1988) note that violent events occur with higher-than-usual frequency during the Christmas or Easter holidays. At these times, the sources of both economic and noneconomic stress

---

BOX 8.1   THE SUPER BOWL MYTH

Shortly before the 1993 Super Bowl, television and newspapers carried stories of research purporting to show that Super Bowl Sunday is the day of the year on which women face the greatest risk of domestic violence. The claim, which was actively promoted by a coalition of media watchdog and antiviolence organizations, was said to be empirically supported by research that provided unequivocal evidence of the Super Bowl effect.

The press actively promoted the story and provided a forum for a variety of "experts" who explained that the spectacle of the Super Bowl includes scantily clad cheerleaders, the legitimate use of physical violence, and highly paid, successful athletes with whom the male viewer at home might compare himself unfavourably. In short, Super Bowl Sunday should show the effects of a national celebration of machismo.

Although most of the press coverage was uncritical, a *Washington Post* writer, Ken Ringle, checked out the sources for the story. He found that the empirical evidence that supposedly provided support for the claim was lacking and that some of the experts who had been cited in the publicity wave that preceded the game had been misquoted. Moreover, those shelters and hotlines that monitored their calls for assistance very closely on Super Bowl Sunday in 1993 reported no variation in the number of calls received.

Despite the lack of evidence to support the claim that a widely watched sports spectacle produces dramatic increases in wife assault, the myth of the Super Bowl effect, like many criminological myths, continues to be widely quoted as fact.

SOURCE: Based on C.H. Sommers, *Who Stole Feminism?* (New York: Simon and Schuster, 1994).

may be especially pronounced. Family members spend more time than usual together and may entertain unrealistically positive expectations about how others will behave. In addition, family celebrations may involve drinking alcohol, which can facilitate the movement toward violence.

PATTERNS OF FAMILY VIOLENCE

Perhaps the most distinctive characteristic of family violence events is their repetitive and cyclical character. In contrast to forms of victimization that result from a chance encounter between victim and offender, the intimate relationships in which family members are involved increase the probability that violent events will reoccur or escalate. Minor acts of violence may be self-reinforcing when those who engage in them come to see violence as an effective means of achieving compliance and when the use of violence carries few sanctions (Johnson, 1996a). While most victims try to resist the physical violence, their resistance is more likely to be passive (reasoning with the offender, trying to get help) than active (Harlow, 1991; Klaus and Rand, 1984). Silverman and Kennedy (1993) note that most spousal homicides are not the result of a sudden "blowup," but rather represent the culmination of serial violence, which is fuelled by drugs and alcohol, a lack of problem-solving skills, and the effects of long-standing quarrels and antagonisms. Many cases of family violence escalate into more serious forms of victimization. At a minimum, the physical violence that does occur is probably part of a much larger pattern that involves a variety of forms of emotional and psychological mistreatment.

The violent events in a household may take on the character of routine activities (low-level conflict) that escalate to violence. The opportunities for this violence are facilitated by the privacy of the home, which protects the offenders from detection and provides them with objects with which to vent their anger. The violence is likely to be repeated (the opportunities for victimization rarely change) at least until the victim decides to flee or seek outside help.

THE AFTERMATH

Family violence may result in severe physical consequences, and even death. In fact, some evidence suggests that violence in the home is more likely than other types of violent episodes to result in injury (Harlow, 1991). This finding may be explained by the repetitive character of family violence and by the relatively limited ability of victims to escape such violent encounters.

SHORT- AND LONG-TERM CONSEQUENCES OF FAMILY VIOLENCE

Violence has emotional and psychological as well as physical effects. Victims of violence in the home, like other victims of violence, experience many forms of fear, trauma, and stress (Wirtz and Harrell, 1987). Indeed, violence in the home may be more likely than other forms of violence to produce these consequences (Gelles and Straus, 1990). Violence may be more threatening if it occurs in environments that individuals have defined as "safe" (Burgess, Holmstrom, and McCausland, 1977). In addition, being victimized by an intimate may produce greater stress since the victim has to cope with the fact that the violence has been at the hands of a trusted individual (Sales, Baum, and Shore, 1984).

Despite the seriousness of their injuries, victims may decline to seek medical aid so as to avoid having to explain to others the sources of the injury. The stigma of being a victim may also keep many from seeking help. Even when they do seek help, they may encounter emergency room personnel who are less than sympathetic. According to Kurz (1987), some ER personnel describe abused wives as "AOBs" (alcohol on breath) and as troublesome people who deserve the predicament in which they find themselves.

Victims of family violence may, for similar reasons, decline to report the incident to the police (Klaus and Rand, 1984). For many female victims of spousal abuse, calling the police is a last resort, even when the violence is severe (Kantor and Straus, 1987). Victimization surveys suggest that the victim's fear that the offender will retaliate through violence against the victim (and possibly against dependent children) figures largely in the decision not to report. The victim may also have concerns about how an arrest may lead to a loss of financial support (Steinman, 1992).

In the past, police have been reluctant to intervene in family situations or, when they did intervene, to remove the offender (most often the husband) from the situation to "cool off." Increasingly, however, the police are taking steps to invoke the law as it applies to family violence. Williams and Hawkins (1986) argue that applying sanctions to offenders may deter future offending. As was pointed out in our review of deterrence theories in Chapter 4, research has shown that there is a considerable stigma associated with arrest (Dutton et al., 1992).

There is also a strong sentiment among victim groups that more must be done to help victims of family violence. The number of safe houses is considered inadequate to meet the needs of women who feel at risk. At a more basic level, some claim, it is unfair that women have to flee their homes for safety's sake. Browne and Williams (1989) attribute the 25 percent reduction in female-perpetrated spousal homicide in the United States since 1980 to the fact that the public is more aware of the difficulties women face when dealing with violent spouses. Accompanying this awareness has been an increase in the resources available to women victims—resources that have enabled them to escape their partner's violence rather than suffer alone or respond with violence themselves.

Providing resources such as shelters is helpful in managing the more serious forms of violence, but the day-to-day problems that people encounter most often do not come to the attention of the authorities. Many of these problems are, however, known to neighbours, friends, and others. We are becoming increasingly aware of situations of serial violence, eventually resulting in homicide, in which outsiders knew of the conflict over a long period but were either reluctant to intervene or were not taken seriously by authorities when they attempted to do so.

One important issue being considered by researchers interested in the aftermath of family violence is the way in which violent behaviour by one family member promotes violent behaviour on the part of others. The fact that courts are becoming increasingly willing to accept the psychological consequences of violence as a defence for killing indicates that we cannot always rely on the notion of rational behaviour when judging why people act as they do. Arguments about acts performed in the "heat of passion" have always been recognized when one partner kills another in a jealous rage. However, the idea that violence begets violence is only now being viewed as contributing to a condition that may constitute a justifiable defence.

FAMILY VIOLENCE AND DELINQUENCY

In a related way, it has been argued that the use of physical violence against children may increase the risk that they will themselves behave in either violent or nonviolent criminal ways (Fleisher, 1995). Although physical punishment may induce conformity in children in the short run, over the longer term it may create the very problems it is intended to prevent (Straus, 1991).

How does physical violence against children increase the risks of their delinquency? Several types of effects may derive from such violence. First, social control theorists have argued that the bonds between juveniles and their parents (and other conformist models) provide a certain insulation against involvement in delinquency. A high degree of parental attachment means that the parent is better able to teach the positive social skills that facilitate an individual's success in the workplace or at school (Currie, 1985; Patterson and Dishion, 1985). Obviously, parental abuse may weaken this bond and lessen the degree of juvenile sensitivity to parental expectations of appropriate behaviour (Rankin and Wells, 1990).

Second, if a parent is abusive, the child or adolescent may seek to avoid contact. To the extent that delinquency is prevented by the ability of the parent to monitor and supervise the behaviour of children, delinquency in such situations may be expected to increase, as predicted by control theory (Gottfredson and Hirschi, 1990; Thornberry, 1987).

Third, violent delinquency may be a form of acting out on the part of the child (Agnew, 1985a). Children may run away from home or engage in other "escape crimes." Their resulting homelessness, combined with a lack of labour market skills, may increase the likelihood that they will make use of whatever delinquent or criminal opportunities present themselves in order to support themselves (McCarthy and Hagan, 1991). In addition, they may behave violently toward classmates or other acquaintances as a way of expressing their frustration about the abusive home situation.

Fourth, growing up in a violent home may provide children with lessons in the use of violence as a means of achieving goals and controlling others (Peek, Fischer, and Kidwell, 1985). A child who witnesses spousal violence may come

---

BOX 8.2 PREDATORY STREET CRIMINALS AND THEIR DEFENSIVE WORLD VIEW

Criminologist Mark S. Fleisher (1995) spent several years engaged in an ethnographic study of predatory street criminals in Seattle and other U.S. cities. His research suggests that the behaviour of these offenders is rooted in a "defensive world view" that finds its origins in the reaction to abusive and neglectful childrearing.

According to Fleisher, this defensive world view consists of six traits:

- a feeling of vulnerability and need to protect oneself
- a belief that no one can be trusted
- a need to maintain social distance
- a willingness to use violence and intimidation to repel others
- an attraction to similarly defensive people
- an expectation that no one will provide aid

While this world view enables youngsters who are threatened by their parents and other adults to protect themselves, it becomes maladaptive when they move into the larger social arena. Years of neglect by parents are followed by rejection by teachers and peers. The fear of interaction that the defensive world view promotes implies an isolation from influences that might encourage moral and cognitive maturity. For Fleisher, the "enculturation" into this world view is a natural and normal process and is unrelated to mental illness or psychopathology and cannot be easily fixed. The only solution is to remove these individuals from their abusive environments before the enculturation process begins.

to see it as a legitimate way of resolving conflict (Fagan and Wexler, 1987; McCord, 1991). According to Hotaling, Straus, and Lincoln (1990), homes in which child assault or spousal assault occurs have higher rates of sibling violence and higher rates of violence by the dependent children against children outside of the home.

CRIMES AGAINST THE HOUSEHOLD

Crimes against the household are very common in Canada (Gartner and Doob, 1994; Greenberg, 1996). Table 8.2 describes the rates of the various forms of household victimization investigated in the 1993 Canadian General Social Survey. Overall, the rate of reported household victimization is 190 incidents per 1000 households. Greenberg reports that even though the officially reported national rate for break and enter has fallen almost 9 percent since 1991, it still accounts for 15 percent of all Criminal Code incidents reported to the police.

PRECURSORS

The routine activities theory of predatory crime, which was described in Chapter 5, explains such crimes in terms of how offenders encounter opportunities for offending. With modern lifestyles forcing people to spend long periods outside of the home working or pursuing leisure activities, the household may remain unoccupied and unguarded, enhancing its appeal as a target for crime.

Not all households are equally likely to be victimized. The patterns of household victimization as revealed by victimization surveys and UCR data suggest that opportunities for property crimes are structured. In general, rates of household crime are higher in urban than in nonurban areas (Cohen and Cantor, 1981; Maguire and Bennett, 1982). For example, the 1993 General Social Survey revealed that the rates of household theft were 56 and 38 incidents per 1000 households for urban and rural areas respectively (Gartner and Doob, 1994). Such differences might be explained by the fact that formal and informal social controls are less effective in urban centres. Alternatively, larger cities may provide a fertile breeding ground for criminal subcultures that provide an intricate network for the distribution of stolen goods.

Not all urban neighbourhoods face the same risk of household crime. Residents of socially disadvantaged areas may face greater risks than do those

Table 8.2 Household Victimization Rates per 1000 Households, by Type of Incident, Urban/Rural Location, and Household Income, Canada 1992

Type of Incident

Household Characteristics	Break and Enter/Attempt	Motor Vehicle Theft/Attempt	Theft, Household and Property/ Attempt	Vandalism	Total Household
Canada	50	37	48	55	190
Urban	56	45	56	64	222
Rural	40	—	38	38	133
Income Groups					
<$15 000	57	—	—	43	154
15 000–29 999	46	—	44	51	172
30 000–39 999	77	54	—	58	239
40 000–59 999	56	51	58	75	240
60 000+	56	42	75	81	254

SOURCE: R. Gartner and A. Doob, "Trends in Criminal Victimization, 1988–1993" (*Juristat*, Statistics Canada, 1994).

who reside in more affluent areas (Evans, 1989; Maguire and Bennett, 1982). Low-income areas may have many characteristics that increase the risks of household crime. Lower income may translate into fewer precautions taken to protect the household—particularly when such precautions involve the use of limited discretionary income. Low-income areas also contain a disproportionate number of single-parent households, leaving children with generally lower levels of adult supervision (Maxfield, 1987; Smith and Jarjoura, 1989). Mixed land use in these areas may mean the presence of bars and stores that bring a large number of strangers through the neighbourhood. Under such conditions, it may be more difficult to know who does and who does not belong in an area (Lynch and Cantor, 1992). Finally, the greater degrees of residential instability and social heterogeneity in poor areas may undermine the development of collective community sentiments and thereby diminish effective informal social control at the local level (Smith and Jarjoura, 1988, 1989). In other words, as people become less tied to one another, they have less reason to worry about what others think and to conform to their expectations.

The fact that poor *areas* have higher rates of household victimization than more affluent ones does not necessarily mean that poorer *households* have higher rates of victimization than their more affluent counterparts (Maguire and Bennett, 1982). In fact, several studies have shown that the risk of many forms of household victimization does not have a clear-cut relationship with household income, and this is supported in the results presented in Table 8.2. Households with income of less than $15 000 reported break and enter rates of 57 incidents per 1000 households. Households with income of $60 000 were burglarized at essentially the same rate—56 incidents per 1000 households. This may be because offenders choose the more affluent targets in less affluent areas or the wealthier homes located near such areas (Waller and Okihiro, 1978; Cohen and Cantor, 1981; Cohen, Kluegel, and Land, 1981).

Victimization research also suggests that some types of housing structures are more susceptible to various forms of household crime than are others (Massey, Krohn, and Bonati, 1989). Most susceptible are those dwellings that offer the thief or the burglar easy access or that provide cover during the commission of the crime. Thus, the risk of breaking and entering is higher when a housing structure offers multiple points of entry, when doors or windows are covered by trees or shrubs, when the house is located on a corner or near a major route that allows easy escape, or when neighbours' houses do not directly overlook the target (Bennett and Wright, 1984; Evans, 1989).

Studies in which burglars themselves have served as informants have also provided information regarding what types of household settings are likely to be "high risk" for this type of victimization (Wright, Logie, and Decker, 1995). In a study with 100 convicted burglars, for example, Reppetto (1974) found that the burglars were able to identify several characteristics that made a household a more (or less) attractive target: ease of access, appearance of affluence, inconspicuous setting, isolation of the neighbourhood, absence of police patrols, and lack of surveillance by neighbours.

Burglary trends also seem to vary somewhat by time of day. Many studies have found burglaries are quite likely to occur when houses are empty, often during daylight hours (Evans, 1989; Mirrlees-Black, Mayhew, and Percy, 1996). The rhythms and tempos of family life affect the risk of household crime in other ways. A good deal of traffic in and out of the home is an expected characteristic of large families. Doors are more likely to be left open or unlocked, and property may not always be put away, which makes such homes an attractive target for thieves (Smith and Jarjoura, 1989). The summer months, which bring warm temperatures, open windows, and houses left empty by vacationers, may also increase the opportunities for household crime (Sacco and Johnson, 1990; Waller and Okihiro, 1978). UCR data show that in 1994, 56 percent of breaking and entering occurred in summer and autumn, while only 44 percent occurred in spring (Chard, 1995).

While we may think about opportunities for crime as an objective feature of the social environment (an open door invites theft), the situation is more complicated than this. Criminal opportunities also have a subjective quality. For criminal events to occur, a potential offender must define the open door as an opportunity for theft. While one person might see the large shrubs blocking a residential window as nothing more than interesting landscaping, another might see this shrubbery as providing cover during a robbery attempt.

What are the characteristics of the property offender? Like many other types of predatory offenders, these individuals tend disproportionately to be young males, many of whom come from socially disadvantaged backgrounds (Maguire and Bennett, 1982; Waller and Okihiro, 1978). Data from the 1994 UCR show that 96 percent of all persons arrested in incidents in which breaking and entering was the most serious offence were males; 31 percent of these were between the ages of 18 and 24, and 24 percent were between the ages of 25 and 34. Similarly, although females made up only 4 percent of those arrested for breaking and entering, 85 percent of these women were under the age of 35 (Chard, 1995).

PROFESSIONAL VS. AMATEUR THIEVES

It is useful to distinguish between two broad types of property offenders (Evans, 1989). On the one hand, there is the professional offender, who is sometimes characterized as the "good burglar" (Shover, 1973, 1983) and as the "elite of the criminal world" (Cromwell, Olson, and Avary, 1991). They have a considerable degree of technical competence and are connected to a network of other thieves and tipsters as well as fences to whom the stolen property is sold. Professional thieves think of themselves as "specialists" and understand their offending in occupational terms; they speak of pulling a "job" or "working" a particular area (Maguire and Bennett, 1982). The crimes in which they engage are generally said to reflect careful planning that involves a rational assessment of the specific risks and benefits.

The professional offender usually figures very prominently in media portrayals of household crime and police rhetoric about the typical offender. However, several researchers argue that popular images of the cool, calculating, highly specialized, and rational property offender may be exaggerated. According to Cromwell et al. (1991), much of what we know about such offenders comes from interviews with offenders or ex-offenders who may engage in **rational reconstruction.** In other words, in recalling their crimes, they suggest that far more planning took place than was actually the case. While professionals sometimes are said to seek opportunities for crime,

Cromwell and his colleagues maintain that these offenders do not so much seek opportunities as develop a special sensitivity to the opportunities they happen to encounter.

Hough (1987) suggests that, despite the activities of some unspecified number of professional household thieves, these individuals are probably responsible for only a minority of the crimes revealed in victimization surveys. This speculation is supported by the fact that such surveys generally uncover large numbers of crimes that point to amateurish offenders with little technical knowledge or experience (Felson, 1994). Many household crimes are committed by unsophisticated offenders, the majority of whom are probably juveniles. These **occasional offenders** commit crimes when opportunities or situational inducements present themselves (Evans, 1989). Property crimes such as theft and breaking and entering (irrespective of the level of professionalism of the offender) are motivated by instrumental needs (Bennett and Wright, 1984). These crimes do not reflect expressive needs like anger or revenge, but rather are prompted by a desire on the part of the offender to obtain the property of the victim.

Engagement in household theft, as well as movement out of this type of crime with advancing age, can be understood in terms of control theory. Household theft is a crime that easily resists detection (Maguire and Bennett, 1982). Offenders learn from their own and others' experiences that the chances of getting caught in the commission of any particular crime are very slim (Bennett and Wright, 1984). They also recognize, however, that if they become known to the police as thieves and they fail to vary their method of crime commission, their chances of getting caught become greater over time, thus reducing the attractiveness of this form of crime (Cromwell et al., 1991). While the professional thief may be said to have a lengthy criminal career, a substantial number of juvenile offenders commit crimes only rarely, and do so with even less frequency as they get older (Shover, 1983). The number of repeat offenders as measured by the recidivism rate for burglary is higher than that for many other crimes, but many juvenile offenders do not repeat the crime at all (Maguire and Bennett, 1982).

As events, crimes against the household can be relatively uncomplicated affairs. An opportunistic thief may pass a house and notice some item of value lying unguarded on the front lawn or in the driveway (Lynch and Cantor, 1992). Seeing no one about, the thief will grab the item and continue on his or her way. Similarly, under cover of darkness in the early hours of the morning, the thief may happen upon an unlocked car and steal either its contents or the car itself.

The crime of breaking and entering varies in terms of how much planning it requires. In a large number of these events, young offenders target a house not far from their own residence (Brantingham and Brantingham, 1984; Cohen and Cantor, 1981; Hough, 1987). The proximity of the target may reflect two distinct considerations: (1) offenders' relatively limited mobility (they may be too young to drive) and (2) offenders' direct knowledge of both the contents and routine activities of the households they encounter in the course of their own routine activities. In such cases, entry may be "child's play" (Maguire and Bennett, 1982). The offender tests the door and, if it is open, enters the house. (According to the 1994 Uniform Crime Report, 81 percent of breaking and entering crimes involved forcible entry—88 percent for business premises, 79 percent for residential premises.) The thief moves through the house quickly, more interested in getting in and out with something of value than with the wanton destruction of property (Maguire and Bennett, 1982; Waller and Okihiro, 1978). The items stolen may include money, alcohol, and light electronic goods such as portable TV sets or VCRs.

The more professional burglar may select a target more carefully. The selection process may include several stages as the offender makes decisions about which neighbourhood, which block in the neighbourhood, and which house on the block will be victimized (Taylor and Gottfredson, 1986). Relationships may be cultivated with "tipsters" who can provide information about vacant homes and potentially large "scores" (Shover, 1973). Some tipsters may be "fences" who are attempting to boost their inventory, while others may be thieves who for some reason are unable to undertake the crime themselves. Additionally, thieves may, in the course of their regular travels through the neighbourhood, be attentive to homes that appear empty or that promise easy entry. Waiting at a traffic light may provide potential burglars with the opportunity to view potential targets without attracting attention (Cromwell et al., 1991).

RISK, EASE OF ENTRY, AND REWARD

Irrespective of the level of professionalism, burglars who are intent on breaking and entering must consider three questions: (1) Can they get away with the crime (risk)? (2) Can they commit the crime without great difficulty (ease)? and (3) Can they get anything out of it (reward)? (Bennett, 1989). Of these three factors, the first (degree of risk) is probably the most important (Bennett and Wright, 1984). Homes that provide cover from surveillance by other homes present the offender with fewer risks. The mere presence of passersby may not influence the decision to offend, since thieves are concerned not about being seen but about being seen *and* reported (Cromwell et al., 1991).

The occupancy of the household may be the most important aspect of risk. The presence of a car in the driveway or signs of movement or activity in the house may encourage the potential offender to look elsewhere (Bennett, 1989).

Some offenders may engage in more sophisticated **occupancy probes** in order to establish whether the household is vacant.

An occupied home is to be avoided not only because of the risk of detection but also because of a concern on the part of the offender that, if someone is home, the crime of breaking and entering could escalate into a more serious offence. Some researchers (Kennedy and Silverman 1990; Maxfield, 1990) have observed that, although a rare occurrence, there is a higher-than-expected number of homicides involving elderly victims in their homes. This may be due to the fact that the elderly occupy households that appear uninhabited during the day. The burglar surprised by an unexpected encounter may strike out against the elderly person, with fatal consequences. The occurrence of such

---

BOX 8.3   OCCUPANCY PROBES

In their interviews with burglars, Cromwell, Olson, and Avary (1991) discovered that these offenders use several imaginative methods to determine whether anyone is home.

1. If working as part of a team, the most "presentable" burglar knocks on the door or rings the doorbell. If someone answers, the burglar asks for directions or for a nonexistent person.

2. The burglar rings the doorbell and, if someone answers, claims that his or her car broke down and that he or she needs to use the phone. If the resident refuses, the burglar may leave without attracting suspicion. If the resident consents, the burglar may have an opportunity to check out the merchandise in the home as well as whatever security measures may exist.

3. The burglar telephones the residence to be broken into from a nearby phone. The burglar then returns to the residence. If he or she can hear the telephone ringing, it is unlikely that anyone is at home.

4. The burglar targets a house next to a residence that has a "for sale" sign on the front lawn. Posing as a buyer, the burglar can examine the target household from the vantage of the sale property.

One informant in the Cromwell et al. study would dress in a tracksuit, jog to the front door of the target household, remove a piece of mail from the potential victim's mailbox, and ring the doorbell. If anyone answered, he would say that he found the letter and was returning it. The tracksuit suggested a reason why a stranger might be ringing a doorbell in the neighbourhood, while the apparently neighbourly gesture suggested that the burglar was a good citizen and therefore above suspicion.

---

unpremeditated homicides, coupled with uncompleted burglaries due to the presence of the householder, suggests that offenders may not be quite as adept at assessing occupancy as is sometimes thought (Hough, 1987).

The second factor (ease of entry) concerns the relative difficulty burglars encounter in attempting to enter the residence. In general, this factor cannot be assessed until the offence is underway (Bennett and Wright, 1984). In many cases, it is a simple matter to break a door or a window; even the presence of special locks and security hardware may not serve as a strong deterrent (Lynch and Cantor, 1992; Maguire and Bennett, 1982). However, while many professional burglars report that they can, if required, deal effectively with alarms or watchdogs, they also report that the large number of households that are unprotected by such measures makes attempted burglary of protected homes unnecessary (Maguire and Bennett, 1982).

The final factor (the potential reward) is probably the least important consideration. Offenders who engage in breaking and entering may be unable to determine before the commission of the crime whether anything of value is to be gained (Lynch and Cantor, 1992; Miethe and Meier, 1994). As noted previously, information from a tipster may decrease uncertainty, and higher-status households may hold the promise of greater rewards. However, in most situations, the thief can be relatively certain that something of value will be collected in the course of the crime (Cromwell, Olsen, and Avary, 1991).

THE AFTERMATH

Data from the 1994 Uniform Crime Report indicate that 83 percent of residential burglaries reported resulted in some economic/monetary loss; about 50 percent of these involved losses of $500 or more. The most common stolen items included audio-visual equipment (such as televisions and stereos)—these comprised 30 percent of residential burglaries. Some of the net loss for property crimes may be mitigated by either recovery or insurance. Members of lower-income groups, who are less likely to have insurance, generally experience the greatest net loss for household crimes (Chard, 1995).

Such figures provide only a partial picture of the impact of household crime. Incidents of illegal entry that escalate into assaults, robberies, sexual assaults, or homicides have very direct and immediate physical consequences (Warr, 1988). Because incidents of this type are relatively rare, and because household crimes generally involve rather small net losses, these crimes are sometimes assumed to have little psychological impact on victims. Such is not the case, especially with respect to breaking and entering. Many victims—particularly women—may be badly shaken by the event (Maguire and Bennett, 1982).

Figure 8.1   Economic Costs of Residential Burglary, 1994

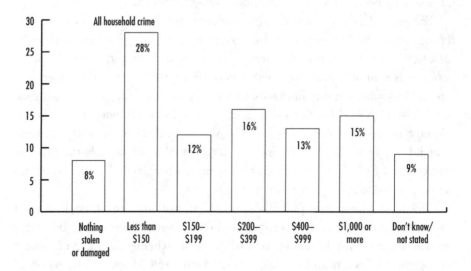

SOURCE: Statistics Canada, *Canadian Crime Statistics*. Annual report (Ottawa: Supply and Services Canada, 1995).
Reproduced with permission of the Ministry of Public Works and Government Services Canada, 1997.

Victims may experience feelings of vulnerability, concern that the offender will
return, and fear of being alone, even in situations that are not directly related
to household crime. They may also experience long-term sleeping disorders or
require tranquillizers for an extended period. Maguire and Bennett (1982)
report that, in a sample of British burglary victims, negative effects were
reported by 65 percent of the victims four to six weeks after the crime.

Like other criminal events, many crimes against the household are not
reported to the police. Data from the 1993 General Social Survey indicate that,
in 1992, about 52 percent of all household crimes were reported (68 percent
of attempted or successful breaking and entering, 52 percent of attempted or
successful motor vehicle theft, 43 percent of attempted or successful theft of
household property, and 46 percent of vandalism) (Gartner and Doob, 1994).
Most people failed to report household crime because they felt it was too
minor (Gartner and Doob, 1994).

Crimes against the household also indicate that it is *what happens to the
victim* rather than *who the victim is* that determines whether an event will be
reported (Evans, 1989). In other words, the likelihood of reporting is not very
strongly related to the social and demographic characteristics of victims.
Instead, the crime is more likely to be reported when it has characteristics that

might be interpreted as indicators of greater seriousness, such as when there is evidence of forced entry or malicious destruction and when the loss is relatively high (Waller and Okihiro, 1978). Thus, unreported household crimes, at least in the legal context, are generally less serious than those that come to the attention of the police (Maguire and Bennett, 1982).

Victims who report household crime do so with the hope that the police will be able to apprehend the offender and recover the stolen property. At a minimum, victims expect that the police will undertake an investigation and treat them with some sympathy (Maguire and Bennett, 1982). In the aftermath of household crime, victims may seek the assistance of a friend, neighbour, or landlord in addition to, or instead of, the police. When losses are substantial, victims may seek compensation through private insurance.

Reported household crimes carry with them a low certainty of arrest. According to Fedorowycz (1992) about three-quarters of break and enters are not "cleared"; among those that are cleared, only 18 percent are cleared by charge. The low clearance rates for such crimes results from the fact that, by the time they are reported to the police, the perpetrator is long gone. In addition, unlike in the typical crime of violence, there is no immediate suspect (Maguire and Bennett, 1982).

In the aftermath of the crime, offenders are probably less concerned with arrest than with the uses to which the stolen merchandise might be put. Cash or alcohol may be used for "partying." Although some stolen merchandise may be kept and used by the offender, there is a limit to how much loot one can put to personal use. Retaining too many stolen goods may also increase the risk of arrest.

Much of what is stolen may be converted into cash through the sale of merchandise. Although a substantial market exists for stolen goods (Cromwell and McElrath, 1994), particularly lightweight electronic goods, offenders recoup a relatively small amount from each item. Some stolen goods are sold directly to private buyers for their own use. Such people may see this exchange not as a criminal activity but as "good business." Their reasoning may be, "It was already stolen and if I don't buy it someone else will" (Cromwell, Olson, and Avary, 1991). Merchandise is also sold to "fences," who purchase the items for the purpose of resale. Some fences are businesspersons who do not have a criminal record, while others are ex-thieves (Maguire and Bennett, 1982).

One popular public response to the increase in property crime has been to make homes less vulnerable to attack. "Target-hardening" activities include installing deadbolt locks and bars on windows, purchasing alarms and watchdogs, and developing programs (such as Neighbourhood Watch) that increase the surveillance of property. Such forms of protection are becoming a routine part of architectural design, with notions of "defensible space" governing how many residential areas are constructed (Newman, 1972).

■ ■ ■

SUMMARY

Violent events within families can be partially attributed to the values that our society places on family privacy. Feminist researchers see family violence as reflecting the differential power within families, whereby men use violence against women and children as a form of control over their actions (Simpson, 1989: 611).

For a more complete understanding of family violence, we must also consider the stresses placed on families, the reluctance of victims to report the violence, the modelling of parental behaviour in managing conflict and anger, the breakdown of social control mechanisms that restrain interpersonal violence, and the paucity of deterrence strategies. The discovery in recent years of the extent of family violence, coupled with changes in societal values, has been influential in defining violent events within families as criminal events. Changes in the laws and in the police enforcement of those laws have come increasingly to reinforce such a definition.

Property crime is a booming business. The target of most of this crime is the household, which is filled with portable appliances that can be easily transported and resold. Much property crime is opportunistic in nature, involving the presence of a thief at a place and time in which property is unguarded and easy to steal. A good deal of the property crime committed by youthful offenders falls into this category. The more complicated crime of breaking and entering, which often requires considerable planning and technical expertise, tends to be committed by professional burglars, who not only take the time to plan the event but also ensure that the merchandise can be disposed of after the fact. Sometimes, due to a miscalculation on the part of the offender, residents may be unexpectedly encountered in the course of a household burglary; the consequences—especially for elderly victims—can be fatal.

Many property crimes are not reported to the police. People who do not report may feel either that there is little that the police can do to solve the crime or that the crime is not serious enough to warrant such action. Increasingly, homeowners are engaging in target-hardening activities intended to discourage both opportunistic and professional burglars.

There is increased interest in dealing with crimes that both occur in and are directed toward the household. Intrafamily violence is attracting a great deal of public concern, and there have been demands that more action (in the form of education and changes in the law) be taken to reduce the likelihood that such violence will occur. Attempts have been made to give victims of family violence greater protection under the law and to provide them with safe havens, as well as to treat offenders. (We will examine these actions in greater detail in Chapter 11.) As our review of family violence has shown, it is important to consider different theoretical approaches to the problem. New perspectives that draw attention to such things as power differentials in the family have become increasingly effective in providing us with explanations of family violence and in suggesting ways in which we should respond to it.

There are many different views about why people are motivated to commit property crimes as well. Obviously, not everyone who is given the opportunity to steal does so. Depending on your view of human behaviour, you might assume that people will steal if they know they won't get caught (social control), if they see others doing the same thing (cultural influence), or if they feel pressured by social circumstances (strain). All of these explanations of motivation rely on the idea that the offender has the opportunity (and some skills) to commit the crime and little fear of apprehension. Limiting opportunities should provide the most effective means of reducing this type of crime.

■ ■ ■

QUESTIONS FOR REVIEW AND DISCUSSION

1. Why has there been so much resistance to the claim that family violence is a serious problem?
2. How can we use strain theory to explain wife assault?
3. Many people would argue that sibling violence is normal and that this kind of violence is very different from the kinds of violence that we label "wife assault" or "child abuse." Do you agree with this statement? Why or why not?
4. Recently, many notorious court cases have revolved around family violence issues (for example, the Lorena Bobbitt, Menendez brothers, and O.J. Simpson cases). Is the high level of media attention devoted to these cases a good thing or a bad thing in your opinion?
5. Marcus Felson has argued that over the past few decades, the decrease in levels of household occupancy and the proliferation of "lightweight durable consumer goods" has resulted in a "deskilling of crime." How valid is this proposition with respect to crimes against the household?
6. With respect to your own residence, how might a potential thief or burglar make decisions about "risk," "ease," and "reward"?

CHAPTER NINE

Leisure

WHAT'S IN CHAPTER NINE

In this chapter, we look at the social domain of leisure to examine the nature of crime that takes place when people pursue recreation and leisure activities. Here, we examine the view that leisure actually acts as a corrupter of youth and makes social control difficult. The contexts in which leisure-based criminal events take place include the street and bars, dating relationships, and vacation travel.

INTRODUCTION

In this chapter, we discuss a second social domain that is significant to the study of criminal events—the leisure domain. As we will see, the relationship between leisure and crime has several interesting dimensions. People who are "at leisure" seem to be particularly susceptible to the risk of many different types of criminal victimization. Moreover, many types of offending—particularly juvenile offending—are themselves forms of leisure. Our language reflects this fact when, for instance, we describe illegal drug use as "recreational drug use" or when we describe stealing a car to use for fun as "joyriding." The leisure preferences of young people may also be seen as a cause of crime. This is evident in periodic scares in our society about the criminogenic effects of violent television, popular music, fantasy role-playing games, and video games.

We will also see that certain leisure settings, such as bars and sports complexes, are frequently scenes of crime and victimization. The street is also a likely location for crime victimization, as we begin to adopt lifestyles that take us away from our homes and into public areas in search of leisure pursuits. We begin our review of the relationship between leisure and criminal activities with a discussion of the concept of leisure.

WHAT IS LEISURE?

Leisure can be defined in a variety of ways (Wilson, 1980). Frequently, we use the term in an objective way to describe the "spare time" or "free time" that is left over after paid work or other obligations (such as child care) have been taken care of (Iso-Ahola, 1980). However, leisure has a subjective as well as objective character. In other words, leisure is not just free time, but rather free time that is used in a particular way—usually for play or recreation. Leisure activity may be regarded as intrinsically satisfying in that it contains its own rewards (Roberts, 1983). In addition, we usually assume that leisure activities are freely chosen and that leisure interaction occurs among peers. By contrast, family- or work-related activities tend to be less voluntaristic and to be characterized by authority relations that are enforced by law or custom.

Like other scarce resources, leisure time is unequally distributed (Jones, 1994). Teenagers and the elderly tend to have more leisure time than young parents or middle-aged individuals. And because household tasks and child care responsibilities reduce free time, men generally have more leisure time than women. People also differ with respect to their leisure preferences and the resources they have to pursue them. Those in higher-income groups are more likely to frequent restaurants, while young people are more likely to go to bars, movies, or video arcades (Provenzo, 1991). The elderly are less likely to go out in the evening for leisure of any kind (Golant, 1984); elderly people who do engage in leisure outside the home tend to visit friends or family.

The amount of leisure time that people have available to them and the uses to which they put it are important elements of what we refer to as lifestyle, a concept introduced in Chapter 5. Moreover, the leisure content of people's lifestyles has important implications for the kinds of criminal events in which they are involved, whether as offenders or victims. Opportunity theories are particularly attentive to the linkage between lifestyle and crime.

PRECURSORS

What does leisure have to do with the timing, location, and relative involvement of particular types of people in particular types of criminal events? There are two answers to this question. One stresses the ways in which specific types of leisure activities motivate offenders toward or free them from constraints against offending. The other suggests that leisure activities and settings facilitate encounters between offenders and potential victims. These perspectives are not contradictory, but they do differ in their fundamental emphases. While the former is offender-centred, the latter is opportunity-centred.

LEISURE AS A CORRUPTER

Arguments about the corrupting influences of leisure have typically been made with respect to the youthful offender. Throughout this century, every major form of youth leisure preference has been characterized by interest groups as a corrupter of young people. Feature films, rock and roll, rap and heavy metal music, video games, comic books, and Saturday morning cartoons have all, at one time or another, been accused of weakening youthful inhibitions, providing negative role models, destroying childhood, and disrupting the bonds between adolescents and adult authority figures (Best, 1990; Gray, 1989; Tanner, 1996).

Literally hundreds of studies have investigated the potentially negative effects of television violence, and the issue has been the focus of attention from the general public as well as Royal Commissions in Canada and presidential panels in the United States. The argument that television violence has some causal relationship with real-life violence would seem to be supported by much anecdotal evidence (in the form of so-called copycat crimes, for example) and by common sense. We know that television is a powerful persuader; otherwise,

BOX 9.1 TELEVISION VIOLENCE

Public concern about television reached another high in the early 1990s. In 1992, a 14-year-old student from Quebec named Virginie Larivière launched a petition drive intended to affect public policy regarding the violent content of Canadian television. The teenager's action was prompted by the rape, robbery, and murder of her 11-year-old sister, actions she attributed to media violence. Her petitions, which were signed by 1.3 million Canadians, were presented to the communications minister and to the prime minister.

On November 18, 1992, the House of Commons referred the petition of Virginie Larivière to the consideration of the Standing Committee on Communications and Culture (1993). After conducting hearings on the subject of television violence, the committee issued its report, *Television Violence: Fraying Our Social Fabric*. Among the committee's findings were the following:

1. Canadians who watch a large number of American television programs are exposed to a high level of television violence.

2. Television violence is one of many factors that may contribute to real-life violence, although these effects are not clear and require further study.

3. The problem of violence should be addressed cooperatively by all the players—including the industry, parents, and government—and with minimal legislative intervention.

4. An amendment of the Criminal Code is needed to control extremely violent forms of entertainment, such as slasher/snuff films and videos.

advertisers would not spend so much money buying commercial time in order to convince consumers to purchase their products. We also know that television is a violent medium and that young people (who are most likely to behave violently) have high levels of exposure to such content.

However, despite anecdotal evidence and commonsense notions, the nature and significance of the effects of televised violence are unclear. The effects of television violence on criminal motivation are likely limited by several factors. First, UCR data indicate that violent crimes make up a small proportion of total crime. Therefore, unless we want to argue that violent portrayals affect nonviolent crime in some as yet undetermined fashion, the amount of crime that could be causally linked to violent content is going to be limited, even if

Much of the concern about leisure as a corrupter of youth is fuelled by perceptions of rising rates of youth violence. According to Doherty and De Souza (1996), people aged 12–17 made up 8 percent of the Canadian population in 1993 but accounted for 14 percent of persons accused of violent incidents and 25 percent of persons accused in property incidents. Of the youths charged with violent offences in 1993, 49 percent were charged with minor assault. Between 1986 and 1993, the number of youths who were charged with violent offences increased at a faster rate than the number of adults who were charged with similar offences. As the authors suggest, this rapid growth in violence among youth appears to be the result of better reporting and less tolerance on the part of government, school, and police officials rather than a true reflection of actual increases in youth crime (Doherty and De Souza, 1996: 237).

the effects on violence are substantial. In fact, some researchers have suggested that the real effects of television may be on property rather than violent crimes (Hennigen et al., 1982). The basis for this argument is that the media emphasis on consumerism raises expectations about the amounts of material goods to which people think they are entitled (Surette, 1992). The link between television and property crime has not, however, received sufficient research attention to warrant firm conclusions.

Second, given that criminal motivation is a complex issue, whatever effects media exposure produces must be understood in the context of many other factors that encourage or restrain offending. The amount of variation attributable to media exposure is likely to be smaller than many observers would argue. Some researchers claim that 5 to 10 percent of the difference between violent and nonviolent behaviour may be attributed to exposure to media violence (Surette, 1992). Whether this means that television violence is a relatively important or unimportant factor in real-life violence remains unresolved.

Third, while many research experiments have been able to show that exposure to violent content in the laboratory setting triggers violent arousal, the same effects are not necessarily produced by media exposure in the real world. In laboratory experiments, subjects may be encouraged to behave violently (or at least not discouraged from doing so); by contrast, violent behaviour in most

**Figure 9.1   Youth Court Cases by Offence Category, Canada, 1986–1987
and 1993–1994**

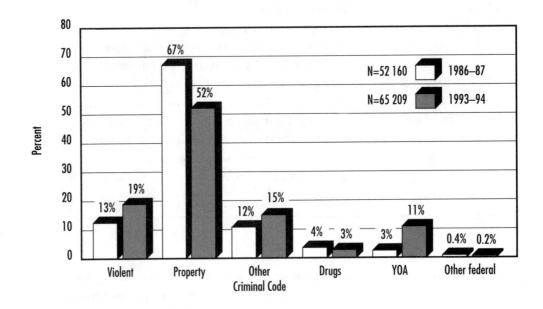

¹ Data for this period exclude Ontario and the Northwest Territories.

SOURCE: Paul De Souza (1995), "Youth Court Statistics, 1993–94 Highlights," Statistics Canada, *Juristat*, Catalogue No. 85-002, Volume 15, Number 9 (January): 7.

social contexts is discouraged. Also, the ways in which violence is measured in the lab (for example, the willingness of children to play with violent toys or of subjects to administer a harmless electrical shock to another person) may not have much to do with the willingness of people to beat, assault, rob, or kill others. Studies that attempt to link television violence to aggressive behaviour in real-life settings have frequently been less successful than those that try to find these effects in the laboratory.

As the preceding discussion suggests, the relationship between television violence and criminal violence is more complicated, and perhaps less substantial, than we sometimes think. Much of the research supports the view that television violence may influence the behaviour of a pool of at-risk individuals who may be particularly susceptible to its effects. In other words, television violence may be most likely to affect the behaviour of individuals already predisposed to behave aggressively. Unfortunately, we lack detailed knowledge of the size of this at-risk pool or of the factors that put them at risk. The effect of media violence may be not to cause interpersonal aggression in any direct way, but rather to reinforce pre-existing tendencies or to shape them in particular ways. In the case of copycat crimes, for instance, media violence may not motivate someone to commit a crime, but it may affect *how* that person commits a crime.

In many cases, the effects of television (or movie) violence may be short-term. Anyone who has ever left a movie theatre feeling excited or energized may intuitively understand the nature of this temporary arousal. We also know that such effects tend to dissipate rather quickly as we return to the family, work, or school responsibilities that structure our lives. Thus, whether people behave violently subsequent to such arousal may have as much to do with the situations and circumstances in which they find themselves as with their level of arousal. It is also important to note, though, that we know relatively less about the long-term effects of high levels of violent content in media on cultural beliefs and social practices.

The work of sociologist David Phillips (1983) illustrates how some of the effects might work. In a number of studies, Phillips has shown that media portrayals of homicide or suicide may exert temporary effects on the rates of such behaviour. In the case of homicide, for instance, Phillips studied what happened to homicide rates after highly publicized prizefights. These media events are particularly interesting because they involve violence that is both widely publicized and generally condoned rather than condemned. In a careful assessment of homicide trends, Phillips was able to show that in the few days immediately following a highly publicized fight, homicide rates increased by about 12 percent and that such effects could not be attributed to seasonal, monthly, or other temporal patterns.

Much of the rancorous public debate about television violence has recently begun to find a parallel expression in debates about video games. Not only is the content of these games typically violent, but, because they are interactive, it is argued that they may be more likely than television viewing to produce delinquency. While we have not yet amassed a significant body of research on the subject of the criminogenic influences of video games, thus far, concerns about the effects of these games on serious criminal offending seem to be overstated (Provenzo, 1991).

Debates about the corrupting influence of popular culture are not restricted to juveniles. Public alarm about the effects of pornography on sex crimes reflects concerns similar to those voiced by the critics of television violence. Yet, in a similar way, attempting to draw direct causal links between violent pornography (for example, "slasher" movies that combine sexual scenes with violent ones) and sex crimes ignores the complexity of the issue. A large body of experimental literature suggests that exposure to such pornography promotes negative attitudes toward women, a greater acceptance of rape myths (for example, that rape victims are to blame for what happens to them), and a decreased sensitivity toward female victims of violence (Malamuth, 1983; Malamuth and Donnerstein, 1984). Yet, as in the case of television violence, the effects of violent pornography on perpetrators of sex crimes may be most evident in men who are already predisposed to behave violently toward women.

LEISURE AND FREEDOM FROM SOCIAL CONTROL

In the case of juveniles, it is sometimes argued that patterns of leisure activity increase the likelihood that crimes will occur by freeing youth from the social controls that might be expected to check or restrain delinquent conduct. This position builds on the arguments suggested in the theories presented in Chapter 4.

Juvenile leisure is most frequently pursued out of the sight of parents or teachers and in the presence of peers (Agnew and Peterson, 1989; Osgood et al., 1996). The modern video arcade, like the pool hall of an earlier era, is off-limits to adults. "Hanging out" at the video arcade or mall or on the street corner may provide the behavioural freedom that makes group delinquency possible. A study by Riley (1987) of juvenile crime in England and Wales found that offenders and nonoffenders engaged in different types of leisure activities. Nonoffenders generally spent more time with parents and around the home, while offenders were more likely to spend their time in peer activities away from home. In addition, offenders were more often out in the evening, were expected home later, and were more likely to spend their money on youth-oriented amusements. Such leisure activities remove some of the obstacles to delinquency by lessening the chances of apprehension and by providing exposure to behavioural contexts that facilitate delinquent action.

By contrast, leisure activities organized by adults or leisure time spent with parents may be expected to decrease the possibilities of delinquency by strengthening social bonds and thereby rendering delinquency less attractive (Agnew, 1985a; Messner and Blau, 1987). One study found that, while "hanging out" and social activities such as dating and partying were associated with higher levels of delinquent involvement, organized leisure was associated with lower levels of delinquent involvement (Agnew and Peterson, 1989). The researchers also reported, however, that it is not sufficient for youths to be engaged in "positive" leisure for a decrease in delinquency to occur—they also must enjoy the activity. In other words, coercive leisure cannot be expected to bring about a decrease in offending behaviour.

The role of leisure in the development or the freeing of delinquent motivation may have more to do with the behaviour of males than of females (Riley, 1987). In part, as power control theory has argued, this is because female adolescents have traditionally been subject to higher levels of control, which restrict their leisure options (Hagan, Gillis, and Simpson, 1985; Singer and Levine, 1988). These gender differences may be rooted in patterns of family socialization. As we saw in Chapter 4, while risk-taking behaviour is encouraged in male children, female children are generally subjected to significantly greater degrees of parental control. Gender differences in delinquent leisure may reflect these patterned gender differences in risk taking and control.

However, according to Tanner (1996), it is important to note that in addition to parental controls, the behaviour of boys exerts a significant effect on the routine leisure activities of female adolescents. Girls are often missing from deviant youth cultures because males exclude them. Male delinquents do not always relish female participation except as ancillaries or as objects of sexual goals. As Tanner points out, there is really no reason to think that delinquent males are any less sexist than nondelinquent males.

LEISURE ACTIVITIES AND OPPORTUNITIES

Leisure activities provide important occasions for criminal events of various types, as evidenced by the times and places at which crimes occur. A large number of personal victimizations occur during the evenings and on weekends when most people are "at rest," when they have dropped their more serious work roles, and when the formal social controls of the school and the workplace are not operative (Luckenbill, 1977; Melbin, 1987). Personal victimizations also occur disproportionately in leisure settings—informal contexts that host a wide range of activities such as drinking, gambling, dancing, and playing games. In a study of high-school youth in Tucson, Arizona, Jensen and Brownfield (1986) found partying, cruising, and visiting bars—in general, the social pursuit of fun—to be significantly related to victimization risk.

Bars are good examples of such **permissive environs.** Not only are bars themselves the site of large numbers of criminal events, but so are the blocks on which they are located (Roncek and Maier, 1991; Roncek and Pravatiner, 1989). There are many reasons for this. Bars do most of their business in the evenings when people are freed from many of the social controls that structure their working days. Bars also deal in cash and liquor, which are easily stolen and easily used by the offender. Further, bars tend to place no real restrictions on who can enter, and they are particularly popular among young people. Finally, for many people, the consumption of alcohol increases the probability of interpersonal conflicts and impairs judgments about the scale of these conflicts (Engs and Hanson, 1994).

More generally, activities that bring people out of their homes in the evening increase the likelihood of personal and household crime (Kennedy and Forde, 1990). Messner and Blau (1987) found that the volume of leisure activity in the home (indexed by levels of reported television viewing) is related to lower rates of victimization, while the volume of leisure activity outside of the home (indexed by the number of sports and theatrical facilities) is related to higher rates of victimization.

A similar and consistent pattern has been revealed by victimization surveys. Violent and household victimization increase as evening activities outside of the home increase, and this relationship is independent of marital status, employment status, and age (Gartner and Doob, 1994; Gottfredson, 1984). Going out on weekends increases these risks more than going out during the week, while engaging in leisure pursuits increases risk more than does going to work or to school (Lasley and Rosenbaum, 1988; Sacco, Johnson, and Arnold, 1993).

In general, leisure can be part of a **risky lifestyle** that has dangerous consequences (Kennedy and Forde, 1990). Some types of leisure are clearly riskier than others. Young single males are more likely than others to go to bars where, as we have seen, the risks are higher. By contrast, elderly people are less likely to leave their homes for leisure in the evening; when they do, they are less likely to come into contact with potential offenders.

Several studies suggest that forms of leisure that are themselves criminal may pose particularly high victimization risks (Gottfredson, 1984; Jensen and Brownfield, 1986; Lauritsen, Sampson, and Laub, 1991; Sampson and Lauritsen, 1990). This is partially because offenders make good victims—they may be unlikely to call the police and, if they do, may likely have difficulty establishing their credibility.

TRANSACTIONS

The content of criminal events varies across leisure settings and activities. Criminologists have focused particular attention on the street, bars, dating, and tourism.

THE STREET

For many youths, the street is itself a leisure setting. For others, it is the route that they take from one setting to another or from these settings to their homes. Criminal events in the street seem to support the argument of opportunity theorists that people are victims of routines that leave them vulnerable to offenders. In fact, research indicates that, despite the horror stories from inner-city areas where people of all ages are vulnerable to crime, the group that is most likely to be involved in these "risky" routines on the street are young males. Their behaviour tends to be more public than that of most other groups, and they frequent the street to a greater degree than others.

YOUNG MALES

As stated previously, the groups most vulnerable to assaults in public places are young, unmarried males who frequent bars, go to movies, go out to work, and spend time out of the house walking or driving around. This lifestyle creates exposure to risk. While violent crime may be spontaneous, its targets tend to be people who are in places that are conducive to violent conflict. This observation does not account for the motivation behind violent crime, but it does explain the high levels of victimization among particular groups based on their exposure to certain settings and activities. Kennedy and Forde (1990) report a similar pattern for robberies: young, unmarried males who frequent bars and who are out walking or driving around are more likely to be victims of this crime.

The behaviour of young males who just hang around on the street is often seen as criminogenic. According to Skogan and Maxfield (1981), urban residents are most afraid of run-down urban areas where teenagers are hanging around on street corners. Even if the loitering is harmless and the individuals who engage in it never become involved in crime, the street is seen as a dangerous place.

If these youths are loosely attached to one another, those whom they encounter in street situations are likely to be acquaintances, and the chances of violence tend to be low. When individuals are more closely affiliated, as in a gang, the chance of violence increases, although, as Kennedy and Baron (1993) report, violence may not be a routine outcome of activity by gangs on the street. Much of the crime engaged in by gangs actually occurs when they come into contact with other gangs. Minor theft and robbery certainly occur, but not to the extent that the public believes. In addition, the view that gangs pursue violence for violence's sake, as would be predicted by the subculture-of-violence theory, is not substantiated by the research.

The same individuals on the street who represent potential offenders can also be victims. Young men in risky areas can easily become targets of assaults and robberies. When alcohol or drugs are involved, spontaneous conflicts may arise between individuals who are complete strangers to one another. Motivation in the violence that occurs among young males, whether in gangs or not, may simply be based on tests of character (Luckenbill, 1977).

Although women may be present in street environments, they are less likely to become involved in conflicts directly, even though they may act as third parties in escalating or defusing the conflict. Women alone tend to avoid those areas they perceive as risky (particularly the street) or situations that may lead to violence or loss of property. Of course, women can be targets of theft just as easily as men—purse snatching is all too common. Nonetheless, street crime appears to be predominantly the domain of young men, both as offenders and victims.

The precursors of assaults or robberies may depend on conflict styles that vary according to the individual personality and the social situation that individuals confront (Hocker and Wilmot, 1985: 38). Hocker and Wilmot assume that people develop patterned responses to conflict. Decisions about response style are based on past experience and learning—by observing others' behaviour and by trying out different responses.

Third parties also play an important role in conflict escalation or de-escalation. Young boys often jokingly exhort their friends to physically restrain them when they are confronting a foe. The opponent is advised, "You're lucky he's holding me back, or you'd be sorry!" While this type of posturing, which is facilitated by third parties, may work to dissipate conflict, it may also have the opposite effect. The joking may become serious, and third parties may promote the conflict instead of acting to reduce its outbreak. However, even when one participant lands a blow that, in legal terms, might be considered criminal assault, it is probably not viewed as such by the parties involved. There is likely too much confusion over the identities of the instigator and the victim (Van Brunschot, 1997). Only when physical harm that requires medical assistance is inflicted do these situations lead to the involvement of a formal third party (i.e., the police).

Kennedy and Baron (1993) found that members of punk gangs would absorb a great deal of verbal abuse but become involved in a fight only when they felt they needed to protect themselves, not when they felt that backing down would make them look foolish. This finding suggests not that the members of punk gangs were unprepared for the violence or that they would just walk away if attacked, but rather that the crime in which they engaged was more likely to be characterized by spontaneous outbursts of violence than by conscious, planned events (Gottfredson and Hirschi, 1990).

VANDALISM

As discussed in Chapter 6, people's attitudes toward city streets may be affected not only by the presence of gangs but by graffiti and other signs of vandalism and decay. When people see these signs, in addition to the patterns of movement around them, their fears tend be awakened. While **vandalism** is not a criminal event in conventional terms (that is, an event in which at least two parties are involved in a criminal action), we can still view it in event terms. Vandalism differs from other criminal events in that there is a time delay between the offence and the victimization.

Criminologists have focused greater attention on the consequences rather than causes of vandalism. Some criminologists (Skogan, 1990b; Kelling and Coles, 1996; Wilson and Kelling, 1982) identify vandalism as a major contributor to the public's declining sense of security in their neighbourhoods. Wilson and Kelling argue that disorder and crime are inextricably linked in a kind of developmental sequence. Wilson (1983: 78) notes that social psychologists and police officers tend to agree that if a building window is broken and left unrepaired, the remaining windows will soon be damaged. Vandalism occurs more frequently in areas in which surveillance is low. In generating what Wilson calls "untended" behaviour, vandalism leads to a breakdown of community controls and the degeneration of the neighbourhood into one that may become criminogenic. The fear that accompanies this degradation may discourage people from routinely using the streets or providing informal surveillance as a way of constraining disorderly behaviour. As vandalism increases and the neighbourhood continues its decline, residents may move to safer, more congenial environments.

While abandoned buildings appear to be the most frequent targets of vandalism, we are witnessing the growth of public vandalism, which involves tagging (writing graffiti) on walls, public vehicles, or whatever else is available. Graffiti-filled trains and stations have long been the scourge of New York public transit and have created the impression of a dangerous system, even though there are fewer incidents of crime on the subway than on the streets of New York. The New York City transportation department has taken extreme steps (discussed later in this chapter) to ban all graffiti on its subway trains. Similar strategies have been used in other cities as well.

While most tagging takes place at night, when there is little possibility of detection, graffiti writers are becoming bolder and are sometimes recognized for their skills at leaving their mark in daylight hours. This bravado may be the natural response of taggers who have come to see themselves as artists; to most people, however, graffiti is nothing more than simple vandalism.

What motivates most vandalism? Thrill seeking and the fact that it doesn't appear to harm anyone are probably significant causative factors. And notwithstanding the efforts made to curtail it in many cities, vandalism is almost impossible to detect and deter.

Bars (taverns, lounges, and so on) are places people go to relax, meet friends, listen to music, and drink. Although most bars escape the frenzied aggressiveness that may lead to crime, some attract it. In these locations, where alcohol and drugs mix with loud music and bravado, violence often erupts. Bar owners are increasingly concerned about this violence but often are confused about what to do to reduce it. They hire private guardians (bouncers) to remove the most raucous of their clients, but sometimes the actions of bouncers incite more violence. When one asks college or university criminology students where they would go to find a fight on any given night, they can easily list two or three notorious bars in town in which violence occurs with regularity. Apparently, these places attract a clientele that tends to be more aggressive than average, a conclusion that supports the subculture-of-violence perspective.

Criminal events that occur in bars generally consist of minor assaults, particularly between young males. These events may also involve vandalism (breaking windows, chairs, and tables). Events that involve interpersonal conflict may conclude without violence, with the protagonists walking away or being pulled away from one another. When there is escalation, violence may erupt. As a member of a band that has played for student gatherings told the authors, a crowd that is docile throughout an entire gig may suddenly become violent when the band finishes its last set. It is, he said, almost as if they can now hear one another speak and don't like what is being said! The jostling and shoving that may occur in these situations may be seen by all parties as harmless, but violence may ensue if the aggressiveness accelerates. While this description suggests that the event is spontaneous, the idea that certain bars attract this type of problem implies that some individuals go there in search of trouble. Luckenbill's (1977) characterization of the "character contest," discussed in Chapter 5, would seem to apply to such situations. The jostling and shoving that precedes a fight might be combined with insults and threats. When the fight breaks out, those around the combatants may add fuel to it by offering encouragement or by joining in.

DATING VIOLENCE

According to popular thinking, adolescent dating is a context for innocent exploration, while violence is a feature of conflict-ridden and constricting marital relationships (Sugarman and Hotaling, 1989). However, in recent years, dating violence has been recognized as existing in some unknown proportion of dating relationships. The efforts of researchers to estimate levels of dating violence are fraught with the same difficulties that characterize attempts to understand violence in families; as a result, estimates of the size of the problem are highly variable. While the term **dating violence,** or courtship violence, has no precise meaning, it generally refers to various forms of sexually and nonsexually assaultive behaviours (Thompson, 1986). In dating behaviour, as in marital relationships, women rather than men typically are the victims of violence (DeKeseredy and Hinch, 1991; Johnson, 1996b).

Most of the contemporary discussion about dating violence has focused on the subject of date rape (Gabor, 1994a). Because such rapes occur in a social context in which consensual sex is a possibility, until recently, the tendency has been to view date rape as something other than "real rape" (Bechhofer and Parrot, 1991). This has led to a victim-blaming strategy, as well as to a widespread willingness to dismiss the injury or trauma experienced by victims. A more realistic appraisal links date rape to culturally supported dating rituals that reflect patriarchal assumptions about male power and privilege (DeKeseredy and Kelly, 1993a; b). Research suggests that male sexual aggression is more likely when males exert greater control over the dating process—that is, when they control the initiation of dating, assume responsibility for expenses and transportation, and choose the dating activity (Harney and Muehlenhard, 1991).

Male control may translate into sexual aggression in two distinct ways. First, many men may interpret a woman's willingness to allow the male to make decisions about where they will go on a date, what they will do, and who will pay for it as a sign of interest in sexual activity (Johnson, Palileo, and Gray, 1982). Such men might reason that if women don't object to coming back to their room or accompanying them to a secluded spot, they must be interested in sex, even if they say otherwise. In particular, a woman's heavy consumption of alcohol may be interpreted by the male as a sign of sexual interest (Benson, Charlton, and Goodhart, 1992; Vogel and Himlein, 1995).

Second, to the extent that the male controls the circumstances of dating, he controls the opportunities for offending. When he controls transportation, for instance, he can effectively impede the ability of the female to escape a situation in which sexual assault is likely. The woman who is in an isolated spot with a sexually aggressive male may be reluctant to leave the car because she has been warned that even greater dangers confront women who are not protected by male companions. Not surprisingly, date rapes typically occur in the home of the offender, inside an automobile, or in some other isolated location (Harney and Muehlenhard, 1991). The Violence Against Women Survey, for instance, found that 20 percent of date-related sexual assaults took place in the home of the male and 25 percent took place in a car; a further 24 percent occurred in the victim's home, while 21 percent occurred in another public

BOX 9.3   DATING VIOLENCE

In 1992, Walter DeKeseredy and Katharine Kelly, two sociologists at Carleton University, undertook a study of woman abuse in Canadian university/college dating relationships. The study (DeKeseredy and Kelly, 1993a) was intended to provide information that would be representative of different types of postsecondary institutions, different regions of the country, and different programs and periods of study.

Two versions of a questionnaire were distributed to students in the classroom. Although both questionnaires included some similar questions, one was designed to elicit women's experiences while the other was designed to elicit the experiences of men. Students were assured that their participation in the survey was strictly voluntary and that all information would be kept confidential.

After the questionnaires were collected, the researchers provided a brief lecture on dating violence and all respondents were given a list of local support services that they could contact if they needed assistance.

The final sample consisted of 1835 women and 1307 men. Among the measures used by the researchers were those derived from the Conflict Tactics Scale. Male and female reports of female victimization tactics are outlined in the table below.

Physical Abuse Incidence Rates

Type of Abuse	Male Respondents (N = 1307)		Female Respondents (N = 1835)	
	%	N	%	N
Physical				
Threw something at her (you)	3.5	40	5.3	85
Pushed, grabbed, or shoved her (you)	11.5	132	19.8	319
Slapped her (you)	2.6	30	5.3	85
Kicked, bit, or hit her (you) with your (his) fist	1.4	16	3.8	61
Hit or tried to hit her (you) with something	1.7	20	3.3	54
Beat her (you) up	0.6	7	1.3	21
Choked you (her)	0.9	10	2.1	32
Threatened her (you) with a knife or a gun	0.8	9	0.6	9
Used a knife or a gun on her (you)	0.7	8	0.1	2

place and 10 percent occurred in someone else's home (Johnson, 1996b). The consequences of male control—misinterpretation of sexual interest and the creation of opportunity—frequently work in concert. For example, "parking" combines privacy, which provides the opportunity for sexual aggression, with the likelihood that the male will overestimate the female's willingness to engage in sexual relations (Muehlenhard and Linton, 1987).

In courtship violence, like marital violence, violence is supported by the patriarchal belief that the use of force by men against women is legitimate (DeKeseredy and Kelly, 1993a, b; Lloyd, Koval, and Cale, 1989). Women who are assaulted by boyfriends frequently cite jealousy or attempts to terminate the relationship as the precipitating factors. Ironically, such dating violence may be viewed as a sign of love by either or both parties.

TOURISM

It is impossible to ignore the growing importance of tourism in our society. Large amounts of money are spent on tourist attractions, and people are allocating increased amounts of their disposable income to travel. Despite the growing awareness that tourists are not immune to crime, however, hotels and travel agencies have been slow to warn tourists about potentially dangerous areas. Tourists tend to be easy targets for the pickpocket or the robber. Nor is it just the property that tourists take with them that is at risk. One scam involves thieves reading the identification tags of departing travellers and then going to their homes to burglarize their now unoccupied homes!

Victimization of travellers is hardly a recent phenomenon. In the Middle Ages, castles were built in the south of France to protect pilgrims who travelled through areas inhabited by thieves and robbers. And although modern tourism has left the impression that tourists are not likely to be victims, they *are,* and they need to take precautions to protect themselves. As tourists become increasingly aware of their vulnerability, many once-popular tourist destinations are finding that visitors are staying away.

Major outbreaks of violence against tourists receive widespread media attention, which may also consist of advice to tourists about special precautions they can take to protect themselves. Attacks on foreign tourists in parts of East Africa and Egypt have led to a worldwide alert to avoid these areas. Canadians have recently received highly publicized warnings about travel in Florida—a popular destination for families and the elderly. Also, travel agencies and tour groups now steer clients away from areas they consider dangerous. The governments of many countries issue warnings to their nationals to avoid certain areas, particularly those characterized by a pattern of violence and robbery against tourists or a great deal of political instability; in the latter situation, travellers may become a target of local anger and frustration. Some countries are responding to crime against tourists by developing programs that enhance security in resort areas and that educate travellers about the hazards they may encounter in certain areas. Tourist-directed crime would seem to be best explained by opportunity theorists, who see tourists as vulnerable targets in areas where surveillance may be low and precautions more difficult to take.

The tourist is more likely to be a victim of theft or robbery than of personal attack. Most commonly, luggage is stolen or pockets are picked. As thieves develop sophisticated techniques for picking or jimmying locks, they increasingly are preying on autos as well. In one scam, the car thief drives along a beach road that is not too crowded and checks out the parked cars. If there are signs of an attractive target (for example, a foreign licence plate or a rental car), and if the owner(s) is nowhere to be seen (and thus presumably down at the beach), the thief parks behind the car, approaches the car, and breaks through the lock (with special tools, this can be accomplished fairly easily). Then the thief quickly searches the car and exits with whatever loot he finds. Slashing a tire prevents the victim from attempting pursuit.

Tourists may also run into problems simply because they do not understand the local customs or language. In one case, a 16-year-old Japanese exchange student was shot and killed in a Louisiana neighbourhood because he did not understand the warning "Freeze!" The youth had been looking for a Halloween party and did not stop when he was accosted by Rodney Peairs, who said that he had felt that his life had been threatened by the costumed youth. Peairs was acquitted under a Louisiana law that allows citizens to use deadly weapons to protect themselves. In response to the student's tragic death, the Japanese government is publishing a guide of helpful phrases for U.S.-bound tourists. The guide will include about thirty phrases that few Japanese learn in their language classes, among them, "Get lost," "Watch out," and "I mean it" (Sanger, 1993: A9). Not only the translations but also the different cultural meanings of the thirty phrases will be imparted as a way of letting the visitors know that the person issuing the warning is serious.

THE AFTERMATH

Victimizations that occur in leisure settings frequently go unreported. The tourist–victim, for instance, may not speak the local language or know how to find the police. If the loss or the injury is not great, the tourist–victim may decide that reporting the incident to the police may not be worth it. Victimizations may also go unreported when the leisure activity is itself regarded as a form of disreputable behaviour. Victims who have been drinking or who encounter offenders in a known "deviant context" may be reluctant to bring the incident to the attention of the police. Given the generally negative attitude toward many forms of youthful leisure activities, it is not surprising that crimes that occur in these settings remain undiscovered or unrecorded by police.

Victims may respond to crimes committed against them in leisure settings in other ways. One response may be to avoid the types of encounters or circumstances in which the victimization occurred. Since leisure activity is, by definition, discretionary activity, it is easier to avoid than home- or work-related activities. Thus, the victim of courtship violence may refrain from dating, and the jogger who is mugged may stop jogging and take up "mall walking," which may be perceived as safer than running on city streets or park paths.

In other instances, a participant in a street fight or barroom brawl may prefer to seek revenge rather than report the crime to police. Of course, the status of such individuals as "victims" may itself be questionable, as they themselves may have struck the initial blow or instigated the fight. In addition, many criminal events involving young males may be of little interest to police. In recent times, police have been encouraged to manage their excessive workloads by assigning a higher priority to the victimization of women and children than to young males.

While the long-term consequences of leisure-related victimizations are not yet evident, it may be that, with the exception of the sexual assaults, the effects are short-lived. For example, the punks that Baron (1989) talked with simply shrugged off their own victimization, regarding it as just a routine hazard of life on the streets. The degree to which individuals are deterred from becoming involved in leisure-related crimes may have more to do with the risk of being hurt than with the risk of being arrested. This is not to suggest that the police do not deter; their presence on the street or in bars plays an important role in keeping such potentially dangerous behaviour under control. The evidence would seem to indicate that the behaviour of young males on the street and in other settings can change from violent to passive fairly easily, particularly given the fact that victims and offenders are often hard to distinguish and that public guardians (police and citizens) are not always available to stop a brewing conflict from becoming serious.

The need for guardianship has long driven the policy whereby police attempt to maintain a high profile on the street. This has been achieved through the use of random patrol (that is, cars cruising neighbourhoods looking for problems). As we discussed in Chapter 7, however, patrol tactics appear to have little influence on the amount of neighbourhood crime. As a result, police departments are now experimenting with neighbourhood mini-stations and increasing foot patrols and neighbourhood consultations—tactics they believe can prevent and deter crime more effectively than can a highly visible police presence in the form of random patrol. Still, the most effective guardians against crime are not the police, but rather other people who frequent leisure settings and who call the police when needed.

Leisure settings are best described as settings in which crimes occur according to opportunity. As we will discuss in Chapter 11, attempts have been made to reduce opportunities for crime by making changes to the environment. Target hardening can include anything from increased and better-situated lighting to surveillance cameras (Newman, 1972). For example, a multimillion-dollar program has been initiated by the New York City Subway Authority to clean all trains of graffiti. After each journey, trains are checked and cleaned of debris. Subway police patrol stations with special night-vision glasses and cameras to catch graffiti artists in the act. Scratch-proof glass on the trains is being developed, and there are plans for paint-resistant exteriors. There is even talk of banning spray cans and wide-tip marker pens in order to limit the resources available to graffiti artists. All of these measures are being taken to increase public confidence in the safety of the subway system.

There have also been attempts to influence the use of leisure as a crime control mechanism. Particularly conspicuous have been efforts to develop **positive leisure** alternatives for young people who are actually or potentially delinquent (Agnew and Peterson, 1989). This approach reflects the maxim, made explicit in social control theory, that "idle hands are the devil's workshop." Youths get themselves into trouble (through various forms of "hanging out") because they lack positive options. The reasoning behind the positive-leisure approach is that summer camps, organized clubs, and other so-called forms of healthy recreation will expose youths to an environment that discourages involvement in crime and delinquency.

A parallel approach focuses on the need to control what are widely viewed in some quarters as negative and corrupting forms of youth leisure. This approach seems to reflect the view that, if they are left to make their own leisure choices, youths will almost always make the wrong ones. The past several decades have witnessed numerous crusades intended to impose legal and social restrictions on the ability of young people to make these choices. These campaigns were directed against feature films in the 1930s; comic books and rock and roll in the 1950s; the presumed drug-influenced protest music of the 1960s; and rap and heavy metal music, fantasy role-playing games (for example, Dungeons and Dragons), and video games in the 1980s and 1990s. Television violence has been the subject of recurrent crusades every five or ten years since the 1960s (Best, 1990; Gray, 1989). However, there is an ironic character to such crusades. According to Tanner (1992: 228) they reflect a perennial tendency on the part of adults to rediscover, to stigmatize and to attempt to control the culture and behaviour of the generations that follow them. Thus, the Elvis Presley and Beatle fans. The Hippies and student radicals of earlier eras express bewilderment and concern about the corruptive nature of the cultural worlds in which they believe their own children to be immersed. Contemporary charges that modern heavy metal music inspires teen suicide and sexual promiscuity or that it promotes mysticism and devil worship tell us more about the ways in which anxieties about youth are reproduced across generations than about the uniquely deviant characteristics of contemporary youth.

■ ■ ■

Summary

When people are "at leisure," they are also at risk of involvement in criminal events, as offenders or victims. The relationships that link leisure activity and criminal activity are highly varied. Some forms of leisure might be seen as causes of crime. The content of youth-oriented media, for instance, may seem to provide the motives for crime. Alternatively, engagement in peer activities may suggest freedom from the social controls that might be expected to inhibit offending.

Much leisure activity takes place in public spaces. Street crime involves people who are passing through areas in transit from one place to another or who are simply "hanging out." In these contexts, crime might itself constitute leisure, as appears to be the case with vandalism and graffiti writing. In leisure settings such as streets and bars, it is often difficult to distinguish the offenders from the victims when a conflict escalates into assault or other forms of violence. This form of opportunity crime tends to be based on the risky lifestyles of the individuals involved and is more likely to be deterred by retribution than by reporting the crime to the police.

In date rape, the routine activity of courtship takes on a criminal character when aggressive behaviour translates into sexual assault against an unwilling participant. Much of this behaviour also goes unreported. Tourism crime targets people who are at leisure in unfamiliar places, where their lack of understanding of what areas are safe or unsafe may put them at risk. It is often difficult for tourists who have been victimized to find someone to whom to report the crime. They may decide that they simply do not want the hassle of getting involved with police in a foreign country. Travel agencies and governments are increasingly briefing tourists on how to travel safely and advising them of areas that should be avoided altogether. A tourist's most effective deterrent against crime is to not travel in unsafe areas at all, thereby removing the opportunity for crime.

Some types of leisure pursuits place people at particular risk of victimization. The risky lifestyles in which people engage may make the search for a "good time" result in a "bad time." It must be emphasized that, in the leisure domain, as in other domains, the processes that we are describing are not deterministic. In other words, exposure to criminogenic influences or to threats of victimization does not guarantee the development of a criminal event, but rather only increases its probability by bringing together opportunities for crime and motivations to offend.

■ ■ ■

QUESTIONS FOR REVIEW AND DISCUSSION

1. Why are bars the site of so much crime? Can you name some bars in your area that are associated with high rates of crime?
2. Is dating violence a serious problem on your campus? What measures (if any) have been taken by school officials to deal with the problem?
3. How do you account for the recurrent tendency on the part of adults to view the cultural trappings of adolescents as troublesome?
4. In what way can vandalism be understood as a juvenile form of leisure activity?
5. How do patterns of leisure activity change over the life cycle, and what implications do these changes have for victimization risk?
6. Why are many of the crimes committed against tourists never reported to the police?

CHAPTER TEN

Crime and Work

WHAT'S IN CHAPTER TEN

In this chapter, we discuss the work domain from three different perspectives: victimization and work, crime and legitimate work, and crime as work. First, we examine how different types of work can expose individuals to varying forms and levels of victimization risk. Second, we examine how people who are employed in legitimate work activities take advantage of their positions to commit crimes. Third, we look at crime that takes on the character of work in the context of an ongoing illegal enterprise.

INTRODUCTION

In this chapter, we consider the social domain of the workplace. As we will see, among the characteristics in which jobs differ is the accessibility to criminal opportunities and risks they entail. Our discussion is organized around two broad topics. The first is the relationship between participation in the legitimate labour force and the occurrence of criminal events. Two major issues concern us here. First, in what ways are patterns of victimization associated with patterns of employment? In other words, how do the jobs we have affect the victimization risks we face? Second, in what ways does seemingly honest work make available opportunities for criminal behaviour, involving either employers (or employees) or members of the general public?

The second major theme to be explored in this chapter is crime as a type of occupational activity. Here, we examine "enterprise crime," which involves the exploitation of opportunities for the development of criminal business.

CRIME, EMPLOYMENT, AND UNEMPLOYMENT

The Canadian labour force has undergone several important changes in the past few decades. The unemployment rate, which was 11.8 percent in 1983. had fallen to 7.8 percent in 1989. By 1997, however, unemployment was again hovering around the 10 percent mark. Unemployment is particularly prevalent among young people and minorities—groups that, as we already know, are at high risk for involvement in criminal events as both victims and offenders. Female labour force participation has increased greatly in recent years, especially among married women.

The types of jobs available have also changed in the last two decades. While employment in the manufacturing sector has fallen since 1979, the availability of jobs in the service sector has increased. Compared with goods-producing jobs, however, service jobs tend to be lower paying and to more frequently involve part-time work.

In addition to the size and nature of the work force, the nature of work itself has undergone important changes. Many of these changes are attributable to various types of technological innovations, particularly in computer technology. While these changes are intended to make the workplace more efficient (and, from the employer's viewpoint, more profitable), they affect the pacing and timing of jobs. Employees may have computer hookups in their homes that allow them to reduce the amount of time required at their formal places of work. Fax machines quicken the pace at which information can be transmitted, and cellular telephones have worked to blur, for many, the distinction between private time and work time.

EMPLOYMENT AND VICTIMIZATION

How do patterns of employment or experiences in the labour force relate to patterns of involvement in criminal events? One approach to this question is to ask whether employed and unemployed individuals have different victimization risks. This question is not as straightforward as it may initially appear. Part of the problem concerns how we choose to define the reference group against whom the employed should be compared. If we define this group broadly, including not only those who are unemployed but also those who are retired, institutionalized, or sick, or who define their main activity in surveys as "homemakers," then the victimization risks associated with being employed are generally higher for most types of crime (Miethe, Stafford, and Long, 1987). This is because those who constitute this other broad reference group are likely to be people whose social and demographic characteristics are usually associated with lower victimization rates. However, when we compare those who are employed with those who are unemployed, the disadvantages associated with employment diminish in many surveys. In other words, unemployment is associated with higher victimization risks (Miethe and Meier, 1994).

UNEMPLOYMENT AND OFFENDING

The relationship between unemployment and offending is studied much more frequently than the relationship between unemployment and victimization. Most of the theories of offending that we reviewed in Chapters 3 and 4 would lead us to expect that risks of offending are greater for unemployed people. Theories that emphasize the role of social inequality in the generation of crime quite naturally suggest that not having a job may encourage the development of criminal motivations. Moreover, this view is perfectly consistent with common sense.

We would expect measures of unemployment to be related, in empirical studies, to measures of criminal offending, for many reasons. First, some property crimes may be committed out of a sense of need or desire for things that people want but cannot buy. If people lack a stable income, they may experience greater temptations to take what is not theirs. Second, occupational status arguably is an important mechanism for integrating people into conventional society; that is, jobs provide a "stake in conformity" (Toby, 1974). Not having a job may weaken the hold that conformist institutions have over people. Third, being unemployed may result in the adoption of behaviours, such as drug use, that are themselves associated with criminal offending (Hartnagel and Krahn, 1989). Fourth, unemployment may be related to family instability and thus to the ability of parents to monitor the criminal behaviour of dependent children (Sampson, 1987). Fifth, since rates of unemployment are high among young people, who seem to be most "crime prone," we might expect the criminogenic effects of unemployment to be particularly strongly related to offending among this segment of the population.

Despite these theoretical and commonsense connections between unemployment and offending, several criminologists question the validity of this relationship (Chiricos, 1987; Freeman, 1983; Gottfredson and Hirschi, 1990). While many criminologists would argue that unemployment is causally related to crime, they are unsure of the size and significance of the effect. Others dispute whether being unemployed has any independent causal influence on the propensity to behave criminally.

Sorting out the relationship between unemployment and offending is no simple task. First, just as efforts to measure crime are fraught with difficulties, it is also quite difficult to measure unemployment in a valid way (Gramling, Forsyth, and Fewell, 1988). Unemployment is usually measured in terms of the number of people who are not employed but who are actively looking for work. Such measures thus exclude those who have "dropped out" of the labour pool. This bias in our measures of unemployment may have the effect of including those who are most highly motivated to gain entry to the "conventional world" and excluding those who are least motivated. The overall effect may be to weaken the measured relationship between crime and unemployment.

Second, some researchers have argued that not only unemployment per se but also the quality of labour force experiences is related to criminal offending (Allan and Steffensmeier, 1989; Hartnagel and Krahn, 1989). Precarious, low-paying jobs that offer few of the advantages generally associated with employment are counted as "employment" in labour force surveys, despite the fact that such jobs might not provide a strong cushion against the various criminogenic influences to which the jobholder may be exposed. Third, many researchers attempt to study the relationship between unemployment and crime at the aggregate level (for example, by asking if the national unemployment rate is related to the national crime rate) (Chiricos, 1987). However, this may be too broad a level for the investigation of this issue in that it may obscure relationships that exist at the community or neighbourhood level.

Despite the popular view of the relationship between unemployment and crime, studies support alternative interpretations. Some researchers have suggested, for instance, that delinquent involvement is greater among employed teenagers than among unemployed ones (Tanner, 1996). The former group, it is argued, may be less susceptible to parental controls and more susceptible to delinquent peer influences. Other researchers have suggested that crime causes unemployment (not the other way around) in that people who are criminally inclined are less interested in conforming to the routines demanded by legitimate labour force participation (Wilson, 1983). Still others maintain that the relationship between crime and unemployment is "spurious" in the sense that no real relationship exists between them; the appearance of a relationship is created by the fact that being unemployed and behaving criminally are both related to a "common cause" such as a low degree of self-control (Gottfredson and Hirschi, 1990).

Ultimately, it may be impossible to generalize about the relationship between unemployment and crime. The nature of the relationship may depend on the type of crime, the social characteristics of the labour force group, and the social policies in place to assist those who are not employed (Allan and Steffensmeier, 1989; Currie, 1985). Cantor and Land (1985) have argued, moreover, that the rate of unemployment may have more than one type of effect on the overall rate of crime. Consistent with arguments made previously in this chapter, they suggest that unemployment may encourage the development of criminal motivation among some people. This implies that unemployment will be positively related to the crime rate such that the crime rate increases as the unemployment rate increases. However, Cantor and Land also argue that the unemployment rate may have a negative effect on the crime rate. This effect is related not to criminal motivation but to criminal opportunity. According to Cantor and Land, the unemployed are much less likely to engage in routine activities that take them away from the home for predictable and extended periods. In other words, unemployment may be related to increases in the level of guardianship exercised over persons and property. In addition, because the unemployment rate can be understood, at least in part, as a general indicator of the overall well-being of the economy, we can assume that when the unemployment rate is high, there will be fewer goods in circulation for thieves to steal. Cantor and Land's analysis of American UCR data for the period 1946 to 1982 supports the argument that both types of effects may be possible.

We have reviewed the relationship between the general effects of employment and unemployment on the likelihood of committing crime. Now we can examine how particular forms of labour force participation make crime possible. Two issues concern us here. The first is the relationship between the jobs people have and the victimization risks they face. The second is the ways in which the jobs that people have give them opportunities to behave criminally.

VICTIMIZATION AND WORK

Public awareness of **workplace stress** has been increasing in recent years. According to a Canadian government survey, 38 percent of people who had a job or were self-employed had encountered a work situation within the previous year (1991) that had caused them excess stress or worry (Geran, 1992). American studies have estimated that approximately 15 percent of the U.S work force will experience health problems due to stress (*Business and Health,* 1994). Worker's compensation claims for stress-related problems tripled in the 1980s (Karasek and Theorell, 1990). In the U.S., stress-related losses are estimated to cost the economy as much as $150 billion per year (Freudenheim, 1987). Work-related stressors include job demands and hours of work, the threat of layoff, poor interpersonal relations, the risk of accident or injury, harassment, discrimination—and even fear for one's life.

BOX 10.1   MURDER IN THE WORKPLACE

From the office manager who just fired an employee to the emergency room nurse who fears the stabbing victim's shady companion is fingering a weapon, workers are increasingly worried about being murdered on the job.

By some estimates homicide may now be the third highest work-related cause of death in the United States, according to Joseph Kinney of the Chicago-based National Safe Workplace Institute.

Such crimes are sometimes page one news:

- In Tampa, Fla., a disgruntled former employee killed three men at lunch who were once his supervisors, wounded two others, then took his own life.
- Seven workers at a fried chicken restaurant in suburban Chicago were mowed down during a robbery after the store closed for the evening.
- In 1986 and 1991, two postal workers, one fired and the other threatened with dismissal, took out their rage on postal centres in Oklahoma and Michigan. Nineteen died in all.

But other cases rate only a line or two on the evening news—typically a rejected suitor or ex-spouse stalking his or her mate to a violent death in the office or shop.

"Violence in the workplace is escalating and I think there are two root causes," Kinney says.

"One is a feeling of increased vulnerability that workers and managers now feel. In fact, at least a million managers have lost their jobs because of corporate downsizing or mergers in the last 10 years.

BOX 10.1	MURDER IN THE WORKPLACE (CONT.)

"The other thing is just the increased willingness of people to use violence in our society—to deal with emotions and problems. Stress is rising all over the place."

He says he expects these kinds of violent reactions to escalate.

"Just a generation ago, workers and managers expected to have one employer for life. Now, not only can we expect to have multiple employers, but there is talk about having two or three career changes during a lifetime.

"But, we don't have in place yet the kind of social and educational institutions, public and private, that are responsive to this increased feeling of vulnerability and disloyalty."

Eric Hickey of California State University says mass murders in public places are running at the rate of two or three per month in the United States.

Usually the killer "is making a final statement to the world," he says. "The ultimate motivation is the same—having control over other people when you don't have control over your own life."

Paul Levy of the department of psychology at the University of Akron says he is not 100 percent sure that workplace violence has increased as dramatically as it seems.

"But there probably has been some increase," he says. "When our competence or our security at work is undermined, that causes a great deal of stress and frustration. In addition, the economic situation is so bad that people feel very insecure in their jobs."

Job loss, Levy says, is nearly as stressful as facing the death of a loved one.

SOURCE: "Murder in the Workplace on the Increase in U.S.," *The Toronto Star,* February 9, 1993, p. F10. Reprinted by permission of Reuters America Inc.

INDIVIDUAL AND OCCUPATIONAL CHARACTERISTICS

Although it is not generally recognized as such, the threat of criminal victimization may be an important source of job stress for many people. Victimization surveys tell us that the chances of being a victim of crime are not randomly distributed across occupational groups. While work roles may have much in common, irrespective of the unique characteristics of particular jobs, there are dramatic differences in what types of work people do, where they do it, and with whom it brings them into contact. As we will see, the characteristics of some jobs increase risk while the characteristics of other jobs decrease risk. Such differences may be obscured when the victimization experiences of the employed are compared with those of the unemployed.

Yet, even when we compare the victimization risks associated with different occupations, it may be difficult to determine whether it is the job itself or the characteristics of the people who hold such jobs that affect the risk of victimization. For instance, if we were to discover that part-time employees of fast-food restaurants faced particularly high risks of victimization, we would not necessarily be justified in concluding that there is something about cooking or serving hamburgers that makes one more vulnerable to criminal danger (although there may be!). Fast-food employees tend to be teenagers and, in view of the relationship between age and victimization, the higher risks may involve age-related rather than work-related factors. In fact, we might not even be surprised to discover that, while these employees report higher rates of crime, the experiences that they tell us about typically occur outside of work rather than on the job. Thus, a cursory review of victimization risks and occupation may be misleading.

Information about how victimization risks vary across occupations is hard to come by. This is because the statistical rarity of victimization incidents does not, in many cases, allow survey researchers to compute separate victimization rates for a detailed inventory of occupations. Some research indicates that risks are higher for members of the military (Harlow, 1991), probation officers (Linder and Bonn, 1996), police officers, welfare workers, and those who work in bars (Mayhew, Elliott, and Dowds, 1989) and other occupations that involve regular and frequent contact with high-risk populations.

Perhaps the most comprehensive study of this type was undertaken by Block, Felson, and Block (1984), who calculated the victimization rates for 426 different occupations using data on 108 000 crime incidents reported to U.S. National Crime Survey interviewers between 1973 and 1981. For the five offences these researchers examined (robbery, assault, burglary, larceny, and automobile theft), victimization risk was inversely related to "occupational status," which they defined as the average income for each occupation. In other words, as the average income of an occupation increased, the risks of being victimized decreased. More specifically, the study revealed marked differences in levels of victimization risk. For instance, amusement and recreation workers and restaurant workers such as busboys, dishwashers, and servers were among the five highest-risk occupations for all offences. Sheriffs and police officers had the highest assault rates, while taxi drivers and newspaper vendors were among the most frequently robbed. The lowest rates of victimization were found among certain farm workers, as well as telephone and electrical workers, opticians, stenographers, and radio operators.

The authors readily acknowledge that data of this sort are difficult to interpret:

On the one hand, better jobs tend to provide more good things in life, presumably including safety and security from crime. More income and credit allow people to purchase security devices, safer locations to live in, better parking spots and the like. Better jobs may also help people avoid public transit and unfavourable hours for trips to work and elsewhere. Better credit allows avoidance of cash. In general, more resources, including money, credit and control over time, should help people to obtain security from crime.

On the other hand, better jobs may bring with them more luxury goods to attract offenders. Higher strata individuals may also go out more at night, enjoying sport and cultural events or visiting restaurants or other night spots. Good jobs are often found within a metropolis rather than in rural areas with lower risk. One suspects that modern offenders have little trouble finding the higher occupational strata in order to victimize them, security efforts notwithstanding. (Block, Felson, and Block, 1984: 442)

Thus, while analyses of the victimization rates of different occupational groups are interesting and informative, they do not necessarily tell us very much about crimes that occur in the workplace. This requires a more focused investigation of the crimes that happen while people are at work.

PRECURSORS

In very general terms, workplace settings have characteristics that both encourage and inhibit victimization. On the one hand, full-time employees spend many hours "at risk" of whatever threats the workplace presents. On the other hand, workplace settings tend to be much more highly structured than, for instance, leisure settings and thus more subject to a variety of social controls that discourage victimization. Some degree of order and control is usually deemed necessary if the organizational goals of the workplace are to be achieved in an efficient fashion.

How much crime occurs in the workplace? As stated, answers to this question are not easy to derive from most kinds of existing data sets, which are usually intended to answer more general kinds of questions. Data from a twenty-year analysis of American National Crime Survey Data provide some clarification (Zawitz et al., 1993). That analysis revealed that with respect to violent crime about 14 percent of the incidents occurred while the victim was working or "on duty." In contrast, 16 percent of the incidents occurred while the victim was participating in an activity at home (rather than sleeping) and 29 percent occurred while the victim was engaged in a leisure activity away from home. In the case of burglary, 21 percent occurred while the victim was at work (as compared with 15 percent while the victim was sleeping and 25 percent while the victim was pursuing a leisure activity away from home). For crimes of theft, the two most common activities for victims at the time the crime was committed were leisure away from home (21 percent) and working (19 percent). However, these data underestimate the relative proportion of workplace crime in that they represent proportions of the total number of incidents—that is, incidents involving those who are and who are not members of the paid labour force.

Data from the 1988 British Crime Survey allow us to separate out the proportion of workplace crimes reported by employed respondents (Mayhew, Elliott, and Dowds, 1989). These findings reveal that 71 percent of the thefts, 22 percent of the assaults, 11 percent of the robberies, and 13 percent of the vehicle thefts occurred while respondents were at work. In all cases, the vast majority of the crimes occurred while the victims were inside the workplace rather than in some other work-related location, such as out of doors at work or on the street near the workplace.

One type of worksite for which detailed information regarding the nature of victimization risk is readily available is the school. In recent years, much attention has been focused on schools as settings that pose serious criminal dangers to both students and teachers (Toby, 1983; Hanke, 1996). American National Crime Survey data (1985–1988) indicate that, with respect to teenage victims aged 12–15, 37 percent of the crimes of violence and 81 percent of the crimes of theft occurred while the victims were at school (Whitaker and Bastian, 1991). A special survey of school crime undertaken by the Department of Justice as a supplement to the 1989 National Crime Survey found that an estimated 9 percent of students aged 12–19 were victims of crime in or around their schools over a six-month period; 2 percent reported experiencing one or more violent crimes; and 7 percent reported at least one property crime (Bastian and Taylor, 1991). Sixteen percent of the respondents claimed that a student had attacked or threatened a teacher at their school in the six months prior to the interview. The violent crimes typically involved "simple assaults" (for example, schoolyard fights) that did not involve weapons and that resulted in relatively minor injuries. A survey of 881 Ontario schools suggests that much school crime involves not only students but also teachers and other school staff (Ontario Teachers Federation, 1992).

How do workplace characteristics relate to variations in the levels of workplace danger? Do these risks, for instance, have something to do with the nature of the work or with the location of the workplace? Answers to such questions are still fragmentary. Respondents in the 1988 British Crime Survey blamed the nature of their jobs for nearly one-quarter of the violent and theft incidents they experienced. The "public" rather than fellow employees were blamed for nearly three-quarters of the violent incidents and one-half of the thefts.

Data from victimization surveys have been used to describe the types of workplace conditions that seem to facilitate employee victimization (Collins, Cox, and Langan, 1987; Lynch, 1987). These studies suggest that the risks of becoming a crime victim on the job are greater in the following circumstances:

- when the job involves face-to-face contact with large numbers of people on a routine basis (if the workplace restricts access to authorized persons, the risks of crime are lower);
- when the job involves handling money;
- when the job involves overnight travel or travel between worksites; and
- when the job involves the delivery of passengers and goods.

The importance of these factors becomes apparent when they are assessed in reference to routine activities theory and associated concepts such as exposure and guardianship. People who work in settings that leave them unprotected and at the same time exposed to large numbers of people (some of whom may be "motivated offenders") are more likely to be victimized in the workplace.

Victimization studies also indicate that it is the nature of the work, rather than the characteristics of the victims (such as sex and age), that affects an individual's likelihood of becoming a crime victim in the workplace. In the case of schools, the structure of the school population might lead us to expect more crime than we observe. Schools, after all, are settings that concentrate on a daily basis the age groups at greatest risk of offending and victimization. Toby (1983) argues that the risks associated with school populations are compounded by the requirement of compulsory attendance. Disruptive or troublesome students who do not wish to attend school are required to do so. For this reason, he suggests, junior high schools have more serious rates of victimization than do senior high schools.

In addition, until recently, schools have been relatively open settings, easily accessible to potential offenders who do not attend them. These "intruders," as they are usually referred to by school officials, might include not only the stereotypical predator but also the angry parent or the student who is disgruntled at having been expelled. Although schools are capable of exercising some degree of guardianship against victimization, a school of above-average size that allows students considerable freedom of movement may provide many settings that facilitate criminal activity. Within school buildings, more victimizations typically take place in less supervised areas, such as hallways and restrooms, than in more controlled places such as classrooms and libraries (Garofalo, Siegel, and Laub, 1987).

The routine activities associated with some work locations also tend to make them less vulnerable to crime. Based on his study of robbery, for instance, Desroches (1995) argues that while department stores and super-markets are known to carry large amounts of cash, they are generally not viewed as desirable targets by robbers. Not only are supermarkets likely to have security equipment but it is also the case that there are often many people in the store at any one time. The high shelves in most grocery stores do not allow the potential thief an unobstructed view of the setting, and because there are usually two exits, it is difficult to control movement in and out of the store. The separation of the cash registers by relatively wide aisles makes the collection of the stolen money a time-consuming activity. In short, such targets offer too many risks for too little money.

TRANSACTIONS

Much of the violent victimization that occurs in the workplace results from conflicts between employees and customers or clients. These situations include the bartender who tells the inebriated customer that he is "cut off," the teacher who tries to enforce classroom discipline, the sales clerk who refuses to accept returned merchandise, and the police officer who tries to intervene in an argument.

This pattern of employee–customer conflict is reflected in British Crime Survey data that describe "verbal abuse" at work. Fourteen percent of respondents in a survey by Mayhew, Elliott, and Dowds (1989) said that they had been verbally abused by someone other than a co-worker during the fourteen-month period preceding the survey. Although not strictly criminal, verbal abuse can contain threatening statements and may precipitate a conflict that escalates to violence. Although male and female workers were about equally likely to be abused in this way, younger women appeared to be particularly susceptible. While incidents involving abuse by an adult were more likely to involve a single offender, incidents involving adolescents were about as likely to involve a group as a single offender. Intoxication was a factor in almost one-tenth of the incidents. In 80 percent of the incidents, workers were sworn at, and insulting comments about job performance were made in 40 percent of the cases.

The nature of the situational context of much workplace victimization is revealed in a study by Salinger and colleagues (1993) of assaults of flight attendants. This study found that flight attendants have rates of assault as much as ten times higher than the average person. Most assaults involved a conflict between the passenger and the attendant over some mandatory aspect of the flight, such as baggage arrangements or food or drink service. The researchers discovered that first-class passengers, who comprise only 10 percent of the travelling public, accounted for 20 percent of the assaults, a finding that may be explained by the higher expectations of service, passengers' perception of their status relative to that of the attendant, and the amount of alcohol that is typically consumed. The study also found that assaults are most likely to occur during takeoff or landing, the most distressing time for passengers who are afraid of flying. In addition, at takeoff, the authority role of the attendant may not yet be clearly understood.

Violent school crimes, except perhaps those involving intruders, are probably more likely than other workplace crimes to include as participants offenders and victims who are known to each other (Whitaker and Bastian, 1991). According to Garofalo, Siegel, and Laub (1987) many of these events result from:

> frictions from peers arising from normal daily activities. School grounds and trips to and from school provide ample opportunities for interactions that can escalate into relatively minor victimizations. "Weapons" often consist of available items grabbed on the spur of the moment. Items stolen from victims often seem to be the targets of malicious, even mischievous motivations. (333)

BOX 10.2   WEAPON USE IN SCHOOLS

A report prepared for the federal Solicitor General by Sandra Gail Walker (1994) attempted to assess the nature and extent of weapon use in Canadian schools. The study used a variety of methods (focus groups, interviews, and mail out surveys) to collect information from police, educators, and customs officials. While the study did not collect data directly from students, the results are informative. Findings from the focus groups and interviews include the following:

- Knives are the weapons of choice in schools, and many are made at home or in shop class. In some schools (in municipalities of 250 000 or more) such weapons are confiscated on a daily basis.
- Firearms are rare in most Canadian schools.
- Weapons are not only carried and used for aggressive purposes, they are also carried for protection against assault, as "status symbols," for peer approval, or to intimidate other students.

BOX 10.2   WEAPON USE IN SCHOOLS (CONT.)

- Gangs were not seen as a problem in most schools. However, in some regions, gangs actively recruit from schools. Gang members may not themselves attend school but use school networks to exert influence.
- Although schools are quick to report firearms, they are, for a variety of reasons, less likely to report other types of weapons.

THE AFTERMATH

Victimizations that occur in the workplace do not seem to differ appreciably from other categories of crime in terms of their levels of property loss and injury (Garofalo, Siegel, and Laub, 1987; Mayhew, Elliott, and Dowds, 1989; Whitaker and Bastian, 1991). One important factor that probably reduces the potential severity of much workplace crime is the presence of other co-workers, who can provide or summon assistance.

As in the case of other social domains, much of the crime that occurs in the workplace is not reported to the police (Mayhew, Elliott, and Dowds, 1989). At least two specific characteristics of the work domain may discourage such reporting. First, many work environments may have alternative means for dealing with crime. The handling of an incident might proceed no further than bringing it to the attention of a supervisor or private security officer. Businesses, restaurants, and even schools may choose to avoid the publicity associated with the visit of a police patrol car by using informal processing or nonprocessing to deal with the majority of less serious incidents.

Second, employees who are victimized as a result of their dealings with the public may be persuaded by their employers that such incidents only occur when they are not doing their job properly. In other words, they may come to believe that among their job responsibilities is "cooling off" belligerent customers or clients. Even in more severe cases, the victim may fear being blamed for having started the incident by behaving rudely toward the customer (Salinger et al., 1993).

Jobs can become hazardous when they expose employees to clients and situations that may provide an opportunity for crime. One step that can be taken to deter these crimes is to provide employees with the resources they need to deal with client-related problems. Employers must further resolve to react strongly to crimes that occur on their premises, thereby ensuring that their employees can do their job with a greater sense of security.

CRIME AND LEGITIMATE WORK

We have seen that the relationship between crime and unemployment is less straightforward than is commonly supposed. Being employed is no guarantee of immunity from crime or victimization. In this section, we explore some of the ways in which work makes offending possible. Put simply, how do particular types of work routines and particular forms of the social organization of work relate to particular styles of offending?

WHAT IS OCCUPATIONAL CRIME?

The scope of work-related crime is potentially as broad as the types of jobs that exist within an economic system (Croall, 1987). Employees who have unsupervised access to the stock of their employers may find that their work role allows them a unique opportunity for theft. Physicians and lawyers may charge for services that are not performed (Arnold and Hagan, 1992). Stores may use illegal sales practices to defraud the public. Large corporations may engage in the sale and manufacture of dangerous products, pollute the environment, and maintain unsafe working conditions. Work-related crime ranges from pilfering by a disgruntled employee to the gargantuan thefts associated with the Savings and Loans Scandal in the United States.

Modern interest in the concept of work-related crime is usually traced back to the writings of the famous American criminologist Edwin Sutherland (see Chapter 3). Sutherland (1940) used the term **white-collar crime** to refer to a crime committed by a person of respectability and high status in the course of one's occupation. Sutherland saw a need to correct the imbalance in criminological thinking that associated crime almost exclusively with the actions of the poor and the powerless. Through a study of major American corporations, he sought to prove that individuals who were fully and gainfully employed, and whose jobs accorded them considerable power and economic security, were frequently responsible for serious breaches of the law.

Since Sutherland's time, the concept of white-collar crime has undergone adjustments that reflect changes in the meaning of white-collar work. For Sutherland, the term *white-collar crime* denoted the criminal conspiracies of major corporations. Today, many forms of white-collar work (for example, sales or computer programming) do not involve manual labour, but they cannot be considered positions in some sort of economic or corporate elite. Criminologists have attempted to capture important distinctions in the study of crime and legitimate work by introducing such terms as *professional crime, elite deviance, corporate crime, organizational crime, respectable crime,* and *business crime.* Our interest in social domains as the context of criminal events requires us to focus attention not only on the crimes of powerful jobholders but also on the crimes of those whose jobs denote lower-ranked positions. Encompassing both types of crime is the term **occupational crime,** which Akers (1985: 228) defines as the "violation of legal norms governing lawful occupational endeavours."

Occupational crimes may be distinguished in two important ways. First, they differ with respect to the nature of the offender–victim relationship. Some kinds of crimes are intended to provide only the jobholder with direct benefits. The person who pilfers from an employer does so for personal benefit, as does the bank teller who embezzles or the systems analyst who steals computer time. In such cases, the agency or organization is the victim, and the employee is the offender.

In other cases, the organization may be understood not as the victim but as a weapon that is used against those outside of the organization or at the bottom of the organizational hierarchy. In the context of such criminal events, the crime may profit the jobholder indirectly in that direct benefits accrue to the organization itself. Included among the victims might be other business organizations (a corporation hires industrial saboteurs to steal competitors' secrets), clients or customers (a corporation engages in deceptive advertising or sells untested pharmaceutical or food products), or low-level organizational members (employers maintain unsafe working conditions or violate laws relating to labour relations). Finally, we can recognize more general patterns of victimization with respect to offenders who inflict harm on very broad segments of society. Such crimes include political bribery, which undermines the political system; tax frauds, through which people indirectly distribute their losses to members of the tax-paying public; and industrial pollution, which threatens the air, land, and water.

A second way in which occupational crimes differ concerns the nature of the organizational settings in which they occur. Some types of occupational crime involve an offender who acts alone or only a small number of offenders. Medical fraud or dishonest household repair schemes might each involve the actions of a single offender who deals directly with victims and whose activities are not dependent on institutional support from co-workers. At the other extreme, **corporate crime** might involve "large vertical slices" of complex organizations (Snider, 1993: 321). In such cases, it may be difficult to say who did and who did not behave criminally, since each individual's actions contribute in small ways to the criminal event.

BOX 10.3   FRAUDULENT BUSINESS PRACTICES: LET THE BUYER BEWARE

While a "caveat emptor" (let the buyer beware) attitude may be seen to characterize many business transactions, the law sets limits on the ways in which companies can (and cannot) do business. While no one knows exactly how much consumer fraud takes place, fraudulent business practices clearly are far from uncommon. Christopher Stone describes one blatantly fraudulent practice in his book *Where the Law Ends: The Social Control of Corporate Behavior.* The case involved Holland Furnace Company, an organization clearing about $30 million in sales annually. One of the ways in which Holland boosted sales of its furnaces, however, involved flagrant fraud.

A Holland representative, posing as an inspector from the gas company, would visit private homes, ostensibly to inspect the furnace. The "inspector" would dismantle the furnace and then refuse to reassemble it because of an alleged safety violation. In the ensuing confusion, a second representative of Holland Furnace would appear at the door, conveniently selling furnaces in the neighbourhood. The distraught householder quite often proceeded to purchase a new heating unit from Holland.

After twenty-two years of legal wranglings, three company executives were found guilty of criminal contempt. The company's president was subsequently sentenced to six months in jail.

SOURCE: Based on William Coleman, *The Criminal Elite,* 3rd ed. (New York: St. Martin's Press, 1994); and Christopher Stone, *Where the Law Ends: The Social Control of Corporate Behavior* (New York: Harper & Row, 1975).

We now examine the social organization of work routines in order to understand how and why occupational crimes occur.

PRECURSORS

The relationship between work routines and criminal offending may be understood with reference to the concepts of opportunity and motivation (Coleman, 1987, 1991). In other words, the social organization of work may give people the means with which to violate the law, while their feelings about their jobs or employers may supply them with the reasons for doing so.

In terms of opportunity, some work routines give employers or employees access to people and things to victimize. Doctors have access to patients, lawyers have access to clients, corporations have access to markets, and bank tellers have access to "other people's money" (Calavita and Pontell, 1991). While such access does not necessarily result in criminal action, it does make such action possible.

According to Coleman (1987, 1991), at least four factors influence the evaluation of opportunities to commit white-collar crime. The first factor is the perception of how large a gain can be expected from using the opportunity. The second is the perception of potential risks associated with the opportunity. The exploration of criminal opportunities is more likely when effective control is lacking. Many professional groups, for example, claim to be self-regulating and discourage the efforts of government agencies to assume an investigative function, except in the most extreme cases. Many crimes that are associated with large corporations are so complex that they are policed only with great difficulty. Some observers have argued that the power of professional groups and large corporations discourages effective enforcement by state agencies (Hagan, 1992). The third factor is the degree of compatibility between the use of the opportunity and the potential offender's beliefs, attitudes, and ethical view of the situation. Finally, the evaluation of the opportunity is based on the potential offender's perception of the benefits of one opportunity relative to other opportunities to which the person has access.

The motivations for occupational crime are a matter of considerable debate. Some observers claim that these motivations reside in the nature of work itself or in the wider socioeconomic setting of the workplace. Insofar as capitalism promotes a "culture of competition" that encourages the pursuit of economic profit, the profit motive may be said to be the criminal motive (Calavita and Pontell, 1991). However, the ways in which particular businesses and industries are organized may also serve as important motivating factors. Industries that experience severe competition, that are engaged in the sale or distribution of potentially dangerous—and therefore highly regulated—goods, or that operate in an uncertain economic environment may feel pressure to operate unlawfully as a means of achieving organizational goals (Coleman, 1991; Keane, 1996; Snider, 1993).

In very large corporations or businesses, the pressures to behave criminally may be accentuated by the pressure placed on underlings to achieve organizational goals. In what Simon and Eitzen (1993) describe as "corporate Frankensteins," senior management may establish goals or quotas that everyone knows cannot be achieved within the limits imposed by current regulations. At the same time, management may be able to insulate itself from any covert criminal action that results from the establishment of such corporate objectives (Hagan, 1992). Those who make decisions about criminal wrongdoing may be actively or passively discouraged from reporting their activities to senior management (Coleman, 1987; Hagan, 1985). If the acts are discovered by enforcement agencies or the public, management can disavow any knowledge of wrongdoing. If the acts are not discovered, management can claim credit for the high profit yields (Snider, 1993).

By way of illustration, Farberman (1975) argues that the North American automobile industry is characterized by a **criminogenic market structure.** He maintains that the economic organization of the automobile industry almost necessitates criminal behaviour on the part of car dealers. The large automobile manufacturers require dealership franchises to sell cars in large numbers but at comparatively low prices. A small profit markup per unit on a large number of units benefits the car manufacturer, but not the dealer, who, as a result, feels compelled to compensate for financial losses by resorting to dishonest repair schemes and other forms of fraud.

The role of market forces in shaping criminal events in the automobile industry is even more clearly illustrated in the case of the Ford Pinto. This car was placed on the market in 1970, largely in response to feared competition from Japanese car manufacturers. Lee Iacocca, who was president of Ford at the time, told his engineers that they had to produce a car that weighed less than 2000 pounds and that cost less than $2000. While the Pinto met these specifications, it also contained serious design flaws. Most critical was the placement of the gas tank, which increased the likelihood that the car would explode in a rear-end collision. It was subsequently discovered that the corporate officers had known about this design flaw and about the actions that could be taken to correct it. Rather than act on this knowledge, however, they calculated the cost of these modifications and compared them with the costs likely to be incurred in lawsuits resulting from injuries to or deaths of Pinto drivers. Because the costs of the improvements were estimated to be greater than the costs associated with death and injury, Ford decided not to repair the defect.

Despite organizational and market pressures and a culture that seems to extol success at any cost, not everyone uses his or her occupational role to achieve criminal ends. Criminologists have stressed the significant role played by "definitions of the situation" that favour criminal offending (Benson, 1985). Coleman (1987) proposes the following six such definitions:

1. defining acts of theft as "borrowing"
2. denying that white-collar crimes result in any real harm
3. claiming that the laws that prohibit the behaviour are unfair or unjust
4. claiming that certain types of criminal behaviour are necessary if organizational goals are to be achieved

5. claiming that the behaviour is normal and "everybody does it"
6. claiming that employee theft is not really stealing since the money was owed (for example, uncharged overtime)

Thus, acts that may be seen as criminal by others may be seen as excusable behaviours by the embezzler who defines theft as "borrowing" and by the corporate executive who defines the violation of fair labour laws as "just good business."

Much of the debate about the motivations to commit occupational crime has centred on questions about the distinctiveness of occupational offenders. Many criminologists have long argued that white-collar offenders differ from street criminals in important ways that influence the likelihood of law violation. Many white-collar offenders are neither poor nor powerless. Their crimes are not impulsive, irrational, or the product of inadequate planning. Thus, many factors that are usually associated with crime and criminals would seem to have little to do with the behaviour of those white-collar offenders, particularly those at the top of corporate hierarchies. Therefore, the causes of these types of crime must lie elsewhere.

By contrast, the architects of the "general theory of crime," Gottfredson and Hirschi (1990), argue that the similarities between street criminals and occupational criminals are more important than the differences. For Gottfredson and Hirschi, the key explanatory mechanism for both groups is "self-control." Special theories are no more necessary to explain the criminal in a legitimate business than they are to explain the criminal in the university, the military, or the church. People who have low self-control are likely to engage in a variety of types of crime and deviance, as the opportunities to do so present themselves.

Because occupations that present significant criminal opportunities tend to be occupations that require a considerable degree of self-control, Gottfredson and Hirschi argue that the rates of occupational crime are lower than is popularly believed. Moreover, they suggest that when differences in opportunity are taken into account, demographic correlates of street and occupational crime are similar. They conclude that there is no need to presume special motivational circumstances in the case of the occupational offender, such as "the culture of competition" or other types of factors described here. Instead, they assert that "the distinction between crime in the street and crime in the suite is an *offence* rather than an *offender* distinction [and] that offenders in both cases are likely to share similar characteristics" (Gottfredson and Hirschi, 1990: 200).

Benson and Moore (1992) used data on the sentencing patterns for a large number of white-collar crimes (bank embezzlement, bribery, income tax evasion, false claims, and mail fraud) and common crimes (narcotics offences,

postal forgery, and bank robbery) to test some of the implications of
Gottfredson and Hirschi's theory. Specifically, they attempted to determine
whether white-collar offenders were as "criminally versatile" as common
offenders and whether they were as prone to as wide a range of deviant activities. They found that, while a minority of white-collar offenders behaved as
the theory predicted, the majority did not.

According to Benson and Moore, low self-control is not the only path to
occupational crime. Offenders with high self-control may employ it to pursue
ego gratification in an aggressive and calculating manner. The culture of
competition rewards such individuals by giving them positions of trust and
opportunities for committing serious but frequently undetected crimes. In
between those with high self-control and those with low self-control are individuals who may take advantage of occupational opportunities depending on
their personal situations. For these individuals, fear of economic or occupational failure may create a circumstance in which a previously adequate level
of self-control may become inadequate; as a result, the individual's ability to
resist occupational opportunities for crime may be weakened.

TRANSACTIONS

It is very difficult to determine the amount of crime that is committed in the
course of legitimate work, for many reasons. Above all, the nature of much of
this crime ensures that it will never be discovered. Corporate crimes that
victimize consumers, clients, or members of the general public are very often
"invisible" (Coleman, 1987). For example, people do not necessarily know
that some of the illnesses they experience are the result of inadequately tested
drugs. Workers who are injured by hazardous working conditions may be
inclined to blame themselves rather than their employers for their injuries
(Croall, 1987). Our terminology encourages this tendency—we routinely call
such occurrences "accidents" rather than "assaults."

Unlike more garden variety forms of offending, occupational crimes are
largely hidden from public view. The employee who has access to opportunities for offending may escape public scrutiny. The offender who uses the
computer to embezzle may do so in such a way that the crime goes undetected
by the employer, co-workers, or enforcement agencies. Corporate conspiracies
are even less visible. Evidence about corporate decisions regarding offending is
not accessible to those outside the corporation. Moreover, because a
corporate crime may involve actions by members at all levels of the organization, many of those who participate in the event may not even be aware of the
true character of their actions.

As is the case with other categories of crime, occupational crimes do not come to the attention of policing or regulatory agencies as a result of vigorous enforcement practices. At the same time, victims may be poorly positioned to know about—and respond to—the occupational crimes that victimize them. The regulatory agencies that are supposed to police and scrutinize corporate behaviour face many obstacles. According to Snider (1992), these obstacles include the following:

- the massive economic and political power of corporations that favour nonenforcement
- lack of staff and funds
- frequent lack of support from the governments that appoint them
- the high cost of investigating each complaint
- support only from weak consumer or labour groups
- minimal accountability to public or media scrutiny

A consequence of these obstacles is that many kinds of occupational crimes that are discovered are not reported. A business that learns that its employees have been embezzling funds may not wish the matter to be widely known because it would in all likelihood reduce public trust in the company. Thus, the long-range negative consequences of reporting may be seen to outweigh the immediate benefits of doing so.

Police data on occupational offences are of only limited use. Not only are such offences underreported, but in many cases (for example, fraud) it is not possible to determine whether the crimes occurred in the context of work roles. This is due in part to the fact that occupational crime is a conceptual rather than a legal category. While victimization surveys may supplement official record-keeping systems, they, too, are limited, given the absence in many cases of a "direct victim" as well as the inability of the victim to recognize occupational and corporate offending.

THE AFTERMATH

Our best estimates suggest that the crimes committed by people in the course of legitimate occupational activities result in considerable levels of financial and physical harm and loss of life (Simon, 1996). Snider (1993) argues that "corporate crime is a major killer, causing more deaths in a month than all the mass murderers combined do in a decade." According to one estimate, Canadians are ten times more likely to die as a result of unsafe or unhealthy workplace conditions as they are to be murdered (Reasons, Ross, and Paterson, 1981). It is estimated that the economic costs of corporate crime also

BOX 10.4   PUBLIC PERCEPTIONS OF COMMERICAL CRIME

Frank Pearce (1991) describes a British victimization survey (the Second Islington Crime Survey) that asked respondents not only about their experiences with "conventional" crime but also about their experiences with several forms of "commercial" crime. Of 889 community residents:

- 9 percent believed that they had been given misleading information about goods or services. As a result, 45 percent complained and 49 percent received some kind of compensation;

- 19 percent believed that they had been deliberately overcharged for goods or services. Of these, 68 percent complained and in 67 percent of cases received some kind of compensation; and

- 25 percent believed that they had paid for goods or work that turned out to be defective. Of these, 74 percent complained and 72 percent received some kind of compensation.

exceed the costs of "street" crimes like burglary or larceny. In the United States, one particularly notorious case of corporate offending, the Savings and Loans Scandal, will probably end up costing American taxpayers as much as $500 billion (Gabor, 1994a).

Controlling crimes that occur in the context of legitimate work roles is no easy task. It is sometimes assumed that members of the public are less concerned about occupational crimes than about more direct forms of predatory crime; however, this does not appear to be the case (Hans and Ermann, 1989). Nonetheless, the fact remains that the low level of visibility associated with occupational crimes makes effective deterrence difficult (Coleman, 1987). Some studies suggest that the threat of legal sanction has less impact on corporate crime than does the market environment in which companies operate (Keane, 1996; Simpson and Koper, 1992).

ENTERPRISE VERSUS ORGANIZED CRIME

In some cases, crime can itself be thought of as an occupation or business. We can define **enterprise crimes** as the "sale of illegal goods and services to customers who know that the goods or services are illegal" (Haller, 1990: 207). The nature of such goods or services may be highly varied and ultimately depend on what the law disallows. The sale of illegal drugs or pornography, the operation of illegal gambling houses, loan sharking, and "contract killing" are all examples of enterprise crime.

What we call enterprise crime is usually referred to by criminologists and noncriminologists alike as "organized crime." This concept conjures up a number of familiar images gleaned from movies like *The Godfather*, novels, and newspaper coverage of "mob trials" (exemplified by the trial of John Gotti). However, for reasons that will become clear, the concept of organized crime obscures rather than enhances our understanding of the types of events in which we are interested.

WHAT IS ORGANIZED CRIME?

In popular usage, the study of enterprise crime has been compromised by what some writers have referred to as the "official myth of organized crime" (Kappeler, Blumberg, and Potter, 1993). In this context, the term *organized crime* has been most often used to refer to long-term, highly organized criminal syndicates that are involved in a number of criminal businesses. These syndicates are said to be organized along ethnic lines and to function in much the same way as legitimate business corporations (Cressey, 1969). In this sense, they have well-established patterns of recruitment and authority.

The most widely discussed group of organized criminals in the criminological and popular literature on the subject is the Mafia, also known as **La Cosa Nostra**. This particular form of criminal conspiracy is said to be the major such group operating in North America (Abadinsky, 1987). It is said by many observers to have its origins in the Sicilian Mafia and to have been imported to Canada and the United States along with the waves of European immigration in the latter days of the nineteenth century (Carrigan, 1991; Smith, 1975).

BOX 10.5   TYPES OF ORGANIZED CRIME GROUPS

In her recent analysis of organized crime in Canada, sociologist Margaret Beare (1996) argues that organized crime groups can be distinguished with respect to their differing degrees of dependence on organized crime activity. She suggests that this typology is not only useful in helping us distinguish groups at any one point in time, but that it also describes the various forms that any one group might take at different points in time.

**Table 10.1 The Commitment of Legitimate and Illegitimate
Groups to Crime**

Existence of group is independent of, and therefore separate from, OC activity ➡		➡	*Existence of group is dependent on, and therefore explained by, OC activity*
Characteristics	**Characteristics**	**Characteristics**	**Characteristics**
Criminal activity is secondary to the ongoing purpose of the existing group structure. Existing structure or circumstantial advantages may facilitate the OC activity, but OC is not the reason the group exists. Group is seen to be legitimate in spite of OC activity. Group activities are much broader.	Structure is in place for political/ideological or task-oriented reason. OC may be used to provide the funds to reach the goals. OC activity is accepted as a necessary part of the operation of these groups. However, without the OC activity, the groups would change but continue to exist.	The sense of tradition/ethnic cohesion is provided within the continuation of a historical structure that may have been created originally around a political ideology. The group's main reason now for existing is to carry out OC.	Groups are created strictly for the purpose of efficiently carrying out OC crimes. If OC was no longer a group activity, the group would have no reason to exist. This category tends to include the newer OC groups that are still in a state of flux.
Examples	**Examples**	**Examples**	**Examples**
Aboriginal groups that engage in OC criminal activity.	Terrorist groups involved in OC to generate funds. Outlaw motorcycle gangs.	Asian triads/Mafia.	Russian, Jamaican, and Nigerian OC groups. Colombian cartels.

SOURCE: M.E. Beare, *Criminal Conspiracies* (Scarborough, ON: Nelson Canada, 1996).

Observers further claim that the modern Mafia has its origins in the so-called "Black Hand" gangs that operated in the ethnic enclaves of major Canadian and American cities. These gangs were simply groups of extortionists who preyed on their fellow émigrés (Pitkin and Cordasco, 1977; Dubro, 1985). Their name derived from the fact that they would send their victims letters signed with a black hand print. The American experiment with national prohibition of liquor in the 1920s allegedly gave organized crime groups an opportunity to consolidate their economic power. Throughout the 1930s, the theory asserts, these gangs developed into a national federation that came to control the operation of illegal business in all regions of the continent.

This view of organized crime has been legitimated in the stories told by former Mafiosi (Kirby and Renner, 1986; Maas, 1968), in the reports of undercover law enforcement officers, journalists (Edwards and Nicasco, 1993) in federal investigations of organized crime (Moore, 1974; Smith, 1975), and in the writings of academic criminologists (Galliher and Cain, 1974). The major academic architect of this view was the sociologist Donald Cressey (1969), who, as a consultant to the President's Commission on Law Enforcement and the Administration of Justice in the late 1960s, wrote a highly influential report on the nature and influence of organized crime groups in the United States. In a revised version of that report, published in 1969, Cressey argued that any attempt to understand American organized crime required recognition of eight "facts":

1. A nationwide alliance of at least twenty-four tightly knit crime "families" exists in the United States.
2. The members of these "families" are all Italians and Sicilians, or of Italian and Sicilian descent, and those on the eastern seaboard, especially, call the entire system "Cosa Nostra."
3. The names, criminal records, and principal criminal activities of about five thousand of the participants have been assembled.
4. The persons occupying key positions in the skeletal structure of each "family" are well known to law enforcement officials.
5. The "families" are linked to one another and to non–Cosa Nostra syndicates by understandings, agreements, and "treaties," as well as by mutual deference to the "Commission," which is made up of the leaders of the most powerful families.
6. The boss of each family directs the activities (especially the illegal ones) that are undertaken by the members of his "family."
7. The organization as a whole controls all but a tiny part of illegal gambling, loan sharking, and narcotics importation.
8. Information about the Commission, the "families," and family activities has come from detailed reports made by a wide variety of police observers, informants, wiretaps, and electronic "bugs."

In Canada, as in the United States, a similar image of the problem has been constructed by the police, journalists, and some members of the academic community (Beare, 1996; Carrigan, 1991; Dubro, 1985; Kirby and Renner,

1986). It is generally acknowledged that the Cosa Nostra has never become as firmly entrenched in Canadian as in American society. Instead, it is argued that much of the activity of organized crime groups in Toronto, Hamilton, and Montreal has, like much of the legitimate economy, operated as branch plants of powerful American families located in New York City and Buffalo (Dubro, 1985). As one recent law enforcement report states:

> There are approximately 14 traditional organized crime groups in Ontario
> with an estimated membership of 280. These groups are branches of the
> American La Cosa Nostra. They are involved in legitimate businesses
> which enable them to launder the profits obtained from their illegal activi-
> ties. Their illegal ventures include extortion, fraud, gambling, loanshark-
> ing, counterfeiting, murder and trafficking in drugs. (Canadian
> Association of Chiefs of Police, 1992: 40)

It is claimed in both countries by advocates of the view that organized crime is an organized conspiracy that these groups are not the only ones involved in organized crime (Abadinsky, 1987). In Canada, for instance, increasing attention is being focused on the activities of Chinese or Vietnamese groups, as well as those of outlaw motorcycle gangs. In a similar way, American observers have expressed concern about the increasing involvement of Cuban, Afro-American, Jamaican, Russian, and Aboriginal groups in organized crime activities (Beare, 1996).

Despite the popularity of the view of organized crime just outlined, many researchers have called into question both its accuracy and value. Several shortcomings have been noted. First, the view of organized crime as an "organized parasitic conspiracy" deflects our attention from any critical assessment of the ways in which our own society makes such crime possible. Despite the obvious implications of this view, it has been shown that the types of activity associated with La Cosa Nostra have not developed in all societies that have large numbers of Italian immigrants. Second, researchers over the past two decades have called into question every one of Cressey's eight "facts" as well as the orthodox history of organized crime that is told and retold in the works of popular and academic writers (Kappeler, Blumberg, and Potter, 1993; Smith, 1975).

Third, and most basically, the concept of organized crime is itself confusing and misleading (Friedrichs, 1996). Logically, we might suggest that it refers to any type of activity that involves more than one offender acting in coordinated fashion. From this point of view, two juveniles who break into a house could be said to have engaged in organized crime. However, the term is almost never used this way. Instead, it is used to refer to large-scale criminal efforts that are

According to law enforcement authorities, "outlaw motorcycle gangs" have become a major force in enterprise crime. Police intelligence pictures the regional distribution of gang activity as follows:

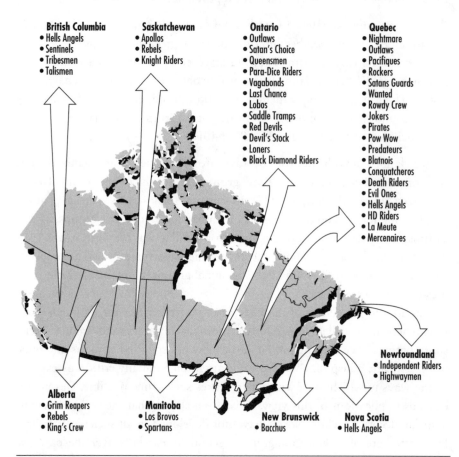

British Columbia
• Hells Angels
• Sentinels
• Tribesmen
• Talismen

Saskatchewan
• Apollos
• Rebels
• Knight Riders

Ontario
• Outlaws
• Satan's Choice
• Queensmen
• Para-Dice Riders
• Vagabonds
• Last Chance
• Lobos
• Saddle Tramps
• Red Devils
• Devil's Stock
• Loners
• Black Diamond Riders

Quebec
• Nightmare
• Outlaws
• Pacifiques
• Rockers
• Satans Guards
• Wanted
• Rowdy Crew
• Jokers
• Pirates
• Pow Wow
• Predateurs
• Blatnois
• Conquatcheros
• Death Riders
• Evil Ones
• Hells Angels
• HD Riders
• La Meute
• Mercenaires

Alberta
• Grim Reapers
• Rebels
• King's Crew

Manitoba
• Los Brovos
• Spartans

New Brunswick
• Bacchus

Nova Scotia
• Hells Angels

Newfoundland
• Independent Riders
• Highwaymen

SOURCE: Canadian Association of Chiefs of Police, *Organized Crime Committee Report* (Ottawa: Criminal Intelligence Service Canada, 1992).

diverse in nature and that seem to have little in common beyond the fact that we associate them with particular stereotypical notions of who organized criminals are. Adding to the confusion, the term *organized crime* is sometimes used to refer to a particular type of activity (as in the statement, "Gambling is a form of organized crime") and other times to particular groups of criminals (as in the statement, "We must prosecute members of organized crime"). Such usage results in circular reasoning (Maltz, 1976). If we say, for example, "Organized crime is involved in the drug trade," we have not really said anything because, by definition, the drug trade is an organized crime and any group involved in this activity must necessarily be involved in organized crime. Recently, Margaret Beare (1996) has argued that the most useful way to think of organized crime is to view it as a "process" rather than as a structure or a group. Organized crime is thus viewed as a way of committing crimes rather than as a type of crime.

One way to circumvent some of these definitional difficulties is to shift our attention away from the focus on alien, parasitic conspiracies and "organized crime" and toward the study of enterprise crime.

PRECURSORS

As previously defined, enterprise crime involves the sale and distribution of illegal goods and services. What kinds of social conditions make enterprise crime likely? The first such condition, of course, is the existence of laws prohibiting the goods and services in question. In other words, enterprise crime is made possible when the reach of law creates market opportunities. Prohibition, which was in force in the United States between 1920 and 1933, in a very real sense created the opportunity for financial gain that could be exploited by criminal entrepreneurs (Packer, 1969; Schelling, 1967). In a similar way, attempts to use the law to control the availability of illicit drugs—such as marijuana or cocaine—or to use high rates of taxation to control the availability of legal drugs such as tobacco, make enterprise crime possible. The gap between what people want and what the law allows them to legitimately have suggests an important way in which our society provides the sources of enterprise crime. This point is obscured when we think of such crime as merely the product of an alien, parasitic conspiracy.

The second such factor is systematic corruption. To the degree that enterprise criminals have access to police or political officials who are interested in the development of cooperative ventures with these entrepreneurs, the effects of agencies of legal control may be neutralized. Bribery and corruption may afford some enterprise criminals protection from the law, while others may discover that they are the objects of much more aggressive enforcement. Just as occurs in the more legitimate sectors of the economy, the establishment of cozy relationships between those who do the policing and those who are supposed to be policed may facilitate the conditions by which greater market control is assured. In the absence of such mutually advantageous relationships, criminal enterprise markets are more unstable.

A third precondition for the establishment of stable enterprise crime is the existence of partnership arrangements. Such arrangements have the same role in illegal businesses that they have in legal business ventures. They allow entrepreneurs to share risks (especially the risk of business failure), and they allow people with different types of resources to pool these resources. This means that individuals who have political influence, capital, or managerial skills can combine their talents in a way that increases the potential for profit.

This emphasis on partnerships suggests that, rather than being hierarchically or bureaucratically organized, enterprise crime is much more likely to involve informal styles of association (Albini, 1971; Ianni and Reuss-Ianni, 1972). Partnerships may arise when they are deemed necessary or desirable for business purposes, and they may be dissolved when they have served their purpose or when they cease to be profitable. Moreover, Haller (1990) notes, not everyone need be thought of as equal in these partnerships. Some entrepreneurs exercise much more power than others because they have the political or economic resources that allow them to participate in several enterprises simultaneously. In Nicholas Pileggi's book *Wiseguy* (on which the movie *Goodfellas* was based), ex-mobster Henry Hill describes the influence of mob boss Paul Vario in terms that clearly indicate the nature of these partnership arrangements:

> There were hundreds of guys who depended on Paulie for their living, but he never paid out a dime. The guys who worked for Paulie had to make their own dollar. All they got from Paulie was protection from other guys looking to rip them off. That's what it's all about. That's what the FBI can never understand—that what Paulie and the organization offer is protection of the kinds of guys who can't go to the cops. They're like the police department for wiseguys. (Pileggi, 1985: 56–57)

More generally, Haller (1990) suggests that, like the Chamber of Commerce or Rotary Club, La Cosa Nostra should be viewed, not as an organization that operates illegal (or legal) businesses, but as an association that businesspeople join partly to further their business careers.

Finally, Haller notes, many types of economic factors shape the structure of illegal enterprises—factors that serve both to enhance and to reduce cooperation (Schelling, 1967). Enterprises that involve the importation of drugs like cocaine or heroin may involve a high degree of cooperation among many groups located in both the exporting and receiving countries. Drug networks also exist at the local level. In addition, substantial drug transactions may require a large initial capital investment. Factors of this type may encourage the development of monopolistic tendencies, since relatively few groups are

able to marshal the economic resources or possess the contacts needed to facilitate large-scale arrangements. By contrast, the illegal market for marijuana
may be structured quite differently (Rogers, 1973). This illicit commodity does
not have to be imported and can be distributed on a small-scale basis by inde-

---

BOX 10.7   THE DRUG BUSINESS

The sale and distribution of drugs represents a major form of enterprise crime. In
the 1980s, the concern about drugs dominated much of the discussion about crime
and violence in North America.

The reporting of drug crimes differs from the reporting of crimes that involve a
direct and immediate victim. Given that both sides are willing participants in a drug
transaction, no one is likely to notify the police that a crime has been committed.
Drug users, like other types of offenders, are interested in ensuring that their
behaviour has low visibility. This means that official data on drug crimes are likely to
reflect the vigour with which policing agencies pursue such crime.

According to the Canadian Centre for Justice Statistics (Wolff, 1991), supply
offences (trafficking, importation, and cultivation) have increased as a proportion of
total drug crimes since 1977. At the same time, recorded crimes of possession
have fallen, although possession still represents the major type of drug offence.

**Figure 10.1   Cocaine and Cannabis as a Proportion of Trafficking Offences,
Canada, 1977–1993**

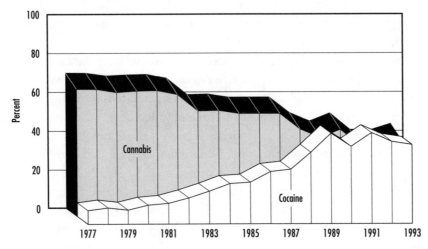

Figure 10.2   Possession and Supply Offences

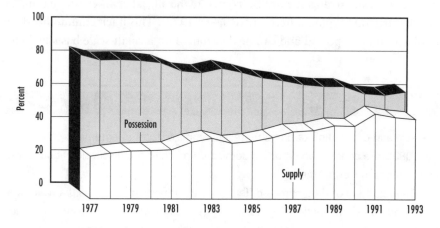

SOURCE (Figures 10.1 and 10.2): Uniform Crime Reporting survey, Canadian Centre for Justice Statistics, 1993.

pendent entrepreneurs who cater to the needs of a small, local clientele. Markets of this type are much more resistant to monopolization.

TRANSACTIONS

If we think about enterprise crime as a type of business, then the questions to which we seek answers are not unlike the questions we might ask about more legitimate businesses. What is the nature of the market? How are goods and services produced and distributed? What are the sources of capital that underwrite the costs of doing business? How do the various groups involved in these businesses cope with changing markets? What types of people are attracted to this particular line of work, and why?

Criminologists are particularly concerned, however, with the fact that the business is illegal (Haller, 1990). As economist Thomas Schelling (1967) notes, when a business is made illegal, entry into the marketplace is restricted to those who are willing and able to behave criminally. In other words, the illegal nature of the business is perhaps most attractive to those who have no strong reservations about involvement in behaviours that are prohibited by law.

As we pointed out previously, much has been made of the ethnic character of organized crime. Apart from La Cosa Nostra, commonly cited groups include the Chinese Triad, the Jamaican Posse, and associations loosely referred to in the popular press as the Colombian, Irish, and Vietnamese mafias. This emphasis on ethnicity has frequently served to reinforce the popular view that criminal enterprise is an "alien" problem because it is associated with ethnic groups.

In rejecting this view, sociologist Daniel Bell (1953) argued over four decades ago that organized crime functions as a "queer ladder of social mobility" in societies that emphasize material success but fail to provide all racial and economic groups with equal opportunities for achieving it. Like Robert Merton (1938), Bell maintained that, as a result of the pressure to achieve social goals, groups that find the legitimate channels of upward mobility blocked may turn to illegal alternatives. A key implication of this argument is that enterprise crime, seen as a form of economic activity, is most attractive to those located at or near the bottom of the social hierarchy.

Ianni (1974), like Bell before him, argued that involvement in enterprise crime is characterized by an ethnic succession rather than by an enduring criminal conspiracy. Particular ethnic groups may dominate organized crime until legitimate channels of upward mobility become generally accessible. At this point, the influence of any particular group may decline as other groups move in to fill the void created by the outward movement. Thus, the Italian presence in organized crime, which peaked in the period immediately before Prohibition, was preceded by an Irish and Jewish presence and succeeded by a Cuban and African-American presence (Ianni, 1974). The emergence in Canada of Vietnamese and Chinese gangs may illustrate a similar process of ethnic succession.

This is not to say that the domination of enterprise crime by any particular group is irrelevant to the ways in which markets are structured or exploited (Light, 1977). Members of ethnic groups may be able to draw on their cultural capital in ways that enable them to be especially effective in particular types of enterprise crime. They may also share in particular forms of cultural traditions that facilitate criminal organization. According to Ianni (1971), the significance of the family as a central organizing theme in Italian culture has contributed to the creation of criminal enterprises—structured along kinship lines—that are remarkably durable.

A second important implication that flows from the illegal nature of criminal enterprises relates to the role of regulation. Obviously, when a market is declared illegal, it cannot be controlled by the government agencies responsible for the mediation of disputes or the resolution of conflicts (Reuter, 1984b). As Henry Hill's earlier remarks make clear, criminal entrepreneurs are unable to seek recourse for harm done against them by going to the police or initiating lawsuits. One mobster cannot sue another because a promised shipment of heroin was not delivered or because a promise to influence the vote of a labour union was not kept. It is for such reasons that violence, or the threat of violence, looms so large in the business affairs of criminal entrepreneurs.

Violence represents one of the few means by which contracts can be enforced and compliance with agreements can be assured (Black, 1983; Reuter, 1984b).

The types of criminal events that are central to enterprise crime—the acquisition and distribution of illegal goods and services—are complicated affairs, but much popular thinking on the subject glosses over these complexities. We are used to thinking about enterprise crime as nothing more than the acts of vicious gangsters whose ways of thinking and acting are foreign to the societies in which we find them. While this makes for good pulp fiction, it is not very illuminating. Organized crime events are shaped by the societal context and are in no fundamental way alien to it. The gap between popular demand and efforts to legally control supply makes illegal markets possible in the first place. By declaring these markets off-limits to legal regulation, society helps to create circumstances in which the potential for violence is considerable. The stratified nature of society and the restrictions it imposes on upward mobility cause some who are adversely affected to see enterprise crime as a viable means of achieving the goals toward which their societies encourage them to aspire.

THE AFTERMATH

Public reactions to enterprise crime often fail to take account of the wider context, which, we have argued, is necessary if we hope to achieve an appropriate understanding of this type of crime (Morash, 1984). When we read about a gangland killing in an urban ethnic restaurant or a police seizure of drug assets, we rarely consider the social character of these crimes. We are encouraged to think about organized crime as a force at war with "decent society," as it preys on citizens and threatens to corrupt our public officials and undermine our basic social institutions. Rarely are we encouraged to think about criminal enterprise as a logical product of prevalent social conditions. As McIntosh (1975) argues, criminal entrepreneurs are part of a larger configuration that includes not only the criminal but also victims, the police, politicians, customers, and others. The activities of the criminal entrepreneur cannot be understood by focusing on the entrepreneur alone. As these larger configurations change, so do the types of events in which criminal entrepreneurs are likely to be involved. In the absence of this more complex and detailed understanding, enterprise crime will be seen as alien and parasitic.

One important implication of traditional views of enterprise crime relates to the means by which such crime is to be controlled. The image of enterprise crime as an alien, parasitic conspiracy, rather than as a social product, supports the position that this type of crime is a law enforcement problem. From this perspective, enterprise crime is best controlled through the aggressive prosecution of criminal entrepreneurs. And yet, when we conceptualize the problem in terms of criminal enterprise rather than in terms of organized crime, we recognize that this "gangbuster mentality" has serious limitations. If enterprise crime really does function like other economic markets, then the removal of criminal entrepreneurs (through arrest and imprisonment) will not significantly affect market operation, since such actions have no effect on the demand for illegal goods. We recognize this fact quite explicitly in the case of legal markets. When an entrepreneur who sells legal goods—for instance, shoes—is removed from the market as a result of death, illness, or retirement, shoes remain available (Van den Haag, 1975). This is because the demand for shoes will prompt others to enter the market to fill the void. In fact, it might even be argued that, because an aggressive policy of prosecution increases the risks of doing business, the going rate for goods and services will increase and the profits to be gained may increase accordingly.

■ ■ ■

SUMMARY

We have seen in this chapter that the roles we play in the workplace domain structure the kinds of involvement we are likely to have in various types of criminal events. Some jobs increase employees' risks of criminal victimization, while others provide them with opportunities to victimize others, be they subordinates, co-workers, clients, customers, or society at large. Alternatively, illegal though they may be, various types of enterprise crime nevertheless constitute a form of work.

Throughout much of its history, criminology has focused attention on how exclusion from the world of legitimate work motivates criminality. While this remains an important (if unresolved) issue, it is equally important to understand how the organization of the domain of work facilitates or hinders the development of criminal events within this domain. Theories that emphasize the role of social inequality in the generation of crime quite naturally suggest that not having a job may encourage the development of criminal motivations. Victimization risks differ between those who are employed and those who are not. More importantly, particular forms of labour force participation make crime possible. Relevant here are two factors: (1) the relationship between the jobs people have and the victimization risks they face and (2) the ways in which jobs provide people with opportunities to behave criminally.

Victimization risk at work is inversely correlated to occupational status, measured by income, with those in lower-income occupations being more vulnerable. However, occupation alone is not enough to define victimization risk. Workplace settings can be very important in influencing the opportunity for crime. Risk can be heightened by the fact that money is available to be stolen. Sometimes, the nature of the job has a provoking effect on customers, who may vent their anger and frustration at the employee. Crimes that occur in these circumstances are not easy to deter and are underreported. In the aftermath of violent encounters, employees may accept the blame or assume that the employer will blame them for handling the situation poorly. Alternatively, these incidents may be handled informally to avoid the problems associated with police involvement.

Work-related crime may range all the way from pilfering by a disgruntled employee to the gargantuan thefts associated with the Savings and Loans Scandal in the United States. Sutherland (1940) used the term *white-collar crime* to refer to crimes committed by a person of respectability and high status in the course of one's occupation. He saw a need to correct the imbalance in criminological thinking that associated crime almost exclusively with the actions of the poor and the powerless.

Occupational crimes may be distinguished in two important ways. First, they differ with respect to the nature of the offender–victim relationship. Some kinds of crimes are intended to provide direct benefits only for the jobholder, as in the case of the employee who steals. In such instances, the agency or organization is the victim and the employee is the offender. In other cases, the organization may be used to attack those outside of the business or at the bottom of the organizational hierarchy. With respect to these criminal events, the crime may profit the jobholder indirectly in that more direct benefits accrue to the organization itself. Finally, more general patterns of victimization result from crimes that inflict harm on very broad segments of society. Such crimes include political bribery, tax fraud, and industrial pollution.

Occupational crimes differ according to the nature of the organizational settings in which they occur. Some types of occupational crime involve either a lone offender or a small number of offenders, as is exemplified by medical frauds and dishonest household repair services. At the other extreme, corporate crime might involve "large vertical slices" of complex organizations. In such cases, it may be difficult to say who did and did not behave criminally, since each individual's actions constitute only a small portion of the criminal event.

Gottfredson and Hirschi (1990) argue that the mechanism of self-control is equally applicable to understanding the behaviour of the occupational criminal as it is to understanding the behaviour of the street criminal. What distinguishes occupational crime from street crime is, in Gottfredson and Hirschi's view, not the offender but rather the offence. People who have low self-control are likely to engage in a variety of types of crime and deviance, as the opportunities to do so present themselves. Despite the significant financial and physical harm caused by occupational crimes, their low visibility makes them difficult to detect and deter.

We can also view crime as operating in a marketplace in which illicit substances and services are sold to customers who know that they are illegal. Rather than view such activity in terms of ethnically based organized crime, we instead use the term *enterprise crime* to refer to this type of criminal activity. Enterprise crime occurs as a result of laws that prohibit certain goods and services. In other words, enterprise crime is made possible when the reach of law creates market opportunities. More than requiring a definition of illegality, however, enterprise crime needs the presence of systematic corruption, partnership arrangements between illegal and legal businesses, and favourable market conditions such as a monopoly on the illegal goods.

When we conceptualize the problem of "organized crime" in terms of criminal enterprise rather than in terms of organized crime, it becomes apparent that law enforcement responses to crime have serious limitations. If enterprise crime functions like other economic markets, removing criminal entrepreneurs (through arrest and imprisonment) will not significantly affect market operation or reduce the demand for illegal goods.

■　■　■

QUESTIONS FOR REVIEW AND DISCUSSION

1. What criminological factors would help to explain why taxi drivers tend to experience high rates of robbery?

2. What measures could be taken to reduce the problems of crime and victimization in high schools? Do these solutions interfere with the basic mission of schools to provide education?

3. Do you agree with the view that corporate crime is a more serious problem than street crime? How do corporations discourage us from adopting this view?

4. In reference to a job you currently hold (or perhaps a past summer job), what opportunities for crime did your employment make available to you?

5. How do television and movie portrayals of organized crime distort public understanding of the problem? Can you think of some specific examples?

6. "Despite their differences, most offender-based theories lead us to expect a higher rate of crime among people who are unemployed than among people who are employed." Discuss this statement.

PART SIX

RESPONSES TO CRIME

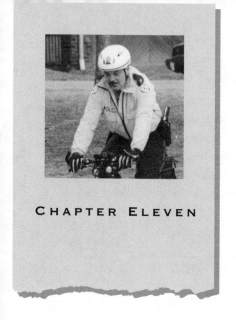

CHAPTER ELEVEN

Summary and Review of Public Policy Responses to Crime

WHAT'S IN CHAPTER ELEVEN

In this chapter, we begin by reviewing the criminal event. We then examine potential public policy responses to the crime problem from an event perspective, focusing on public health and public safety issues and crime prevention through social development. We conclude by discussing recent initiatives in community policing.

INTRODUCTION

The objectives of this chapter are (1) to summarize what we have learned in previous chapters about the nature, causes, and consequences of criminal events, and (2) to sketch some of the major policy responses available to us. These objectives are interrelated in that what we can do about criminal events should follow logically from a detailed understanding of their causes and content.

SUMMARY OF FINDINGS ON THE CRIMINAL EVENT

We began in Chapter 1 by discussing some important concepts that guide the study of criminal events. Most notably, we emphasized that there are no simple answers to the questions, What is crime? and How is crime to be studied? It is too glib to say that crime is simply behaviour that violates the law; such a definition obscures our view of the complex social realities that demand our attention. We emphasized a need to recognize that there is more to crime than the behaviour of a lawbreaker. As social events, crimes involve not only offenders but other participants as well, including victims, the police, witnesses, and bystanders, all of whom act and react within particular social and physical circumstances.

Chapter 1 sketched a general picture of crime in Canada. We saw that the amount of crime has increased fourfold over the past thirty years and that the majority of crime is directed against property rather than against people. Public views of crime, as articulated in the mass media and day-to-day conversations, influence our views of crime. Unfortunately, media images of crime tend to exaggerate the frequency of serious violent crime and to emphasize the sensationalist character of both crime and the solutions to crime.

In Chapter 2, we introduced the criminal event framework. Most fundamentally, we observed that criminal events are social events in that they involve interaction between human beings. The dynamics of this interaction shape the content of the event and thus the consequences of the event for those involved. We discussed the roles played by the principal protagonists in criminal events: offenders, victims, bystanders, and the police. In examining the social and demographic characteristics of victims and offenders, we noted that, for many categories of crime, offenders and victims have much in common (a finding contrary to what media reporting sometimes leads us to expect). Both victims

333

*Summary and
Review of
Public Policy
Responses
to Crime*

and offenders tend to be young, socially disadvantaged, and, for many categories of crime, males. There are, of course, important exceptions to this pattern. For obvious reasons, corporate crimes are not typically perpetrated by disadvantaged young males, and many forms of violence uniquely victimize women. We also pointed out that criminal events do not occur with equal frequency in all types of communities or within communities, or at all types of locations.

Chapters 3 to 6 described the major theoretical orientations that have dominated criminology in recent decades. We defined criminological theories as generalized explanations of criminal phenomena. We look to theories to make sense of our observations of the empirical world. Conversely, we look to the empirical world for confirmation or refutation of our theoretical views.

Theoretical interest in crime has generally meant theoretical interest in offenders. For this reason, we devoted two chapters to describing alternative conceptualizations of the offender. Chapter 3 focused on theories that derive from "positivist" views of the offender, while Chapter 4 presented explanations that find their origins in "classical" thought. The distinction between positivist and classical views, which we introduced in Chapter 1, has to do with the degree to which human will is thought to dominate social action. Broadly stated, positivist theories seek to understand the factors that cause offenders to do what they do, while classical theories emphasize the significance of rational choice in influencing the behaviour of the criminal offender.

Chapter 3 discussed many of the causal theories that have been offered to explain criminal behaviour. While some of these theories emphasize biological, constitutional, or genetic causes of criminal conduct, most emphasize the role of social factors. We examined two major types of social explanations. The first considers the ways in which socially induced frustration can contribute to the development of criminal motivations. Robert Merton discerned in the gap between the things that people are encouraged by their culture to want and what is actually available to them a major source of frustration that manifests itself in criminal conduct.

The second social explanation of criminal motivation stresses the role of culture. Subcultural theories suggest that people learn the motivations to behave criminally in the same way that they learn motivations to do anything else. The emphasis here is on the immediate environment in which offenders operate and on how these environments encourage or facilitate the learning of cultural lessons that support criminal behaviour. The foremost architect of this view was Edwin Sutherland, whose theory of differential association stressed an understanding of crime as a learned behaviour. While Sutherland and the subcultural theorists who followed him encourage us to think about the relationship between criminal behaviour and exposure to criminal cultures, theorists like David Matza and Gresham Sykes have argued for the need to appreciate how lessons that might motivate offending can be learned from mainstream culture.

In Chapter 4, we focused on offenders' decision-making processes rather than their motivations. For theorists who adhere to the classical school, there is little to be gained from attempts to search for unique factors that motivate offending behaviour. Instead, they suggest that such behaviour is better understood in relation to the formal and informal social controls that might be expected to restrain offending behaviour. When these controls are ineffective or when individuals are insensitive to them, potential offenders are primed to become actual offenders. In such circumstances, people are free to act in ways that, criminal though they may be, also reflect rational self-interest. Social controls that discourage individuals from engaging in the criminal pursuit of self-interest include their social bonds to conformist others, their relationships with their communities, and the sanctions promised by the legal system.

The theoretical explanations discussed in Chapter 5 differ in a fundamental way from those presented in previous chapters. Specifically, they do not focus on the behaviour of offenders, but rather on the opportunities to which offenders have access and on the situations in which they find themselves. According to these theories, an individual who is ready, willing, and able to break the law will not necessarily do so. Other elements must come into play, and depending on how these elements come together, the offender may end up committing one type of crime rather than another.

Opportunity theories suggest that the ways in which people distribute their time and energies over time and across space either increase or decrease the number of opportunities to violate the law that are presented to them. Lifestyle exposure theory argues that, for individuals who pursue lifestyles that bring them into contact with people who have offender characteristics or that put them in places where crimes frequently occur, the risks of becoming crime victims increase. Similarly, routine activities theory suggests that crimes result when motivated offenders, suitable targets, and an absence of capable guardianship converge in time and space. Other theories reviewed in Chapter 5 focus on the ways in which the interactions between offenders and their victims influence criminal outcomes. Relatively simple theories that speak of "victim precipitation" have been replaced in recent years by theories about crime as a situated transaction that is the product not only of an offender's will or motivation but also of social interaction.

Chapter 6 discussed theories and research relating to the aftermath of the criminal event. We examined the variety of ways—obvious and not so obvious—in which involvement in such events may affect victims and offenders. Labelling theorists maintain, for instance, that the societal reaction to minor or petty acts of nonconformity may result in stigmatization, which frustrates the labelled person and thereby contributes indirectly to more serious violations of the law. We also discussed how the effects of crime extend beyond the immediate victim. The fear of crime, for example, can have important implications for the well-being of individuals and their communities. In extreme cases, the public response in the aftermath of criminal events may approximate a panic situation.

Our theoretical elaboration of criminal events led us to conclude that there is value to be derived from investigating these events in the context of particular social domains. Social domains can be defined as the major spheres of life in which we spend most of our time and energy. Three such domains—the family and the household, recreation and leisure, and the workplace—provided the organizing themes for the substantive analysis of criminal events presented in Chapters 8 to 10. We argued that a comprehensive examination of criminal events in these domains requires us to focus on three important components: precursors, the transaction, and its aftermath. This approach helps us to understand (1) how social arrangements affect the distribution and timing of criminal events, (2) why some groups in society are more likely than others to be involved in criminal events, whether as offenders or victims, (3) why particular types of criminal events have the content that they have, and (4) how victims and others are affected by these events.

Our analyses of criminal events were grounded in empirical data, the sources of which we investigated in Chapter 7. In that chapter, we saw that the data on crime derive principally from two types of investigative strategies: observations and reports. Some researchers attempt to gather information about crime through their observations of crime in naturalistic settings and/or experimental and quasi-experimental settings. Most contemporary research, however, focuses on reports of crime from police, victims, and offenders. While there is much debate about the innate superiority of one type of report over another, we suggested that each type must be appreciated in terms of its own particular strengths and weaknesses. Each type of report provides us with different perspectives on and data about criminal events. Their variable nature does not make these data unusable; however, we should be critical and judicious in employing them.

Our discussion of criminal events in specific social domains in Chapters 8 to 10 enabled us to apply the theoretical and research lessons that emerged from earlier chapters. In Chapter 8, we took up the issue of criminal events in the home. Two general categories of events were discussed. The first involved interpersonal violence in the context of familial relationships. As we saw, such violence emerges from and reflects the social organization of family life. The very factors that lead us to idealize family life—intimacy and privacy—increase the risks of danger to more vulnerable family members. The data clearly indicate that women and children suffer most from violence in the home.

The second major type of criminal event in the family and household domain is property crime. Breaking and entering and the theft of household goods are very common crimes, and they result in substantial financial loss. As we suggested, much of this crime is opportunistic in nature, involving as it does rational offenders who encounter opportunities for theft. Our discussion of family life and family organization revealed how routine activities create such opportunities.

In Chapter 9, we took up several issues relating to criminal events in the leisure domain. We saw that (particularly in the case of juveniles) leisure is frequently understood as a "cause" of crime. It has been argued that many leisure pursuits in which youths engage promote criminal conduct directly or indirectly. This argument has been made most passionately with respect to television violence, but it also encompasses most other leisure activities pursued by young people. We also saw how leisure pursuits among youths may free them from social controls while at the same time providing them with opportunities for offending. Finally, we investigated how particular leisure contexts—the street, bars and taverns, dating, and tourism—provide settings for criminal events.

A final social domain, the workplace, was discussed in Chapter 10. Here, we saw that the nature and degree of people's involvement in the work domain has important implications for the kinds of criminal events in which they might find themselves. Two major issues emerged from our discussion of the work domain. The first concerned the relationship between involvement in the legitimate world of work and involvement in criminal events. We saw that particular kinds of work expose employees to particular kinds of victimization and offending risks. In the former case, jobs that involve handling money, travel between remote worksites, or regular exposure to high-risk populations increase the risks people face at work. Highly publicized homicides in the workplace have brought this issue into sharp relief. The jobs people have may also provide them with unique opportunities to break the law. For instance, corporate criminals have access to highly profitable offending opportunities and very frequently remain insulated from controls that are supposed to deter their behaviour.

The second major issue discussed in Chapter 10 has to do with crime as a form of work. Like legitimate business enterprises, criminal enterprises are sensitive to market conditions, endeavour to forge stable partnership arrangements, and attempt to manage their relationships with state agencies that try to control their activities.

337

*Summary and
Review of
Public Policy
Responses
to Crime*

Over the course of this book, we have developed an appreciation for the variety and the complexity of criminal events. The fact that these events occur in diverse social domains and involve different categories of actors does not mean that they are not amenable to criminological analysis. Throughout our analysis of criminal events, the same fundamental questions have kept recurring: Why do offenders and victims come together when they do, as they do, and where they do? Why does the event evolve as it does? What are the consequences of what transpired in the event for its participants? Instead of seeking highly specific answers to these questions, we have attempted to link specific concerns to theoretical ones. Moreover, we have been attentive to the pictures of criminal events that are revealed to us by the major criminological data sources. We conclude with a brief consideration of how the criminological understanding of these events helps us to make sense of public attempts to deal with the problem of crime.

RESPONDING TO CRIME

Criminal events occur because offenders encounter opportunities to violate the law. Controlling the occurrence of these events might involve attempts to discourage potential offenders. Depending on our theoretical model, we may wish to remove the factors that we believe motivate offending, or we may wish to make crime appear less rewarding to those who regard it as a rational course of action. With respect to the latter strategy, we have commented repeatedly on the role of legal deterrence.

Rather than attempt to prevent criminal events by controlling offenders, we might try instead to empower victims in ways that make them more resistant to victimization. One way of achieving this would be to develop policies that allow potential victims greater access to law or that teach them about measures they can take to make themselves less vulnerable to crime. Similarly, we might try to reduce the numbers of criminal opportunities available to offenders by manipulating the physical environments or social situations in which crimes occur.

THE 'GET-TOUGH' APPROACH

These preliminary observations suggest several fronts along which any campaign against crime might be conducted. Too often, however, our thinking about crime is less imaginative than it might be. Fed by sensationalist media reporting and political rhetoric, we tend to think of the appropriate response to crime as what some call the "get-tough" approach: hire more police, hand down longer sentences, and build more prisons.

In a similar vein, police forces respond to the rising dangers in their jobs with requests for greater firepower. For example, the police in Winnetka, Illinois, have recently proposed the purchase of Uzi submachine guns to replace their shotguns. These machine guns, which can shoot through walls and fire up to ten rounds a second, are being demanded by a force that patrols a village of 13 000 residents.

Concerns about police safety have risen in response to changes in the nature of street crimes involving drugs. In the aftermath of a sting operation that went awry, resulting in a police officer being wounded, the special narcotics prosecutor in New York City commented, "The rules of engagement in the drug war have changed ... It's getting vicious out there" (*New York Times,* 1989: B2). He attributed this new attitude to the youthfulness of the members of the drug-dealing organizations. Whereas experienced drug dealers tend to flee when confronted with a police officer, teenage gunmen seem to believe that they can escape prosecution by killing the officer. This attitude leaves the police more inclined to take strong precautions when dealing with gun-toting offenders, including the option of shooting first. "Deadly force" options probably deter, but they may also heighten feelings of desperation in those who see them as just another risk of criminal activity.

The use of deadly force raises concerns about breaches in a criminal justice system that theoretically promises fair treatment for all. Still, there appears to be public support for a get-tough response to crime. Are these responses justified, or are they symptomatic of a traumatized society more afraid of the mythology of crime than its reality? This is a difficult question to answer, particularly for people who feel that they have high chances of victimization.

Mandatory charging and sentencing practices that remove discretion from the police and courts have been implemented in some jurisdictions in the belief that greater certainty of punishment will create greater deterrence. In addition, there has been a determined effort in some American states to implement the death penalty as the appropriate sanction for capital crimes. The severity of the sentence has not been complemented by swiftness of imposition as the queue on death rows gets longer (in some cases, inmates have waited up to ten years for punishment).

Some observers have argued that get-tough responses to the problem of crime are inherently limited (Donzinger, 1996; Schwendinger and Schwendinger, 1993; Standing Committee on Justice and the Solicitor General,

339

*Summary and
Review of
Public Policy
Responses
to Crime*

BOX 11.1 PRINCIPLES FOR CRIME PREVENTION

Michael R. Gottfredson and Travis Hirschi (1995) have used their "general theory of crime" to develop some crime control principles. Their recommendations include the following:

Rule 1.   Do not attempt to control crime by incapacitating adults.

Rule 2.   Do not attempt to control crime by rehabilitating adults.

Rule 3.   Do not attempt to control crime by altering the severity of penalties available to the justice system.

Rule 4.   Restrict the unsupervised activities of teenagers.

Rule 5.   Limit proactive policing.

Rule 6.   Question the characterization of crime offered by agents of the criminal justice system and uncritically repeated by the media.

Rule 7.   Support programs designed to provide early education and effective child care.

Rule 8.   Support policies that promote and facilitate two-parent families and that increase the number of caregivers relative to the number of children.

1993). As they see it, the problem is twofold. First, there seems to be little convincing evidence that we effectively control crime when we simply invest more resources in the criminal justice system (Graham, 1990). Second, when we view the criminal justice system as the principal social mechanism for responding to crime, we approach the problem in a reactive rather than a proactive manner and thus never really address the underlying factors associated with crime and criminality.

As with other social problems, it is perhaps more sensible to think about strategies of prevention. **Crime prevention** has been defined as "the anticipation, recognition and appraisal of a crime risk and the initiation of some action to reduce or remove it" (National Crime Prevention Institute, 1986: 2). Clearly, the criminal justice system is itself part of an overall crime prevention strategy in that (1) the threat of legal penalty is meant to deter potential offenders and (2) prison terms, in their capacity to either punish or rehabilitate, are intended to prevent reoffending.

Get-tough approaches to crime tend to involve options that are specifically associated with the criminal justice system. As used by criminologists, the term *crime prevention* is more broadly based, referring to strategies or tactics that, while they might involve the police (or other criminal justice functionaries), are rooted in the physical and social character of the local community (Lab, 1992; van Dijk and de Waard, 1991). From this perspective, crime prevention involves a range of strategies, including installing lights on city streets, initiating citizen police patrols, developing Neighbourhood Watch programs, mounting public information campaigns, locking doors, carrying weapons or alarms, and introducing programs aimed at reducing unemployment or poverty.

WHAT DOES IT MEAN?

Crime Prevention

Crime prevention refers to strategies or tactics that, while they might involve the police (or other criminal justice functionaries), are rooted in the physical and social character of the local community.

PUBLIC HEALTH AND PUBLIC SAFETY

Public policy in the area of health care suggests interesting parallels to the issue of crime prevention (Anderson, Grandison, and Dyson, 1996). One way society can deal with medical problems is to wait until people get sick and then make health-care services available to them. Similarly, we can wait until people commit crimes and then take action by using criminal justice resources to catch and then confine or treat them. The use of the word *rehabilitation* in reference to prison programs suggests a quite literal application of the medical model to our thinking about crime and punishment.

In the area of public health, however, most policy planners recognize the value of applying limited resources in a preventive rather than a reactive manner. If we can prevent illness, we won't need to treat it after the fact. For this reason, we are advised to get regular medical checkups, exercise, and watch our diets. We might view the problem of crime in a similar way. It is more sensible to take action *before* crimes occur than after harm has been done.

Borrowing from the language of public health, we can think of crime prevention as having primary, secondary, and tertiary dimensions (Brantingham and Faust, 1976; Lab, 1992; van Dijk and de Waard, 1991). Primary prevention includes programs aimed at either the entire community or the population at risk. Exemplifying primary prevention are crime prevention programs that teach risk-reducing skills to the large audiences (Davis and Smith, 1994; Sacco and Silverman, 1982). Pamphlets, brochures, and posters providing information on family violence are examples of (mass media) primary prevention. Secondary prevention refers to programs aimed at those segments of the population that are at particularly high risk (or, in public health language, that show early symptoms of the problem). Examples of

341

*Summary and
Review of
Public Policy
Responses
to Crime*

BOX 11.2 THE CRIME PREVENTION ARMCHAIR VARIABLES

Sociologist Marcus Felson (1992) has proposed four "armchair variables" that help us to summarize much of what we do, or could do, in the area of crime prevention. He presents these variables as dichotomies, although he indicates that they are better understood as continuous dimensions:

1. *Strategy vs. tactics.* These are military terms that describe the nature of our organizational efforts. A strategy is an overall plan to deal with a problem, while a tactic is a more detailed procedure for carrying out the strategy. Crime prevention tactics may work at cross-purposes if we lack an overall strategy; and a crime prevention strategy may fail if our tactics are not part of a strategic plan.

2. *Simple vs. complex.* Strategies or tactics may be simple or complex. Felson advises us that "making automobiles more difficult to steal" is a simple strategy but one that may involve many complex tactics, such as the use of anti-theft computers or policing strategies.

3. *Small area vs. large area.* Some crime prevention efforts may target a single building or a single neighbourhood. Others may address crime on a citywide or national basis.

4. *Narrow vs. broad.* Some types of programs might be directed toward a very narrow range of crimes or a single type of crime (e.g., shoplifting), while others (e.g., social development approaches) might be intended to prevent a wide variety of crimes.

---

secondary prevention include targeting high-crime areas for special treatment (such as neighbourhood redevelopment or Neighbourhood Watch programs) and installing security equipment in schools that have experienced problems with intruders. Finally, tertiary prevention refers to strategies that are intended to prevent the recurrence of crime. Examples of tertiary prevention include victim–offender mediation, training courses for drunk drivers, treatment programs for wife assaulters, and various forms of diversion and community service.

There have been efforts in the United States to focus on violent crime as one would certain forms of disease (Anderson et al., 1996; Meredith, 1984). James Mason, then the head of the Atlanta-based Centers for Disease Control (CDC)—which studies violent crime as a form of life-threatening disease—has stated that public health measures have been successful in treating poverty-related problems (for example, venereal disease, lead poisoning, and tuberculosis) *in the absence of* attempts to alleviate the social ills associated with them. The campaign against smoking has been particularly successful. Warnings about the health hazards, the political activism of nonsmokers, demands for nonsmoking areas, and interest in public fitness are all factors that have forced smokers to reconsider their habits (Meredith, 1984: 48).

According to Mason, we can do something about violence without first having to come up with solutions to poverty (Meredith, 1984: 45). Among his recommendations for reducing violence are developing programs that teach people how to handle conflict and restricting the availability of handguns.

The gun control debate is highly contentious. It ranges from the facile observation that "guns don't kill people, people kill people" to evidence that gun control laws appear to have little effect on the amount of homicide by firearms that we see in Canada to claims that firearms are important crime deterrents (Mauser, 1996; Mundt, 1990; Silverman and Kennedy, 1992). Nonetheless, controlling guns is viewed by the CDC as a major factor in the successful eradication of violence in the United States.

Guns are the most popular means of committing homicide in both Canada (Silverman and Kennedy, 1993) and the United States. The issue of gun control is complicated by those who argue that they have a right to use guns for sporting purposes. Despite such protests, guns provide a symbolic as well as real threat to the well-being of crime-racked societies. As Silverman and Kennedy (1993) point out, the debate about gun control in Canada intensified in the aftermath of Marc Lepine's murder of fourteen women at the Université de Montréal's École Polytechnique in December 1989. Lepine used a semi-automatic weapon to shoot the women and then turned it on himself. The event generated a storm of public sentiment in favour of restrictions on the availability of multishot or assault weapons. Bill C17, which was passed in 1992, allowed for the ownership of these guns, but put strong emphasis on their control. Of particular note is the requirement that the guns be securely stored, with strong penalties for noncompliance (Silverman and Kennedy, 1993: 245).

Under new legislation—C68, the Firearms Control Act, passed in 1995—strict controls are being put in place to require the mandatory registration of all guns. Further, the list of restricted weapons that cannot be legally owned has been lengthened. Public opinion polls conducted during the time the new gun control law was debated in the House of Commons showed strong national support for these restrictions, although there were loud outcries from gun-owning groups who viewed the law as an attack on individual freedom and rights.

Despite the valuable insights that the public health model provides, its application to crime prevention is problematic (Graham, 1990). First, the

343

*Summary and
Review of
Public Policy
Responses
to Crime*

BOX 11.3   CHANGES IN CANADIAN GUN LAWS

Recent changes in Canadian gun laws have been highly controversial. While public opinion polls have shown widespread support for the tightening of laws to control the use of weapons, gun owners have expressed strong concerns about the extent to which their personal liberties will be compromised by these laws. They believe that these laws give the police too much power, allowing them to target gun owners unfairly in their efforts to control firearm ownership. What exactly do these new regulations involve? Here is a summary from the Canadian Firearms Centre outlining the requirements that will be made of gun owners under the new Firearms Control Act:

Canadian individuals who already possess firearms must obtain a firearms licence by January 1, 2001. An acquisition licence may be obtained at any time. Those who do not wish to acquire any additional firearms may obtain a possession only licence. Individuals falling into this category do not have to take the Canadian Firearms Safety Course or test. They will get a licence to possess, but not to acquire firearms. People who now have a firearms acquisition certificate (FAC) may continue to use it to acquire a firearm until its expiry date or until January 1, 2001, whichever is earlier. After January 1, 2001, possession and acquisition licences will replace FACs completely. Individuals who do not own a firearm by that date, but who subsequently wish to acquire firearms may apply for a licence to possess and acquire firearms.

Successful completion of the Canadian Firearms Safety Course or test is essential for any person wishing to obtain a licence to possess and acquire firearms. However, anyone who has already completed the course or test will not have to take it again unless they are the subject of a firearms prohibition order. In the provinces of Manitoba and Quebec, anyone who has taken a safety course or test approved by the Attorney General of a province between January 1, 1993, and December 31, 1994, will also not have to complete the Canadian Firearms Safety Course or test unless they are the subject of a firearms prohibition order.

Firearms licences must be renewed every five years. The screening to obtain a licence will be similar to that for obtaining a Firearms Acquisition Certificate. On November 27, 1996, the Minister of Justice

BOX 11.3   CHANGES IN CANADIAN GUN LAWS   (CONT.)

tabled proposed regulations before Parliament. These provide for a fee of $10 to obtain a five-year possession only (non-acquisition) licence. The fees will rise on a sliding scale to a maximum of $60 in the last year of the phase-in period. For sustenance hunters, there will be no fee for either the acquisition licence or the non-acquisition licence. The proposed regulations also provide for a $10 fee during the first year of implementation to register any number of non-restricted firearms, provided that they are registered at the same time. The fee will rise to a maximum of $18 in the last year of the phase-in period. Sustenance hunters will not be required to pay a registration fee.

Registration certificates are valid for as long as the owner owns the firearm. Owners must continue to renew their firearms licence every five years, as required.

SOURCE: Department of Justice Web site, Canadian Firearms Centre.

model is so wide-ranging that it is unclear where we should draw the boundaries between what is and what is not a crime prevention practice. Second, the distinctions between primary, secondary, and tertiary prevention are frequently less clear in practice than they are in theory. Third, the attempt to classify crime prevention practices in this way assumes that our understanding of what causes crime (and, therefore, of how it can be prevented) is more scientifically precise than it really is. Harries (1990) further cautions that public health as an institution has, at present, neither the resources nor the personnel to make a lasting impression on the problem of crime incidence.

In the remainder of this section and in the two sections that follow, we examine three major approaches to crime prevention that extend well beyond traditional get-tough approaches. Each picks up an important theme in the study of criminal events and, in combination, they form the basis for what many would argue is a comprehensive approach to crime prevention. **Opportunity reduction** focuses on how social and environmental factors might be brought to bear on the reduction of crime opportunities. **Social development** approaches attempt to create social conditions that discourage long-term serious offending and empower potential victims while at the same time contributing to the rebuilding of communities. Finally, **community-based policing** (or problem-oriented policing) considers ways in which the policing role may be expanded beyond the narrow reactive role that brings the police into criminal events only when such events are either already underway or finished.

CRIME PREVENTION THROUGH OPPORTUNITY REDUCTION

As we have seen, the event conceptualization of crime stresses the importance of opportunity in elucidating where and when crimes occur. Only when people who are ready, willing, and able to offend encounter conditions favourable to offending are criminal events likely to develop. From a policy standpoint, therefore, actions that control the appearance or accessibility of opportunities to engage in crime may help to prevent much crime (see Table 11.1). The important implication of this approach is that we can manage the risks of crime without changing the character of offenders. Because the emphasis in opportunity reduction is on the modification of the situations in which crimes occur, crime prevention through opportunity reduction is sometimes referred to as **situational crime prevention** (Clarke, 1993).

Situational prevention is based on two important assumptions. The first is that crimes are most effectively prevented when we are attentive to their particular characteristics (Brantingham and Brantingham, 1990; Gottfredson and Hirschi, 1995). Thus, the first step in opportunity reduction is careful crime analysis: Who commits these crimes? When are they committed? Where do they most frequently occur? What do offenders hope to achieve by committing crimes? How might certain characteristics of the physical environment contribute to these events? Are there natural forces of guardianship that might be activated in the situations in which crimes typically occur? The answers to such questions help crime prevention planners tailor specific solutions to specific crime problems.

The second key assumption relates to the nature of the offender. Opportunity reduction approaches reflect the model of the rational offender (Cornish and Clarke, 1986). In other words, offenders' decisions are based on their assessment of the various costs and benefits associated with a particular course of action. How easily can a crime be committed? Is anyone who might take action to prevent the crime standing guard? Are there less risky ways of obtaining the rewards that the commission of the crime promises? Offenders will seek answers to such questions and behave in ways that reflect their best interests. If the opportunities conducive to crime can be made less attractive or less plentiful, many types of crimes (particularly those that are largely opportunistic in nature) may occur much less frequently. According to Clarke (1992), situational

Table 11.1   Safety Precautions Taken by Canadians

Respondents to the 1993 General Social Survey were asked whether they routinely take precautions intended to increase their safety from crime.

Precaution	Percent Taking Precaution
Lock doors for safety when alone in car	
Total population	54
Men	40
Women	68
Check backseat for intruders	
Total population	46
Men	33
Women	58
Plan route with safety in mind	
Total population	46
Men	33
Women	58
Stay home at night	
Total population	14
Men	3
Women	24
Carry something to defend yourself	
Total population	12
Men	7
Women	17

SOURCE: V.F. Sacco (1995), "Fear and Personal Safety," Statistics Canada, *Juristat*, Catalogue No. 85-002, Volume 15, Number 9.

prevention involves increasing the risks and decreasing the rewards associated with crime. As offending situations become more difficult, riskier, and less rewarding, rational offenders will be discouraged from offending.

One obvious way in which people increase the difficulties associated with crime is through target hardening, which refers to those measures that decrease the vulnerability of personal or household property. Entry into a house with locked doors and windows is more difficult than entry into a house in which such measures have not been taken. Various forms of access control, such as

BOX 11.4   CASE STUDIES IN SITUATIONAL PREVENTION

Canadian criminologists Patricia L. Brantingham and Paul Brantingham are international experts in the area of situational crime prevention. Their research (1990) provides the following examples, which clearly illustrate the logic and the value of the approach:

SITE/SITUATION-SPECIFIC EXAMPLES

Example 1: In a large suburban municipality, there was a brewer's warehouse that experienced repeated problems with people breaking into their delivery vans at night. The vans were empty, but backed up to the loading bay doors and locked up overnight as if they contained merchandise. Offenders, apparently in search of beer, repeatedly cut through a fence on the perimeter of the warehouse lot and broke into the vans. No beer was stolen, since the vans were empty, but there were continuous repair costs to fix the damaged fence and delivery vans. The crime prevention officer convinced the warehouse manager to keep the delivery vans away from the loading bay doors (which were themselves very secure) and unlocked overnight. The vans were opened at night on a few subsequent occasions, but they were not damaged as before.

Example 2: At a convenience store, there was a less serious, but more common problem. A high school was located opposite a church. On the street behind the church there was a convenience store. As might be expected, students from the high school walked through the church parking lot to get to and from the convenience store. Lots of litter was left in the church parking lot, producing calls for police service and complaints. Church members were upset by the mess, but unable to stop either the trespassing teenagers or their littering.

The crime prevention officer found an effective, low-cost solution. He convinced the church to dig a ditch across the front of its property (except for an entrance way) and arranged a direct pathway from school to convenience store to be built along one edge of the church property. The new pathway had a tall cedar fence (2.5 metres) on one side to separate it from adjacent houses and a chain link fence to enhance its appearance. The littering on the church grounds stopped and, perhaps surprisingly, the student pathway stayed clear of litter and graffiti. General research on littering and graffiti finds that keeping the area "clean" is a deterrent to further problems.

Example 3: There is an international example of something that has happened in video stores. To eliminate shoplifting, video stores are switching how they display the videos they have for rental. Early on, they tended to place the actual VHS or Beta rental cassettes out on the shelves. People selected a cassette and carried it to a central desk for rental. This is similar to the situation found in many smaller lending libraries. It has the virtue of reducing staff time spent on telling customers whether

BOX 11.4   CASE STUDIES IN SITUATIONAL PREVENTION (CONT.)

particular videos are still available for rental: if they are on the shelves they are available; if they are not on the shelves, they are not available.

The situation has now largely changed: most stores display the small empty boxes that the videos originally came in, or they display small plastic display cards with advertising material. The customer must go to the central desk to determine whether a particular video is available and, if so, rent it before actually taking possession of the cassette. This is similar to the controlled stacks situation found in major research libraries: it occupies more staff time, but cuts casual user pilferage.

locked gates and entry phones, also increase the degree of effort needed to commit certain crimes.

The risks involved in the commission of crime may be increased by measures that make it more likely (or, at least, make it *appear* more likely) that the offender will be discovered and apprehended. A high level of surveillance by security guards, citizen patrols, and security cameras clearly is intended to serve this purpose. Perhaps less obvious is the role played by other types of

BOX 11.5   CRIME AND THE PHYSICAL ENVIRONMENT

How can locations be made more resistant to crime-related problems? Assuming that crimes are committed by rational offenders, Taylor and Harrell (1996) suggest four possible approaches to this problem:

1. *Housing design or block layout.* This involves reducing the availability of crime targets and the removal of barriers that would prevent the easy detection of crimes in progress.

2. *Land use and circulation patterns.* This involves reducing the routine exposure of potential offenders to crime targets through consideration of such factors as walkways, paths, streets, and traffic patterns as well as the location and hours of operation of public places.

3. *Territorial features.* This means encouraging the use of territorial markers and signalling to potential offenders that a location is occupied by vigilant residents. Organized spring cleanups, for example, can signify the extent to which residents identify with and announce control of the local environment.

4. *Physical deterioration.* Physical improvements can reduce the signs of vulnerability and increase commitment to joint protective activities.

crime prevention measures, such as locks. As Felson (1992: 32) argues, "The strategic role of a lock is not to prevent entry! Rather, its strategic role is to force the offender to make a lot of noise, in hope that others will hear that noise. Ideally, the potential offender will take a look at the lock, note the noise it will force him to make, fear the consequences of that noise, and decide against committing the crime."

349

*Summary and
Review of
Public Policy
Responses
to Crime*

The role of prevention goes beyond the introduction of defensible space. According to Merry (1981), a neighbourhood may be architecturally designed to discourage crime but still not be adequately defended, because it has little or no social cohesion. Krupat and Kubzansky (1987: 61) note that "even when buildings are low and the entrances and public spaces focus around a small set of families, people will not react to crime when they believe that they are on someone else's turf, when they do not consider the police effective or when they fear retribution."

Among the most popular measures intended to activate natural surveillance at the local level are Block Watch or Neighbourhood Watch programs that are sponsored by the local police. These programs are supposed to encourage neighbourhood residents to "share information about local crime problems, exchange crime prevention tips, and make plans for engaging in surveillance ('watching') of the neighbourhood and crime-reporting activities" (Rosenbaum, 1987: 104). Surveillance programs increase interaction among neighbours at the same time as they remove opportunities for crime.

In the United States, the Bureau of Justice Statistics reported in 1986 that about 1 family in 5 lives in a neighbourhood with a surveillance program and that, in those areas, 38 percent of residents participate (Garofalo and McLeod, 1988). In Canada, evidence suggests that while awareness of these programs has been high, actual levels of participation have been somewhat lower (Solicitor General, 1984).

While opportunity for crime can be thwarted by the self-help actions of potential victims, individuals who take the law into their own hands may do so in a manner that constitutes vigilantism (Rosenbaum and Sederberg, 1976). Black (1983) describes "self-help crime" as a potent and frequently used form of punishment and deterrence. The equation of guns with independence and security is evident in the sales pitch for LadySmith, a handgun designed to meet the "physical requirements of women." Here, a potential victim is provided the means with which to enact summary justice on her assailant. A National Rifle Association ad that appeared in *USA Today* in 1987 justifies the arming of women by arguing that only 3 percent of rape attempts are completed against victims carrying weapons.

Self-help deterrence can become outright retribution. Bernard Goetz (the "subway vigilante") admitted to having purposely carried a gun when riding on the New York subways in search of trouble. He found trouble when a number of youths carrying screwdrivers approached him and demanded money. Goetz shot at them, hitting one youth in the back as he was running away. Initially proclaimed a hero for standing up to his "assailants," he was not convicted of the original charge of attempted murder (though he was found guilty of possessing a hidden weapon). Goetz's image was badly tarnished by his admission that he had been seeking revenge for an earlier mugging. What had first appeared a defensive strategy was in fact an offensive act. Goetz had tried to assume the role of police officer, the difference being that the police are normally constrained by professional codes of conduct and due process of the law. In a more recent development, however, a civil trial brought against Goetz by a survivor of his shooting resulted in a $43 million settlement for the pain and suffering brought about by the bullet wound. While the criminal jury felt that the circumstances of the case warranted the use of violence, the civil jury clearly did not.

Finally, crime may be made less attractive by reducing the rewards associated with the offence. For example, requiring bus riders to have exact change decreases the amount of money that must be handled by any particular bus driver and makes the robbery of drivers a less attractive proposition. Similarly, markings that identify individual ownership of property may discourage the conspicuous use of stolen merchandise and seriously hurt the chances for resale. As we saw in Chapter 5, the amount of money available in 7-Eleven stores at any given time is another way in which the rewards for criminality can be curtailed.

Unquestionably, opportunity reduction has proved to be effective in a variety of specific settings (Clarke, 1993, 1994). However, this approach is not without its critics. Some have suggested that removing opportunity is more likely to displace crime than to prevent it (Gabor, 1990b). In other words, if we make it difficult for a motivated offender to offend in one situation, he or she might simply find another situation more conducive to offending. If one store takes precautions to prevent theft, can we really be sure that the would-be thief will not simply seek out targets where such precautions are not taken? The evidence suggests that displacement may be a problem with particular types of crime and particular types of offenders. However, many forms of opportunity reduction do in fact prevent crimes rather than just displace them (Brantingham and Brantingham, 1990).

More specific forms of opportunity reduction invite more specific criticisms. Various target-hardening methods, such as installing locks on doors and bars on windows, may be faulted for encouraging a "fortress mentality" that enhances the fear of crime in society (Graham, 1990). Some critics see the use of electronic surveillance as part of a gradual shift toward a "surveillance society" (Clarke, 1992). Critics of Neighbourhood Watch programs claim that, despite the highly favourable publicity they receive and the high regard in which they are held by police and politicians, little evidence suggests that they accomplish what they are supposed to accomplish. According to Rosenbaum (1987):

> There is some evidence to suggest (a) if given the opportunity to participate, residents in the majority of high-crime neighbourhoods would not participate, and (b) when citizens do participate, the social interaction that occurs at meetings may lead to increases (rather than decreases) in fear of crime, racial prejudice and other crime-related perceptions or feelings. More important, there is little evidence that these block/neighbourhood meetings cause local residents to engage in neighbourhood surveillance, social interaction, and bystander intervention—behaviours that are posited as the central mechanism for strengthening informal social controls and reducing opportunities for crime. (127)

Perhaps the most frequent and general criticism of opportunity reduction approaches is that, by placing so much emphasis on reducing opportunities for crime, they ignore the underlying causes of crime (Waller and Weiler, 1984). It has been argued that, because these strategies do not address the root causes of crime, the best they can hope to achieve is short-term benefits. If we wish to consider these root causes, we must turn to another major approach—crime prevention through social development.

CRIME PREVENTION THROUGH SOCIAL DEVELOPMENT

Crime prevention through social development focuses not on the criminal act, but on the serious, repeat offender (Gabor, 1990a). As we saw in previous chapters, research suggests that a relatively small number of offenders are responsible for a disproportionately large number of crimes. These offenders begin their criminal careers early in life and end them (if at all) late in life. Over the course of their offending careers, they commit a wide variety of predatory offences. The research also indicates that these individuals tend to come from disadvantaged backgrounds, that they abuse alcohol and other drugs, and that they have experienced serious family problems as well as school- and employment-related problems.

A range of social problems, from family victimization to poverty and racism, can provide a fertile breeding ground for crime. The building of communities is seen by advocates of the social development approach to

BOX 11.6   A SOCIAL DEVELOPMENT APPROACH TO YOUTH CRIME

In 1995, members of the Youth Justice Committee of the National Crime Prevention Council organized meetings with 100 young men and women and 180 adults who work with young people. The meetings were held in six centres across Canada. The ideas generated by the meetings reflect principles of the social development approach. A report based on these meetings recommended certain conditions that would help young people avoid trouble with the law:

- opportunities and responsibilities to go along with rights
- fair, clear, consistent, and meaningful consequences for their actions
- lives free from abuse
- physical and emotional support
- freedom from other types of harm
- accurate and complete information about their rights and responsibilities and about the consequences of their actions
- positive role models
- a voice in what happens to them
- a chance to be part of the solution

SOURCE: National Crime Prevention Council, *Clear Limits and Real Opportunities: The Key to Preventing Youth Crime* (Ottawa: National Crime Prevention Council Secretariat, 1995).

provide a comprehensive strategy that reduces crime by discouraging potential offenders while at the same time strengthening potential victims. The aim of crime prevention through social development is to correct the criminogenic social conditions that are assumed to be the root causes of crime (National Crime Prevention Council, 1995, 1996). Oriented toward the achievement of long-range prevention, this approach seeks to eliminate the underclass from which serious, repeat offenders typically emerge (Standing Committee on Justice and the Solicitor General, 1993).

The notion that crime can be prevented by eliminating the social ills that breed crime (particularly teenage crime) is not new. There is a long history of social reformism that argues that we can best fight crime by fighting poverty, racism, unemployment, and other forms of social disadvantage (Graham, 1990; Rosenbaum, 1988). The social development approach differs from these older approaches in its more systematic efforts to identify and attack the root causes of crime.

Because predatory crime is part of a "tangle of pathologies" (Wilson, 1987) that characterizes the lives of the socially disadvantaged, our policy approaches to crime prevention must extend beyond the criminal justice system into the areas of family, educational, housing, and health policy (Canadian Criminal Justice Association, 1989; Graham, 1990). One important theme emphasizes **resource mobilization,** which addresses crime issues in terms of whether the law helps people—especially the poor and powerless—protect themselves against victimization. Browne and Williams (1989) note that the enactment of domestic violence legislation (which makes arrest of offenders more likely), coupled with high levels of resource mobilization (including the provision of shelters for battered women), tended to reduce the rate of female-perpetrated homicide. That is, the more women feel empowered to deal with violence directed against them, the less likely they are to react with fatal violence.

Browne and Williams admit that some issues remain unclear. They cannot establish the degree of individuals' awareness of available resources. In addition, they have no way of measuring individual women's accessibility to the mandated resources. Further, it is not clear how many people actually use the resources that are available or how effective these resources are in meeting individual needs (Browne and Williams, 1989: 91–92). What *is* clear from this research, however, is that, where these resources are available, criminal victimization from fatal assaults is lower. This finding provides a strong argument for the need to assess the extent to which society can provide alternatives to women that will enable them to avoid becoming victims.

Advocates of the social development approach see crime prevention not as the exclusive domain of any one social or governmental agency. Instead, they place considerable emphasis on the need to establish crime prevention councils at both the federal and municipal levels. These councils would bring together those responsible for health, family, employment, and housing policy, as well as the police and voluntary agencies that are concerned with a broad range of social welfare issues. The idea behind such an arrangement is that, by sharing the ownership of the crime problem, more comprehensive solutions will be developed.

While the social development approach has proved more popular in some European countries than in North America, it is clearly gaining momentum in Canada and the United States (Donzinger, 1996; Waller, 1989). However, some advocates of opportunity reduction maintain that the social development strategy fails to recognize that crime is not a homogeneous event and that different crimes require different intervention strategies (Brantingham, 1989).

Other critics question whether we have the political will or, if in times of fiscal restraint, we are truly prepared to make the financial commitments that a comprehensive social development approach might entail. We might also ask if the linkages that social development advocates draw between factors such as family upbringing, employment, and school experience are as obvious and as straightforward as they are sometimes made out to be. The list of causative factors to which the social development approach draws our attention is long and unwieldy, and as we have seen, there is honest debate among criminologists about the relative importance of these factors (Graham, 1990).

While for purposes of presentation we have drawn a distinction between opportunity reduction and social development, there is not really an inherent conflict between these two approaches. In the same way that we have borrowed from different theories to explain criminal events, we can borrow from these different perspectives to create an integrated approach to crime prevention. In fact, many policymakers have advocated a combination of these strategies in what has come to be known as the "safer cities" approach to crime prevention (Canadian Criminal Justice Association, 1989; Standing Committee on Justice and the Solicitor General, 1993).

How will changes in the nature of our communities condition our ability to implement crime prevention strategies in the future? Some general trends are apparent. For example, the development of new information technologies clearly is transforming the nature of social life, and in so doing is suggesting the possibility of new prevention opportunities. Cellular telephones allow people to intervene anonymously in a variety of situations that would not have been possible before. Computer terminals in patrol cars allow police to tap databases that provide instant information about known offenders and unsafe locations.

Other trends that bring with them increases in the levels of guardianship and decreases in levels of victimization risk include the growth of remote worksites, which can reduce commuting time; the spread of computer technologies, which allow many people to spend part of the working day at home; the expansion of part-time work in the service economy; and the increasing popularity of video and other home entertainment technologies. All of these changes suggest that the shift in routine activities away from the home may be undergoing a reversal. While the long-term impact of such changes on the community remains to be seen, they may eventually permit some forms of community prevention that were not viable in the past.

Felson (1987) provides an interesting example of how our prevention planning must be informed by careful social forecasting. He argues that metropol-

355

*Summary and
Review of
Public Policy
Responses
to Crime*

itan areas in North America are undergoing profound changes that involve the emergence of the "metroquilt" as the new dominant urban form. Within the context of the metroquilt, the city becomes "a patchwork of coterminous facilities intervening between homes, business and the larger society. The metroquilt would divide urban space among a large set of corporations, whose facilities managers would be responsible for organizing everyday movements, including security" (Felson, 1987: 920). This patchwork is apparent in the landscape of any major city. Stores are replaced by malls, single-family dwellings by condominiums and apartment complexes, and businesses and factories by industrial parks. In the metroquilt, Felson maintains, we have decreasing need to walk from one place to another and increasing need to drive from the parking lot of one facility to the parking lot of another facility.

In Felson's view, the growth of the metroquilt has far-reaching implications for crime prevention. As facilities develop, the distinction between public urban space and private space becomes increasingly blurred. As people spend increasing amounts of their time shopping in malls, working in office complexes, and visiting friends and relatives in apartment complexes, private businesses rather than the government assume greater responsibility for their safety. As a result, the facility could become the major organizational tool for crime prevention. Felson is optimistic about these developments because they seem to suggest the possibility that prevention can be rationalized and that security can be planned. He maintains that safety will become part of the marketing strategy because, as facilities compete for customers and tenants, private developers will have a strong incentive to make environments more crime-free (see also Shearing and Stenning, 1983; Walsh and Donovan, 1989).

However, there is a more disturbing side to all of this. If the production of safety is increasingly the domain of the private developer, then safety becomes a commodity accessible only to those who can afford it (Bayley and Shearing, 1996). The patron of the upscale shopping centre, the resident of the luxurious condo, and the employee in a gleaming office tower may find safety more accessible than those who spend most of their time in facilities where profit motives or government cost-cutting militate against extensive crime prevention planning. The risk that safety may become a commodity to be bought and sold, rather than a public good, suggests that issues other than technical effectiveness must inform prevention efforts. The prevention of crime must involve not only logistical matters but also matters of justice and equality. This concern is one that police are now facing as they attempt to adopt crime prevention as a primary focus of their activities.

Gottfredson and Hirschi (1995) argue that the natural limits of law enforcement are set by the spontaneous nature of crime: the offender sees that he or she can get something for nothing and seizes the opportunity. No increases in law enforcement, they suggest, can truly deter this type of behaviour. Research in Canada (Koenig, 1991) and elsewhere (Bayley, 1985; Jackson, 1989) has provided strong evidence that there is no relationship between the level of crime in a society and the number of police available to control this crime. Gottfredson and Hirschi (1990: 270) maintain that, in the overwhelming majority of robberies, burglaries, assaults, homicides, thefts, and drug deals, "the offender does not know or care about the probability of being observed by the police." The primary role of the police, they suggest, is to respond to criminal activity and to maintain social control; there is no evidence that increasing police tactical resources has the effect of reducing crime rates.

Unfortunately, police resources have become scarcer, and what the police do primarily is respond to complaints (not crime), maintain visibility in neighbourhoods, and control traffic. In a study of police activity, Lawson (1982) discovered that the police spend only 10–15 percent of their time engaged in actual law enforcement. Bayley (1994) reports that patrol officers, who are responsible for most contacts with the general population, rarely make an arrest. In the United States, there is less than one arrest per officer every fifteen working days. In Canada, according to Ericson and Shearing (1986), police officers on average make one criminal arrest a month and encounter a recordable criminal offence only once a week. The police spend the rest of their time on order maintenance.

The pressures of order maintenance and restricted resources have forced police agencies to begin to rethink their strategy of law enforcement. The police role has expanded partly as a result of the fact that the police belong to the only twenty-four-hour social agency that is easy to reach and that will make house calls. As we discussed earlier, the police emergency line (911) leaves police overwhelmed with calls that require them to serve not a law enforcement function, but rather a regulatory or order maintenance function (Kennedy and Veitch, 1997). As Bayley (1994) points out, most of the time the police do not use the criminal law to restore calm and order:

> The police "sort out" situations by listening patiently to endless stories about fancied slights, old grievances, new insults, mismatched expectations, indifference, infidelity, dishonesty, and abuse. They hear about all the petty, mundane, tedious, hapless, sordid details of individual lives.

None of it is earthshaking, or worthy of a line in a newspaper—not the stuff that government policy can address, not even especially spicy: just the begrimed reality of the lives of people who have no one else to take their problems to. (20)

In addition, the police are being called upon to become more actively involved in crime prevention, partly as a response to the increased levels of unease that people feel in urban areas. Given the assumption of routine activities theory that crime is made possible not only by the availability of offenders and victims but also by the absence of visible guardians (such as the police), it is hard to believe that the police have *no* effect on deterring crime. However, hiring more police does not necessarily lower crime, for many reasons. In previous chapters, we examined the police role in defining criminal events. The criteria that the police use in determining whether to arrest a person are shaped by a number of factors, including the nature of the police organization and its strategies of policing, differing interpretations of criminal events and differing assessments of the characteristics and motivations of participants in these events, and variations in the interpretations of the law and the cooperation of the public. We will examine how each of these factors can influence the new problem-oriented strategies (referred to as community-based policing) that are intended to assist the police in dealing with crime. But first, we will consider the changes that have taken place in the ways in which the police have functioned over the years.

The original mandate of the police in the nineteenth century was order maintenance (Wilson, 1983). The order maintenance or compliance role of the police was coterminous with "community relations." The police were to protect the community from disorderly behaviour and to control conflict where they found it (Monkkonen, 1983). This role required them to act as "watchmen," keeping track of the comings and goings in the community and looking out for behaviour that might constitute a threat to public order. The compliance role is associated with the "proactive" policing we discussed in Chapters 1 and 5. As Klockars (1985: 106–7) has stated, the police are not law enforcement agencies, but rather regulatory institutions—their job is not to enforce the laws but to regulate relationships between people.

The principal objective of compliance law enforcement is to secure conformity with the law by resorting to means that induce that conformity (Reiss, 1984). Compliance systems return to the original mandate of the police whereby one seeks to create law-abidingness through preventive or remedial actions. Under these systems, the primary focus of policing shifts from detecting and penalizing violators to providing incentives to individuals to comply with the law. Compliance-based policing also recognizes the need to include the public in controlling social disorder, beyond merely reporting crime to the police. The public is encouraged to include the police as intermediaries in situations of community conflict (Normandeau and Leighton, 1993).

The public has demanded more social order since at least the 1850s (Monkkonen, 1983). In fact, in comparison with crime control, order control as practised by the police has had a long and successful record. As Monkkonen states, Victorian morality has triumphed in most of North America's city streets. We expect, and get, quiet and predictable behaviour from almost everyone. Vice is no longer highly visible. Yet the dramatic rise in crime rates, and the apparent ineffectiveness of the police in dealing with crime and its consequences, has again raised concerns about social order. Monkkonen attributes the increases in crime rates to a number of factors, including urbanization and changes in the demographic composition of the population. The effect of these increases early in this century was to narrow the focus of police agencies to crime control alone, leaving the problems of general order maintenance to other agencies.

The principal objective of crime control or deterrence law enforcement is to detect violations of the law, identify offenders responsible for violations, and penalize perpetrators. This is done to diminish the chance of future offences both by the offender (specific deterrence) and by others who may contemplate the same criminal act (general deterrence) (Reiss, 1984: 91). Until recently, contemporary policing has had as a stated objective the apprehension of offenders through arrest, which has led to the form of "reactive" policing that dominates the way that police agencies operate (Reiss, 1984: 84).

Police have now begun to realize that crime control, by necessity, requires broadening their mandate once again to include order maintenance or compliance law enforcement. However, this notion is being resisted by police agencies that still regard law enforcement as their principal mandate. The internal workings of police organizations are such that peacekeeping and order maintenance functions are seen as residual matters (Bayley, 1994: 34). Real policing, some argue, involves arrest. The philosophy of community-based policing challenges this view, but the problem remains that many compliance-based actions are still without legitimation in police organizations. In addition, little training is provided for compliance-based operations. As Mastrofski (1983: 34) notes, the crime-fighting and the noncrime public service functions coexist uneasily in the police profession. The former dominates training curricula, career incentives, and organization evaluations, while the latter dominates the workload.

Notwithstanding this trend, according to Murphy (1993) community-based policing has replaced professional crime control policing as the dominant ideological and organizational model of progressive policing in Canada. Bayley (1988: 226) identifies four major features of community-based policing: (1) community-based crime prevention, (2) proactive servicing, as opposed to emergency response, (3) public participation in the planning and supervision of police operations, and (4) the shifting of command responsibility to lower-level ranks. Accompanying these organizational and procedural changes is an emphasis on identifying and solving problems, which are defined in terms of breaches of both law and social order. Further, the solutions to these problems do not merely reside in the rules and regulations of the police service; they must also acknowledge the concerns and desires of the community in which the problems occur.

359

*Summary and
Review of
Public Policy
Responses
to Crime*

According to Goldstein (1990), community-based policing requires at least five major adjustments in current thinking. First, to do their job well, police officers must be encouraged to search for alternatives to law enforcement. This encouragement must be reflected in a consistent, agencywide commitment to improving the quality of police service. Second, the police must not restrict their attention to those actions that have a potential for reducing crime. In some cases, crime is only the final consequence of unresolved noncrime-related problems. Third, consistent with the view that policing encompasses all of a community's problems, those that do not fit strict law enforcement criteria must also be addressed. Fourth, some effort must be made to understand the nature of the problems that are encountered in any given area before setting out alternatives. Too often, alternatives are prescribed that simply do not work because they are not suited to the area being policed. Like any other large organization, police have difficulty resisting internal pressures to follow established but rigid objectives and procedures. Fifth, police must be open to the idea of allowing other agencies to fulfill the job in conjunction with (or in place of) the police. According to Goldstein (1990: 104), this strategy "is intended to dissuade the police from applying a generic response to a generic problem, or to applying a single response haphazardly to a wide range of different types of problems."

Bayley (1988: 226) suggests that, if implemented correctly, community-based policing will constitute the most fundamental change in policing since the rise in police professionalism early in this century. However, while community-based policing appears to be gaining acceptance in police circles, few attempts have been made to understand how it actually works or to evaluate its overall performance (Kennedy, 1991). This means that the police may simply be doing the same thing as before but labelling it as something else, or doing something differently but not as well as before.

At the heart of the community-based policing concept is neighbourhood team policing, which involves the long-term assignment of officers to a particular area (for a discussion of the experience in Halifax with this strategy, see Clairmont, 1990). This strategy allows officers to make a commitment to an area and to assume a broader level of authority in providing policing that is more sensitive to community needs. Neighbourhood team programs have not been embraced by many police managers, however, who see the decentralization that is associated with them as limiting their control over their officers (Scheingold, 1984: 134). In addition, aggressive patrol tactics used in crime control may diminish police rapport with the public, thereby undermining the effectiveness of community-based policing (Scheingold, 1984: 135). Finally, their fear of being seen as indecisive may cause many officers to play the role of enforcer rather than that of peacemaker (Palenski, 1984: 35).

Police must look to community members to support them in their efforts to bring about order in the community. This support can take the form of self-help, as discussed earlier, or it can involve a kind of coproduction, whereby the police use community members as supporters of police activity (Krahn and Kennedy, 1985). Coproduction can range from passive responses, such as locking doors, to more active responses, such as participating in crime prevention programs or acting as informants (Skolnick, 1966). As Black (1980) points out, since the typical criminal act occurs at an unpredictable time and place, the police must rely on citizens (most often the victims of a crime) to involve them.

Providing resources for community-based policing (outside of community support) has proved to be problematic. Police budgets still depend on caseloads of calls for service and on crime rates. Community-based policing activity, directed as it is at problem solving and referral to outside programs, may create an impression of reduced activity, which, in turn, would suggest a need for lower budgets. The use of alternative programs also brings the police into conflict with other agencies, which makes it more difficult for them to define their role in the community and obtain the resources they need to realize their objectives (Kennedy and Veitch, 1997). Despite these problems, the solutions that have been offered for handling the demands of the public, including the development of different means of accessing police resources through such initiatives as the building of community police stations, have proved to be quite successful. Walker and Walker (1993) document the positive experiences with mini-stations in Victoria, which have worked to reduce strain on centralized police functions and have increased the police department's ability to solve problems at the community level.

Further, it is very difficult for some police agencies to remain apolitical when fighting for budget allocations and arguing for certain policing strate-

361

*Summary and
Review of
Public Policy
Responses
to Crime*

gies. The lobbying by communities and by volunteers in community-based policing programs may make the police appear more politically active than local politicians would want them to be, thereby making their requests for more funds even more tenuous. Police chiefs are thus confronted with a plethora of community constraints. These constraints need to be overcome before the chiefs can show that they are fulfilling the objectives of compliance-based policing. In her discussion of policing programs in Britain, Shaffer (1980: 38) argues that improving police–community relations is a crucial first step. The members of a community must get to know the police as concerned and sympathetic individuals as well as controlling and disciplining law officers. Without communication and cooperation between the police and the public, she concludes, "policing in a democratic society is impossible."

■ ■ ■

SUMMARY

One response to crime is to see it as a public health problem that is best addressed by removing some of the major instruments that bring about injury (for example, guns). A second view advocates the mobilization of social institutions and resources as a means of empowering victims to defend themselves against criminal attack. Given the already formidable challenges that public health institutions face in dealing with diseases and injuries that originate from noncrime sources, our heavy reliance on the police to confront the crime problem is unlikely to change (at least in the near future).

We can look at prevention from the viewpoint of opportunity reduction or social development. Prevention can include a number of factors, ranging from target hardening to increased surveillance. It can also set as a priority the targeting of violence and offer ways in which violence can be averted. Situational prevention is based on two important assumptions. The first is that crime is most effectively prevented when we attend to the particular characteristics of the type of crime in question. The second is that, in most cases, we are dealing with a rational offender, who calculates such things as risks, benefits, and ease of accomplishment before committing a crime. It follows from this that raising the costs associated with crimes (which are largely opportunistic in nature) may reduce the frequency with which they occur. Neighbourhood Watch and Block Watch programs assume that crime can be prevented by increasing surveillance and, by extension, the risk of detection and apprehension, as it is perceived by the potential offender.

In contrast to the other prevention strategies, crime prevention through social development focuses on the serious, repeat offender. A relatively small number of offenders may be responsible for a disproportionately large number of crimes. These individuals tend to have in common many social and demographic characteristics. The aim of crime prevention through social development is to correct the criminogenic social conditions that are assumed to be important causes of crime. The focus of the social development approach is on long-range outcomes that enhance social security and reduce crime incidence.

Combining opportunity reduction and social development is a new approach known as community-based policing. The police are shifting their attention from crime fighting (that is, deterrence-based policing) to compliance policing, which is more directly integrated into the community. The principal objective of compliance law enforcement is to secure conformity with law through systems that encourage community participation in defining and solving problems. The former emphasis on the detection and punishment of violators has given way to an emphasis on the need to provide incentives to individuals as a means of encouraging them to comply with the law.

Compliance-based policing recognizes the need to include the public in controlling social disorder, beyond merely reporting crime to the police. Bringing together a number of services within the community, as well as community members, can help to form a multipronged attack on crime involving reeducation, mediation, opportunity removal, resource mobilization, the targeting of the roots of crime, and problem solving. Our success in controlling crime and diminishing the incidence of criminal events depends on our ability to understand where crime comes from and on our commitment to expend resources in broadening our responses to it.

■ ■ ■

QUESTIONS FOR REVIEW AND DISCUSSION

1. Why is there a popular tendency to think about "more police and more prisons" as the *obvious* solution to the crime problem?
2. What similarities are there in the ways in which Canadian society approaches the problem of crime and the problem of disease?
3. With reference to the community in which you reside, what are some of the implications for crime prevention of Felson's analysis of changing urban forms?
4. How do policies of situational prevention emerge logically from theoretical ideas that emphasize "rational offenders" and "social control"?
5. What does it mean to say that "there is much more to community-based policing than law enforcement"?
6. According to critics, what are some of the more important limitations of traditional responses that assign the central responsibility for crime control to the criminal justice system?

REFERENCES

Abadinsky, H. 1987. *Organized Crime,* 2nd ed. Chicago: Nelson-Hall.

Agnew, R. 1985a. "A Revised Strain Theory of Delinquency." *Social Forces* 64(1): 151–67.

Agnew, R. 1985b. "Neutralizing the Impact of Crime." *Criminal Justice and Behavior* 12: 221–39.

Agnew, R. 1990. "The Origins of Delinquent Events: An Examination of Offender Accounts." *Journal of Research in Crime and Delinquency* 27(3): 267–94.

Agnew, R. 1992. "Foundation for a General Strain Theory of Crime and Delinquency." *Criminology* 30: 47–87.

Agnew, R. 1993. "Why Do They Do It? An Examination of the Intervening Mechanisms between 'Social Control' Variables and Delinquency." *Journal of Research in Crime and Delinquency* 30(3): 245–66.

Agnew, R., and S. Huguley. 1989. "Adolescent Violence toward Parents." *Journal of Marriage and the Family* 51: 699–711.

Agnew, R., and A.R. Peters. 1986. "The Techniques of Neutralization: An Analysis of Predisposing and Situational Factors." *Criminal Justice and Behavior* 13: 81–97.

Agnew, R., and D.M. Peterson. 1989. "Leisure and Delinquency." *Social Problems* 36(4): 332–50.

Agnew, R., and H.R. White. 1992. "An Empirical Test of General Strain Theory." *Criminology* 30: 475–99.

Akers, R.L. 1985. *Deviant Behavior: A Social Learning Approach.* Belmont, CA: Wadsworth.

Akers, R.L. 1994. *Criminological Theories.* Los Angeles: Roxbury Publishing Co.

Albini, J.L. 1971. *The American Mafia: Genesis of a Legend.* New York: Irvington.

Allan, E.A., and D.J. Steffensmeier. 1989. "Youth, Underemployment and Property Crime: Differential Effects of Job Availability and Job Quality on Juvenile and Young Adult Arrest Rates." *American Sociological Review* 54: 107–23.

Amir, M. 1971. *Patterns of Forcible Rape.* Chicago: University of Chicago Press.

Anderson, J., and L. Whitten. 1976. "Auto Maker Shuns Safer Gas Tank." *The Washington Post* (December 30), p. B7.

Anderson, J.F., T. Grandison, and L. Dyson. 1996. "Victims of Random Violence and the Public Health Implication: A Health Care or Criminal Justice Issue." *Journal of Criminal Justice* 24(5): 379–91.

Arneklev, B.J., H.G. Grasmick, C.R. Tittle, and R.J. Bursik. 1993. "Low Self-Control and Imprudent Behavior." *Journal of Quantitative Criminology* 9(3): 225–47.

Arnold, B.L., and J. Hagan. 1992. "Careers of Misconduct: Prosecuted Professional Deviance among Lawyers." *American Sociological Review* 57(6): 771–80.

Bala, N. 1991. "The Young Offenders Act: A Legal Framework." In R.A. Silverman, J.J. Teevan, and V.F. Sacco, *Crime in Canadian Society,* 4th ed. Toronto: Butterworths.

Baldassare, M. 1986. "The Elderly and Fear of Crime." *Sociology and Social Research* 70: 218–21.

Balkin, S. 1979. "Victimization Rates, Safety and Fear of Crime." *Social Problems* 26(3): 343–58.

Bandura, A.A., D. Ross, and S.A. Ross. 1963. "Imitation of Film-Mediated Aggressive Models." *Journal of Abnormal and Social Psychology* 66: 3–11.

Barnhorst, R., S. Barnhorst, and K.L. Clarke. 1992. *Criminal Law and the Canadian Criminal Code,* 2nd ed. Toronto: McGraw-Hill Ryerson.

Baron, S. 1989. "The Canadian West Coast Punk Subculture: A Field Study." *Canadian Journal of Sociology* 14(3): 289–316.

Baron, S.W. 1997. "Risky Lifestyles and the Link between Offending and Victimization." *Studies on Crime and Crime Prevention* 6(1): 53–71.

Baron, S.W., and T.F Hartnagel. 1996. "'Lock em up': Attitudes towards Punishing Juvenile Offenders. " *Canadian Journal of Criminology* 38: 191–212.

Bastian, L.D., and B.M. Taylor. 1991 (September). *School Crime: A National Crime Victimization Survey Report.* Washington, DC: U.S. Department of Justice.

Baumer, T.L. 1978. "Research on Fear of Crime in the United States." *Victimology* 3: 254–64.

Baunach, P.J. 1990. "State Prisons and Inmates: The Census and Survey." In D.L. Mackenzie, P.J. Baunach, and R.R. Roberg (eds.), *Measuring Crime: Large-Scale, Long-Range Efforts.* Albany: State University of New York.

Bayley, D.H. 1985. *Patterns of Policing: A Comparative International Analysis.* New Brunswick, NJ: Rutgers University Press.

Bayley, D.H. 1986. "The Tactical Choices of Police Patrol Officers." *Journal of Criminal Justice* 14: 329–48.

Bayley, D.H. 1988. "Community Policing: A Report from the Devil's Advocate." In J.R. Greene and D. Mastrofski (eds.), *Community Policing: Rhetoric or Reality.* New York: Praeger.

Bayley, D. 1994. *Police for the Future.* New York: Oxford University Press.

Bayley, D., and C.D. Shearing. 1996. "The Future of Policing." *Law and Society Review* 30(3): 585-606.

Beare, M.E. 1996. *Criminal Conspiracies.* Scarborough, ON: Nelson Canada.

Bechhofer, L., and A. Parrot. 1991. "What Is Acquaintance Rape?" In A. Parrot and L. Bechhofer (eds.), *Acquaintance Rape: The Hidden Crime.* New York: John Wiley.

Becker, H.S. 1963. *Outsiders: Studies in the Sociology of Deviance.* New York: Free Press.

Bell, D. 1953. "Crime as an American Way of Life." *The Antioch Review* 13 (June): 131–54.

Bell, D.J. 1987. "The Victim–Offender Relationship: A Determinant Factor in Police Domestic Dispute Dispositions." *Marriage and Family Review* 12(1/2): 87–102.

Bennett, T. 1989. "Burglars' Choice of Targets." In D.J. Evans and D.T. Herbert (eds.), *The Geography of Crime.* London: Routledge.

Bennett, T., and R. Wright. 1984. *Burglars on Burglary.* Brookfield, VT: Gower.

Benson, D., C. Charlton, and F. Goodhart. 1992. "Acquaintance Rape on Campus: A Literature Review." *College Health* 40 (January): 157–65.

Benson, M.L. 1985. "Denying the Guilty Mind: Accounting for Involvement in a White-Collar Crime." *Criminology* 23(4): 583–607.

Benson, M.L., and E. Moore. 1992. "Are White Collar and Common Offenders the Same? An Empirical and Theoretical Critique of a Recently Proposed General Theory of Crime." *Journal of Research in Crime and Delinquency* 29(3): 251–72.

Bequai, A. 1987. *Technocrimes.* Lexington, MA: D.C. Heath.

Bernard, T.J. 1981. "The Distinction between Conflict and Radical Criminology." *Journal of Criminal Law and Criminology* 72(1): 362–79.

Best, J. 1988. "Missing Children: Misleading Statistics." *The Public Interest* 92 (Summer): 84–92.

Best, J. 1990. *Threatened Children.* Chicago: University of Chicago Press.

Best, J. 1995. *Images of Issues*. New York: Aldine de Gruyter.

Birkbeck, C., and G. LaFree. 1993. "The Situational Analysis of Crime and Deviance." *Annual Review of Sociology* 19: 113–37.

Black, D. 1970. "Production of Crime Rates." *American Sociological Review* 35: 733–47.

Black, D. 1971. "The Social Organization of Arrest." *Stanford Law Review* 23: 1087–1111.

Black, D. 1976. *The Behavior of Law*. New York: Academic Press.

Black, D. 1980. *The Manners and Customs of the Police*. New York: Academic Press.

Black, D.J. 1983. "Crime as Social Control." *American Sociological Review* 48 (February): 34–45.

Black, D.J., and A.J. Reiss. 1967. "Patterns of Behavior in Police and Citizen Transactions." In *U.S. President's Commission on Law Enforcement and the Administration of Justice, Studies in Crime and Law Enforcement in Major Metropolitan Areas, Field Surveys III*, Vol. 2. Washington, DC: U.S. Government Printing Office.

Blau, J.R., and P.M. Blau. 1982. "The Cost of Inequality: Metropolitan Structure and Violent Crime." *American Sociological Review* 4 (February): 114–29.

Block, C.R., and R.L. Block. 1984. "Crime Definition, Crime Measurement, and Victim Surveys." *Journal of Social Issues* 40(1): 137–60.

Block, R. 1974. "Why Notify the Police?: The Victim's Decision to Notify the Police of an Assault." *Criminology* 11(4): 555–69.

Block, R., M. Felson, and C.R. Block. 1984. "Crime Victimization Rates for Incumbents of 246 Occupations." *Sociology and Social Research* 69(3): 442–51.

Blumstein, A., J. Cohen, and D.P. Farrington. 1988a. "Criminal Career Research: Its Value for Criminology." *Criminology* 26(1): 1–36.

Blumstein, A., J. Cohen, and D.P. Farrington. 1988b. "Longitudinal and Criminal Career Research: Further Clarifications." *Criminology* 26(1): 57–74.

Blumstein, A., J. Cohen, and R. Rosenfeld. 1992. "The UCR-NCS Relationship Revisited: A Reply to Menard." *Criminology* 30(1): 115–24.

Bockman, L.S. 1991. "Interest, Ideology and Claims-Making Activity." *Sociological Inquiry* 61(4): 452–70.

Bograd, M. 1988. "How Battered Women and Abusive Men Account for Domestic Violence: Excuses, Justifications or Explanations." In G.T. Hotaling, D. Finkelhor, J.T. Kirkpatrick, and M.A. Straus (eds.), *Coping with Family Violence*. Newbury Park, CA: Sage.

Bohm, R.M. 1997. *A Primer on Crime and Delinquency*. Belmont, CA: Wadsworth.

Boritch, H. 1992. "Gender and Criminal Court Outcomes: An Historical Analysis." *Criminology* 30(3): 293–325.

Boritch, H. 1997. *Fallen Women: Female Crime and Criminal Justice in Canada*. Scarborough, ON: Nelson Canada.

Bottomley, A.K., and K. Coleman. 1981. *Understanding Crime Rates: Police and Public Roles in the Production of Official Statistics*. Farnborough, U.K.: Gower.

Bottomley, A.K., and K. Pease. 1986. *Crime and Punishment—Interpreting the Data*. Philadelphia: Open University Press.

Box, S. 1981. *Deviance, Reality, and Society*. London: Holt, Rinehart & Winston.

Boyd, N. 1996. "Canadian Criminal Law." In R.A. Silverman, J.J. Teevan, and V.F. Sacco (eds.), *Crime in Canadian Society*, 5th ed., pp. 36–47. Toronto: Harcourt Brace.

Braithwaite, J. 1981. "The Myth of Social Class and Criminality Reconsidered." *American Sociological Review* 46 (February): 36–57.

Braithwaite, J. 1989. *Crime, Shame and Reintegration.* Cambridge: Cambridge University Press.

Brantingham, P.J., and P.L. Brantingham. 1984. *Patterns in Crime.* New York: Macmillan.

Brantingham, P.J., and S.T. Easton. 1996. *The Crime Bill: Who Pays and How Much?* Vancouver: The Fraser Institute.

Brantingham, P.J., and F.L. Faust. 1976. "A Conceptual Model of Crime Prevention." *Crime and Delinquency* 22: 284–96.

Brantingham, P.J., S. Mu, and A. Verma. 1995. "Patterns in Canadian Crime." In M.A. Jackson and C.T. Griffiths (eds.), *Canadian Criminology*, pp. 187–245. Toronto: Harcourt Brace.

Brantingham, P.L. 1989. "Crime Prevention: The North American Experience." In D.J. Evans and D.T. Herbert (eds.), *The Geography of Crime.* London: Routledge.

Brantingham, P.L., and P.J. Brantingham. 1990. "Situational Crime Prevention in Practice." *Canadian Journal of Criminology* 32(1): 17–40.

Brezina, T. 1996. "Adapting to Strain: An Examination of Delinquent Coping Responses." *Criminology* 34(1): 39–60.

Brillon, Y. 1985. "Public Opinion about the Penal System: A Cynical View of Criminal Justice." In D. Gibson and J.K. Baldwin (eds.), *Law in a Cynical Society? Opinion and Law in the 1980s.* Calgary: Carswell.

Brinkerhoff, M.B., and E. Lupri. 1988. "Interspousal Violence." *Canadian Journal of Sociology* 13(4): 407–34.

Bromley, D.G. 1991. "Satanism: The New Cult Scare." In J.T. Richardson, J. Best, and D.G. Bromley (eds.), *The Satanism Scare.* New York: Aldine de Gruyter.

Browne, A., and K. Williams. 1989. "Exploring the Effect of Resource Availability and the Likelihood of Female-Perpetrated Homicides." *Law and Society Review* 23(1): 75–94.

Brunvand, J.H. 1981. *The Vanishing Hitchhiker: American Urban Legends and Their Meaning.* New York: Norton.

Brunvand, J.H. 1984. *The Choking Doberman and Other "New" Urban Legends.* New York: Norton.

Brunvand, J.H. 1986. *The Mexican Pet.* New York: Norton.

Brunvand, J.H. 1989. *Curses! Broiled Again!* New York: Norton.

Brunvand, J.H. 1993. *The Baby Train.* New York: Norton.

Burgess, A.W., L.L. Holmstrom, and M.P. McCausland. 1977. "Child Sexual Assault by a Family Member: Decisions Following Disclosure." *Victimology: An International Journal* 2(2): 236–50.

Bursik, R.J., Jr., and H.G. Grasmick. 1993. *Neighborhoods and Crime: The Dimensions of Effective Community Control.* New York: Lexington Books.

Burt, M.R., and B.L. Katz. 1985. "Rape, Robbery and Burglary: Responses to Actual and Feared Criminal Victimization with Special Focus on Women and the Elderly." *Victimology* 10: 325–58.

Business and Health. 1994. "Helping to Eliminate Stress in the Workplace." 12(4) (Depression Supplement): 28–31.

Cain, M., and K. Kulscar. 1981–82. "Thinking Disputes: An Essay on the Origins of the Dispute Industry." *Law and Society Review* 16(3): 375–402.

Calavita, K., and H.N. Pontell. 1991. "'Other People's Money' Revisited: Collective Embezzlement in the Savings and Loan Insurance Industries." *Social Problems* 38(1): 94–112.

Calhoun, T.C. and G. Weaver. 1996. "Rational Decision-Making among Male Street Prostitutes." *Deviant Behavior* 17: 209–27.

Campbell, G. 1990. "Women and Crime." *Juristat Service Bulletin* 10(20). Ottawa: Canadian Centre for Justice Statistics.

Canada. 1982. *The Criminal Law in Canadian Society.* Ottawa: Government of Canada.

Canadian Centre for Justice Statistics. 1990a. *The Development of Data Quality Assessment Procedures for the Uniform Crime Reporting Survey: A Case Study of Calgary-Edmonton.* Ottawa: Statistics Canada.

Canadian Centre for Justice Statistics. 1990b. *The Future of Crime Statistics from the UCR Survey.* Ottawa: Statistics Canada.

Canadian Criminal Justice Association. 1989. "Safer Communities: A Social Strategy for Crime Prevention in Canada." *Canadian Journal of Criminology* 31(4): 359–63.

Cantor, D., and K.C. Land. 1985. "Unemployment and Crime Rates in the Post–World War II United States: A Theoretical and Empirical Analysis." *American Sociological Review* 50 (June): 317–32.

Carrigan, D.O. 1991. *Crime and Punishment in Canada: A History.* Toronto: McClelland and Stewart.

Carter, D.L. 1985. "Hispanic Perceptions of Police Performance: An Empirical Assessment." *Journal of Criminal Justice* 13: 487–500.

Cater, J., and T. Jones. 1989. "Crime and Disorder." In J. Cater and T. Jones (eds.), *Social Geography—An Introduction to Contemporary Issues.* New York: Routledge, Chapman & Hall.

Cavender, G., and L. Bond-Maupin. 1993. "Fear and Loathing on Reality Television: An Analysis of 'America's Most Wanted' and 'Unsolved Mysteries.'" *Sociological Inquiry* 63(3): 305–17.

Chaiken, J., and M. Chaiken. 1982. *Varieties of Criminal Behavior.* Rand Report r-2814-NIJ. Santa Monica, CA: Rand Corporation.

Chambliss, W. 1975. "On the Paucity of Original Research on Organized Crime: A Footnote to Galliher and Cain." *The American Sociologist* 10: 36–39.

Chambliss, W.J. 1986. "On Lawmaking." In S. Brickey and E. Comack (eds.), *The Social Basis of Law.* Toronto: Garamond Press.

Chard, J. 1995. "Breaking and Entering in Canada." *Juristat.* Statistics Canada.

Chibnall, S. 1977. *Law-and-Order News.* London: Tavistock.

Chilton, R. 1991. "Images of Crime: Crime Statistics and Their Impact." In J.F. Sheley (ed.), *Criminology: A Contemporary Handbook,* pp. 45–65. Belmont, CA: Wadsworth.

Chiricos, T.G. 1987. "Rates of Crime and Unemployment: An Analysis of Aggregate Research Evidence." *Social Problems* 34(2): 187–242.

Clairmont, D. 1990. *To the Forefront: Community-Based Zone Policing in Halifax.* Ottawa: Canadian Police College.

Clark, R.D. 1988. "Celerity and Specific Deterrence: A Look at the Evidence." *Canadian Journal of Criminology* 30(2): 109–20.

Clarke, R.V. 1992. "Introduction." In R.V. Clarke (ed.), *Situational Crime Prevention.* Albany, NY: Harrow & Heston.

Clarke, R.V. 1993. *Crime Prevention Studies,* vol. 1. Monsey, NY: Criminal Justice Press.

Clarke, R.V. 1994. *Crime Prevention Studies,* vol. 2. Monsey, NY: Criminal Justice Press.

Clarke, R.V., P. Ekblom, M. Hough, and P. Mayhew. 1985. "Elderly Victims of Crime and Exposure to Risk." *Journal of Criminal Justice* 23: 1–9.

Clarke, R.V., and M. Felson. 1993a. "Introduction: Criminology, Routine Activity, and Rational Choice." In R.V. Clarke and M. Felson (eds.), *Routine Activity and Rational Choice.* New Brunswick, NJ: Transaction.

Clarke, R.V., and M. Felson. 1993b. *Routine Activity and Rational Choice. Advances in Criminological Theory*, vol. 5. New Brunswick, NJ: Transaction Publishers.

Cloward, R.A. 1959. "Illegitimate Means, Anomie, and Deviant Behavior." The Bobbs-Merrill Reprint Series in the Social Science. Reprinted by permission of *American Sociological Review* 24 (April): 164–76.

Cloward, R.A., and L.E. Ohlin. 1960. *Delinquency and Opportunity.* New York: Free Press.

Cohen, A.K. 1955. *Delinquent Boys: The Culture of the Gang.* New York: Free Press.

Cohen, L.E., and D. Cantor. 1981. "Residential Burglary in the United States: Lifestyle and Demographic Factors Associated with the Probability of Victimization." *Journal of Research in Crime and Delinquency* 18(1): 113–27.

Cohen, L.E., D. Cantor, and J.R. Kleugel. 1981. "Robbery Victimization in the U.S.: An Analysis of a Non-Random Event." *Social Science Quarterly* 62(4): 644–57.

Cohen, L.E., and M. Felson. 1979. "Social Change and Crime Rate Trends: A Routine Activity Approach." *American Sociological Review* 44 (August): 588–608.

Cohen, L.E., J.R. Kluegel, and K.C. Land. 1981. "Social Inequality and Predatory Criminal Victimization: An Exposition and Test of a Formal Theory." *American Sociological Review* 46 (October): 505–24.

Cohen, S. 1972. *Folk Devils and Moral Panics.* London: MacGibbon & Kee.

Coleman, J.W. 1987. "Toward an Integrated Theory of White-Collar Crime." *American Journal of Sociology* 93(2): 406–39.

Coleman, J.W. 1991. "Respectable Crime." In J.F. Sheley (ed.), *Criminology: A Contemporary Handbook,* pp. 219–39. Belmont, CA: Wadsworth.

Collins, J.J., B.G. Cox, and P.A. Langan. 1987. "Job Activities and Personal Crime Victimization: Implications for Theory." *Social Science Research* 16: 345–60.

Conklin, J.E. 1975. *The Impact of Crime.* New York: Macmillan.

Cook, F.L., and W.G. Skogan. 1990. "Agenda Setting and the Rise and Fall of Policy Issues: The Case of Criminal Victimization of the Elderly." *Environment and Planning C: Government and Policy* 8: 395–415.

Cook, P.J. 1977. "Punishment and Crime: A Critique of Current Findings Concerning the Preventive Effects of Punishment." *Law and Contemporary Problems* 41(1): 164–204.

Cornish, D.B., and R.V. Clarke (eds.). 1986. *The Reasoning Criminal.* New York: Springer-Verlag.

Cornwall, A., and H.N. Bawden. 1992. "Reading Disabilities and Aggression: A Critical Review." *Journal of Learning Disabilities* 25(5): 281–88.

Corrado, R.R., and A. Markwart. 1996. "The Evolution of Juvenile Justice in Canada." In R.A. Silverman, J.J. Teevan, and V.F. Sacco (eds.), *Crime in Canadian Society*, 5th ed., pp. 25–35. Toronto: Harcourt Brace.

Cressey, D.R. 1969. *Theft of the Nation.* New York: Harper & Row.

Croall, H. 1987. "Who Is the White-Collar Criminal?" *British Journal of Criminology* 29(2): 157–74.

Cromwell, P., and K. McElrath. 1994. "Buying Stolen Property: An Opportunity Perspective." *Journal of Research in Crime and Delinquency* 31(3): 295–310.

Cromwell, P.F., J.N. Olson, and D.W. Avary. 1991. *Breaking and Entering: An Ethnographic Analysis of Burglary.* Newbury Park, CA: Sage.

Cullen, F.T., B.G. Link, and C.W. Polanzi. 1982. "The Seriousness of Crime Revisited: Have Attitudes Towards White-Collar Crime Changed?" *Criminology* 20(1): 83–102.

Culliver, C., and R. Sigler. 1991. "The Relationship between Learning Disabilities and Juvenile Delinquency." *International Journal of Adolescence and Youth* 3(1–2): 117–28.

Cumberbatch, G., and A. Beardsworth. 1976. "Criminals, Victims and Mass Communications." In E.C. Viano (ed.), *Victims and Society.* Washington, DC: Visage Press.

Currie, E. 1985. *Confronting Crime: An American Challenge.* New York: Pantheon Books.

Cusson, M. 1993. "Situational Deterrence: Fear During the Criminal Event." In R.V. Clarke (ed.), *Crime Prevention Studies,* vol. 1. Monsey, NY: Criminal Justice Press.

Daly, M., and M. Wilson. 1988. *Homicide.* Chicago: Aldine de Gruyter.

Davis, C.R., and B. Smith. 1994. "Teaching Victims Crime Prevention Skills: Can Individuals Lower Their Costs of Crime?" *Criminal Justice Review* 19(1): 56–68.

Davis, N.J. 1988. "Battered Women: Implications for Social Control." *Contemporary Crises* 12: 345–72.

Davis, P.W. 1991. "Stranger Intervention into Child Punishment in Public Places." *Social Problems* 38(2): 227–46.

Davis, P.W. 1994. "The Changing Meaning of Spanking." In J. Best (ed.), *Troubling Children,* pp. 133–53. New York: Aldine de Gruyter.

Dechenes, E.P. 1990. "Longitudinal Research Designs." In K.L. Kempf (ed.), *Measurement Issues in Criminology,* pp. 152–66. New York: Springer-Verlag.

DeKeseredy, W.S., and R. Hinch. 1991. *Woman Abuse: Sociological Perspectives.* Ottawa: Thompson Educational Publishing.

DeKeseredy, W., and K. Kelly. 1993a. "The Incidence and Prevalence of Woman Abuse in Canadian University and College Dating Relationships." *Canadian Journal of Sociology* 18(2): 137–59.

DeKeseredy, W., and K. Kelly. 1993b. "Woman Abuse in College and University Dating Relationships: The Contribution of the Ideology of Family Patriarchy." *Journal of Human Justice* 4(2): 25–52.

Desroches, F.J. 1991. "Tearoom Trade: A Law Enforcement Problem." *Canadian Journal of Criminology* 33(1): 1–21.

Desroches, F.J. 1995. *Force and Fear: Robbery in Canada.* Toronto: Nelson Canada.

Devereaux, M.S. 1990. "Decline in the Number of Children." *Canadian Social Trends* 18 (Autumn): 32–34.

DiIulio, J.J. 1989. "The Impact of Inner-City Crime." *Public Interest* 96: 28–46.

Doherty, G., and P. De Souza. 1996. "Youth Crime." In L.W. Kennedy and V. Sacco, (eds.), *Crime Counts: A Criminal Event Perspective,* pp. 231–55. Scarborough, ON: Nelson Canada.

Dominick, J.R. 1978. "Crime and Law Enforcement in the Mass Media." In C. Winick (ed.), *Deviance and Mass Media.* Beverly Hills, CA: Sage.

Donzinger, S.R. 1996. *The Real War on Crime: The Report of the National Criminal Justice Commission.* New York: HarperPerennial.

Doob, A.N. 1982. "The Role of Mass Media in Creating Exaggerated Levels of Fear of Being the Victim of a Violent Crime." In P. Stringer (ed.), *Confronting Social Issues: Applications of Social Psychology.* Toronto: Academic Press.

Doob, A.N., and G.E. MacDonald. 1976. "Television Viewing and Fear of Victimization: Is the Relationship Causal?" *Journal of Personality and Social Psychology* 37: 170–79.

Dorfman, A. 1984. "The Criminal Mind." *Science Digest* 92(10): 44–47, 98.

Douglas, J.D., and F.C. Waskler. 1982. *The Sociology of Deviance*. Boston: Little, Brown.

DuBow, F., E. McCabe, and G. Kaplan. 1979. *Reactions to Crime: A Critical Review of the Literature*. Washington, DC: U.S. Department of Justice.

Dubro, J. 1985. *Mob Rule: Inside the Canadian Mafia*. Toronto: Macmillan.

Durkheim, E. 1933. *The Division of Labor in Society*. Trans. G. Simpson. Glencoe, IL: Free Press.

Durkheim, E. 1964. *The Rules of Sociological Method*. New York: Free Press. (Orig. pub. in 1938.)

Dutton, D.G. 1987. "The Criminal Justice Response to Wife Assault." *Law and Human Behavior* 11(3): 189–206.

Dutton, D., S. Hart, L.W. Kennedy, and K. Williams. 1992. "Arrest and the Reduction of Repeat Wife Assault." In E. Buzawa and C. Buzawa (eds.), *Domestic Violence: The Changing Criminal Justice Response*. Westport, CT: Greenwood Press.

Edwards, P., and A. Nicasco. 1993. *Deadly Silence: Canadian Mafia Murders*. Toronto: Macmillan Canada.

Elliott, D.S., and S.S. Ageton. 1980. "Reconciling Race and Class Differences in Self-Reported and Official Estimates of Delinquency." *American Sociological Review* 45 (February): 95–110.

Ellis, L. 1982. "Genetics and Criminal Behavior." *Criminology* 20(1): 43–66.

Engs, R.C., and D.J. Hanson. 1994. "Boozing and Brawling on Campus: A National Study of Violent Problems Associated with Drinking over the Past Decade." *Journal of Criminal Justice* 22(2): 171–80.

Ericson, R.V. 1982. *Reproducing Order: A Study of Police Patrol Work*. Toronto: University of Toronto Press.

Ericson, R.V. 1991. "Mass Media, Crime, Law, and Justice: An Institutional Approach." *The British Journal of Criminology* 31(3): 219–49.

Ericson, R.V., P.M. Baranek, and J.B.L. Chan. 1987. *Visualizing Deviance*. Toronto: University of Toronto Press.

Ericson, R.V., P.M. Baranek, and J.B.L. Chan. 1989. *Negotiating Control: A Study of News Sources*. Toronto: University of Toronto Press.

Ericson, R.V., P.M. Baranek, and J.B.L. Chan. 1991. *Representing Order: Crime, Law, and Justice in the News Media*. Toronto: University of Toronto Press.

Ericson, R., and C. Shearing. 1986. "The Scientification of Police Work." In G. Boehme and N. Stehr (eds.), *The Knowledge Society*, pp. 129–59. Dordrecht: D. Reidel.

Evans, D.J. 1989. "Geographical Analyses of Residential Burglary." In D.J. Evans and D.T. Herbert (eds.), *The Geography of Crime*. London: Routledge.

Fagan, J., and S. Wexler. 1987. "Family Origins of Violent Delinquents." *Criminology* 25: 643–69.

Farberman, H.A. 1975. "A Criminogenic Market Structure: The Automobile Industry." *Sociological Quarterly* 16: 438–57.

Farrington, D.P. 1989. "Implications of Longitudinal Studies for Social Prevention." *Canadian Journal of Criminology* 31(4): 453–63.

Farrington, D.P., S. Bowen, A. Buckle, T. Burns-Howell, and J. Burrows. 1993. "An Experiment on the Prevention of Shoplifting." In R.V. Clarke (ed.), *Crime Prevention Studies*, pp. 93–119. Monsey, NY: Criminal Justice Press.

Fattah, E.A. 1991. *Understanding Criminal Victimization*. Scarborough, ON: Prentice-Hall.

Fattah, E.A. 1993. "The Rational Choice/Opportunity Perspectives as a Vehicle for Integrating Criminological and Victimological Theories." In R.V. Clarke and M. Felson (eds.), *Routine Activity and Rational Choice*, pp. 225–28. New Brunswick, NJ: Transaction.

Fattah, E.A., and V.F. Sacco. 1989. *Crime and Victimization of the Elderly*. New York: Springer-Verlag.

Fedorowycz, O. 1992. "Break and Enter in Canada." *Juristat Service Bulletin* 12(1).

Fedorowycz, O. 1996. "Homicide in Canada—1995." *Juristat* 16(11).

Fekete, J. 1994. *Moral Panic: Biopolitics Rising*. Montreal: Robert Davies Publishing.

Felson, M. 1986. "Linking Criminal Choices, Routine Activities, Informal Control, and Criminal Outcomes." In D.B. Cornish and R.V. Clarke (eds.), *The Reasoning Criminal*. New York: Springer-Verlag.

Felson, M. 1987. "Routine Activities and Crime Prevention in the Developing Metropolis." *Criminology* 25(4): 911–31.

Felson, M. 1992. "Routine Activities and Crime Prevention." *Studies in Crime and Crime Prevention Annual Review* 1(1): 30–34.

Felson, M. 1994. *Crime and Everyday Life*. Newbury Park, CA: Pine Forge Press.

Felson R.B., W.F. Baccaglini, and S.A. Ribner. 1985. "Accounting for Criminal Violence: A Comparison of Official and Offender Versions of the Crime." *Sociology and Social Research* 70(1): 93–101.

Felson, R.B., A.E. Liska, S.J. South, and T.L. McNulty 1994. "The Subculture of Violence and Delinquency: Individual vs. School Context Effects." *Social Forces* 73(1): 155–73.

Felson, R.B., and S. Messner. 1996. "To Kill or Not to Kill: Lethal Outcomes in Injurious Attacks." *Criminology* 34(4): 519–45.

Ferraro, K.J. 1989. "Policing Woman Battering." *Social Problems* 36(1): 61–74.

Ferraro, K.J., and J.M. Johnson. 1983. "How Women Experience Battering: The Process of Victimization." *Social Problems* 30: 325–35.

Fischer, C.S. 1975. "The Effect of Urban Life on Traditional Values." *Social Forces* 53: 420–32.

Fischer, C.S. 1976. *The Urban Experience*. New York: Harcourt Brace Jovanovich.

Fischer, C.S. 1981. "The Public and Private Worlds of City Life." *American Sociological Review* 46 (June): 306–16.

Fisher, B., and J.L. Nasar. 1995. "Fear Spots in Relation to Microlevel Physical Cues: Exploring the Overlooked." *Journal of Research in Crime and Delinquency* 32(2): 214–39.

Fishman, M. 1978. "Crime Waves as Ideology." *Social Problems* 25(5): 531–43.

Fishman, M. 1981. "Police News: Constructing an Image of Crime." *Urban Life* 9(4): 371–94.

Fleisher, M.S. 1995. *Beggars and Thieves: Lives of Urban Street Criminals*. Madison: University of Wisconsin Press.

Flowers, R.B. 1989. *Demographics and Criminality: The Characteristics of Crime in America*. New York: Greenwood Press.

Forde, D., and L.W. Kennedy. 1997. "Risky Lifestyles, Routine Activities, and the General Theory of Crime." *Justice Quarterly* 14(2): 301–31.

Freeman, R.B. 1983. "Crime and Unemployment." In J.Q. Wilson (ed.), *Crime and Public Policy*. San Francisco: ICS Press.

Freudenheim, M. 1987. "Business and Health." *New York Times.* (May 26).

Friedrichs, D.O. 1996. *Trusted Criminals*. Belmont, CA: Wadsworth.

Frieze, I.H., and A. Browne. 1989. "Violence in Marriage." In L. Ohlin and M. Tonry (eds.), *Family Violence*. Chicago: University of Chicago Press.

Frinell, D.E., E. Dahlstrom III, and D.A. Johnson. 1980. "A Public Education Program Designed to Increase the Accuracy and Incidence of Citizens' Reports of Suspicious and Criminal Activities." *Journal of Police Science and Administration* 8(2): 160–65.

Furstenberg, F. 1971. "Public Reactions to Crime in the Streets." *The American Scholar* 40: 601–10.

Gabor, T. 1990a. "Crime Prevention: The Agenda." *Canadian Journal of Criminology* 32(1): 1–7.

Gabor, T. 1990b. "Crime Displacement and Situational Prevention: Toward the Development of Some Principles." *Canadian Journal of Criminology* 32(1): 41–73.

Gabor, T. 1994a. *Everybody Does It: Crime by the Public*. Toronto: University of Toronto Press.

Gabor, T. 1994b. "The Suppression of Crime Statistics on Race and Ethnicity: The Price of Political Correctness." *Canadian Journal of Criminology* 36(2): 153–63.

Gabor, T., and A. Normandeau. 1989. "Armed Robbery: Highlights of a Canadian Study." *Canadian Police College Journal* 13(4).

Galliher, J.F., and J.A. Cain. 1974. "Citation Support for the Mafia Myth in Criminology Textbooks." *The American Sociologist* 9 (May): 68–74.

Gans, H. 1962. *The Urban Villagers*. New York: Free Press.

Garofalo, J. 1981a. "Crime and the Mass Media: A Selective Review of Research." *Journal of Research in Crime and Delinquency* (July): 319–50.

Garofalo, J. 1981b. "The Fear of Crime: Causes and Consequences." *The Journal of Criminal Law and Criminology* 72: 839–57.

Garofalo, J., and M. McLeod. 1988. *Improving the Use and Effectiveness of Neighborhood Watch Programs*. Washington, DC: U.S. Department of Justice.

Garofalo, J., L. Siegel, and J. Laub. 1987. "School-Related Victimizations among Adolescents: An Analysis of National Crime Survey (NCS) Narratives." *Journal of Quantitative Criminology* 3(4): 321–38.

Garofalo, R. 1914. *Criminology*. Boston: Little, Brown.

Gartner, R., and A. Doob. 1994. "Trends in Criminal Victimization: 1988–1993." *Juristat* 14(13). Statistics Canada.

Gartner, G., and B. McCarthy. 1996. "The Social Distribution of Femicide in Urban Canada: 1921–1988." In R.A. Silverman, J.J. Teevan, and V.F. Sacco (eds.), *Crime in Canadian Society*, 5th ed., pp. 177–85. Toronto: Harcourt Brace.

Gates, L.B., and W.M. Rohe. 1987. "Fear and Reactions to Crime: A Revised Model." *Urban Affairs Quarterly* 22: 425–53.

Gauthier, P. 1994. "Canada's Seniors." In *Canadian Social Trends: A Canadian Studies Reader*, pp. 17–21. Toronto: Thompson Educational Publishing.

Gelles, R.J., and M.A. Straus. 1988. *Intimate Violence*. New York: Simon & Schuster.

Gelles, R.J., and M.A. Straus. 1990. "The Medical and Psychological Costs of Family Violence." In M.A. Straus and R.J. Gelles (eds.), *Physical Violence in American Families: Risk Factors and Adaptations to Violence in 8,145 Families*. New Brunswick, NJ: Transaction.

Geran, L. 1992. "Occupational Stress." *Canadian Social Trends* 26 (Autumn): 14–17.

Gibbons, D.C. 1988. "Some Critical Observations on Criminal Types and Criminal Careers." *Criminal Justice and Behavior* 15: 8–23.

Gibbs, J.P 1966. "Conceptions of Deviant Behavior: The Old and the New." *Pacific Sociological Review* 9: 9–14.

Gibbs, J.P. 1981. *Norms, Deviance, and Social Control: Conceptual Matters.* New York: Elsevier.

Gibbs, J.P., and M.L. Erikson. 1976. "Crime Rates of American Cities in an Ecological Context." *American Journal of Sociology* 82(3): 605–20.

Gilbert, N. 1991. "The Phantom Epidemic of Sexual Assault." *The Public Interest* 103 (Spring): 54–65.

Gillespie, C. 1989. *Justifiable Homicide: Battered Women, Self Defense, and the Law.* Columbus: Ohio State University Press.

Gillespie, D.L., and A. Leffler. 1987. "The Politics of Research Methodology in Claims-Making Activities: Social Science and Sexual Harassment." *Social Problems* 34(5): 490–501.

Gilsinan, J.F. 1989. "They Is Clowning Tough: 911 and the Social Construction of Reality." *Criminology* 27(2): 329–44.

Gilsinan, J.F. 1990. *Criminology and Public Policy: An Introduction.* Englewood Cliffs, NJ: Prentice-Hall.

The Globe and Mail. 1993. "Westray Charges Thrown Out" (July 21), p. A1; "Injected with HIV While Asleep, Alberta Man Says" (July 21), p. A4; "Calgary Teen Given Life Sentence for Schoolyard Stabbing of Boy, 13" (July 21), p. A3.

Goff, C., and N. Nason-Clark. 1989. "The Seriousness of Crime in Fredericton, New Brunswick: Perceptions Toward White-Collar Crime." *Canadian Journal of Criminology* 31(1): 19–34.

Goffman, E. 1959. *The Presentation of Self in Everyday Life.* Garden City, NJ: Doubleday.

Goffman, E. 1963. *Stigma: Notes on the Management of Spoiled Identity.* Englewood Cliffs, NJ: Prentice-Hall.

Golant, S.M. 1984. "Factors Influencing the Nighttime Activity of Old Persons in Their Community." *Journal of Gerontology* 39: 485–91.

Gold, M. 1970. *Delinquent Behavior in an American City.* Belmont, CA: Brooks/Cole.

Goldstein, H. 1990. *Problem-Oriented Policing.* Philadelphia: Temple University Press.

Gondolf, E.W., and J.R. McFerron. 1989. "Handling Battering Men and Police Action in Wife Abuse Cases." *Criminal Justice and Behavior* 16: 429–39.

Goode, E., and N. Ben-Yehuda. 1994. *Moral Panics: The Social Construction of Deviance.* Oxford: Blackwell.

Goodstein, L., and R.L. Shotland. 1982. "The Crime Causes Crime Model: A Critical Review of the Relationship between Fear of Crime, Bystander Surveillance, and Changes in the Crime Rate." *Victimology* 5(2–4): 133–51.

Gordon, M.T., and L. Heath. 1981. "The News Business, Crime and Fear." In D.A. Lewis (ed.), *Reactions to Crime.* Beverly Hills, CA: Sage.

Gordon, M.T., and S. Riger. 1989. *The Female Fear.* New York: Free Press.

Gordon, R.M., and J. Nelson. 1996. "Crime, Ethnicity, and Immigration." In R.A. Silverman, J.J. Teevan, and V.F. Sacco (eds.), *Crime in Canadian Society,* 5th ed., pp. 234–44. Toronto: Harcourt Brace.

Gorelick, S.M. 1989. "'Join Our War': The Construction of Ideology in a Newspaper Crimefighting Campaign." *Crime and Delinquency* 35(3): 421–36.

Gottfredson, M.R. 1984. "Victims of Crime: The Dimensions of Risk." A Home Office Research and Planning Unit Report. London: HMSO Books.

Gottfredson, M.R., and D. Gottfredson. 1988. *Decisionmaking in Criminal Justice,* 2nd ed. New York: Plenum.

Gottfredson, M.R., and T. Hirschi 1986. "The True Value of Lambda Would Appear to Be Zero: An Essay on Career Criminals, Criminal Careers, Selective Incapacitation, Cohort Studies, and Related Topics." *Criminology* 24(2): 213–34.

Gottfredson, M.R., and T. Hirschi 1988. "Science, Public Policy and the Career Paradigm." *Criminology* 26: 37–55.

Gottfredson, M.R., and T. Hirschi. 1990. *A General Theory of Crime.* Stanford, CA: Stanford University Press.

Gottfredson, M.R., and T. Hirschi. 1995. "National Crime Prevention Policies." *Society* 32(2): 30–36.

Gould, L.C. 1989. "Crime, Criminality, and Criminal Events." Paper presented at the Annual Meetings of the American Society of Criminology, Reno, Nevada.

Gove, W.R. 1975. *The Labelling of Deviance: Evaluating a Perspective.* New York: Sage.

Gove, W.R., M. Hughes, and M. Geerken. 1985. "Are Uniform Crime Reports a Valid Indicator of the Index Crimes? An Affirmative Answer with Minor Modifications." *Criminology* 23(3): 451–501.

Graber, D.A. 1980. *Crime News and the Public.* New York: Praeger.

Graham, J. 1990. *Crime Prevention Strategies in Europe and North America.* Helsinki: Helsinki Institute for Crime Prevention and Control.

Grainger, B. 1996. "Data and Methodology in the Area of Criminal Justice." In L.W. Kennedy and V.F. Sacco (eds.), *Crime Counts*, pp. 3–19. Toronto: Nelson Canada.

Gramling, R., C. Forsyth, and J. Fewell. 1988. "Crime and Economic Activity: A Research Note." *Sociological Spectrum* 8: 187–95.

Gray, H. 1989. "Popular Music as a Social Problem: A Social History of the Claims against Popular Music." In J. Best (ed.), *Images of Issues.* New York: Aldine de Gruyter.

Greenberg, D.F. 1992. "Comparing Criminal Career Models." *Criminology* 30(1): 141–47.

Greenberg, M.S., R.B. Ruback, and D.R. Westcott. 1982. "Decision Making by Crime Victims: A Multimethod Approach." *Law and Society Review* 17: 47–84.

Greenberg, P. 1996. "Break and Enter." In L.W. Kennedy and V.F. Sacco (eds.), *Crime Counts: A Criminal Event Analysis,* pp. 153–65. Scarborough, ON: Nelson Canada.

Gurr, T.R. 1980. "Development and Decay: Their Impact on Public Order in Western History." In J. Inciardi and C.E. Faupel (eds.), *History and Crime.* Beverly Hills, CA: Sage.

Gusfield, J. 1963. *Symbolic Crusade: Status Politics and the American Temperance Movement.* Urbana: University of Illinois Press.

Gusfield, J. 1989. "Constructing the Ownership of Social Problems: Fun and Profit in the Welfare State." *Social Problems* 36(5): 431–41.

Hackler, J., and K. Don. 1990. "Estimating System Biases: Crime Indices that Permit Comparisons across Provinces." *Canadian Journal of Criminology* 32(2): 243–64.

Hagan, J. 1980. "The Legislation of Crime and Delinquency: A Review of Theory, Method and Research." *Law and Society Review* 14(3): 603–28.

Hagan, J. 1985. *Modern Criminology.* New York: McGraw-Hill.

Hagan, J. 1989. *Structural Criminology.* New Brunswick, NJ: Rutgers University Press.

Hagan, J. 1992. "White Collar and Corporate Crime." In R. Linden (ed.), *Criminology: A Canadian Perspective.* Toronto: Harcourt Brace Jovanovich.

Hagan, J., A.R. Gillis, and J.H. Simpson. 1979. "The Sexual Stratification of Social Control: A Gender-Based Perspective on Crime and Delinquency." *British Journal of Sociology* 30(1): 25–38.

Hagan, J., A.R. Gillis, and J.H. Simpson. 1985. "The Class Structure of Gender and Delinquency: Toward a Power-Control Theory of Common Delinquent Behavior." *American Journal of Sociology* 90(6): 1151–78.

Hagan, J., J. Simpson, and A.R. Gillis. 1987. "Class in the Household: Deprivation, Liberation and a Power-Control Theory of Gender and Delinquency." *American Journal of Sociology* 92(4): 788–816.

Hagan, J., J. Simpson, and A.R. Gillis. 1988. "Feminist Scholarship, Relational and Instrumental Control, and a Power-Control Theory of Gender and Delinquency." *The British Journal of Sociology* 39(3): 301–36.

Haller, M.H. 1990. "Illegal Enterprise: A Theoretical and Historical Interpretation." *Criminology* 28(2): 207–35.

Hamlin, J.E. 1988. "The Misplaced Role of Rational Choice in Neutralization Theory." *Criminology* 26: 425–38.

Hanke, P. 1996. "Putting School Crime into Perspective: Self Reported School Victimizations of High-School Seniors." *Journal of Criminal Justice* 24(3): 207–26.

Hanmer, J., and S. Saunders. 1984. *Well-Founded Fear: A Community Study of Violence to Women.* London: Hutchinson, in association with The Explorations in Feminism Collective, an affiliation of the Women's Research and Resources Centre.

Hans, V.P. 1990. "Law and the Media: An Overview and Introduction." *Law and Human Behavior* 14(5): 399–407.

Hans, V.P., and D. Ermann. 1989. "Responses to Corporate versus Individual Wrongdoing." *Law and Human Behavior* 13(2): 151–66.

Hansel, M.K. 1987. "Citizen Crime Stereotypes—Normative Consensus Revisited." *Criminology* 25: 455–85.

Harlow, C.W. 1991. *Female Victims of Violent Crime.* Washington, DC: U.S. Department of Justice.

Harney, P.A., and C.L. Muehlenhard. 1991. "Factors That Increase the Likelihood of Victimization." In A. Parrot and L. Bechhofer (eds.), *Acquaintance Rape: The Hidden Crime.* New York: John Wiley.

Harries, K.D. 1990. *Serious Violence.* Springfield, IL: Charles C. Thomas.

Harris, M.K. 1991. "Moving into the New Millennium: Toward a Feminist Vision of Peace." In H.E. Pepinsky and R. Quinney (eds.), *Criminology as Peacemaking.* Bloomington: Indiana University Press.

Hartman, D.P., D.M. Gelfand, B. Page, and P. Walder. 1972. "Rates of Bystander Observation and Reporting of Contrived Shoplifting Incidents." *Criminology* (November): 247–67.

Hartnagel, T.F. 1996. "Correlates of Criminal Behaviour." In R. Linden (ed.), *Criminology: A Canadian Perspective*, 3rd ed., pp. 95–137. Toronto: Harcourt Brace.

Hartnagel, T.F., and H. Krahn. 1989. "High School Dropouts, Labor Market Success, and Criminal Behavior." *Youth and Society* 20(4): 416–44.

Hasell, M.J., and F.D. Peatross. 1990. "Exploring Connections between Women's Changing Roles and House Forms." *Environment and Behavior* 22(1): 3–26.

Health and Welfare Canada. 1989. *National Survey on Driving and Drinking, 1988: Overview Report.* Ottawa: Supply and Services Canada.

Heath, L. and K. Gilbert. 1996. "Mass Media and Fear of Crime." *American Behavioral Scientist* 39(4): 379–86.

Hendrick, D. 1996. "Canadian Crime Statistics." *Juristat* 16(10).

Hennigen, K.M., L. Heath, J.D. Wharton, M.L. Del Resario, T.D. Cook, and B.J. Calder. 1982. "Impact of the Introduction of Television on Crime in the United States: Empirical Findings and Theoretical Implications." *Journal of Personality and Social Psychology* 42(3): 461–77.

Henshel, R.L., and R.A. Silverman. 1975. *Perception in Criminology.* Toronto: Methuen.

Hickey, E. 1991. *Serial Murderers and Their Victims.* Belmont, CA: Wadsworth.

Hicks, R.D. 1991. *In Pursuit of Satan.* Buffalo: Prometheus Books.

Hindelang, M.J., M.R. Gottfredson, and J. Garofalo. 1978. *Victims of Personal Crime: An Empirical Foundation for a Theory of Personal Victimization.* Cambridge, MA: Ballinger.

Hindelang, M.J., T. Hirschi, and J. Weis. 1981. *Measuring Delinquency.* Beverly Hills, CA: Sage.

Hirschi, T. 1969. *Causes of Delinquency.* Berkeley: University of California Press.

Hocker, J.L., and W.W. Wilmot. 1985. *Interpersonal Conflict,* 2nd ed. Dubuque, IA: William C. Brown.

Hollinger, R.C., and L. Lanza-Kaduce. 1988. "The Process of Criminalization: The Case of Computer Crime Laws." *Criminology* 26(1): 101–13.

Horowitz, A.V. 1990. *The Logic of Social Control.* New York: Plenum.

Hotaling, G.T., and D. Finkelhor. 1990. "Estimating the Number of Stranger-Abduction Homicides of Children: A Review of Available Evidence." *Journal of Criminal Justice* 18: 385–99.

Hotaling, G.T., and M.A. Straus (with A.J. Lincoln). 1990. "Intrafamily Violence and Crime and Violence Outside the Family." In M.A. Straus and R.J. Gelles (eds.), *Physical Violence in American Families: Risk Factors and Adaptations to Violence in 8,145 Families.* New Brunswick, NJ: Transaction.

Hough, M. 1985. "The Impact of Victimisation: Findings from the British Crime Survey." *Victimology* 10: 488–97.

Hough, M. 1987. "Offenders' Choice of Target: Findings from Victim Surveys." *Journal of Quantitative Criminology* 3(4): 355–70.

Humphries, D. 1981. "Serious Crime, News Coverage, and Ideology: A Content Analysis of Crime Coverage in a Metropolitan Paper." *Crime and Delinquency* 27(2): 191–205.

Hunt, J. 1985. "Police Accounts of Normal Force." *Urban Life* 13(4): 315–41.

Ianni, F.A.J. 1971. "The Mafia and the Web of Kinship." *The Public Interest* 16: 78–100.

Ianni, F.A.J. 1974. *Black Mafia.* New York: Simon & Schuster.

Ianni, F.A.J., and E. Reuss-Ianni. 1972. *A Family Business: Kinship and Social Control in Organized Crime.* New York: Russell Sage Foundation.

Innes, C.A., and L.A. Greenfeld. 1990. "Violent State Prisoners and Their Victims." *Bureau of Justice Statistics Special Report.* Washington, DC: U.S. Department of Justice.

Iso-Ahola, S. 1980. *The Social Psychology of Leisure and Recreation.* Dubuque, IA: William C. Brown.

Jackson, P.G. 1990. "Sources of Data." In K.L. Kempf (ed.), *Measurement Issues in Criminology.* New York: Springer-Verlag.

Jackson, P.I. 1989. *Minority Group Threat, Crime, and Policing.* New York: Praeger.

Jacobs, N. 1965. "The Phantom Slasher of Taipei: Mass Hysteria in a Non-Western Society." *Social Problems* 12: 318–28.

Janoff-Bulman, R., and I.H. Frieze. 1983. "A Theoretical Perspective for Understanding Reactions to Victimization." *Journal of Social Issues* 39(2): 1–17.

Jeffery, C.R. 1990. *Criminology: An Interdisciplinary Approach*. Englewood Cliffs, NJ: Prentice-Hall.

Jenkins, P. 1992. *Intimate Enemies: Moral Panic in Great Britain*. New York: Aldine de Gruyter.

Jenkins, P. 1994. *Using Murder: The Social Construction of Serial Homicide*. New York: Walter de Gruyter.

Jenkins, P., and D. Meier-Katkin. 1992. "Satanism: Myth and Reality in a Contemporary Moral Panic." *Crime, Law and Social Change* 17: 53–75.

Jensen, G.F., and D. Brownfield. 1986. "Gender, Lifestyles, and Victimization: Beyond Routine Activity." *Violence and Victims* 1(2): 85–99.

Johnson, D.M. 1945. "The 'Phantom Anesthetist' of Mattoon: A Field Study of Mass Hysteria." *Journal of Abnormal and Social Psychology* 40: 175–86.

Johnson, G.D., G.J. Palileo, and N.B. Gray. 1992. "Date Rape on a Southern Campus." *Sociology and Social Research* 76(2): 37–41.

Johnson, H. 1995. "Children and Youths as Victims of Violent Crime." *Juristat* 15(15).

Johnson, H. 1996a. *Dangerous Domains*. Scarborough, ON: Nelson Canada.

Johnson, H. 1996b. "Violence against Women: A Special Topic Survey." In R.A. Silverman, J.J. Teevan, and V.F. Sacco (eds.), *Crime in Canadian Society*, 5th ed., pp. 210–21. Toronto: Harcourt Brace.

Johnson, H., and V. Sacco. 1995. "Researching Violence against Women: Statistics Canada National Survey." *Canadian Journal of Criminology* 37(3): 281–304.

Jones, M. 1994. "Time Use of the Elderly." In *Canadian Social Trends: A Canadian Studies Reader*, pp. 349–51. Toronto: Thompson Educational Publishing.

Junger, M. 1987. "Women's Experiences of Sexual Harassment: Some Implications for Their Fear of Crime." *British Journal of Criminology* 27(4): 358–83.

Jupp, V. 1989. *Methods of Criminological Research*. London: Unwin Hyman.

Kantor, G.K., and M.A. Straus. 1987. "The Drunken Bum Theory of Wife Beating." *Social Problems* 34(2): 213–30.

Kapferer, J.N. 1989. "A Mass Poisoning Rumor in Europe." *Public Opinion Quarterly* 53: 467–81.

Kappeler, V.E., M. Blumberg, and G.W. Potter. 1993. *The Mythology of Crime and Criminal Justice*. Prospect Heights, IL: Waveland Press.

Karasek, R., and T. Theorell. 1990. *Healthy Work*. New York: Basic Books.

Karmen, A. 1996. *Crime Victims: An Introduction to Victimology*. Belmont, CA: Wadsworth.

Katz, J. 1987. "What Makes Crime 'News.'" *Media, Culture and Society* 9: 47–75.

Katz, J. 1988. *Seductions of Crime: Moral and Sensual Attractions in Doing Evil*. New York: Basic Books.

Katz, J. 1993. "Guns, Guns, Guns: The War in the United States." *Globe and Mail* (July 2), p. A15.

Keane, C. 1995. "Victimization and Fear: Assessing the Role of Offender and Offence." *Canadian Journal of Criminology* 37(3): 431–55.

Keane, C., P.S. Maxim, and J.J. Teevan. 1996. "Testing a General Theory of Crime." In R.A. Silverman, J.J. Teevan, and V.F. Sacco (eds.), *Crime in Canadian Society*, 5th ed., pp. 169–76. Toronto: Harcourt Brace.

Keane, K. 1996. "Corporate Crime." In R.A. Silverman, J.J. Teevan, and V.F. Sacco (eds.), *Crime in Canadian Society*, 5th ed., pp. 282–92. Toronto: Harcourt Brace.

Kelling, G.L., and C.M. Coles. 1996. *Fixing Broken Windows*. New York: The Free Press.

Kelling, G., T. Pate, D. Dieckman, and C.E. Brown. 1974. *The Kansas City Preventive Patrol Experiment: A Summary Report*. Washington, DC: The Police Foundation.

Kempf, K.L. 1987. "Specialization and the Criminal Career." *Criminology* 25: 399–420.

Kennedy, L.W. 1988. "Going It Alone: Unreported Crime and Individual Self-Help." *Journal of Criminal Justice* 16(5): 403–12.

Kennedy, L.W. 1990. *On the Borders of Crime: Conflict Management and Criminology*. New York: Longman.

Kennedy, L.W. 1991. "Evaluating Community Policing." *Canadian Police College Journal* 15(4): 275–90.

Kennedy, L.W., and S. Baron. 1993. "Routine Activities and a Subculture of Violence: A Study of Violence on the Street." *Journal of Research in Crime and Delinquency* 30(1): 88–112.

Kennedy, L.W., and D.G. Dutton. 1989. "The Incidence of Wife Assault in Alberta." *Canadian Journal of Behavioral Science* 21(1): 40–54.

Kennedy, L.W., and D.R. Forde. 1990. "Routine Activities and Crime: An Analysis of Victimization in Canada." *Criminology* 28(1): 101–15.

Kennedy, L.W., and R.A. Silverman. 1990. "The Elderly Victim of Homicide: An Application of the Routine Activities Approach." *Sociological Quarterly* 31(2): 307–19.

Kennedy, L.W., and R.A. Silverman. 1985. "Significant Others and Fear of Crime among the Elderly." *International Journal of Aging and Human Development* 20(4): 241–56.

Kennedy, L.W., and D. Veitch. 1997. "Why Are the Crime Rates Going Down? A Case Study in Edmonton." *Canadian Journal of Criminology* 39(1): 51–69.

Kinderlehrer, J. 1983. "Delinquent Diets: Partners in Crime." *Prevention* (October): 141–44.

Kirby, C., and T.C. Renner. 1986. *Mafia Assassin: The Inside Story of a Canadian Biker, Hitman and Police Informer*. Toronto: Methuen.

Kitsuse, K.I. 1962. "Societal Reaction to Deviant Behavior: Problems of Theory and Method." *Social Problems* 9: 247–56.

Klaus, P.A., and M.R. Rand. 1984. *Family Violence*. Washington, DC: Bureau of Justice Statistics.

Kleck, G., and S. Sayles. 1990. "Rape and Resistance." *Social Problems* 37(2): 149–62.

Klockars, C.B. 1985. *The Idea of Police*. Beverly Hills, CA: Sage.

Koenig, D.J. 1991. *Do Police Cause Crime?: Police Activity, Police Strength, and Crime Rates*. Ottawa: Canadian Police College.

Kong, R., and K. Rodgers. 1995. "Victims' Use of Police and Social Services." *Juristat* 15(6).

Kornhauser, R. 1978. *Social Sources of Delinquency*. Chicago: University of Chicago Press.

Krahn, H., and L.W. Kennedy. 1985. "Producing Personal Safety: The Effects of Crime Rates, Police Force Size, and Fear of Crime." *Criminology* 23(4): 697–710.

Krohn, M.D., L. Lanza-Kaduce, and R. Akers. 1984. "Community Context and Theories of Deviant Behavior: An Examination of Social Learning and Social Bonding Theories." *The Sociological Quarterly* 25: 353–71.

Krupat, E., and P. Kubzansky. 1987. "Designing to Deter Crime." *Psychology Today* (October): 58–61.

Kurz, D. 1987. "Emergency Department Responses to Battered Women: Resistance to Medicalization." *Social Problems* 34(1): 69–81.

Lab, S.P. 1992. *Crime Prevention: Approaches, Practices and Evaluations*, 2nd ed. Cincinnati, OH: Anderson.

LaGrange, R.L., and K.F. Ferraro 1987. "The Elderly's Fear of Crime: A Critical Examination of the Research." *Research on Aging* 9: 372–91.

LaGrange, R.L., and K.F. Ferraro. 1989. "Assessing Age and Gender Differences in Perceived Risk and Fear of Crime." *Criminology* 27: 697–719.

LaGrange, R.L., K.F. Ferraro, and M. Supancic. 1992. "Perceived Risk and Fear of Crime: Role of Social and Physical Incivilities." *Journal of Research in Crime and Delinquency* 29: 311–34.

Langan, P.A. 1983. "Career Patterns in Crime." *Bureau of Justice Statistics: Special Report.* Washington, DC: U.S. Department of Justice.

LaNovara, P. 1994. "Changes in Family Living." In *Canadian Social Trends: A Canadian Studies Reader*, pp. 171–73. Toronto: Thompson Educational Publishing.

Lasley, J.R., and J.L. Rosenbaum. 1988. "Routine Activities and Multiple Personal Victimization." *Sociology and Social Research* 73(1): 47–50.

Laub, J.H. 1987. "Data for Positive Criminology." In M.R. Gottfredson and T. Hirschi (eds.), *Positive Criminology*. Newbury Park, CA: Sage.

Laub, J.H. 1990. "Patterns of Criminal Victimization in the United States." In A.J. Lurigio, W.G. Skogan, and R.C. Davis (eds.), *Victims of Crime: Problems, Policies and Programs*. Newbury Park, CA: Sage.

Laub, J.H., and R.J. Sampson. 1993. "Turning Points in the Life Course: Why Change Matters to the Study of Crime." *Criminology* 31(3): 301–25.

Lauritsen, J.L., R.J. Sampson, and J.H. Laub. 1991. "The Link between Offending and Victimization among Adolescents." *Criminology* 29(2): 265–92.

Lawson, P.E. 1982. *Solving Somebody Else's Blues*. Latham, MD: University Press of America.

Lejeune, R., and N. Alex. 1973. "On Being Mugged." *Urban Life and Culture* 2(3): 259–83.

Lemert, E.M. 1951. *Social Pathology*. New York: McGraw-Hill.

Lenton, R.L. 1990. "Techniques of Child Discipline and Abuse by Parents." *Canadian Review of Sociology and Anthropology* 27(2): 157–85.

Leroux, T.G., and M. Petrunik. 1990. "The Construction of Elder Abuse as a Social Problem: A Canadian Perspective." *International Journal of Health Services* 20(4): 651–63.

Letkemann, P. 1973. *Crime as Work*. Englewood Cliffs, NJ: Prentice-Hall.

Levi, K. 1981. "Becoming a Hit Man: Neutralization in a Very Deviant Career." *Urban Life* 10: 47–63.

Light, I. 1977. "The Ethnic Vice Industry, 1880–1944." *American Sociological Review* 42 (June): 464–79.

Lindner, C., and R.L. Bonn. 1996. "Probation Officer Victimization and Fieldwork Practices: Results of a National Study." *Federal Probation* 60(2): 16–23.

Lindner, C., and R.J. Koehler. 1992. "Probation Officer Victimization: An Emerging Concern." *Journal of Criminal Justice* 20(1): 52–62.

Lindquist, J.H., and J.M. Duke. 1982. "The Elderly Victim at Risk." *Criminology* 20(1): 115–26.

Liska, A.E., and W. Baccaglini. 1990. "Feeling Safe by Comparison: Crime in the Newspapers." *Social Problems* 37(3): 360–74.

Liska, A.E., and B.D. Warner. 1991. "Functions of Crime: A Paradoxical Process." *American Journal of Sociology* 6: 1441–63.

Lizotte, A.J. 1985. "The Uniqueness of Rape: Reporting Assaultive Violence to the Police." *Crime and Delinquency* 31(2): 169–90.

Lloyd, S.A., J.E. Koval, and R.M. Cale. 1989. "Courtship and Violence in Dating Relationships." In M.A. Pirog-Good and J.E. Stets (eds.), *Violence in Dating Relationships*. New York: Praeger.

Loftus, E.F. 1979. *Eyewitness Testimony*. Cambridge, MA: Harvard University Press.

Logan, R., and J. Belliveau. 1995. "Working Mothers." *Canadian Social Trends* 36: 24–28.

Loseke, D.R. 1989. "'Violence' Is 'Violence' ... or Is It?: The Social Construction of 'Wife Abuse' and Public Policy." In J. Best (ed.), *Images of Issues: Typifying Contemporary Social Problems*. New York: Aldine de Gruyter.

Loucks, A., and E. Zamble. 1994. "Some Comparisons of Female and Male Serious Offenders." *Forum on Corrections Research* 6(1): 22–25.

Luckenbill, D.F. 1977. "Criminal Homicide as a Situated Transaction." *Social Problems* 25(2): 176–86.

Luckenbill, D.F. 1984. "Murder and Assault." In R.F. Meier (ed.), *Major Forms of Crime*. Beverly Hills, CA: Sage.

Luckenbill, D.F., and J. Best. 1981. "Careers in Deviance and Respectability: The Analogy's Limitation." *Social Problems* 29: 197–206.

Lurigio, A.J. 1987. "Are All Victims Alike? The Adverse, Generalized and Differential Impact of Crime." *Crime and Delinquency* 33: 452–67.

Lurigio, A.J., and P.A. Resick. 1990. "Healing the Psychological Wounds of Criminal Victimization: Predicting Postcrime Distress and Recovery." In A.J. Lurigio, W.G. Skogan, and R.C. David (eds.), *Victims of Crime: Problems, Policies and Programs*. Newbury Park, CA: Sage.

Luxton, M. 1988. "Thinking About the Future." *Family Matters: Sociology and Contemporary Canadian Families*. Toronto: Methuen.

Lynch, J.P. 1987. "Routine Activity and Victimization at Work." *Journal of Quantitative Criminology* 3(4): 283–300.

Lynch, J.P., and D. Cantor. 1992. "Ecological and Behavioral Influences on Property Victimization at Home: Implications for Opportunity Theory." *Journal of Research in Crime and Delinquency* 29(3): 335–62.

Maas, P. 1968. *The Valachi Papers*. New York: Putnam.

McCarthy, B., and J. Hagan. 1991. "Homelessness: A Criminogenic Situation?" *British Journal of Criminology* 31(4): 393–410.

McClearly, R.M., B.C. Nienstedt, and J.M. Erven. 1982. "Uniform Crime Reports as Organizational Outcomes: Three Time Series Experiments." *Social Problems* 29(4): 361–72.

McCord, J. 1991. "Family Relationships, Juvenile Delinquency, and Adult Criminality." *Criminology* 29(3): 397–417.

McDaniel, S. 1994. *General Social Survey Analysis Series: Family and Friends*. Ottawa: Ministry of Industry, Science and Technology.

McIntosh, M. 1975. *The Organization of Crime*. London: Macmillan.

Macmillan, R. 1995. "Changes in the Structure of Life Courses and the Decline of Social Capital in Canadian Society: A Time Series Analysis of Property Crime Rates." *Canadian Journal of Sociology* 20(1): 51–79.

Maguire, M., with T. Bennett. 1982. *Burglary in a Dwelling: The Offence, the Offender and the Victim*. London: Heinemann.

Malamuth, N.M. 1983. "Factors Associated with Rape as Predictors of Laboratory Aggression against Women." *Journal of Personality and Social Psychology* 45: 432–42.

Malamuth, N.M., and E. Donnerstein. 1984. *Pornography and Sexual Aggression.* Orlando: Academic Press.

Maltz, M.D. 1976. "On Defining 'Organized Crime': The Development of a Definition and a Typology." *Crime and Delinquency* 22: 338–46.

Marsh, H.L. 1991. "A Comparative Analysis of Crime Coverage in Newspapers in the United States and Other Countries from 1960–1989: A Review of the Literature." *Journal of Criminal Justice* 19: 69–79.

Martin, R., R.J. Mutchnick, and W.T. Austin. 1990. *Criminological Thought: Pioneers Past and Present.* New York: Macmillan.

Martin, M., and L. Ogrodnik. 1996. "Canadian Crime Trends." In L.W. Kennedy and V.F. Sacco, *Crime Counts*, pp. 43–58. Scarborough, ON: Nelson Canada.

Massey, J.L., M.D. Krohn, and L.M. Bonati. 1989. "Property Crime and the Routine Activities of Individuals." *Journal of Research in Crime and Delinquency* 26(4): 378–400.

Mastrofski, S. 1983. "The Police and Noncrime Services." In G. Whitaker and C.D. Phillips (eds.), *Evaluating Performance of Criminal Justice Agencies.* Beverly Hills, CA: Sage.

Matza, D., and G.M. Sykes. 1957. "Techniques of Neutralization: A Theory of Delinquency." *American Sociological Review* 5: 1–12.

Matza, D., and G.M. Sykes. 1961. "Juvenile Delinquency and Subterranean Values." *American Sociological Review* 26: 712–19.

Mauser, G. 1996. "Armed Self-Defence." *Journal of Criminal Justice* 24(5): 393–406.

Maxfield, M.G. 1987. "Household Composition, Routine Activity, and Victimization: A Comparative Analysis." *Journal of Quantitative Criminology* 3(4): 301–20.

Maxfield, M.G. 1990. "Homicide Circumstances, 1976–1985: A Taxonomy Based on Supplementary Homicide Reports." *Criminology* 28: 671–95.

Mayhew, P., D. Elliott, and L. Dowds. 1989. *The 1988 British Crime Survey: A Home Office Research and Planning Unit Report.* London: HMSO Books.

Mayhew, P., N. Maung, and C. Mirrlees-Black. 1993. *The 1992 British Crime Survey.* London: HMSO Books.

Mednick, S., T. Moffitt, and S. Stack. 1987. *The Causes of Crime: New Biological Approaches.* New York: Cambridge University Press.

Meier, R., and G. Geis. 1997. *Victimless Crimes?: Prostitution, Drugs, and Abortion.* Los Angeles: Roxbury.

Melbin, M. 1987. *Night as Frontier.* New York: The Free Press.

Menard, S. 1995. "A Developmental Test of Mertonian Anomie Theory." *Journal of Research in Crime and Delinquency* 32(2): 136–74.

Menard, S., and H.C. Covey. 1988. "UCR and NCS: Comparisons over Space and Time." *Journal of Criminal Justice* 16: 371–84.

Meredith, N. 1984. "The Murder Epidemic." *Science* (December): 41–48.

Merry, S.E. 1981. *Urban Danger.* Philadelphia: Temple University Press.

Merton, R.K. 1938. "Social Structure and Anomie." *American Sociological Review* 3: 672–82.

Messner, S. 1989. "Economic Discrimination and Societal Homicide Rates: Further Evidence on the Cost of Inequality." *American Sociological Review* 54: 597–611.

Messner, S.F., and J.R. Blau. 1987. "Routine Leisure Activities and Rates of Crime: A Macro-Level Analysis." *Social Forces* 65: 1035–51.

Messner, S., and R. Rosenfeld. 1997. *Crime and the American Dream*, 2nd ed. Belmont, CA: Wadsworth.

Michalowski, R.J., and E.W. Bohlander. 1976. "Repression and Criminal Justice in Capitalist America." *Sociological Inquiry* 46(2): 95–106.

Miethe, T.D. 1982. "Public Consensus on Crime Seriousness: Normative Structure or Methodological Artifact?" *Criminology* 20: 515–26.

Miethe, T.D., and G.R. Lee. 1984. "Fear of Crime among Older People: A Reassessment of the Predictive Power of Crime-Related Factors." *The Sociological Quarterly* 25: 397–415.

Miethe, T.D., and R.F. Meier. 1994. *Crime and Its Social Context*. Albany: State University of New York Press.

Miethe, T.D., M.C. Stafford, and J.S. Long. 1987. "Social Differentiation in Criminal Victimization: A Test of Routine Activities/Lifestyle Theories." *American Sociological Review* 52 (April): 184–94.

Miller, G. 1978. *Odd Jobs*. Englewood Cliffs, NJ: Prentice-Hall.

Miller, J.L., and A.B. Anderson. 1986. "Updating the Deterrence Doctrine." *Journal of Criminal Law and Criminology* 77(2): 418–38.

Miller, L.J. 1990. "Violent Families and the Rhetoric of Harmony." *British Journal of Sociology* 41(2): 263–88.

Miller, W. 1958. "Lower Class Culture as a Generating Milieu of Gang Delinquency." *Journal of Social Issues* 14: 5–19.

Minor, W.W. 1981. "Techniques of Neutralization: A Reconceptualization and Empirical Examination." *Journal of Research in Crime and Delinquency* 18: 295–318.

Mirrlees-Black, C., P. Mayhew, and A. Percy. 1996. "The 1996 British Crime Survey." *Home Office Statistical Bulletin* (September 24).

Moeller, G.L. 1989. "Fear of Criminal Victimization: The Effects of Neighborhood Racial Composition." *Sociological Inquiry* 59: 208–21.

Moffitt, T.E., D.R. Lynam, and P.A. Silva. 1994. "Neuropsychological Tests Predicting Persistent Male Delinquency." *Criminology* 32(2): 277–300.

Monkkonen, E.H. 1983. "The Organized Response to Crime in Nineteenth- and Twentieth-Century America." *Journal of Interdisciplinary History* 14(1): 113–28.

Moore, W.H. 1974. *The Kefauver Commission and the Politics of Crime, 1950–1952*. Columbia: University of Missouri Press.

Morash, M. 1984. "Organized Crime." In R.F. Meier (ed.), *Major Forms of Crime*. Beverly Hills, CA: Sage.

Morin, E. 1971. *Rumor in Orleans*. New York: Pantheon.

Morris, N., and G. Hawkins. 1970. *The Honest Politician's Guide to Crime Control*. Chicago: University of Chicago Press.

Morrison, P. 1996. "Motor Vehicle Crime." In L.W. Kennedy and V. Sacco, *Crime Counts*, pp. 195–213. Scarborough, ON: Nelson Canada.

Moysa, M. 1992. "Crown Backs Off Murder Charge." *Edmonton Journal* (February 12), p. A1.

Muehlenhard, C.L., and M.A. Linton. 1987. "Date Rape and Sexual Aggression in Dating Situations: Incidence and Risk Factors." *Journal of Counseling Psychology* 34(2): 186–96.

Mundt, R.J. 1990. "Gun Control and Rates of Firearm Violence in Canada and the United States." *Canadian Journal of Criminology* 32(1): 137–54.

Murphy, C. 1993. "The Development, Impact, and Implications of Community Policing in Canada." In J. Chacko and S.E. Nancoo (eds.), *Community Policing in Canada*, pp. 13–26. Toronto: Canadian Scholar's Press.

Murray, C., and R. Herrnstein. 1994. *The Bell Curve*. New York: Free Press.

Naffine, N. 1987. *Female Crime: The Construction of Women in Criminology*. Sydney: Allen & Unwin.

Nagin, D.S., and R. Paternoster. 1993. "Enduring Individual Differences and Rational Choices of Crime." *Law and Society Review* 27(3): 467–96.

National Crime Prevention Council. 1995. *Clear Limits and Real Opportunities: The Keys to Preventing Youth Crime*. Ottawa: National Crime Prevention Council Secretariat.

National Crime Prevention Council. 1996. *Safety and Savings: Crime Prevention through Social Development*. Ottawa.

National Crime Prevention Institute. 1986. *Understanding Crime Prevention*. Boston: Butterworths.

Nelson, B. 1984. *Making an Issue of Child Abuse*. Chicago: University of Chicago Press.

Nettler, G. 1984. *Explaining Crime*. New York: McGraw-Hill.

Newman, G.R. 1990. "Popular Culture and Criminal Justice: A Preliminary Analysis." *Journal of Criminal Justice* 18: 261–74.

Newman, O. 1972. *Defensible Space: Crime Prevention through Urban Design*. New York: Macmillan.

New York Times. 1989. "Two Men Arrested in Shooting of Officer" (May 7), p. B2.

Normandeau, A. 1987. "Crime on the Montreal Metro." *Sociology and Social Research* 71(4): 289–92.

Normandeau, A., and B. Leighton. 1993. "A Growing Canadian Consensus: Community Policing." In J. Chacko and S.E. Nancoo (eds.), *Community Policing in Canada*, pp. 27–34. Toronto: Canadian Scholar's Press.

O'Brien, R.M. 1985. *Crime and Victimization Data*, vol. 4. Law and Criminal Justice Series. Beverly Hills, CA: Sage.

O'Brien, R.M. 1986. "Rare Events, Sample Sizes and Statistical Problems in the Analysis of the NCS City Surveys." *Journal of Criminal Justice* 14: 441–48.

Oderkirck, J., and C. Lockhead. 1994. "Lone Parenthood: Gender Differences." In *Canadian Social Trends: A Canadian Studies Reader*, pp. 189–92. Toronto: Thompson Educational Publishing.

O'Grady, B. 1989. "Crime Violence and Victimization: A Newfoundland Case." *Canadian Criminology Forum* 10: 1–16.

O'Keefe, G.J. 1984. "Public Views on Crime: Television Exposure and Media Credibility." In R.N. Bostrom (ed.), *Communication Yearbook 8*. Beverly Hills, CA: Sage.

Ontario Teachers' Federation. 1992. *The Safe School Task Force Resource Kit*, vol. 1 (June). Toronto: OTF.

Osborne, J.A. 1995. "The Canadian Criminal Law." In M.A. Jackson and C.T. Griffiths (eds.), *Canadian Criminology*, pp. 273–306. Toronto: Harcourt Brace.

Osgood, D.W., J.K. Wilson, P.M. O'Malley, J.G. Bachman, and L.D. Johnston. 1996. "Routine Activities and Individual Deviant Behaviour." *American Sociological Review* 61: 635–55.

Packer, H.L. 1969. *The Limits of the Criminal Sanction*. Stanford, CA: Stanford University Press.

Pagelow, M.D. 1989. "The Incidence and Prevalence of Criminal Abuse of Other Family Members." In L. Ohlin and M. Tonry (eds.), *Family Violence.* Chicago: University of Chicago Press.

Palenski, J.E. 1984. "The Use of Mediation by Police." *Mediation Quarterly* 5: 31–38.

Pandiani, J.A. 1978. "Crime Time TV: If All We Know Is What We Saw ..." *Contemporary Crises* 2: 437–58.

Papadopoulos, C. 1997. *A Comparison of Crime in the U.S. and Canada.* Unpublished MA thesis. Edmonton: University of Alberta.

Parsons, T. 1951. *The Social System.* Glencoe, IL: Free Press.

Paternoster, R., and P. Mazzerole. 1994. "General Strain Theory and Delinquency: A Replication and Extension." *Journal of Research in Crime and Delinquency* 31(3): 235–63.

Patterson, G.R., and T.J. Dishion. 1985. "Contributions of Families and Peers to Delinquency." *Criminology* 23: 63–79.

Pearce, F. 1991. *Second Islington Crime Survey: Commercial and Conventional Crime in Islington.* Kingston, ON: Queen's University.

Peek, C.W., J.L. Fischer, and J.S. Kidwell. 1985. "Teenage Violence toward Parents: A Neglected Dimension of Family Violence." *Journal of Marriage and the Family* 47: 1051–58.

Pepinsky, H., and P. Jesilow. 1984. *Myths That Cause Crime.* Cabin John, MD: Seven Locks Press.

Pfohl, S. 1977. "The Discovery of Child Abuse." *Social Problems* 24(3): 315–21.

Pfuhl, E.H. 1986. *The Deviance Process,* 2nd ed. Belmont, CA: Wadsworth.

Phelps, T.G. 1983. "The Criminal as Hero in American Fiction." *Wisconsin Law Review* 6: 1427–54.

Phillips, D.P. 1983. "The Impact of Mass Media Violence on U.S. Homicides." *American Sociological Review* 48 (August): 560–68.

Pileggi, N. 1985. *Wiseguy: Life in a Mafia Family.* New York: Simon & Schuster.

Pillemer, K.A. 1985. "The Dangers of Dependency: New Findings on Domestic Violence against the Elderly." *Social Problems* 33: 146–58.

Pillemer, K.A., and D. Finkelhor. 1988. "The Prevalence of Elder Abuse: A Random Sample Survey." *The Gerontologist* 28(1): 51–57.

Pitkin, T.M., and F. Cordasco. 1977. *The Black Hand: A Chapter in Ethnic Crime.* Totowa, NJ: Littlefield, Adams.

Podnieks, E. 1990. *National Survey on Abuse of the Elderly in Canada.* Toronto: Ryerson Polytechnic Institute.

Pound, R. 1943. "A Survey of Social Interests." *Harvard Law Review* 53: 1–39.

Provenzo, E.F. 1991. *Video Kids: Making Sense of Nintendo.* Cambridge, MA: Harvard University Press.

Quinn, M.J., and S.K. Tomita. 1986. *Elder Abuse and Neglect: Causes, Diagnosis and Intervention Strategies.* New York: Springer-Verlag.

Quinney, R., and J. Wildeman. 1991. *The Problem of Crime: A Peace and Social Justice Perspective.* Mountain View, CA: Mayfield.

Randall, D.M., L. Lee-Sammons, and P.H. Hagner. 1988. "Common versus Elite Crime Coverage in Network News." *Social Science Quarterly* 69(4): 910–29.

Rankin, J.H., and L.E. Wells. 1990. "The Effect of Parental Attachments and Direct Controls on Delinquency." *Journal of Research in Crime and Delinquency* 27(2): 140–65.

Reasons, C.E., L. Ross, and C. Paterson. 1981. *Assault on the Worker: Occupational Health and Safety in Canada.* Toronto: Butterworths.

Reckless, W. 1967. *The Crime Problem,* 4th ed. New York: Meredith.

Reiman, J.H. 1990. *The Rich Get Richer and the Poor Get Prison,* 3rd ed. New York: Macmillan.

Reiss, A.J., Jr. 1984. "Consequences of Compliance and Deterrence Models of Law Enforcement for the Exercise of Police Discretion." *Law and Contemporary Problems* 47(4): 83–122.

Reiss, A.J., Jr. 1986a. "Official and Survey Crime Statistics." In E.A. Fattah (ed.), *From Crime Policy to Victim Policy—Reorienting the Justice System.* London: Macmillan.

Reinarman, C., and H.G. Levine. 1989. "The Crack Attack: Politics and Media in America's Latest Drug Scare." In J. Best (ed.), *Images of Issues.* New York: Aldine de Gruytger.

Reiss, A.J., Jr. 1986b. "Policy Implications of Crime Victim Surveys." In E.A. Fattah (ed.), *From Crime Policy to Victim Policy—Reorienting the Justice System.* London: Macmillan.

Reppetto, T. 1974. *A Residential Crime.* Cambridge, MA: Ballinger.

Resick, P.A. 1987. "Psychological Effects of Victimization: Implications for the Criminal Justice System." *Crime and Delinquency* 33: 468–78.

Reuter, P. 1984a. "The (Continued) Vitality of Mythical Numbers." *Public Interest* 75: 135–47.

Reuter, P. 1984b. "Social Control in Illegal Markets." In D. Black (ed.), *Toward a General Theory of Social Control, Volume 2: Selected Problems.* Orlando: Academic Press.

Rice, T.W., and C.R. Goldman. 1994. "Another Look at the Subculture of Violence Thesis: Who Murders Whom under What Circumstances?" *Sociological Spectrum* 14: 371–84.

Richardson, J.T., J. Best, and D.G. Bromley. 1991. *The Satanism Scare.* New York: Aldine de Gruyter.

Riley, D. 1987. "Time and Crime: The Link between Teenager Lifestyle and Delinquency." *Journal of Quantitative Criminology* 3(4): 339–54.

Roberts, K. 1983. *Youth and Leisure.* London: George Allen & Unwin.

Rodgers, K., and R. Kong. 1996. "Crimes against Women and Children in the Family." In L.W. Kennedy and V. Sacco (eds.), *Crime Counts: A Criminal Event Analysis,* pp. 115–32. Scarborough, ON: Nelson Canada.

Rodgers, K., and G. Roberts. 1995. "Women's Non-Spousal Multiple Victimization: A Test of the Routine Activities Theory." *Canadian Journal of Criminology* 37(3): 363–91.

Rogers, A.J. 1973. *The Economics of Crime.* Hinsdale, IL: Dryden Press.

Roncek, D.W. 1981. "Dangerous Places." *Social Forces* 60: 74–96.

Roncek, D.W., and P.A. Maier. 1991. "Bars, Blocks and Crimes Revisited: Linking the Theory of Routine Activities to the Empiricism of 'Hot Spots.'" *Criminology* 29(4): 725–53.

Roncek, D.W., and M.A. Pravatiner. 1989. "Additional Evidence That Taverns Enhance Nearby Crime." *Sociology and Social Research* 73(4): 185–88.

Rosenbaum, D.P. 1987. "The Theory and Research behind Neighborhood Watch: Is It a Sound Fear and Crime Reduction Strategy?" *Crime and Delinquency* 33(1): 103–34.

Rosenbaum, D.P. 1988. "Community Crime Prevention: A Review and Synthesis of the Literature." *Justice Quarterly* 5(3): 323–95.

Rosenbaum, H.J., and P.C. Sederberg. 1976. "Vigilantism: An Analysis of Establishment Violence." In H.J. Rosenbaum and P.C. Sederberg (eds.), *Vigilante Politics*. Philadelphia: University of Pennsylvania Press.

Rosnow, R.L. 1988. "Rumour as Communication: A Contextual Approach." *Journal of Communication* 38(1): 12–28.

Rosnow, R.L., and G.A. Fine. 1976. *Rumor and Gossip*. New York: Elsevier.

Ross, R., and G.L. Staines. 1972. "The Politics of Analyzing Social Problems." *Social Problems* 20(1): 18–40.

Rossi, P.H., E. Waite, C.E. Bose, and R.E. Berk. 1974. "The Seriousness of Crimes: Normative Structure and Individual Differences." *American Sociological Review* 39: 224–37.

Rountree, P.W., and K.C. Land. 1996. "Burglary Victimization, Perceptions of Crime Risk, and Routine Activities: A Multilevel Analysis across Seattle Neighbourhoods and Census Tracts." *Journal of Research in Crime and Delinquency* 33(2): 147–80.

Ruback, R.B., M.S. Greenberg, and D.R. Wescott. 1984. "Social Influence and Crime-Victim Decision Making." *Journal of Social Issues* 40(1): 51–76.

Rubington, C., and M.S. Weinberg. 1987. *Deviance: The Interactionist Perspective*. New York: Macmillan.

Rush, G. 1994. *The Dictionary of Criminal Justice*, 4th ed. Guilford, CT: Dushkin.

Sacco, V.F. 1990. "Gender, Fear and Victimization: A Preliminary Application of Power-Control Theory." *Sociological Spectrum* 10: 485–506.

Sacco, V.F. 1995. "Media Constructions of Crime." *The Annals of the American Academy of Political and Social Science* 539: 141–54.

Sacco, V.F., and B.J. Fair. 1988. "Images of Legal Control: Crime News and the Process of Organizational Legitimation." *Canadian Journal of Communication* 13: 113–22.

Sacco, V.F., and H. Johnson. 1990. *Patterns of Criminal Victimization in Canada*. Ottawa: Minister of Supply and Services.

Sacco, V.F., H. Johnson, and R. Arnold. 1993. "Urban–Rural Residence and Criminal Victimization." *Canadian Journal of Sociology* 18(4): 431–51.

Sacco, V.F., and R.A. Silverman. 1982. "Crime Prevention through Mass Media: Prospects and Problems." *Journal of Criminal Justice* 10: 257–69.

Sacco, V.F., and E. Zureik. 1990. "Correlates of Computer Misuses: Data from a Self-Reporting Sample." *Behaviour and Information Technology* 9(5): 353–69.

Sagarin, E. 1975. *Deviants and Deviance*. New York: Praeger.

St. John, C., and T. Heald-Moore. 1996. "Racial Prejudice and Fear of Criminal Victimization by Strangers in Public Settings." *Sociological Inquiry* 66(3): 267–84.

Sales, E., M. Baum, and B. Shore. 1984. "Victim Readjustment Following Assault." *Journal of Social Issues* 40(1): 117–36.

Salinger, L.R., P. Jesilow, H.N. Pontell, and G. Geis. 1993. "Assaults against Airline Flight Attendants: A Victimization Study." In H.N. Pontell (ed.), *Social Deviance*. Englewood Cliffs, NJ: Prentice-Hall.

Sampson, R.J. 1985. "Race and Criminal Violence: A Demographically Disaggregated Analysis of Urban Homicide." *Crime and Delinquency* 31(1): 47–82.

Sampson, R.J. 1987. "Urban Black Violence: The Effect of Male Joblessness and Family Disruption." *American Journal of Sociology* 93(2): 348–82.

Sampson, R.J., and W.B. Groves. 1989. "Community Structure and Crime: Testing Social Disorganization Theory." *American Journal of Sociology* 94: 774–802.

Sampson, R.J., and J.H. Laub. 1990. "Crime and Deviance over the Life Course: The Salience of Adult Social Bonds." *American Sociological Review* 55: 609–27.

Sampson, R.J., and J.L. Lauritsen. 1990. "Deviant Lifestyles, Proximity Crime, and the Offender–Victim Link in Personal Violence." *Journal of Research in Crime and Delinquency* 27(2): 110–39.

Sanger, D.E. 1993. "How to Visit America and Get Out Alive." *Globe and Mail* (June 18), p. A9.

Sasson, T. 1995. *Crime Talks*. New York: Aldine de Gruyter.

Saunders, D.G. 1989. "Who Hits First and Who Hurts Most?: Evidence for the Greater Victimization of Women in Intimate Relationships." Paper presented at the Annual Meeting of the American Society of Criminology, Reno, Nevada.

Savitz, L.D. 1978. "Official Police Statistics and Their Limitations." In L.D. Savitz and N.Johnston (eds.), *Crime in Society*. New York: John Wiley.

Scheingold, S.A. 1984. *The Politics of Law and Order: Street Crime and Public Policy*. New York: Longman.

Schelling, T.C. 1967. "Economic Analysis of Organized Crime." In *President's Commission on Law Enforcement and Administration of Justice Task Force Report: Organized Crime, Annotations and Consultant's Papers*, pp. 114–26. Washington, DC: U.S. Government Printing Office.

Scheppele, K.L., and P.B. Bart. 1983. "Through Women's Eyes: Defining Danger in the Wake of Sexual Assault." *Journal of Social Issues* 39: 63–81.

Schissel, B. 1992. "The Influence of Economic Factors and Social Control Policy on Crime Rate Changes in Canada, 1962–1988." *Canadian Journal of Sociology* 17(4): 405–28.

Schlesinger, P., et al. 1992. *Women Viewing Violence*. London: BFI.

Schneider, V.W., and B. Wieresma. 1990. "Limits and Use of the Uniform Crime Reports." In D.L. MacKenzie, P.J. Baunach, and R.R. Roberg (eds.), *Measuring Crime: Large-Scale, Long-Range Efforts*. Albany: State University of New York Press.

Schur, E.M. 1965. *Crimes without Victims*. Englewood Cliffs, NJ: Prentice-Hall.

Schur, E.M. 1979. *Interpreting Deviance*. New York: Harper & Row.

Schwartz, M.D. 1988. "Ain't Got No Class: Universal Risk Theories of Battering." *Contemporary Crises* 12: 375–92.

Schwendinger, H., and J. Schwendinger. 1993. "Giving Crime Prevention Top Priority." *Crime and Delinquency* 39(4): 425–46.

Scott, M., and S. Lyman. 1968. "Accounts." *American Sociological Review* 33: 42–62.

Scully, D., and J. Marolla. 1984. "Convicted Rapists' Vocabulary of Motive: Excuses and Justifications." *Social Problems* 31(5): 530–44.

Sedlak, A.J. 1988. "The Effects of Personal Experiences with Couple Violence on Calling It 'Battering' and Allocating Blame." In G.T. Hotaling, D. Finkelhor, J.T. Kirpatrick, and M.A. Straus (eds.), *Coping with Family Violence*. Newbury Park, CA: Sage.

Sellin, T. 1938. "Culture Conflict and Crime." A Report of the Subcommittee on Delinquency of the Committee on Personality and Culture. *Social Science Research Council Bulletin* 41.

Shaffer, E.B. 1980. *Community Policing*. London: Croom Helm.

Shaw, C.R., and H.D. McKay. 1942. *Juvenile Delinquency in Urban Areas*. Chicago: University of Chicago Press.

Shearing, C.D., and P.C. Stenning. 1983. "Private Security: Implications for Social Control." *Social Problems* 30: 493–506.

Sheldon, W.H. 1949. *Varieties of Delinquent Youth: An Introduction to Constitutional Psychiatry*. New York: Harper & Brothers.

Sheley, J.F. 1991. "Conflict in Criminal Law." In J.F. Sheley (ed.), *Criminology: A Contemporary Handbook,* pp. 21–39. Belmont, CA: Wadsworth.

Sherman, L. 1992. *Policing Domestic Violence: Experiments and Dilemmas.* New York: Free Press.

Sherman, L., and R. Berk. 1984. "The Specific Deterrent Effects of Arrest for Domestic Assault." *American Sociological Review* 49: 261–72.

Sherman, L., J. Schmidt, D. Rogan, and C. DeRiso. 1991. "Predicting Domestic Homicide: Prior Police Contact and Gun Threats." In Michael Steinman (ed.), *Woman Battering: Policy Responses.* Cincinnati: Anderson.

Sherman, L., P.R. Gartin, and M.E. Buerger. 1989. "Routine Activities and the Criminology of Place." *Criminology* 27(1): 27–55.

Shibutani, T. 1966. *Improvised News: A Sociological Study of Rumor.* Indianapolis, IN: Bobbs-Merrill.

Shotland, R.L. 1976. "Spontaneous Vigilantism: A Bystander Response to Criminal Behavior." In H.J. Rosenbaum and P.C. Sederberg (eds.), *Vigilante Politics.* Philadelphia: University of Pennsylvania Press.

Shotland, R.L., and L.I. Goodstein. 1984. "The Role of Bystanders in Crime Control." *Journal of Social Issues* 40(1): 9–26.

Shotland, R.L., and M.K. Straw. 1976. "Bystander Response to an Assault: When a Man Attacks a Woman." *Journal of Personality and Social Psychology* 34: 990–99.

Shover, N. 1973. "The Social Organization of Burglary." *Social Problems* 201 (Spring): 499–513.

Shover, N. 1983. "The Later Stages of Ordinary Property Offender Careers." *Social Problems* 30: 208–18.

Sigler, R.T., and M. Johnson. 1986. "Public Perceptions of the Need for Criminalization of Sexual Harassment." *Journal of Criminal Justice* 14: 229–37.

Silverman, I., and S. Dinitz. 1974. "Compulsive Masculinity and Delinquency: An Empirical Investigation." *Criminology* 11: 498.

Silverman, R.A., and L.W. Kennedy. 1992. "Interpersonal Relations and Means of Lethal Violence in Canada." In A. Kuhl (ed.), *Homicide: The Victim–Offender Connection.* Cincinnati: Anderson.

Silverman, R.A., and L.W. Kennedy. 1993. *Deadly Deeds: Murder in Canada.* Scarborough, ON: Nelson Canada.

Silverman, R.A., and M.O. Nielsen. 1992. *Aboriginal Peoples and Canadian Criminal Justice.* Toronto: Butterworths.

Silverman, R.A., J.J. Teevan, and V.F. Sacco (eds.). 1996. *Crime in Canadian Society,* 5th ed. Toronto: Harcourt Brace.

Simon, D.R. 1996. *Elite Deviance,* 5th ed. Boston: Allyn and Bacon.

Simon, D.R., and D.S. Eitzen. 1993. *Elite Deviance,* 4th ed. Boston: Allyn & Bacon.

Simpson, S.C., and C.S. Koper. 1992. "Deterring Corporate Crime." *Criminology* 30(3): 347–75.

Simpson, S.S. 1989. "Feminist Theory, Crime and Justice." *Criminology* 27(4): 605–31.

Singer, S.I., and M. Levine. 1988. "Power-Control Theory, Gender and Delinquency: A Partial Replication with Additional Evidence on the Effect of Peers." *Criminology* 26: 627–47.

Skaret, D., and C. Wilgosh. 1989. "Learning Disabilities and Juvenile Delinquency: A Causal Relationship." *International Journal for the Advancement of Counselling* 12: 113–23.

Skinner, B.F. 1948. *Walden Two.* New York: Macmillan.

Skipper, J.K. 1985. "Nicknames of Notorious American Twentieth Century Deviants: The Decline of the Folk Hero Syndrome." *Deviant Behavior* 6: 99–114.

Skogan, W.G. 1976. "Citizen Reporting of Crime: Some National Panel Data." *Criminology* 13(4): 535–49.

Skogan, W.G. 1977. "Dimensions of the Dark Figure of Unreported Crime." *Crime and Delinquency* 23: 41–50.

Skogan, W.G. 1981. "On Attitudes and Behavior." In D.A. Lewis (ed.), *Reactions to Crime*. Beverly Hills, CA: Sage.

Skogan, W.G. 1986. "Methodological Issues in the Study of Victimization." In E.A. Fattah (ed.), *From Crime Policy to Victim Policy—Reorienting the Justice System*. London: Macmillan.

Skogan, W.G. 1987. "The Impact of Victimization on Fear." *Crime and Delinquency* 33: 135–54.

Skogan, W.G. 1990a. "The National Crime Survey Redesign." *Public Opinion Quarterly* 54: 256–72.

Skogan, W.G. 1990b. *Disorder and Decline*. New York: Free Press.

Skogan, W.G. 1993. "The Various Meanings of Fear." In W. Bilsky, C. Pfeiffer, and P. Wetzels (eds.), *Fear of Crime and Criminal Victimization*. Stuttgart, Germany: Ferdinand Enke Verlag.

Skogan, W.G., and M.G. Maxfield. 1981. *Coping with Crime: Individual and Neighborhood Reactions*. Beverly Hills, CA: Sage.

Skogan, W.G., and M.A. Wycoff. 1987. "Some Unexpected Effects of a Police Service for Victims." *Crime and Delinquency* 33: 490–501.

Skolnick, J. 1966. *Justice without Trial*. New York: John Wiley.

Smith, D. 1975. *The Mafia Mystique*. New York: Basic Books.

Smith, D.A. 1987. "Police Response to Interpersonal Violence: Defining the Parameters of Legal Control." *Social Forces* 65(3): 767–82.

Smith, D.A., and G.R. Jarjoura. 1988. "Social Structure and Criminal Victimization." *Journal of Research in Crime and Delinquency* 25: 27–52.

Smith, D.A., and G.R. Jarjoura. 1989. "Household Characteristics, Neighborhood Composition and Victimization Risk." *Social Forces* 68(2): 621–40.

Smith, L.N., and G.D. Hill. 1991. "Victimization and Fear of Crime." *Criminal Justice and Behavior* 18: 217–39.

Smith, M.D. 1988. *Woman Abuse in Toronto: Incidence, Prevalence and Demographic Risk Markers*. Toronto: Institute for Social Research and the LaMarsh Research Programme.

Smith, S.J. 1982. "Victimization in the Inner City." *British Journal of Criminology* 22: 386–401.

Snider, L. 1992. "Commercial Crime." In V.F. Sacco (ed.), *Deviance: Conformity and Control in Canadian Society,* 2nd ed. Scarborough, ON: Prentice-Hall.

Snider, L. 1993. *Bad Business: Corporate Crime in Canada*. Scarborough, ON: Nelson Canada.

Solicitor General of Canada. 1983. *Canadian Urban Victimization Survey Bulletin 1: Victims of Crime*. Ottawa: Programs Branch/Research and Statistics Group.

Solicitor General of Canada. 1984. *Canadian Urban Victimization Survey Bulletin 3: Crime Prevention Awareness and Practice*. Ottawa: Programs Branch/Research and Statistics Group.

Solicitor General of Canada. 1985. *Canadian Urban Victimization Survey Bulletin 4: Female Victims of Crime*. Ottawa: Programs Branch/Research and Statistics Group.

Sorenson, A.M., and D. Brownfield. 1995. "Adolescent Drug Use and a General Theory of Crime: An Analysis of Theoretical Integration." *Canadian Journal of Criminology* 37(1): 19–37.

Sparks, R. 1992. Television and the Drama of Crime. Buckingham: Open University Press.

Spector, M., and J.I. Kitsuse. 1977. *Constructing Social Problems*. Menlo Park, CA: Cummings.

Stafford, M.C., and J.P. Gibbs. 1980. "Crime Rates in an Ecological Context: Extension of a Proposition." *Social Science Quarterly* 61(3–4): 653–65.

Stafford, M.C., and O.R. Galle. 1984. "Victimization Rates, Exposure to Risk, and Fear of Crime." *Criminology* 22(2): 173–85.

Stafford, M.C., and M. Warr. 1993. "A Reconceptualization of General and Specific Deterrence." *Journal of Research in Crime and Delinquency* 30(2): 123–35.

Standing Committee on Communications and Culture. 1993. *Television Violence: Fraying Our Social Fabric*. Ottawa: House of Commons.

Standing Committee on Justice and the Solicitor General. 1993. *Crime Prevention in Canada: Toward a National Strategy*. Ottawa: Queen's Printer.

Stanko, E. 1985. *Intimate Intrusions: Women's Experience of Male Violence*. London: Routledge & Kegan Paul.

Stark, R. 1987. "Deviant Places: A Theory of the Ecology of Crime." *Criminology* 25(4): 893–909.

Statistics Canada. 1985. *Canadian Crime Statistics*. Ottawa: Supply and Services Canada.

Statistics Canada. 1995. Canadian Crime Statistics. Annual report.

Steffensmeier, D., and E. Allan. 1995. "Criminal Behaviour: Gender and Crime." In J.F. Sheley (ed.), *Criminology: A Contemporary Handbook*, 2nd ed., pp. 83–113. Belmont, CA: Wadsworth.

Steffensmeier, D.J., and R.H. Steffensmeier. 1977. "Who Reports Shoplifters?: Research Continuities and Further Developments." International Journal of Criminology and Penology 3: 79–95.

Steffensmeier, D.J., and R.M. Terry. 1973. "Deviance and Respectability: An Observational Study of Reactions to Shoplifting." *Social Forces* 51: 417–26.

Steinman, M. 1992. "Going Beyond Arrest: Police Responses to Domestic Violence." Paper presented at the Annual Meeting of the American Society of Criminology, New Orleans.

Steinmetz, S. 1977–78. "The Battered Husband Syndrome." *Victimology: An International Journal* 2: 499–509.

Steinmetz, S. 1986. "The Violent Family." In M. Lystad (ed.), *Violence in the Home: Interdisciplinary Perspectives*. New York: Brunner/Mazel.

Stoddart, K. 1996. "It's Easier for the Bulls Now: Official Statistics and Social Change in a Canadian Heroin-Using Community." In R.A. Silverman, J.J. Teevan, and V.F. Sacco (eds.), *Crime in Canadian Society*, 5th ed., pp. 111–20. Toronto: Harcourt Brace.

Stoker, B. 1975. *The Annotated Dracula*. Annotated by L. Wolf. New York: Clarkson N. Potter.

Stone, S.D. 1993. "Getting the Message Out: Feminists, the Press and Violence against Women." *Canadian Review of Sociology and Anthropology* 30(3): 377–400.

Straus, M.A. 1990b. "Social Stress and Marital Violence in a National Sample of American Families." In M.A. Straus and R.J. Gelles (eds.), *Physical Violence in*

American Families: Risk Factors and Adaptations to Violence in 8,145 Families. New Brunswick, NJ: Transaction.

Straus, M.A. 1991. "Discipline and Deviance: Physical Punishment of Children and Violence and Other Forms of Crime in Adulthood." *Social Problems* 38(2): 133–52.

Straus, M.A., and R.J. Gelles. 1990a. "How Violent Are American Families?: Estimates from the National Family Violence Resurvey and Other Studies." In M.A. Straus and R.J. Gelles (eds.), *Physical Violence in American Families: Risk Factors and Adaptations to Violence in 8,145 Families.* New Brunswick, NJ: Transaction.

Straus, M.A., and R.J. Gelles. 1990b. *Physical Violence in American Families: Risk Factors and Adaptations to Violence in 8,145 Families.* New Brunswick, NJ: Transaction.

Straus, M.A., and C. Smith. 1990. "Family Patterns and Child Abuse." In M.A. Straus and R.J. Gelles (eds.), *Physical Violence in American Families: Risk Factors and Adaptations to Violence in 8,145 Families.* New Brunswick, NJ: Transaction.

Strike, C. 1995. "Women Assaulted by Strangers." *Canadian Social Trends* 36: 2–6.

Sugarman, D.B., and G.T. Hotaling. 1989. "Dating Violence: Prevalence, Context and Risk Markers." In M.A. Pirog-Good and J.E. Stets (eds.), *Violence in Dating Relationships.* New York: Praeger.

Sumser, J. 1996. *Morality and Social Order in Television Crime Drama.* Jefferson, NC: McFarland and Co.

Surette, R. 1992. *Media, Crime, and Criminal Justice: Images and Realities.* Pacific Grove, CA: Brooks/Cole.

Sutherland, E.H. 1940. "White-Collar Criminality." *American Sociological Review* 5: 1–12.

Sutherland, E.H. 1947. *Principles of Criminology,* 4th ed. Chicago: Lippincott.

Sutherland, E.H. 1961. *White Collar Crime.* New York: Holt, Rinehart & Winston.

Suttles, G. 1972. *The Social Construction of Communities.* Chicago: University of Chicago Press.

Taber, J.K. 1980. "A Survey of Computer Crime Studies." *Computer Law Journal* 2: 275–328.

Tanioka, I. 1986. "Evidence Links Smoking to Violent Crime Victimization." *Sociology and Social Research* 71(1): 58ff.

Tanner, J. 1992. "Youthful Deviance." In V.F. Sacco (ed.), *Deviance: Control and Conformity in Canadian Society,* 2nd ed. Scarborough, ON: Prentice-Hall.

Tanner, J. 1996. *Teenage Troubles.* Scarborough, ON: Nelson Canada.

Taylor, R.B., and S. Gottfredson. 1986. "Environmental Design and Prevention: An Examination of Community Dynamics." In A.J. Reiss, Jr., and M. Tonry (eds.), *Communities and Crime.* Chicago: University of Chicago Press.

Taylor, R.B., and A.V. Harrell. 1996. *Physical Environment and Crime.* Washington DC: U.S. Department of Justice.

Taylor, S.E., J.V. Wood, and R.R. Lichtman. 1983. "It Could Be Worse: Selective Evaluation as a Response to Victimization." *Journal of Social Issues* 39: 19–40.

Thompson, W.E. 1986. "Courtship Violence: Toward a Conceptual Understanding." *Youth and Society* 18(2): 162–76.

Thornberry, T.P. 1987. "Toward an Interactional Theory of Delinquency." *Criminology* 25(4): 863–92.

Thornberry, T.P., A.J. Lizotte, M.D. Krohn, M. Farnworth, and S.J. Jang. 1991. "Testing Interactional Theory: An Examination of Reciprocal Causal

Relationships Among Family, School, and Delinquency." *Journal of Criminal Law and Criminology* 82(1): 3–33.

Tibbetts, S.G., and D.C. Herz. 1996. "Gender Differences in Factors of Social Control and Rational Choice." *Deviant Behavior: An Interdisciplinary Journal* 17: 183–208.

Tierney, K. 1982. "The Battered Women Movement and the Creation of the Wife Beating Problem." *Social Problems* 29: 207–20.

Timmer, D.A., and W.H. Norman. 1984. "The Ideology of Victim Precipitation." *Criminal Justice Review* 9: 63–68.

Toby, J. 1974. "The Socialization and Control of Deviant Motivation." In Daniel Glaser (ed.), *Handbook of Criminology*. Chicago: Rand McNally.

Toby, J. 1983 (December). "Violence in Schools." *National Institute of Justice: Research in Brief*. Washington, DC: U.S. Department of Justice.

Tracy, P.E., and J.A. Fox. 1989. "A Field Experiment on Insurance Fraud in Auto Body Repair." *Criminology* 27: 509–603.

Traub, S.H., and C.B. Little (eds.). 1980. *Theories of Deviance*, 2nd ed. Itasca, IL: F.E. Peacock.

Tunnell, K.D. 1992. *Choosing Crime: The Criminal Calculus of Property Offenders*. Chicago: Nelson-Hall.

Turk, A. 1976. "Law as a Weapon in Social Conflict." *Social Problems* 23: 276–292.

Turner, P.A. 1993. *I Heard It Through the Grapevine*. Berkeley: University of California Press.

Tyler, T. 1990. *Why People Obey the Law*. Chicago: University of Chicago Press.

Unger, D.G., and A. Wandersman. 1985. "The Importance of Neighbors: The Social, Cognitive, and Affective Components of Neighboring." *American Journal of Community Psychology* 13(2): 139–69.

U.S. Department of Justice. 1988. *Report to the Nation on Crime and Justice*, 2nd ed. Washington, DC: Bureau of Justice Statistics.

Van Brunschot, E. 1997. *The Assault Event: Individuals, Interactions, and Interpretations*. Unpublished Ph.D. dissertation. Edmonton: University of Alberta.

Van den Haag, E. 1975. *Punishing Criminals: Concerning a Very Old and Painful Question*. New York: Basic Books.

van Dijk, J.J.M., and J. de Waard. 1991. "A Two-Dimensional Typology of Crime Prevention Projects with a Bibliography." *Criminal Justice Abstracts* (September).

Victor, J.S. 1993. *Satanic Panic*. Chicago: Open Court.

Visher, C.A. 1991. "Career Offenders and Selective Incapacitation." In J.F. Sheley (ed.), *Criminology: A Contemporary Handbook*, pp. 459–77. Belmont, CA: Wadsworth.

Vogel, R.E., and M.J. Himlein. 1995. "Dating and Sexual Victimization: An Analysis of Risk Factors among Precollege Women." *Journal of Criminal Justice* 23(2): 153–62.

Vold, G., and T.J. Bernard. 1986. *Theoretical Criminology*, 3rd ed. New York: Oxford University Press.

Voumvakis, S.E., and R.V. Ericson. 1984. *News Accounts of Attacks on Women: A Comparison of Three Toronto Newspapers*. Toronto: Centre of Criminology, University of Toronto.

Wachs, E. 1988. *Crime-Victim Stories: New York City's Urban Folklore*. Bloomington and Indianapolis: Indiana University Press.

Walker, S. 1994. *Sense and Nonsense about Crime: A Policy Guide*, 2nd ed. Pacific Grove, CA: Brooks/Cole.

Walker, S.G. 1994. *Weapons Use in Canadian Schools*. Ottawa: Solicitor General.

Walker, S.G., and C.R. Walker. 1993. "The Victoria Community Police Stations: An Exercise in Innovation." In J. Chacko and S.E. Nancoo (eds.), *Community Policing in Canada*, pp. 47–89. Toronto: Canadian Scholar's Press.

Walklate, S. 1989. *Victimology: The Victim and the Criminal Justice System*. London: Unwin Hyman.

Waller, I. 1982. "Victimization Studies as Guides to Action: Some Cautions and Suggestions." In H.J. Schneider (ed.), *The Victim in International Perspective*. New York: Aldine de Gruyter.

Waller, I. 1989. *Current Trends in European Crime Prevention: Implications for Canada*. Ottawa: Department of Justice Canada.

Waller, I., and N. Okihiro. 1978. *Burglary: The Victim and the Public*. Toronto: University of Toronto Press.

Waller, I., and R. Weiler. 1984. *Crime Prevention through Social Development*. Ottawa: Canadian Council on Social Development.

Walsh, W.F., and E.J. Donovan. 1989. "Private Security and Community Policing: Evaluation and Comment." *Journal of Criminal Justice* 17: 187–97.

Walters, G.D., and T.W. White. 1989. "Heredity and Crime: Bad Genes or Bad Research." *Criminology* 27(3): 455–58.

Warr, M. 1985. "Fear of Rape among Urban Women." *Social Problems* 32: 238–50.

Warr, M. 1988. "Rape, Burglary, and Opportunity." *Journal of Quantitative Criminology* 4(3): 275–88.

Warr, M. 1989. "What Is the Perceived Seriousness of Crime?" *Criminology* 27: 795–821.

Warr, M. 1990. "Dangerous Situations: Social Control and Fear of Victimization." *Social Forces* 68(3): 891–907.

Warr, M. 1991. "America's Perceptions of Crime and Punishment." In J.F. Sheley (ed.), *Criminology: A Contemporary Handbook*, pp. 5–19. Belmont, CA: Wadsworth.

Warr, M. 1996. "Organization and Instigation in Delinquent Groups." *Criminology* 34(1): 11–37.

Warr, M., and M.C. Stafford. 1983. "Fear of Victimization: A Look at Proximate Causes." *Social Forces* 61: 1033–43.

Webb, V.J., and I.H. Marshall. 1989. "Response to Criminal Victimization by Older Americans." *Criminal Justice and Behavior* 16(2): 239–58.

Weed, F. 1995. *Certainty of Justice: Reforms in the Crime Victim Movement*. New York: Aldine de Gruyter.

Weeks, E.L., J.M. Boles, A.P. Garbin, and J. Blount. 1986. "The Transformation of Sexual Harassment from a Private Trouble to a Public Issue." *Sociological Inquiry* 56: 432–55.

Weis, J.G. 1989. "Family Violence Research Methodology and Design." In L. Ohlin and M. Tonry (eds.), *Family Violence, Crime and Justice—A Review of Research*, vol. 11. Chicago: University of Chicago Press.

Wellford, C. 1975. "Labelling Theory and Criminology: An Assessment." *Social Problems* 22: 332–45.

Wellman, B., and B. Leighton. 1979. "Networks, Neighborhoods, and Communities: Approaches to the Study of the Community Question." *Urban Affairs Quarterly* 14: 363–90.

Wells, L.E., and J.H. Rankin. 1986. "The Broken Homes Model of Delinquency: Analytical Issues." *Journal of Research in Crime and Delinquency* 23(1): 68–93.

Wells, L.E., and J.H. Rankin. 1988. "Direct Parental Controls and Delinquency." *Criminology* 26: 263–85.

Wells, L.E., and J.H. Rankin. 1991. "Families and Delinquency: A Meta-Analysis of the Impact of Broken Homes." *Social Problems* 38(1): 71–93.

West, D.J., and D.P. Farrington. 1977. *The Delinquent Way of Life*. London: Heinemann.

Whitaker, C.J., and L.D. Bastian. 1991. *Teenage Victims*. A National Crime Survey Report. Washington, DC: U.S. Department of Justice.

Will, J.A., and J.H. McGrath 1995. "Crime, Neighborhood Perceptions, and the Underclass: The Relationship between Fear of Crime and Class Position." *Journal of Criminal Justice* 23(2): 163–76.

Williams, K.R., and R.L. Flewelling. 1988. "The Social Production of Criminal Homicide: A Comparative Study of Disaggregated Rates in American Cities." *American Sociological Review* 53: 421–31.

Williams, K.R., and R. Hawkins. 1986. "Perceptual Research on General Deterrence: A Critical Review." *Law and Society Review* 20: 545–72.

Wilson, J. 1980. "Sociology of Leisure." *Annual Review of Sociology* 6: 21–40.

Wilson, J.Q. 1983. *Thinking About Crime*. New York: Vintage.

Wilson, J.Q., and R.J. Herrnstein. 1985. *Crime and Human Nature*. New York: Simon & Schuster.

Wilson, J.Q., and G.L. Kelling. 1982. "Broken Windows." *Atlantic Monthly* (March): 29–38.

Wilson, M., M. Daly, and C. Wright. 1993. "Uxoricide in Canada: Demographic Risk Patterns." *Canadian Journal of Criminology* 35: 263–91.

Wilson, P.R., R. Lincoln, and D. Chappell. 1986. "Physician Fraud and Abuse in Canada: A Preliminary Examination." *Canadian Journal of Criminology* 28(2): 129–46.

Wilson, W.J. 1987. *The Truly Disadvantaged: The Inner City, the Underclass, and Public Policy*. Chicago: University of Chicago Press.

Wirth, L. 1938. "Urbanism as a Way of Life." *American Journal of Sociology* 44: 3–24.

Wirtz, P.W., and A.V. Harrell. 1987. "Police and Victims of Physical Assault." *Criminal Justice and Behavior* 14: 81–92.

Wolf, D. 1991. *The Rebels: A Brotherhood of Outlaw Bikers*. Toronto: University of Toronto Press.

Wolff, L. 1991. "Drug Crimes." *Canadian Social Trends* 20: 27–29.

Wolfgang, M. 1958. *Patterns in Criminal Homicide*. Philadelphia: University of Pennsylvania Press.

Wolfgang, M., and F. Ferracuti. 1967. *The Subculture of Violence: Towards an Integrated Theory in Criminology*. Beverly Hills, CA: Sage.

Wolfgang, M., R.M. Figlio, and T. Sellin. 1972. *Delinquency in a Birth Cohort*. Chicago: University of Chicago Press.

Wright, J.D., and P. Rossi. 1986. *Armed and Considered Dangerous: A Survey of Felons and Their Firearms*. Hawthorne, NY: Aldine de Gruyter.

Wright, R., and T. Bennett. 1990. "Exploring the Offender's Perspective: Observing and Interviewing Criminals." In K.L. Kempf (ed.), *Measurement Issues in Criminology*. New York: Springer-Verlag.

Wright, R., R.H. Logie, and S.H. Decker. 1995. "Criminal Expertise and Offender Decision Making: An Experimental Study of the Target Selection Process in Residential Burglary." *Journal of Research in Crime and Delinquency* 32(1): 39–53.

Yin, P. 1980. "Fear of Crime among the Elderly: Some Issues and Suggestions." *Social Problems* 27: 492–504.

Yin, P. 1982. "Fear of Crime as a Problem for the Elderly." *Social Problems* 30: 240–45.

Zawitz, M.W., P.A. Klaus, R. Bachman, L.D. Bastian, M.M. DeBerry, Jr., M.R. Rand, and B.M. Tayler. 1993. *Highlights from 20 Years of Surveying Crime Victims.* Washington: Bureau of Justice Statistics.

Ziegenhagen, E.A., and D. Brosnan. 1985. "Victims' Responses to Robbery and Crime Control Policy." *Criminology* 23: 675–95.

AUTHORS INDEX

Abadinsky, H., 314, 317
Ageton, S.S., 221,
Agnew, R.S., 59, 64, 73, 102, 113, 102, 113, 118, 175, 244, 255, 276, 288
Akers, R.L., 19, 25, 306
Albini, J.L., 320
Alex, N., 63, 170, 174
Allan, E.A., 55, 294, 295
Amir, M., 157, 158
Anderson, A.B., 135
Anderson, J., 51
Anderson, J.F., 340, 341
Arneklev, B.J., 95
Arnold, B.L., 305
Auger, R.P., 54
Austin, W.T., 9, 159
Avary, D.W., 73, 259, 166, 185

Baccaglini, W.F., 33, 59, 166, 185
Bala, N., 14
Baldassare, M., 181
Balkin, S., 235
Bandura, A.A., 204
Baranek, P.M., 33, 36, 37
Barnhorst, R., 52
Barnhorst, S., 52
Baron, S., 73, 134, 160, 218, 279, 280, 287
Bart, P.B., 64
Bartol, C.R., 91
Bastian, L.D., 300, 303, 304
Baum, M., 173, 253
Baumer, T.L., 181, 182, 183, 184
Baunach, RJ., 216
Bawden, H.N., 95
Bayley, D-H., 67, 355, 356, 358, 359
Beare, M.E., 8, 314, 315, 316, 317, 319
Beardsworth, A., 184
Beccaria, Cesare, 9
Becker, H.S., 104, 136, 176, 188
Beckman, L.S., 20
Bell, D.J., 67, 226, 323
Belliveau, J., 243
Bennett, T., 216, 218, 222, 256, 257, 258, 259, 260, 261, 263, 264, 265
Ben-Yemuda, N., 190, 192

Benson, D., 283
Benson, M.L., 60, 309, 310, 311
Bentham, J., 9
Bequai, A., 219
Berk, R.F., 67, 203, 204
Bernard, T.J., 10, 24
Best, J., 39, 40, 142, 188, 191, 232, 244, 271, 288
Birkbeck, C., 53, 136
Black, D.J., 17, 28, 57, 59, 67, 200, 206, 324, 349, 360
Blau, J.R., 98, 276, 278
Blau, P.M., 98
Block, C.R., 73, 222, 232, 298, 299
Block, R.L., 29, 30, 73, 222, 232, 298, 299
Blumberg, M., 42, 314, 317
Blumstein, A., 139, 233
Bograd, M., 60
Bohm, R.M., 9, 84
Bolander, E.W., 24
Bonati, L.M., 258
Bond-Maupin, L., 38
Bonn, R.L., 298
Bonta, J., 141
Boritch, H., 55, 67
Bottomley, A.K., 231, 232
Braithwaite, J., 135, 221
Brantingham, P.J., 13, 69, 167, 261, 340, 345, 347, 350
Brantingham, P.L., 69, 261, 345, 347, 350, 353
Brezina, T., 102
Brillon, Y., 134
Bromley, D.G., 191
Brosnan, D., 50, 166
Browne, A., 248, 253, 353
Brownfield, D., 121, 277, 278
Brunvand, J.H., 40, 41
Buerger, M.E., 50, 70, 154, 253
Bursik, R.J., 127, 128, 184
Burt, M.R., 170, 173

Cain, J.A., 316
Cain, M., 21
Calavita, K., 308

Cale, R.M., 285
Campbell, G., 55
Cantor, D.L, 73, 226, 256, 257, 258, 260, 261, 263, 295
Carrigan, D.O., 314, 316
Carter, D.L., 173
Cater, J., 70
Cavender, G., 38
Chaiken, J., 141
Chaiken, M., 141
Chambliss, W., 24, 218
Chan, J.B.L., 33, 36, 37
Chappel, D., 52
Chard, J., 258, 259, 263
Charlton, C., 283
Chibnall, S., 36
Chilton, R., 220
Chiricos, T.J., 294
Clairmont, D., 360
Clark, R.D., 131
Clarke, K.L, 52
Clarke, R.V., 136, 137, 155, 235, 345, 350, 351
Cloward, R., 100, 101, 102, 146
Cohen, A.K., 99, 100, 114
Cohen, J., 139, 223
Cohen, L.E., 63, 73, 151, 152, 154, 187, 256, 258, 261
Cohen S., 190
Coleman, W., 111, 112, 232, 307, 308, 309, 311, 313
Coles, C.M., 53, 184, 281
Collin, J.J., 73, 301
Conklin, J.E., 65, 185, 187
Cook, F.L., 181
Cook, P.J., 135
Cordasco, F., 315
Cornish, D.B., 136, 345
Cornwall, A., 95
Corrado, R.R., 14
Covey, H.C., 224
Cox, B.G., 73, 201
Cressey, D.R., 314, 317
Croall, H., 305, 311
Cromwell, P.F., 73, 259, 260, 261, 262, 263, 265
Cullen, F.T., 21
Culliver, C., 94, 95
Cumberbatch, 184
Currie, E., 134, 254, 295
Cusson, M., 133, 134

Dahlstrom, E., 203
Daly, M., 87, 249
Davis, C.R., 340
Davis, P.W., 65, 245, 246, 340
Dechenes, E.P., 143
Decker, S.H., 258
DeKeseredy, W.S., 73, 225, 229, 247, 283, 284, 285
De Sousa, P., 273, 274
Desroches, F., 66, 106, 170, 302
Deveraux, M., S., 242
de Waard, J., 340
Dilulio, J.J., 186
Dinitz, S., 26
Dishion, T.J., 119, 254
Doherty, G., 273
Dominick, J.R., 33, 38
Don, K., 236
Donnerstein, E., 276
Donovan, F.J, 355
Donzinger, S.R., 338, 353
Doob, A.N., 29, 54, 62, 63, 69, 72, 147, 179, 180, 184, 211, 256, 257, 264, 278
Dorfman, A., 92
Douglas, J.D., 105
Dowds, L., 73, 223, 298, 300, 302, 304
DuBow, F., 173, 174
Dubro, J., 315, 316, 317
Duke, J.M., 235
Durkheim, E., 20, 104, 105, 185, 186, 187
Dutton, D.G, 132, 133, 205, 248, 253
Dyson, L., 340

Easton, S.T., 167
Eitzen, D.S., 308
Elliot, D., 73, 212, 223, 298, 300, 302, 304
Ellis, L., 87, 88
Engs, R.C., 72, 277
Ericson, R.V., 33, 36, 37, 66, 200
Erikson, M.L., 234
Erman, D., 313
Erven, J.M., 207
Evans, D.J., 257, 258, 259, 260, 264

Fagan, J., 256
Fair, B.J., 35
Farberman, H.A., 309

Farrington, D.P., 139, 140, 203, 224
Fattah, L.A., 29, 62, 63, 136, 158, 166, 181, 216, 235, 248
Faust, F.L., 340
Fedorwycz, O., 225, 246, 265
Fekete, J., 225
Felson, M., 10, 53, 73, 127, 136, 151, 152, 155, 187, 260, 298, 299, 341, 349, 354, 355
Felson, R.B., 59, 110, 161
Ferracuti, F., 110
Ferraro, K.F., 180, 181, 183
Ferraro, K.J., 63, 200, 226, 227
Fewell, J., 294
Figlio, R.M., 140
Fine, G.A., 39
Finkelhor, D., 233, 247
Fischer, C.S., 69, 72, 85, 125, 182
Fischer, J.L., 255
Fisher, B., 182
Fishman, M., 36, 37
Fleisher, M.S., 218, 254, 255
Flewelling, R.L., 160
Flowers, R.B., 55, 70, 218
Forde, D.R., 95, 121, 154, 235, 278, 279, 356
Forsyth, C., 294
Fox, J.A., 202
Freeman, R.B., 296
Freudenheim, M., 296
Friedrichs, D.O., 317
Frieze, I.H., 170, 248
Frinell, D.E., 203
Furstenberg, F., 178

Gabor, T., 138, 217, 221, 283, 313, 350, 351
Galle, O.R., 235
Galliher, J.F., 316
Gans, H., 85
Garofalo, J., 35, 89, 146, 147, 161, 175, 181, 182, 216, 302, 303, 304, 349
Gartin, P.R., 50, 70, 154
Gartner, R., 29, 62, 63, 69, 72, 147, 179, 180, 211, 225, 250, 256, 257, 264, 278
Gates, L.B., 186
Gauthier, P., 243

Geerkan, M., 67, 206, 207, 221, 222, 223, 224
Geis, G., 61
Gelles, R.J., 52, 70, 71, 228, 229, 245, 249, 250, 251, 253
Geran, L., 296
Gibbons, D.C., 143
Gibbs, J.P., 18, 176, 234
Gilbert, N., 184, 185, 225, 232
Gillespie, C., 28
Gillespie, D.L., 229
Gillis, R., 122, 246, 277
Gilsinan, J.F., 18, 206
Goetz, B., 349
Goff, C., 21
Goffman, E., 158
Golant, S.M., 270
Gold, M., 220
Goldman, C.R., 110
Goldstein, H., 359
Gondolf, E.W., 226
Goode, E., 190, 192
Goodhart, F., 283
Goodstein, L.I., 50, 64, 70, 186, 187, 203
Gordon, M.T., 34, 36, 180, 185
Gordon, R.M., 109
Gorlick, S.M., 36
Gottfredson, D., 29, 30, 67, 206
Gottfredson, M.R., 11, 29, 30, 55, 67, 95, 119, 121, 142, 146, 147, 161, 175, 206, 216, 255, 278, 280, 294, 295, 310, 311, 326, 339, 345, 356
Gottfredson, S., 261
Gould, L.C., 12, 50
Gove, W.R., 67, 177, 206, 221, 222, 223
Graham, J., 339, 343, 350, 352, 353, 354
Grainer, B., 207
Gramling, R., 294
Grandison, T., 340
Grasmick, H.G., 127, 128, 183, 185
Gray, H., 271, 288
Gray, N.B., 283
Greenberg, D.F., 143
Greenberg, M.S., 63, 174
Greenberg, P., 256
Greenfeld, L.A., 216
Grossman, M.G., 54

Groves, W.B., 125
Gurr, T.R., 68
Gusfield, J., 18, 24, 38

Hackler, J., 236
Hagan, J., 111, 122, 188, 246, 255, 277, 305, 308, 309
Hagner, P.H., 35, 37
Haller, M.H., 313, 320, 322
Hamlin, J.E., 113
Hanke, P., 300
Hanmer, J., 229
Hans, V.P., 35, 38, 313
Hansel, M.K., 21
Hanson, D.J., 72, 277
Harlow, C.W., 246, 252, 298
Harney, P.A., 283
Harrell, A.N., 70, 253, 348
Harries, K.D., 344
Harris, M.K., 25, 26, 55
Hartman, D.P., 65
Hartnagel, T., 55, 134, 294
Hasell, M.J., 244
Hawkins, R., 132, 253
Heald-Moore, T., 181
Heath, L., 34, 36, 184, 185
Hendrick, D., 32, 55, 57, 211, 224
Hennigen, K.M., 273
Henshel, R.L., 133
Herrnstein, R.J., 87, 89, 90, 93, 114, 123
Herz, D.C., 122
Hickey, E., 95, 96
Hicks, R.D., 191
Hill, G.D., 172
Himlein, M.J., 283
Hinch, R., 225, 229, 247, 283
Hindelang, M.J., 146, 147, 150, 161, 175, 190, 216, 221, 224
Hirschi, T., 11, 55, 95, 119, 120, 121, 122, 125, 142, 221, 224, 225, 280, 294, 295, 310, 311, 326, 339, 345, 356
Hocker, J.L., 280
Hollinger, R.C., 188
Holmstrom, L.L., 253
Horowitz, A.N., 105, 126
Hotaling, G.T., 232, 256, 282
Hough, M., 172, 173, 260, 261, 263
Hughes, M., 67, 206, 222, 223
Huguley, S., 244

Humphries, D., 35
Hunt, J., 59

Ianni, F.A.J., 218, 320, 323
Innes, C.A., 216
Iso-Ahola, S., 270

Jackson, P.G., 222, 224
Jackson, P.I., 356
Jacobs, N., 39
Janoff-Bulman, R., 170
Jarjoura, G.R., 257, 258
Jeffrey, C.R., 96
Jenkins, P., 24, 191, 192
Jensen, G.F., 277, 278
Jesilow, P., 25
Johnson, D.A., 203
Johnson, D.M., 39
Johnson, G.D., 283
Johnson, H., 8, 63, 64, 67, 73, 169, 170, 171, 180, 211, 212, 229, 230, 247, 248, 250, 252, 258, 264, 278, 283, 285
Johnson, J.M., 64, 226
Johnson, M., 21
Jones, T., 70, 270
Junger, M., 229
Jupp, V., 222

Kantor, G.K., 253
Kapferer, J.N., 40
Kaplan, G., 173
Kappeler, V.E., 42, 314, 317
Karasek, R., 296
Karmen, A., 158
Katz, B.L., 170, 173
Katz, J., 34, 35, 37, 59
Keane, C., 121, 170, 308, 313
Kelling, G.L. 53, 184, 203, 281
Kelly, K., 73, 283, 284, 285
Kennedy, L.W., 8, 21, 22, 29, 30, 39, 63, 73, 95, 121, 126, 154, 206, 235, 248, 249, 252, 262, 278, 279, 280, 342, 356, 359, 359, 360
Kidwell, J.S., 255
Kindererhrer, J., 92
Kirby, C., 316
Kitsuse, J.I., 188, 189
Kitsuse, K.I., 176
Klaus, P.A., 246, 248, 252, 253
Kleck, G., 50, 166

Klockars, C.B., 357
Kluegel, J.R., 63, 154, 258
Koehler, R.J., 73
Koenig, D.J., 356
Kong, R., 174, 247, 248, 249
Koper, C.S., 313
Kornhauser, R., 125
Koval, J.F., 285
Krahn, H., 294, 360
Krohn, M.D., 125, 258
Krupat, E., 154, 349
Kubzansky, P., 154, 349
Kulsar, K., 21
Kurz, D., 253

Lab, S.T., 340
LaFree, G., 53, 136
LaGrange, R.L., 180, 181, 183
Land, K.C., 63, 154, 258, 295
Langan, P.A., 73, 143, 301
La Novara, P., 243
Lanza-Kaduce, L., 125, 188
Lasley, J.R., 149, 278
Laub, J.H., 63, 123, 216, 220, 278,
   302, 303, 304
Lauritsen, I.L., 160, 278
Lawson, P.E., 356
Lee, G.R., 183
Lee-Sammons, L., 35, 37
Leffler, A., 229
Leighton, R., 126, 358
Lejeune, R., 63, 170, 174
Lenton, R., 250
Lemert, E.M., 177
Leroux, T.G., 244
Letkemann, P., 139
Levi, K., 59
Levine, H.G., 191
Levine, M., 277
Lichtman, R.R., 175
Light, L., 323
Lincoln, A.J., 256
Lincoln, R., 51
Lindner, C., 73, 298
Lindquist, J.H., 235
Link, B.G., 21
Linton, M.A., 285
Lipinski, S., 141
Liska, A.E., 33, 166, 185, 187, 188
Little, C.B., 107

Lizotte, A.J., 227
Lloyd, S.A., 285
Loftus, E.F., 65
Logan, R., 243
Logie, R.H., 258
Lombroso, C., 9, 10
Long, J. S., 154, 293
Luckenbill, D.F., 53, 59, 73, 142, 158,
   159, 160, 161, 277, 279, 282
Lurigio, A.J., 53, 174
Luxton, M., 242
Lyman, S., 59
Lynam, D.R., 93, 95
Lynch, J.P., 71, 257, 260, 263, 301

Maas, P., 316
MacDonald, G.E., 184
MacMillan, R., 124
Maguire, K., 256, 257, 258, 259, 260,
   261, 263, 264, 265
Malamuth, N.M., 204, 276
Maltz, M.D., 319
Markwart, A., 14
Marolla, J., 59, 60
Marsh, H.L., 35
Marshall, I.H., 50
Martin, M., 30, 141
Martin, R., 9, 159
Massey, J.L., 258
Mastrofski, S., 358
Matza, D., 112, 113, 115, 175, 334
Maung, N., 170
Mauser, G., 342
Maxfield, M.G., 35, 39, 40, 154, 180,
   181, 184, 185, 257, 262, 279
Maxim, P.S., 121
Mayhew, P., 8, 63, 73, 170, 178, 223,
   258, 298, 302, 304
Mazzerole, P., 102
McCabe, E., 173
McCarthy, B., 225, 250, 255
McCausland, M.P., 253
McClearly, R.M., 207
McCord, J., 256
McDaniel, S., 243
McElrath, K., 265
McFerron, I.R., 226
McGrath, J.H., 181
McIntosh, M., 324
McKay, H.D., 101, 124, 125

McLeod, M., 349

Mednick, S., 87, 89

Meier, R.F., 11, 50, 61, 154, 155, 213, 263, 293

Meier-Katkin, D., 191, 192

Melbin, M., 277

Menard, S., 102, 224

Meredith, N., 341, 342

Merry, S.E., 349

Merton, R.K., 97, 98, 99, 100, 102, 103, 114, 323

Messner, S.F., 99, 103, 161, 276, 278

Michalowski, R.J., 24

Miethe, T.D., 11, 21, 50, 154, 155, 183, 213, 263, 293

Miller, G., 139

Miller, J.I., 135

Miller, L.J., 242, 244

Miller, W., 108, 109, 110

Minor, W.W., 113

Mirrlees-Black, C., 8, 63, 170, 178, 258

Moeller, G.L., 181, 182

Moffitt, T.E., 87, 89, 93, 94, 95

Monkkonnen, E.H., 357, 358

Moore, E., 310, 311

Moore, V.H., 316

Morash, M., 324

Morin, F., 39

Morris, N., 126

Morrison, P., 153

Moysa, M., 12

Mu, S., 13

Muehlenhard, C.L., 283, 285

Mundt, R.J., 342

Munro, J., 17

Murphy, C., 359

Murray, C., 93

Mutchnik, R.J., 9, 159

Naffine, N., 26, 27

Nagin, D.S., 136, 155

Nasar, J.L., 182

Nason-Clark, N., 21

Nelson, B., 244

Nelson, J., 109

Nettler, G., 11, 13, 14, 18, 168, 230

Newman, G.R., 38

Newman, O., 70, 152, 266, 288

Nicasco, A., 316

Nielson, M.O., 55, 57

Nienstedt, B.C., 207

Norman, W.H., 158

Normandeau, A., 70, 138, 358

O'Brien, R.M., 200, 211, 220, 222, 224

O'Grady, B., 226

Ogrodnik, L., 30

Ohlin, L., 100, 101, 102, 146

O'Keefe, G.J., 184

Okihiro, N., 73, 258, 259, 261, 265

Olson, J.N., 73, 259, 262, 262, 263, 265

Osborne, J. A., 13

Osgoode, D.W., 57, 73, 155, 276

Packer, H.L., 319

Pagelow, M.D., 244, 251

Palenski, J.E., 360

Palileo, G.J., 283

Pandiani, J.A., 38

Papdopoulos, C., 103

Parrot, A., 283

Parsons, T., 20

Paternoster, R., 102, 136, 155

Paterson, C., 312

Patterson, G.R., 119, 254

Pearce, F., 313

Pease, K., 231

Peatross, F.D., 244

Peek, C.W., 255

Pepinsky, H., 25

Percy, A., 8, 63, 178, 258

Peters, A.R, 113

Peterson, D.M., 73, 276, 288

Petrunik, M., 244

Pfohl, S., 188, 244

Phelps, T.G., 135

Phillips, D., 275

Pileggi, N., 320

Pillemer, K.A., 227

Pitkin, T.M., 315

Podnicks, E., 252

Polanzi, C.W., 21

Pontell, H.N., 308

Potter, G.W., 42, 314, 317

Pound, R., 20

Pravatiner, M.A., 72, 277

Provenzo, E.F., 271, 275

Quin, M.J., 247
Quinney, R., 25

Rand, M.R., 232, 246, 248, 252, 253
Randal, D.M., 35, 37
Rankin, J.H., 119, 243, 254
Reasons, C.E., 312
Reckless, W., 119
Reiman, J.H., 24, 99
Reinerman, C., 191
Reiss, A.J., Jr., 200, 205, 220, 221, 223, 230, 357, 358
Renner, T.C., 316
Reppetro, T., 258
Resick, P.A., 52
Reuss-Ianni, E., 218, 320
Reuter, P., 233, 323, 324
Ribner, S.A., 59
Rice, T.W., 110
Richardson, J.T., 191
Riger, S., 180, 185, 155, 276, 277
Riley, D., 155, 276, 277
Roberts, G., 154
Rodgers, K., 154, 174, 247, 248, 249
Rogers, A.J., 321
Rohe, W.M., 186
Roncek, D.W., 69, 70, 72, 277
Rosenbaum, D.P., 147, 173, 349, 351, 352
Rosenbaum, H.J., 349
Rosenbaum, J.L., 278
Rosenfeld, R., 103, 223
Rosnow, R.L., 39
Ross, D., 204
Ross, L., 312
Ross, R., 188, 189
Ross, S.A., 204
Rossi, P.H., 21, 216
Rountree, P.W., 154
Ruback, R.B., 63, 174
Rubington, C., 176
Rush, G., 15

Sacco, V.F., 29, 35, 62, 63, 166, 169, 172, 180, 181, 184, 205, 211, 212, 219, 220, 229, 233, 235, 236, 248, 249, 258, 264, 258, 264, 278, 340, 346
Sagarin, E., 177

St. John, C., 181
Sales, E., 50, 173, 175, 253
Salinger, L.R., 302, 304
Sampson, R.J., 57, 123, 125, 160, 278, 294
Sanger, D.E., 286
Sasson, T., 38
Saunders, D.G., 247
Saunders, S., 229
Savitz, L.D., 223
Sayles, S., 166
Scheingold, S.A., 360
Schelling, T.C., 319, 320, 322
Scheppele, K.L., 64
Schissel, B., 24
Schlesinger, P., 184
Schneider, V.W., 222
Schur, E.M., 61, 105
Schwartz, M.D., 248
Schwendinger, H., 338
Schwendinger, J., 338
Scott, M., 59
Scully, D., 59, 60
Sederberg, P.C., 349
Sellin, T., 22, 108, 109, 126, 140
Shaffer, E.B., 361
Shaw, C., 101, 124, 125
Shearing, C.D., 355, 356
Sheldon, W.H., 89, 90
Sheley, J.F., 23
Sherman, L., 67, 70, 73, 154, 203, 204
Shibutani, T., 39
Shore, B., 173, 175, 243
Shotland, R.L., 50, 64, 65, 70, 186, 187, 200, 202, 203
Shover, N., 259, 260, 261
Siegel, L., 302, 303, 304
Sigler, R.T., 21, 94, 95
Silva, P.A., 93, 95
Silverman, I., 26
Silverman, R.A., 8, 39, 55, 57, 63, 133, 205, 207, 233, 249, 252, 262, 340, 342
Simon, D.R., 308, 312
Simpson, J.H., 122, 246, 277
Simpson, S.C., 313
Simpson, S.S., 25, 266
Singer, S.L., 277
Skaret, D., 95
Skinner, B.F., 104
Skipper, J.K., 135

Skogan, W.G., 29, 30, 35, 39, 40, 154, 168, 170, 173, 175, 178, 180, 181, 183, 184, 185, 186, 207, 213, 221, 222, 279, 281
Skolnick, J., 360
Smith, B., 340
Smith, C., 248
Smith, D., 314, 316
Smith, D.A., 62, 67, 257, 258
Smith, L.N., 172
Smith, M.D., 248, 249
Smith, S.J., 126
Snider, L., 8, 57, 60, 99, 306, 308, 309, 312
Sommers, C.H., 251
Sorenson, A.M., 121
Sparks, R., 37
Spector, M., 188, 189
Stack, S., 87, 89
Stafford, M.C., 131, 179, 234, 235, 293
Staines, G.L., 188, 189
Stanko, E., 229
Stark, R., 70, 127
Steffenmeier, D.J., 55, 64, 202
Steffensmeier, R.H., 64, 294, 295
Steinman, M., 253
Steinmetz, S., 247, 248
Stenning, P.C., 355
Stoddart, K., 66
Stoker, Bram, 10
Stone, S.D., 36
Straus, M.A., 52, 70, 71, 226, 228, 245, 247, 248, 249, 250, 251, 253, 254, 256
Straw, M.K., 65, 200, 202, 203
Strike, C., 212
Sugarman, D.B., 282
Sumser. J., 37
Supancic, M., 183
Surette, R., 200, 204, 273
Sutherland, E., 101, 105, 106, 115, 305, 326
Suttles, G., 127
Sykes, G., 112, 113, 115, 175, 334

Taber, J.X., 219
Tanioka, I., 150
Tanner, J., 57, 100, 271, 277, 288, 295
Taylor, B.M., 300
Taylor, R.B., 70, 261, 348

Taylor, S.E., 175
Teevan, J.J., 121, 205, 233
Terry, R.M., 200
Theorell, T., 296
Thompson, W.E., 283
Thornberry, T.P., 122, 123, 255
Tibbetts, S.G., 122
Timmer, D.A., 158
Toby, J., 293, 300, 301
Tomita, S.K., 247
Tracy, P.E., 202
Traub, S.H., 107
Tunnell, K.D., 136
Turk, A., 24
Turner, P.A., 40
Tyler, T., 134

Unger, G.G., 126

Van Brunschot, E., 280
Van den Haag, E., 325
van Dijk, J.J.M., 340
Veitch, D., 30, 206, 356, 360
Verma, A., 13
Victor, J.S., 191
Visher, C.A., 141
Vogel, 283
Vold, G., 10
Voumvakis, S.E., 36

Wachs, E., 40, 51, 174
Walker, C.R., 360
Walker, S.G., 42, 303, 360
Walklate, S., 222
Waller, I., 73, 231, 258, 259, 261, 265, 351, 353
Walsh, W.E., 355
Walters, G.D., 89
Wandersman, A., 126
Warner, B.D., 187, 188
Warr, M., 21, 36, 57, 131, 178, 179, 181, 182, 263
Wasklerm, F.C., 105
Webb, V.J., 50
Weed, F., 174
Weeks, E.L., 188
Weiler, R., 351
Weinberg, M.S., 176
Weis, J.G., 220, 221, 224
Wellford, C., 177

Wellman, B., 126
Wells, L.E., 243, 254
Wescott, D.R., 63, 174
West, D.J., 224
Wexler, S., 256
Whitaker, C.J., 300, 303, 304
White, H.R., 102
White, T.W., 89
Whitten, L., 51
Wiersma, B., 222
Wildeman, J., 25
Wilgosh, C., 95
Will, J.A., 181
Williams, K., 132, 160, 253, 353
Wilmot, W.W., 280
Wilson, J.Q., 87, 89, 90, 99, 114, 123,
    281, 295, 353, 357
Wilson, M., 87, 249
Wilson, P.R., 52

Wirth, L., 85, 124, 125
Wirtz, P.W., 253
Wolf, D., 10, 218
Wolff, L., 321
Wolfgang, M., 59, 110, 140, 156, 157
Wood, J.V., 175
Wright, C., 249
Wright, J.D., 216
Wright, R., 216, 218, 222, 258, 260,
    261, 263
Wycoff, M.A., 173

Yin, P., 181

Zamble, E., 58
Zawitz, M.S., 63, 170, 299
Ziegenhagen, E.A., 50, 166
Zureik, E., 219, 220

GLOSSARY/SUBJECT INDEX

Actus reus. See Law

Aftermath events that occur after the committed crime. 49, 53, 63–74, 76–77, 78, 165–194, 326, 334–335, 342
  community setting and, 182–84
  costs of, 166–77
    behavioural consequences of, 173–75
    coping with, 175–76
    emotional consequences of, 170–73
    financial consequences of, 168–69
    physical consequences of, 169–70
    stigma, 176–77
  crimes against households, of, 263–65
  crimes during leisure, of, 286–88
  definition of, 49
  enterprise crime, of, 324–25
  family violence, of, 252–54
  fear of crime, 166–82
  occupational crimes, of, 312–13
  workplace crimes, of, 304

Alcohol. *See* Substance abuse

Alienation, 98, 124

Ambivalence, 134–35

American dream and crime, 97, 103. *See also* **Anomie theory; Cultural goals; Legitimate means**

Anomie theory theory that says anomie occurs when cultural norms and goals break down. 98–99. *See also* American dream, **Cultural goals; Legitimate means**

Antisocial personality, 92–93, 95–96. *See also* Gacy, John Wayne; **Psychopath; Serial murderer; Sociopath**

Assault, 13, 29, 289
  attitudes toward, 59, 60, 106, 113
  bystanders, 65, 162, 280. *See also* **Witnesses**
  correlates of, 62, 223, 279, 282, 303
  deterrence of, 356
  domestic, *see* **Domestic violence**
  financial costs of, 167
  gender of offenders, 58
  homicide and, 12, 110, 353
  media and, 36
  occupation and, 298, 300, 302, 311
  rational choice theories and, 151
  recording of, 209, 212, 237
  reporting of, 29
  sexual, *see* **Sexual assault**
  time and location of, 71
  victimization risk, 298

Atavism the theory that offenders are less likely to conform to the demands of contemporary social life because they are related to a more primitive evolutionary condition. 9–10. *See also* Evolution; Heredity; **Sociobiology**

Attachment the degree to which children are sensitive to the expectations of parents or teachers. 120, 122, 132, 143, 254. *See also* **Belief; Bond; Commitment; Involvement**

Automobile insurance fraud, 202

Autonomic nervous system, 96

Belief the degree to which youths believe that the conformist values of parents and teachers are worthy of respect. 120, 122, 132, 143. *See also* **Attachment; Bond; Commitment; Involvement**

Bond, theory of theory that strong social bonds insulate youths against the delinquent environment. 120–25, 143, 254, 271, 276, 334. *See also* **Attachment; Belief; Commitment; Involvement**

Break and enter, 141, 205, 209, 212, 256, 265
  statistics on, 32, 57, 141, 257

Burglary, 55, 154, 172, 179, 181, 258, 260, 264, 266, 298, 299
  costs of, 264, 313
  prevention of, 263

Bystanders, 50, 53, 64–65, 77–78, 159, 161–62, 186, 202–3, 204, 332. *See also* Third parties; Witnesses

Career criminal. *See* Offender

Character contests, 160–61, 282

Child-rearing, 121–23

Civil liberties, 135

Claimsmaking best exemplified by the crusading reformer who believes that rules must he formulated to combat the evil world. 188–91

moral entrepreneur, 188

natural history model, 189

stages of, 189

Valence issues issues that do not have an adversarial quality. 189

Classical school a school that views the offender as a "rational person" who would he deterred only by the threat of sanction. 8–10, 86. *See also* **Positivist school**; Rationality

Commitment the size of the investment of time and energy that a youth has made to a conventional activity, such as getting good grades. 120, 122, 123, 132, 143. *See also* **Attachment; Belief; Bond; Involvement**

Community policing expansion of the policing role beyond the traditional narrow reactive role. 25, 331–44, 356–61

compliance-based policing, 357–58, 362. *See also* **Police**

deterrence, 358, 362

fear of crime, 350, 351

features of, 359

guardians, 354, 357

teams, 360

order maintenance, 358

peacekeeping, 358

philosophy of, 28, 78, 358

proactive policing, 28, 30, 65, 66, 78, 206, 357

problems of, 358, 360–61

reactive policing, 28, 78, 358

routine activities theory and, 354, 357

social order and, 358, 359

successes of, 30–31

See also **Crime prevention**; Police

Conflict pattern a pattern that occurs in socially disorganized neighbourhoods where youth frequently experience the disparity between legitimate goals and legitimate opportunities that leads to aggressive behaviour. 101. *See also* **Criminal pattern; Illegitimate means; Retreatist pattern**

Conflict tactics scale, 228

criticisms of, 247–48, 250

Conflict theory theory that argues that in a complex society, social groups may pursue different interests, and the achievement of success depends on how powerful they are. Responses to crime are interpreted as part of a larger struggle among groups that attempt to use law, or legal control, in pursuit of their own interests. 23–24, 25. *See also* Marxism, Feminist theories, Peacemaking

Conformist mainstream culture, 111

Consensus theory theory proposing that laws and punishment be enforced in order to maintain the collective interests shared by members of society. 5, 20–22, 43

criticisms of, 21–22

Containment theory theory, based on control theory, that youth are insulated from delinquency by inner and outer containments that constrain nonconformist behaviour. 119. *See also* **Inner containments; Outer containments**

Control theory, 119, 122, 255, 260, 288 *See also* **Bond theory, Power control theory**

corporate crime. *See* Occupational crime

Crime a behaviour that breaks the criminal law and is liable to public prosecution and punishment.

facts of, 76

hidden dimension of, 12–13

mala in se crimes that are perceived historically and cross-culturally as wrong, 13

mala probibita crimes that are condemned through prohibition, 13

public attitudes toward, 29, 32, 134

social context of, 6, 13–15, 57, 60

talking about, 38–40

"typical," 38, 40

See also Actus reus, Mens rea

Crime funnel a "volume-reducing system," meaning that there is a high level of attrition as cases travel through various stages of the criminal justice system. 204–5

Crime prevention the anticipation, recognition, and appraisal of a crime risk and the initiation of some action to reduce or remove it. 125, 174, 232, 331, 337–62
armchair variables of, 341
deadly force and, 338
definition of, 339
get-tough approach to, 337–39, 344
problems of, 338–39
guardianship, levels of, 354
gun control and, 342–43
statistics about, 343
legal threats and, 78, 128, 130, 132, 136
mandatory charging and, 67, 227, 338
metroquilt and, 355
Neighbourhood Watch and, 340, 341, 349, 361, 174
criticisms of, 351
Opportunity reduction focuses on how social and environmental factors might be brought to bear on the reduction of crime opportunities. 344, 345–51, 553, 354, 361, 362
criticisms of, 350–51
primary crime prevention and, 340–41, 344
principles of, 339
prison terms and, 339
problems of, 343, 350, 358, 360
public health approach to, 340–44
public policy and, 331, 340
public safety and, 340
Resource mobilization addressing crime issues in terms of whether law helps people against victimization. 353, 362
secondary, 340–41, 344
self-help crime and, 349, 360
situational, 345–47, 361
Social development approach an approach to crime prevention that attempts to create social conditions that discourage long-term serious offending and empower potential victims, while at the same time contributing to the rebuilding of communities. 331, 344, 351–54, 361, 362
criticisms of, 353, 354
tertiary crime prevention, 354
See also Community policing; Defensible space; Deterrence; Police; Social control; Target Hardening.

Crime rates, 30–31, 70, 84, 103, 109, 124, 186, 231–37
age-specific the crime risk for a certain age group. 234–35
computing, 231–32
demographic composition of, 235
Ecological position incorporates geographic and economic relationships within a community in the analyses of crime rates. 234–35
feminist explanations of, 26–27
measures of risk and, 234–35
nature of, 331–32
population measures and, 232, 235, 236
Rude crime rates the population at risk of being a victim of crime. 234–35
definition of, 231
uses, 232

Crime types, 9

Criminal event includes its precursors, including the locational and situational factors which bring people together in time and space; the event itself involving how the interactions among participants define the outcomes of their actions; and the aftermath of the event including the reporting to the police, their response, the harm done and the redress required, and the long-term consequences of the event in terms of public reactions and the changing of laws.
aftermath of, 76
community setting and, 69–70
definition of, 74
episodic quality of, 53
physical setting of, 70–71

precursors of, 74

social domains of, 71–73

social events and, 6, 11, 50, 52–53, 76–78, 332

social setting and, 68–69

studying of, 73

systematic accidents and 53

transactions of, 74–74

See also **Aftermath, Precursors, Transactions**

social events and, 6, 11, 50, 52, 53, 76, 77, 78, 332

systematic accidents and, 53

Criminal pattern a rational delinquency oriented toward the pursuit of monetary objectives, exemplified by organized theft and the sale of illicit goods or services. 101. *See also* **Conflict pattern; Illegitimate means; Retreatist pattern**

Criminological theories, 84–85, 333. *See also* Interdisciplinary approach

Criminologists, 7–8, 11, 13, 18

Criminology, 7

Cultural baggage, 83, 86, 108, 112, 275

Cultural beliefs, 60

Cultural distance, 123

Cultural goals legitimate objectives held by all or by diversely located members of society. 97, 98, 100, 101, 103, 114, 118. *See also* American dream; **Anomie theory; Individual adaptation; Legitimate means, Illegitimate means**

Cultural learning, 122, 136

Culture of competition a cultural atmosphere in which crime is promoted by competition that defines wealth and success as central goals of human activity. 122, 136. *See also* **Enterprise crime; Occupational crime;** Workplace domain

Defensible space the physical design of a place that may deter or attract an offender. 70, 152, 154, 266, 349. *See also* **Crime prevention; Deterrence; Target hardening**

Demographic characteristics, 57, 148, 160, 204, 212, 217, 234, 243, 264, 293, 310, 332

age and, 14, 20, 38, 55–56, 62, 92, 140, 141, 142, 147, 179, 180–81, 212–13, 218, 235, 243, 273, 278

gender and, 20, 27, 55, 57, 62, 180–81, 212, 218, 226

economically disadvantaged and, 22, 25, 55, 58, 63, 70, 97, 99, 125–26, 146, 180, 257–58

employment and, 35, 58, 73, 99, 105, 140, 142, 176, 278, 292–95, 352

income and, 63, 99, 147, 167, 181–82, 248, 257–58, 263, 271, 298, 325

marital status, 62, 147, 227, 278

race and, 27, 99, 147, 180, 182

statistics on, 218

unemployment and, 58, 99, 105, 114, 140, 142, 151, 207, 292–95

See also Inner city; Lower classes; Poverty; Social disadvantaged; **Underclass;** Workplace domain

Deterrence theory of prevention in which the threat of punishment or retribution is expected to forestall some act from occurring. 128, 131–36

Attachment costs the costs associated with the loss of weakened ties that may make an arrest a fearsome prospect. 132

Commitment costs the possibility that arrest may jeopardize people's investments in some legitimate activity. 132

General deterrence the ways in which individuals, who *see* offenders receiving punishment, will be deterred from breaking the law themselves. 128, 131, 358

Situational deterrence the ways in which the offender's fear of apprehension is related to the specific circumstances of the criminal event. 133–34

Specific/special deterrence the ways that individuals are deterred from offending or re-offending by receiving punishment. 128, 131, 358

Stigma of arrest the belief that apprehension by the police may harm one's reputation. 131–32, 135
See also **Crime prevention; Punishment; Target hardening**

Differential association, theory of a theory that criminal behaviour is learned in the process of interaction with intimate groups. 105–7, 115, 333. *See also* Learned behaviour

Direct observation a technique in which an investigator attempts to develop theory through exploration, or confirm hypotheses through direct participation in and observation of the community or other social grouping being studied. 200–1
methods of, 200
problems of, 200–1
See also **Experimental observation;** Field research; **Participant observation**

Domestic violence, 64, 67, 213, 227–30, 241
Battered Women's Syndrome the sense of helplessness felt by women who come to believe that they can neither leave an abusive relationship nor effectively act to reduce the violence. 15, 27
consequences of, 252–54
children and, 65, 245, 246–47, 250, 251, 254–56
Conflict Tactics Scale and, 230, 248
delinquency and, 254
deterrence of, 253, 266
economic stress and, 247–51
elderly and, 250
family interaction and, 245
family violence, 19, 64, 67, 70, 77, 223
feminism and, 245, 266
gender and, 245
helping victims of, 253–54
interpersonal conflict theory and, 245–46
inequality in relations and, 246–47
isolation stress and, 247–48

legislation, effect of, 353
location of, 250–52
mandatory charge rule and, 67–68, 227
Minneapolis domestic violence experiment, 203–4
patterns of, 252
police intervention and, 244, 245, 253, 227
private settings of, 245, 250
public awareness of, 253
reporting and, 30
routine activities and, 252
social control mechanisms and, 245, 254, 256, 257, 266
spousal homicide and, 74, 246–47, 250, 252, 253
spousal violence and, 71, 246, 255
substance abuse and, 252, 253
timing of, 250–52
tolerance of, 19, 246
wife abuse and, 30, 111, 230, 244
Violence Against Women Survey, 230–31
statistics about, 248
See also **Household domain; Family domain; Routine activities theory;** Tolerance
Double-failures, 162. *See also* **Individual Adaptation; Retreatist pattern**
Dracula, 10
Drugs. *See* Substance abuse

Enterprise crime sale of illegal goods and services to customers who know that the goods and services are illegal. 292
Cressey's eight facts, 316–17
economic factors and, 320
eight facts of American organized crime, 316–17
ethnic character and, 314, 322
ethnic stereotyping and, 315
ethnic succession and, 323
La Cosa Nostra and, 314, 316–17, 320, 322
law and, 305, 306, 307, 309, 310, 314, 316–17, 319, 327, 332, 334
law enforcement responses to, 316, 324

Mafia and, 314–15, 322
monopolization and, 320, 322, 327
organized crime and, 313, 319
parasitic conspiracy and, 317, 319,
    324
partnership arrangements and, 320,
    327, 337
role of regulation of, 323
    social mobility and, 323
systematic corruption and, 319, 327
traditional views of, 324
See also **Culture of competition;
    Occupational crime;** Prohibition;
    Workplace domain
Evolution, human, 9. *See also* **Atavism;**
    Heredity; **Sociobiology**
Excuse denial of responsibility for an
    acknowledged wrongful act. 59–60.
    See also **Justification; Neutralization
    theory**
Experimental observation an experimen-
    tal method, often conducted in labo-
    ratories, in which the experimenter
    creates the conditions necessary for
    observation rather than searches for
    naturally occurring situations. 202,
    204
    auto insurance fraud experiment,
        example of, 202
    problems of, 202–4
    See also **Direct observation;** Field
        research; **Participant observation**

Family domain enduring pattern of
    social relationships through which
    domestic life is organized. 244
    demographic characteristics of, 243
    hierarchical institution, as a, 26, 246,
        247
    social relations and, 242, 243, 244
    See also Domestic violence; **Household
        domain**
Fear of crime, 39, 40, 68, 165, 166,
    170–90, 193, 203, 212, 335, 350,
    351
    age and, 181, 173
    avoidance behaviour and, 179, 186,
        187, 193
    claimsmaking and, 188–90
    collective reactions and, 187
    community reactions and, 185–88

community setting and, 182–83
distinct meanings of, 178–79
elderly and, 181
environmental factors and, 182
gender and, 180–81
incivility and, 183–84
income and, 181–82
information, environmental and,
    184–95
mass media and, 39, 53, 111, 166,
    184, 186
patterns in, 180
protective behaviour and, 187
public, 177, 180
race and, 181–82
social disorder and, 183–84
social outcomes and, 177
statistics on, 179
See also **Moral panic**
Female criminality, 26–27, 55
Feminism, 25–27, 36, 111, 226, 245,
    266
Field research, 202–4
    description of, 202
    problems of, 204
    See also **Direct observation; Participant
        observation**
Focal concerns concerns around which
    life in the lower class is organized:
    trouble, toughness, smartness, excite-
    ment, fare, and autonomy. 109–10
Folk hero syndrome a residual belief
    that the criminal should be admired
    for expressing some degree of resis-
    tance to convention. 135
Free will the guiding principal of the
    classical school—the belief that indi-
    viduals are responsible for their own
    actions and, therefore, punishment is
    an appropriate response if the person
    violated the law. 9–10. *See also*
    Classical school; Rationality
Frustrated ambitions, 97–114
Functionalism the theory that criminal
    activity contributes to the mainte-
    nance of and stability of normal
    behaviour by establishing boundaries
    of acceptable and tolerable limits to
    human actions. 20–22, 42
    criticisms of, 22

Gacy, John Wayne, 96. *See also*
Antisocial personality; **Psychopath**;
Serial murderers; **Sociopath**
Gangs, 6, 101, 110, 219, 279, 280, 304,
315, 316, 317, 323. *See also* Leisure
domain; Territorial marking
General strain theory a focus on negative relationships between people that
promote anger, fear, and frustration,
which may lead to delinquency. 102.
See also Negative relationships;
Strain theory
General theory of crime the theory that
criminal activity appeals to people
who are impulsive, short-sighted,
physical, risk-taking, nonverbal, and,
most importantly, have low self-
control. 95, 121, 310, 339
Geography of crime, 31, 235
violent and property crime geography
statistics, 33
Guardianship, 151, 152, 154, 155, 188,
287, 295, 3011, 345, 354. *See also*
Routine activities theory
Guns. *See* **Crime prevention**; Gun
control and; Guns and youth and

Hedonism, principle of the principle
that the seeking of pleasure and
avoidance of pain are the ultimate
aims and motivating forces of human
action. 9
Heredity, 9. *See also* Atavism;
Evolution, human; Predetermined
behaviour; **Sociobiology**
Homelessness, 221, 255
Homicide, 8, 14, 28, 31, 35, 37, 53, 55,
59, 60, 73, 110, 129, 130, 151,
156–59, 161, 166, 208, 209, 249,
263, 342, 353, 356
aboriginal peoples and, 54
child and, 250
consequences of, 263
elderly and, 262
media and, 275, 336
situated transactions and, 159–60
spousal, 74, 246–47, 250, 252, 253,
254
statistics on, 32, 57, 210, 225, 226,
234

Hot spots high crime areas. 70, 154,
162
Household crime, 63, 69, 73, 221, 225,
241, 256–67
amateur thieves and, 261
certainty of arrest and, 265
control theory and, 260–61
cultural influence and, 267
defensible space and, 266
definition of household, 243
economic costs of, 264
elderly and, 262
escalating of violence and, 256
family and, 242–44
family violence and, 244
statistics on, 249
household locations and, 257
income and, 258
statistics about, 258
Occasional offenders commit crimes
when opportunities or situational
inducements present themselves.
260
Occupancy probes imaginative methods that the offender uses to determine whether anyone is home. 262
opportunity and, 259, 261, 267
potential reward and, 261–263
professional thieves and, 259–61
psychological impact and, 263
Rational reconstruction occurs when
individuals recall their crimes and
suggest there was more planning
than actually took place. 259
recidivism and, 260
reporting of, 264
risk, ease of entry, and reward of,
261–63
seasonality and, 258
selection of target and, 256, 258,
260–61, 266
single-parent households and, 257
statistics about, 251, 257
strain theory and, 267
structures and, 258
target hardening and, 265
timing and, 250, 271
tipsters and, 259, 261
urban neighbourhoods and, 256–57
statistics on, 257

See also Household domain; Routine activities theory; Target hardening

Household domain the social and physical setting within which family life is organized. 71–72, 241–42, 336. *See also* Family domain; Household crime

Household survey, 221, 225, 256, 260, 264. *See also* Reporting crime statistics

Humanitarianism, 68. *See also* Peacemaking; Rehabilitation

Illegitimate means two aspects of the delinquent opportunity structure: opportunity to learn and to play the delinquent role. 100, 101, 102. *See also* Conflict pattern; Criminal pattern; Retreatist pattern

Immigration, 105, 109, 314

Incivility perceptions of social disorder that include physical conditions, such as abandoned buildings, strewn trash, as well as social conditions, such as public drinking or drug use. 183–84. *See also* Social disorganization

Inner city, 35, 40, 151, 279. *See also* Demographic characteristics; Lower classes; Poverty; Underclass

Inner containments the products of effective socialization and the successful internalization of rule regarding acceptable behaviour. 119. *See also* Containment theory; Outer containments

Institutional balance of power, 103

Intelligence and crime, 93–94

Neuropsychological theory the theory that people with identical IQ scores can have very different patterns of mental strengths and weaknesses (e.g., verbal skill, spatial perception) that can influence behaviour. 93–94. *See also* Learning disabilities

Interactional theory the theory that behaviours are characterized by mutual awareness of interactants over time. 122–23

Interactional theory of delinquency the theory that the weakness of ties to conventional others that increase the likelihood of delinquent behaviour can strengthen or weaken over time in response to changing circumstances. 122. *See also* juvenile delinquency

Interdisciplinary approach. 7, 43. *See also* Criminological theories

Interpersonal violence, 67, 74, 110, 245, 266, 336

Interracial relationships, 126

Involvement the participation in the world of conformity such that little time is left for delinquency. 120, 123, 143. *See also* Attachment; Belief; Bond; Commitment

Justification accepting responsibility for the act while denying the immorality of the act. 59–60, 112. *See also* Excuse; Neutralization theory

Juvenile in Canada, anyone under 12 cannot be responsible for their own actions in the criminal sense. Children 12–17 are held culpable for their actions but are held separate from the adults in assessing their criminal responsibilities. 14 *See also* juvenile delinquency

Juvenile delinquency, 94, 112, 120. *See also* Interaction theory of delinquency; juvenile; Learning disabilities

Labelling theory the theory that frustration created by particular social arrangements, such as identifying a person as a criminal, may motivate criminal behaviour. 176–77. *See also* Secondary deviance; Self-fulfilling prophecy; Symbolic interactionism

Law, 7, 9, 11

Actus reus the mere physical criminal act. 12–13

competence, 12, 14, 34–35

Constructive intent constructing the motive, or mens rea, of the crime, or actus reus. 14

crime and, 11–12

federal, 13, 31

Individual accountability the belief, which the law traditionally holds, that able but negligent people are responsible for their actions. 13–14

insanity and, 15–16
legal codes, 68
legal system, 15–16
legal threats, 78, 128, 130–31, 132, 134, 136

Mens rea the willful quality of a criminal act. 5, 12, 13

offender focus, 11–12
self-defense and, 15
social control as, 17
See also Legal defence

Learned behaviour, 106, 115, 333. *See also* **Differential association, theory of**

Learning disabilities difficulties faced by children and youths with dyslexia, dysgraphia, aphasia, perceptual and motor deficits, poor sensory integration, or minimal brain disfunction. 94–95

Differential adjudication hypothesis the theory that delinquents with learning disabilities who are arrested and charged are more likely to be convicted of crimes due to their inability to cope with the process of criminal justice adjudication. 94

Differential arrest hypothesis the theory that learning disabled children are more likely to be apprehended by the police since they are less likely to conceal their activities. 94

Differential disposition hypothesis the theory that learning disabled delinquents have a higher chance of receiving harsher sentences than other delinquents. 94

School failure hypothesis the theory that self-perpetuating academic failure resulting from learning disabilities causes frustration, aggressive behaviour. 94

Susceptibility hypotheses the theory that learning disabled students have unique characteristics, such as impulsiveness and irritability, thereby they are more prone to become delinquent.
See also juvenile delinquency

Legal defense, 13
battered women's syndrome, 27–28

Duress defense some unlawful constraint of influence used to force an individual to commit an act that he/she would otherwise not have committed. 14, 15

insanity defense, 15–16

Self-defense actions taken to protect oneself or one's property in the face of a threat involving reasonable force. 13, 14, 15, 27

Twinkie defense when a defendant experiences diminished mental capacity and is therefore not guilty of criminal behaviour due to an over-consumption of junk food. 92
See also Law

Legitimate means widely accepted routes of achieving cultural goals through institutions. 97, 100–1, 114. *See also* American dream and crime; **Anomie theory; Cultural goals; Individual adaptation**

Leisure activities, 72–73, 256, 269, 270, 271, 276, 277–78, 287, 336. *See also* **Routine activities theory**

Leisure domain, 270, 290, 336
bars and, 72, 150, 213, 257, 269, 270, 271, 277–78, 282
corrupter, as a, 269, 271–72, 273
dating violence, 282–285. *See also* Sexual aggression; Sexual assault
gangs, 279–80
juvenile delinquency, 270, 276
leisure time distribution and, 270–71
permissive environs and, 277
personal and household crime, 278
pornography, 275–76
positive leisure alternatives and, 288
power control theory and, 277
reporting of victimization, 273, 286, 289

risky lifestyle and, 278, 289, 290
routine activity theory and, 289
social bonds and, 276
social control theory and, 269,
    276–77, 288, 289
street crime, 278–79
television violence and, 272. *See also*
    Mass media
tourism and, 285–86
young males and, 279–80
youth violence and, 273
vandalism and, 280–81
victimization risks and, 277, 278
violent crime and, 272–73, 279. *See
    also* Gangs
Life course perspective adult criminality
    is strongly influenced by patterns of
    childhood behaviour, and changes in
    people's lives affect the likelihood of
    involvement in crime. 123–24. *See
    also* **Trajectories; Transitions**
Lifestyle, 8, 11, 24, 93, 122, 145–48,
    150, 155, 161, 162, 169, 175, 181,
    182, 217, 221, 236, 256, 270, 271,
    278, 279, 289, 290, 334. *See also*
    Lifestyle exposure theory
Lifestyle exposure theory focus on
    lifestyle, or patterned ways in which
    people with certain demographic
    characteristics distribute their time
    and energies across a range of activi-
    ties, and its relation with the risk of
    victimization by motivated offenders.
    146, 334. *See also* Life style; Risky
    lifestyles; **Routine activities theory**
Limited rationality, 137
Lower classes, 99. *See also*
    Demographic characteristics; Inner
    city; Poverty; **Underclass**

Marxism, 24
  capitalism and, 24
  class conflict and, 24
  law and, 24
  social classes and, 24
  See also **Conflict theory**
Masculinity theories, 26
Mass media, 33, 38, 39, 53, 111, 166,
    184, 186, 188, 192, 208, 332
  content, 35–36

crime drama and, 37–38
crime news and, 33–35
crime reporting "bias" and, 35–36
Improvised news similar to rumours,
    expresses anxieties and uncertain-
    ties about some aspect of social life.
    39–40
newsworthy, 37, 40
sources of crime news and, 36–37
violence and, 35–36, 38
Mass murder, 160, 312
Mens rea. *See* Law
Middle-class measuring rod the middle-
    class ethic, which people use to
    compare and determine their status,
    that prescribes an obligation to
    strive, by dint of rational, ascetic,
    self-disciplined and independent
    activity to achieve worldly success.
    100
Modernization crime in Western soci-
    eties has been shaped by four aspects
    of modernization: industrialization,
    urbanization, expression of the state's
    power and resources, and the
    humanization of interpersonal rela-
    tions. 68, 105
Morals society's general rules detailing
    what is permissible or normative
    behaviour. 11, 13, 17, 18–19, 20–21,
    35, 40, 43, 49, 59–60
crusades, 68
mores, 20
normative behaviour, 18
Norms rules that govern social activi-
    ties and define social roles, role
    relations, and standards of appro-
    priate conduct. 18, 19, 20, 99,
    104–5, 115, 126, 306
norm violation, 104, 105
See also **Subterranean values**
Moral panic the behaviour of some
    members of society is seen as so
    problematic, evil, or harmful to the
    society that it becomes a social
    imperative to control the behaviour,
    punish the offenders, and repair the
    damage, e.g., the Great European
    Witch Hunts. 165, 190–92, 193, 194

Elite-engineered model argues that moral panics represent the deliberate attempt on the part of the economic or political elite to promote public concern about some issue that does not involve the public's interests. 192

Grassroots model views moral panics as originating in the mood of the general public. 188, 192

Interest-group theory moral panics may be set in motion by the actions of small groups, such as politicians, crusading journalists, or professional associations. 192

See also Fear of crime

National Crime Victimization Survey, 170. *See* Reporting crime statistics

Nature vs. nurture, 87

Negative relationships, 102

Neutralization theory the view that delinquents often use linguistic constructions (i.e., excuse or rationalization) to reduce the guilt resulting from their delinquent behaviour (denial of responsibility or injury, or blaming the victim or the accusers). 112–13. *See also* **Excuse; Justification**

Norms. *See* Morals

Occult crime, 191

Occupational crime violation of legal norms governing lawful occupational endeavours. 305–6

automobile industry, 309

criminogenic market structure and, 309

corporate crime and, 306, 311–13

culture of competition and, 308, 310, 311

definitions of the situation of, 309–10

fraudulent business practices and, 307

level of visibility and, 313

offenders of, 306, 310–11, 326

obstacles of regulatory agencies, 312

opportunity and motivation of white-collar crime, 305, 307–8, 310, 325

reporting of, 309, 312

White-collar crime a crime committed by a person of respectability and high status in the course of their occupation. 25, 305, 308, 309, 310–11, 326

See also **Culture of competition; Enterprise crime;** Workplace domain

Offender, 11, 55–61

behavioural choices of, 86, 90, 118

characteristics of, 6, 55, 57

occasional, 260

perceptions of, 57–61

professional, 137, 219, 259–61, 263, 266

profile of incarcerated, 56

Offender motivation, 8, 9, 43, 83

Opportunity, 67, 95, 97, 98, 100, 101, 111, 119. *See also* Opportunity theories

Opportunity theories, 146, 154–155, 271, 334

Organized crime, 57, 219, 313–19, 322, 323, 324, 325, 327. *See also* **Enterprise crime**

Outer containments aspects of the individual's social environment (e.g., primary groups) that help to ensure that delinquent behaviour does not occur. 119. *See also* **Containment theory; Inner containments**

Participant observation technique of informally participating in and observing the social world of the offender. 119, 200–2. *See* **also Direct observation; Experimental observation;** Field research

Patriarchal families, 112. *See also* **Power control theory**

Peacemaking a process that involves reducing punishment/imprisonment and promoting programs that encourage treatment, rehabilitation, alternatives to incarceration, mediation, and enhanced social justice. 25–26. *See also* Humanitarianism; Rehabilitation

Peer influence, 93, 122, 276, 295, 303

Police, 28

bias, 29
characteristics of victims and offenders
  and, 54–65
crime and, 30–32
discretion, 28, 30, 67, 78, 227, 228,
  338
intervention, 8, 28, 29, 66, 78, 126,
  174, 203
law and, 28, 33
patrol activities, 28, 65, 66, 287–88
practice, 65–66
private policing, 72
Proactive policing police involvement
  in incidents as a result of their own
  investigative or patrol activities
  which bring to their attention
  events that may be designated as
  crimes. 28
Reactive policing the police become
  involved in criminal events when
  requested to do so by a member of
  the general public. 28
ride-alongs, 201
uniform policing, 68
victims and, 28–29
visibility of, 203, 288
See also **Community policing; Crime
  prevention; Social control**
Positivist school the philosophical position, developed by Auguste Comte,
  that scientific knowledge can come
  only from direct observation, experimentation, and provision of quantitative data, e.g., finding the cause of
  crime within the criminal. 5, 8–11,
  19, 86, 91, 114, 333. *See also*
  Classical school
Poverty, 99, 151, 340, 342, 351, 352.
  See also Demographic characteristics;
  Lower classes; Inner city; **Underclass**
Power control theory the theory that
  due to differential control (i.e., girls
  are subject to greater control than
  boys) within the patriarchal family,
  males have a higher propensity to
  engage in risk taking, or delinquent
  behaviour. 122, 246, 277. *See also*
  Patriarchal families
Precursors situational factors that bring
  people together in time and space.

19, 49, 73, 74, 78, 101, 242, 280,
  335
crimes against households, of, 271
definition of, 49
enterprise crimes, 319–22
family violence, of, 244
occupational crimes, of, 307–11
workplace crimes, of, 299–302
Predetermined behaviour, 9, 90. *See also*
  Heredity; **Sociobiology**
Primary relationships small intimate
  groups composed of significant
  others defined by face-to-face interaction. 119, 126–27
Professional offender. *See* Offender
Prohibition, 13, 316, 319, 323. *See also*
  Enterprise crime
Property crime, 30, 31, 35, 43, 55, 70,
  77, 99, 124, 130, 266–67
  statistics on, 33, 210
Psychology, 13
Psychopath a sociopathic disorder characterized by lack of moral development and inability to show loyalty to
  others. 40. *See also* Gacy, John
  Wayne; Serial murderers; **Sociopath**
Psychopathology study of abnormal
  behaviour. 95–96
Punishment confinement, restriction of
  activities, infliction of pain, or other
  measures taken for retribution, to
  enforce compliance, or invoke behavioural changes. 9, 11, 76, 128. *See
  also* Deterrence
celerity (swiftness) of, 76, 131
certainty of, 130, 131, 132, 338
death penalty and, 129, 338
fear of, 143
incarceration and, 135
severity of, 76, 128, 131, 132–33,
  135, 304, 338

Racism, 99, 351, 352
Rational choice theories the focus on the
  offenders' actions and decisions
  based on perceived benefits rather
  than on some precipitating or
  psychological factors. 135–36, 155
Rational reconstruction in interviews,
  recollection by offenders that more

elaborate planning took place during their crime than actually occurred. 259

Rationality, 118, 137. *See also* **Classical school; Free will**

Recidivism repetition or recurrence of delinquent or criminal behaviour or behaviour disorder, especially following punishment or rehabilitation, 133, 260

aboriginal peoples and, 141

Rehabilitation, 25, 68, 176, 340. *See also* Humanitarianism; **Peacemaking**

Reporting of crime, 29, 30, 204

crime funnel and, 204–5

See also Reporting crime statistics

Reporting crime statistics

Clearance status a judgement made by the police based on identification of at least one of the offenders involved in an offense. 209

limitations of crime reports, 221–25

perspective, 222–25

type of criminal event, 221–22

National Crime Victimization Survey, 170

Offender reports data gathered from a sample of known offenders such as, prison inmates. 217

criticisms of, 219

description of, 217

police reports and, 205–7

advantages of, 224

Edmonton and Calgary comparison of, 207

event-based nature of, 206

increase likelihood of reporting, 206

recording crime and, 206

Self-report studies respondents' reports about their involvement as offenders. 219

computer crime as an example of, 220–21

crime data and, 221

criticisms of, 223, 224, 225

description of, 219

Uniform crime reporting system (UCR), police crime data, collected and processed by the FBI, that provide police departments with a consistent set of procedures for collecting information about crime. 207–11

advantages of, 207

criticisms of, 208–11

Victim reports/surveys large-scale studies that ask individuals about their experience with crime

criticisms of, 213, 217

victimization. 211–13

General Social Survey, excerpt of, 214–16

Telescoping, reporting a crime as occurring during the reference period when it actually occurred at an earlier time, 222, 223

Retreatist pattern pattern exhibited by people who are unable to succeed through either legitimate or illegitimate means (double-failures) and resort to delinquency organized around the consumption of drugs. 102. *See also* **Conflict pattern; Criminal pattern;** Double failures; **Illegitimate means**

Retribution, 289, 349. *See also* Self-help crime; Vigilantism

Risky lifestyles, 122, 145, 236, 289, 290. *See also* **Lifestyle exposure theory; Routine activities theory**

Robbery, 37, 55, 58, 70, 106, 138, 140, 154, 286, 302

statistics on, 32, 57, 63, 69, 210, 225, 226

Routine activities theory a theory that besides the presence of a motivated offender, direct-contact predatory violations, a suitable target, and the absence of capable guardianship are all vital components necessary for completion of a crime. 151, 187, 256, 301, 334, 357. *See also* Domestic violence; Guardianship; Household crime; **Lifestyles exposure theory;** Risky lifestyles

Rumour and legend, 39–40

Crime myths distorted and misleading information that nevertheless is accepted as fact. 42–43

fear of crime and, 185

folklore and, 40
rumour, 39, 40, 186
Urban legend captivating and plausible
    fictional oral narratives that are
    widely regarded as true stories. 40
    terror on campus as an example of,
    41

Satanic crime, 40, 191–92
Secondary deviance the theory that the
    effect of feedback that consistently
    provides the message that one is a
    disreputable person may eventually
    lead to the acceptance of the defini-
    tion. 177, 193. *See also* **Labelling
    theory; Self-fulfilling prophecy**
Segregation, 182. *See also* **Underclass**
Self-control, 94–95, 121, 122, 142, 295,
    310–11, 326
Self-fulfilling prophecy the theory that
    people who are thought they are
    beyond redemption will come to act
    as if they are. 177. *See also* **Labelling
    theory; Secondary deviance**
Self-help crime, 349. *See also* Legitimate
    violence; **Subculture of violence;**
    Vigilantism
Self-identity, 177, 193
Serial murderers, 96
Sexual aggression and male control,
    283, 285
Sexual assault 29, 30, 36, 60, 64, 77,
    78, 111, 169, 186, 213, 223,
    227–29, 283
  acquaintance rape, 160
  date rape, 73, 283, 289
  reporting rape, 228, 289
  statistics on, 32, 57, 63, 69, 147, 210,
    212, 225, 226, 249
  See also Dating violence; Leisure
    domain
Situational factors, 11, 73, 74, 111,
    121, 137
Situated transactions process of interac-
    tion involving two or more individu-
    als that lasts as long as they find
    themselves in one another's presence.
    145, 158–61
Small durable product design, 152
Smoking, 150, 342

Social bonds, 117, 120, 122, 123, 125,
    143, 276, 334. *See also* **Bond, theory
    of**
Social conditions, 35, 83, 86, 96, 101,
    114, 184, 319, 324, 344, 362
Social constraints, 105, 147
Social control the regulatory institutions
    of society, particularly the law
    enforcement and judicial systems and
    how they operate, encompassing
    rule-enforcement at all levels. 7, 11,
    15, 17, 18, 22, 27, 59, 68, 78,
    84–85, 101, 103, 117–18, 120,
    122–23, 124–25, 127, 132, 135,
    142, 143, 155, 156, 177, 184–86,
    245, 254, 256–57, 266, 267, 269,
    276–77, 288, 289, 299, 334, 336,
    351, 356, 362
  agencies of, 84
  community and, 68, 85
  feminist interpretation of, 27
  Formal social control conventional
    methods of technology and physical
    coercion, such as the police force,
    used to maintain social order. 117,
    118, 127, 277
  Informal social control casual methods
    of coercion employed by commu-
    nity members to maintain confor-
    mity. 17, 18, 118, 122, 124, 125,
    132, 135, 143, 183, 186, 245, 256,
    257, 334, 351
  legal controls, 11, 15, 17, 22, 72, 78
  lifecourse and, 123
  offending as, 59
  See also **Crime prevention;** Police
Social disadvantaged, 22, 55, 58, 61,
    77, 97, 99, 125, 126, 256, 259, 333,
    351, 353. *See also* Inner city; Lower
    classes; Poverty; **Underclass;**
    Workplace domain
Social disorganization long-term and
    widespread deterioration of social
    order and control in a population.
    101, 105, 125, 127, 143. *See also*
    Incivility; Social organization
Social distance, 179
Social domains major spheres of life in
    which we spend most of our time
    and energy. 71–72, 242, 246,

269–70, 292, 304, 306, 335–37. *See also* **Enterprise crime; Family domain; Household domain; Occupational crime; Workplace domain**

Social exchange, 161–62

Social inequality results when a social group is underprivileged compared with another. 20, 25, 36, 246–47, 293, 325. *See also* Relative inequality

Social interaction, 19, 26, 186, 242, 334, 351

Socialization, 87, 88–89, 90, 93, 95, 99, 104, 119, 143, 180, 277

Social learning theories, 104

Social organization coherence and continuity in the social environment, and rational co-operation among individuals and social institutions. 242, 244, 305, 307, 336. *See also* **Social disorganization**

Social roles, 123–24, 147, 158–59, 160, 162, 203, 277, 297, 312, 325, 332

Sociobiology the study of the biological basis of social behaviour. 88, 114

Adoption studies the behavioural comparison of near-birth adoptees to their genetic and their adoptive parents. 88, 114

Body type in order to determine the relationship between physique and criminality, Sheldon categorized ("somatotyped") three basic types of body build—endomorphic, ectomorphic, and mesomorphic—that are associated with a particular type of temperament. 89–90. 103

Constitutional structure predispositions toward crime are claimed to be expressed by biological factors, such as phenotypes or body types, and psychological propensities. 89
criticisms of, 90

Crime gene the sociobiological perspective that certain genes may be linked to criminality. 87, 89, 93

Diet the concept that the behaviour of certain individuals can be affected by their diet. 92–93, 114, 115, 340

General pedigree studies a non-experimental approach to the study of

intergenerational transmission of genetically predisposed behaviour between related individuals. 88
genetics and, 88
criticisms of, 88, 89
genotypes and, 89
intergenerational genetic defects and, 87

karyotype studies claim that the size, the shape and the number of chromosomes, or karyotypes, in individuals are causal factors to criminality. 88

physiology and, 87
predisposition and, 87, 89, 92

Trace elements mineral content in the subject's body determines episodic violence or antisocial behaviour. 92

Twin studies a non-experimental study designed to research and compare criminal predispositions between dizygotic and monozygotic twins. 88

See also **Atavism;** Evolution; Heredity; Predetermined behaviour

Sociology, 7–8

Sociopath antisocial personality disorder involving a marked lack of ethical or moral development. 95. *See also* Antisocial personality; Gacy, John Wayne; **Psychopath**

Strain theory the theory that the constant emphasis on success in society and its possible attainment consistently contradicts the actual opportunity, facing people, especially at the bottom of society where the greatest amount of crime, or illegitimate adaptive means occurs. 102. *See also* General strain theory

Subculture a group or groups within a host culture with different value, evident from their expression of deviant behaviour. 61, 108–9, 110, 111, 256

Subculture of violence a subculture in which disproportionate rates of criminal violence are a product of a group's commitment to subcultural values and norms that condone violence as acceptable means of resolving interpersonal conflict. 110–11, 279, 282. *See also* Legitimate violence; Self-help crime

Substance abuse, 58
alcohol and, 13, 54, 58, 59, 93, 114, 156, 157, 159, 210, 217, 252–53, 261, 265, 277, 279, 282, 283, 303, 351
drugs and, 40, 59, 93, 101, 102, 114, 159, 166, 191, 210, 252, 279, 282, 314, 317, 319–20, 338, 351

Subterranean values values that are held by many in society, although they may be in conflict with other cherished values. 112. *See also* **Morals**

Symbolic interactionism the role of linguistic interaction in developing a social identity and functioning according to shared norms and values. 159. *See also* **Labelling theory**

Target hardening, increasing protection of premises to deter a criminal through fear of detection or because the target has been made inaccessible. 288, 361. *See also* **Crime prevention; Defensible space; Deterrence**

Tearooms, 66

Territorial marking, 127, 348. *See also* Gangs

Third parties, 8, 49, 162, 280. *See also* Bystanders; Witnesses

Tolerance, 17, 19, 22, 126, 244, 246, 273. *See also* Domestic violence, tolerance of

Trajectories in life course perspective, describes the directions in which lives *seem* to be moving. 123. *See also* **Life course perspective; Transitions**

Transactions the interactions between individuals that have led to the outcome of the crime that transpired. 49, 335
crimes against households, of, 259
definition of, 49
enterprise crime, of, 322–24
family violence, of, 248–50
leisure crimes, of, 278
occupational crimes, of, 311–12
workplace crimes, of, 302–4

Transitions in life course perspective, specific events that might or might not alter trajectories. 123–24. *See also* **Life course perspective; Trajectories**

Underclass a class of society that almost exclusively inhabits segregated, disadvantaged neighbourhoods where social epidemics are highly concentrated, resulting in mutually reinforcing contagion effects. 25, 110, 352. *See also* Demographic characteristics; **Incivility;** Inner city; Lower Classes; Poverty; Segregation

Universal form of crime, 105, 174

Urban crime, 69, 72, 85, 110, 125–26, 128, 166, 256
statistics on, 62, 69, 257

Urbanization, 68, 105, 358

Utopian world (B.F. Skinner), 104

Victimization, costs of, 166–67
behavioural, 173–74
coping costs, 175–76
emotional, 170–73
statistics on, 171
financial, 169, 169
physical, 169, 170
psychological baggage and, 171
stigma, 176
Vulnerability conversion especially for victims of violence, development of a sudden understanding by victims that they are mote susceptible to the dangers of life than they thought. 170

Victimization, female, 169, 226, 227
domestic and sexual assault and, 227–30
measuring, 225–26
patterns of, 226
reporting spousal violence and, 223, 230
statistics, 225, 226, 246
research innovations, 230–31
See also Domestic violence; Sexual aggression and male control; Sexual assault

Victimization survey, 7, 8, 19, 146, 168, 170, 178, 211–14, 217, 219–21, 224–27, 230–31, 238, 246, 248, 253, 256, 260, 278, 297, 301, 312

Canadian Urban Victimization Survey (CUVS), 211, 246

General Social Survey (GSS), 28, 61, 62–63, 173, 211

National Crime Victimization Survey (NCVS), 170

Violence Against Women Survey (VAWS), 170, 211–12, 230, 248

See also Reporting crime statistics

Victimless crimes criminal events where the victim does not exist in any direct and immediate way, such as the personal choice of drug abuse and gambling. 61

Victims, 61

Avoidance behaviour behaviour by which victims seek to distance themselves from the kinds of people or situations they perceive as dangerous. 173

characteristics of, 61–63

statistics on, 62

coping mechanisms of, 173

denial and, 64

perceptions of, 63–64

Victimization and, 62–62, 72–73, 145–48, 154–55, 167–76, 179, 180–81, 193–94, 211–14, 217–19, 270, 278–79, 286–87, 291–93, 298, 299, 301, 325–27

reports, 211–17

research strategies about, 168, 219, 230, 242, 244, 250, 254

risk and, 236, 277, 278, 290, 291, 292, 293, 295, 298, 300, 325, 354

Victim–offender relations/interactions, 6, 64, 67, 74, 77, 155, 227, 306, 326

Victim precipitation occurs when the opportunity for crime is created by some action of the victim. 156–58, 160, 334

Vigilantism, 349. *See also* Self-help crime, Legitimate violence

Violent crime, 30–32, 37, 43, 54, 55, 62, 63, 69, 87, 167, 185, 210, 223, 272–73, 279, 299, 300, 322, 341

statistics about, 33, 35, 170, 210

White-collar crime, 25, 35, 40, 59, 60, 72, 73, 99, 106, 111, 114, 121, 202, 305, 308, 309, 310, 311, 326. See **Occupational crime**

Witnesses, 11, 50, 64–65, 77, 203, 224, 255, 332. *See also* Bystanders; Third parties; Eyewitnesses, accuracy of

Workplace domain, 324

aftermath of workplace crime and, 304

employed vs. unemployed and, 292–93

employee–customer conflict and, 302

employment and victimization and, 293

individual and occupational characteristics of, 297–99

precursors of workplace crime and, 299–302

statistics about, 300

reporting crime and, 304, 309, 312

schools and victimization and, 303

statistics about, 303

stress, 296

transactions of workplace crime and, 302

unemployment and offending and, 294, 295

work and victimization risks and, 296, 301

See also **Culture of competition; Enterprise Crime; Occupational crime; Routine activities theory**

To the owner of this book

We hope that you have enjoyed *The Criminal Event,* and we would like to know as much about your experiences with this text as you would care to offer. Only through your comments and those of others can we learn how to make this a better text for future readers.

School _____ Your instructor's name _____

Course _____ Was the text required? _____ Recommended? _____

1. What did you like the most about *The Criminal Event?*

_____

_____

_____

2. How useful was this text for your course?

_____

_____

_____

3. Do you have any recommendations for ways to improve the next edition of this text?

_____

_____

_____

4. In the space below or in a separate letter, please write any other comments you have about the book. (For example, please feel free to comment on reading level, writing style, terminology, design features, and learning aids.)

_____

_____

_____

Optional

Your name _____ Date _____

May ITP Nelson quote you, either in promotion for *The Criminal Event* or in future publishing ventures?

Yes _____ No _____

Thanks!

You can also send your comments to us via e-mail at
college_arts_hum@nelson.com

- - - - - - - - - FOLD HERE - - - - - - - - -

Nelson

MAIL POSTE
Canada Post Corporation
Société canadienne des postes
Postage paid   Port payé
if mailed in Canada si posté au Canada
Business Reply **Réponse d'affaires**

0066102399   **01**

0066102399-M1K5G4-BR01

ITP NELSON
MARKET AND PRODUCT DEVELOPMENT
PO BOX 60225 STN BRM B
TORONTO ON M7Y 2H1